African Civilizations

This major new revised edition of *African Civilizations* re-examines the physical evidence for developing social complexity in Africa over the last six thousand years. Unlike the two previous editions, it is not confined to tropical Africa but considers the whole continent. Graham Connah focuses upon the archaeological research of two key aspects of complexity, urbanism and state formation, in ten main areas of Africa: Egypt, North Africa, Nubia, Ethiopia, the West African savanna, the West African forest, the East African coast and islands, the Zimbabwe Plateau, parts of Central Africa, and South Africa. The book's main concern is to review the available evidence in its varied environmental settings and to consider possible explanations of the developments that gave rise to it. Extensively illustrated, including new maps and plans, and offering an extended list of references, this book provides essential reading for students of archaeology, anthropology, African history, black studies, and social geography.

GRAHAM CONNAH is Emeritus Professor of Archaeology at the University of New England, Australia, and a visiting fellow at the Australian National University, Canberra. His earlier book *Three Thousand Years in Africa* (1981) won the Amaury Talbot Prize. Other publications include *The Archaeology of Benin* (1975), *The Archaeology of Australia's History* (1993), *Kibiro: The Salt of Bunyoro, Past and Present* (1996), *Transformations in Africa* (1998), *Forgotten Africa: An Introduction to Its Archaeology* (2004), also translated into German, French, Italian, and Portuguese, and *Writing about Archaeology* (2010). He was awarded the Order of Australia in 2000 for his contributions to African and Australian archaeology.

Contents

Figures

African Civilizations

An archaeological perspective

THIRD EDITION

Graham Connah
Australian National University

CAMBRIDGE
UNIVERSITY PRESS

CAMBRIDGE
UNIVERSITY PRESS

32 Avenue of the Americas, New York, NY 10013-2473, USA

Cambridge University Press is part of the University of Cambridge.

It furthers the University's mission by disseminating knowledge in the pursuit of education, learning, and research at the highest international levels of excellence.

www.cambridge.org
Information on this title: www.cambridge.org/9781107621275

First published 2016

Printed in the United Kingdom by Clays, St Ives plc

A catalog record for this publication is available from the British Library.

Library of Congress Cataloging in Publication Data
Connah, Graham, author.
African civilizations : an archaeological perspective / Graham Connah, Australian National University. – Third edition.
    pages   cm
Includes bibliographical references and index.
ISBN 978-1-107-01187-8 (Hardback : alk. paper)
1. Africa, Sub-Saharan–Antiquities.   2. Africa, Sub-Saharan–Civilization.
3. Prehistoric peoples–Africa, Sub-Saharan.   4. Excavations (Archaeology)–Africa, Sub-Saharan.   I. Title.
DT352.3.C66 2016
967'.01–dc23   2015032522

ISBN 978-1-107-01187-8 Hardback
ISBN 978-1-107-62127-5 Paperback

In memory of Nora Fisher McMillan

Preface and acknowledgements

I started to write this book in 1983, with previous editions appearing in 1987 and 2001 and a Japanese translation in 1993. Any book that originated so long ago and has remained in print for so long will become seriously out of date, but this is particularly the case for a publication about later African archaeology, which has seen an enormous increase in research activity in recent years. I am therefore very grateful to Cambridge University Press for the opportunity to provide a third edition. In doing so, I feel it essential to stress two points. First, people are sometimes unconvinced about the newness of new editions, but this really is a new edition and I hope that it will assist those who have ignored the second edition and continued to cite the outdated first edition. Second, preparing a new edition of a book will inevitably be constrained to some extent by the thinking that influenced its original content and form, in this instance many years ago; the only way to prevent this is to write a completely new book.

Failing this, what is new about this 'new' edition? First, it is larger and covers the whole continent, not just tropical Africa, like the two previous editions. This has meant the addition of three completely new chapters, on Egypt, North Africa, and South Africa. Although the book is consequently longer, the extra chapters could only be added by also shortening some of the chapters that already existed. In addition, those chapters have required considerable additions to include recent research, and as a result parts of some of them have been substantially rewritten or subjected to numerous smaller changes. Inevitably this has resulted in the deletion of older source material, wherever it could be replaced by newer information. This has included the replacement of some illustrations, as well as the addition of new ones. The whole process has taken more than three years but I remain concerned about recent publications that might have been missed; in spite of the Internet, accessing sources remains one of the main difficulties for the writers of syntheses. However, as far as possible, I have tried to include a representative sample of recently published material. I hope that not too many people will think that I have ignored their work.

Second, although this does not pretend to be a theoretical study, there are inevitably theoretical implications in the way that its subject matter has been treated. As with previous editions, it has been my intention to examine the archaeological evidence for emerging social complexity in Africa, particularly the evidence for urbanization and the formation of states. These subjects have a very large literature, particularly concerning social theory, and in the previous editions I tried to outline the most significant of the relevant ideas in the opening chapter. Given the main purpose of the book, however, which is to ask of the physical evidence how we know what we think we know, it is impossible to give adequate space to theoretical matters, and in this new edition I have further compressed the relevant material as well as updating some of its more important aspects. One review of the first edition was headed 'Complex societies made simple' and I have never been able to decide whether this was intended as an insult or a compliment. Whatever the case, is it a crime to attempt straightforward explanations of complex data?

In attempting those explanations, the book continues to emphasize geographical and environmental matters, but sociopolitical aspects are now given greater attention than formerly. The changes in human societies that led to the development of cities and states were clearly influenced by many external factors, but in the end it was changes in the societies themselves and the way that they organized themselves that were of greatest importance. Such changes took place in many different ways and sometimes did not happen at all. There is no magic formula to explain their occurrence or absence, and old explanations involving social evolution and the emergence of so-called civilization have ceased to be adequate. Unfortunately, archaeology is often insufficiently informative on these matters, and our understanding is compounded by the variety of ways used by different researchers to extract meaning from the evidence that is available. It is to be hoped that as time passes, the picture will become clearer.

So many colleagues have assisted in my work on this and previous editions that it is impossible to thank them all here. Instead, the text is heavily referenced to the sources used, and the captions of the illustrations acknowledge the origin of those that are not my own or that have been redrawn. Great efforts have been made to obtain permission to reproduce copyright material where necessary, and in cases where copyright holders could not be contacted, usually because of the passage of time, the author would like to hear from them and offers his apologies for the omission. Some line drawings have been updated by Andrew Stawowczyk Long and/or myself, but I remain grateful to Douglas Hobbs, who did the initial work on many of them long ago. Finally, as for previous editions, I remain greatly in debt to Beryl Connah, whose continuing support and encouragement has been vitally important.

In the meantime, a whole generation of Africanist archaeologists has gradually departed the scene, leaving a legacy of research on which a younger and more numerous generation can build, and one that increasingly includes African scholars as well as those from many other parts of the world. I wish them all well in their future endeavours.

Graham Connah
School of Archaeology and Anthropology
Australian National University
Canberra

Chapter 1

The context

Africa is huge; it is so big that you can put the United States and Australia into it and still have a bit left over. It extends from about 37° north to about 35° south and has an altitudinal range from depressions that are below sea level to mountain peaks that exceed 5,000 metres. As a result it has an incredible diversity of environments. It contains some of the driest deserts in the world, and yet has three of the world's major rivers: the Nile, the Niger, and the Congo. Some of the hottest places on earth are in Africa, and yet there are glaciers on its highest mountains. There are steaming rainforests and dry savanna grasslands, low-lying river valleys and high plateaux, extensive deserts and gigantic lakes, mangrove coasts and surf-pounded beaches. This is only an impressionistic picture of the very large number of differing environments in the African continent. In reality the major zones merge into one another, resulting in an even greater variety of conditions that have been further complicated by climatic variation through time.

For at least 2 million years, human beings have been learning how to get the best out of the kaleidoscope of African environments. Those environments have not determined what men and women could do, nor could the latter ignore the environments in which they have lived. Instead there has been a dynamic relationship between the two, in which people have sought to turn to their advantage the opportunities offered by each environment and to come to terms with its constraints. First as hunters, gatherers, and fishers who gradually intensified their exploitation of available resources, then as pastoralists and cultivators, and eventually as city-dwellers, artisans, and traders, men and women have continued to interact with their environment, retaining a remarkable variety of strategies for doing so.

Archaeology is a major source of information about Africa's past. Documentary sources for African history are limited: their coverage often chronologically patchy and geographically fragmented. For large areas of Africa, particularly tropical Africa, their time depth is restricted to the last century or two. A uniform divide between prehistory and history does not exist on the African continent: some peoples and places, such as Pharaonic Egypt and Aksumite Ethiopia, developed writing several millennia ago; others, such as Benin City and Zimbabwe, lacked a written record until recent times; still others, such as Borno and Kongo, had contemporary accounts for a short period in the past, after which there is virtual silence. In addition, many of the documentary sources that do exist are based on the observations of outsiders who did not always understand what they observed or were prejudiced in their assessments. Such documentary evidence that does exist is often invaluable, but Africanist historians have also given considerable attention to oral sources of history. However, it seems unlikely that oral sources can throw much light on periods more than, say, 500 years ago. Indeed, Jan Vansina (1973: xiv) thought that 250 years was often the maximum. In these circumstances, scholars interested in Africa's past have turned to a variety of other information sources. Thus, art and architectural history (Garlake 2002) and linguistics (Blench 2006) have contributed useful information, as have ethnographic and anthropological investigations. In addition, other disciplines have been of assistance, such as investigations of animals and plants in the past, including genetics (van der Veen 1999; Blench and MacDonald 2000). Relevant research has also included ethnoarchaeological studies, in which archaeology is employed to examine contemporary societies in order to test interpretations applied to societies in the past.

Archaeologists have spent a lot of time over the last few decades arguing about the nature of archaeology (Renfrew and Bahn 2008). Basically the subject is concerned with the study of the physical evidence of past human activities, in order to reconstruct those activities or at least *construct* what we think they might have been. This, it is hoped, will enable us to understand the undocumented past or to increase our understanding of inadequately documented periods of the past. Archaeological evidence, however, has its own strengths and weaknesses, and we are still learning ways of gaining the maximum reliable information from it. Its greatest advantage is that it enables us to examine things that were actually made and used by people in the past and allows us to investigate the impact that those people had on their environment. We can discover what human beings actually did, not merely what they or others said that they did. The main disadvantage of archaeological evidence is that it almost always reflects only part of the activities of past men and women. The differential effects of human behaviour, of climate and soil chemistry, and of subsequent disturbance by either natural or human agencies cause most archaeological evidence to be rather like a jigsaw puzzle from which two-thirds of the pieces are lost, whilst many of the rest have the picture worn off or corners missing. These strengths and weaknesses of archaeological evidence can be seen in this book. On the lower and middle Nile, in North Africa, and in the Ethiopian Highlands we have the remains of cities often built of stone or earth, which have clear indications of centralized authority, so that archaeological investigations have added greatly to what is known from documentary sources. In contrast, archaeology has contributed much less information for Central Africa, where urban settlements were constructed mainly of grass, wood, and other organic materials and occupied by people who did not express their identity in more permanent building materials and did not create written records. Unfortunately, however, archaeological evidence has another drawback: it results from human endeavour, and archaeologists (just like other people) tend to vary in the effort that they expend on different problems. Thus it is easy to search for settlement sites in the open grasslands of the African savanna but difficult to do so in the tangled undergrowth of the rainforest. Similarly, it is easier to locate the sites of stone ruins than those of timber buildings and it is easier to excavate mud-brick structures than those of pisé. As a result, African archaeological distribution maps tend to show the distribution of archaeological research, rather than that of archaeological evidence.

Despite these problems, archaeology has powerful research potential. No longer merely concerned with studying artefacts, archaeologists have turned their attention to the study of human behaviour and its change through time. This is as it should be, for over a long time scale it is probably they, increasingly along with geneticists, linguists, and others, who can throw much light on when and how and why human societies changed in the way that they did. This book, for instance, attempts to assess how much archaeology can tell us about two aspects of the development of social complexity in the African continent: the growth of cities and the appearance of states. The purpose is not to dispute with historians or social anthropologists or sociologists or geographers, who have their own ideas and have developed a number of explanatory theories, but to evaluate the archaeological data and to determine what it has to contribute to the debates on these issues. In doing this, it will also become apparent that future archaeological fieldwork will need more sophisticated research designs than has sometimes been the case in the past.

For most of the time that human beings have been in Africa, they scavenged, collected, hunted, and fished for their food, and there were few of them, widely scattered across the landscape. Nevertheless, archaeological evidence (Phillipson 2005) suggests that from about 200,000 years ago people were adapting to virtually all the varied African environments. Subsequently, it is likely that the size of some groups increased and that overall population levels rose. This probably led to pressure on food resources, which during the period between about 18,000 and about 7,000 years ago caused intensified exploitation strategies, such as the harvesting of grass seeds, the use of specialized fishing equipment, and possibly the management of wild animals. These changes occurred at various dates during this overall period, in parts of what is now the Sahara, in parts of the Nile Valley, and in some areas of the East African savanna. It seems likely that they then led to the development of food production, which occurred in the northern half of Africa by about the sixth millennium BC. Thus Africans have been farmers for less than half of 1 percent of their history, but the development of farming has had a major accelerating effect on the evolution of human culture and on social organization. The domestication of sorghum, millet, teff, African rice, wheat, barley, yam, and a host of other plants, plus the domestication of cattle, sheep, and goats, resulted in larger human populations, greater densities of population, and a growth in human sedentism. The development of food production in Africa arose from both indigenous experimentation and influences from South-West Asia. The evidence indicates that much of the plant domestication was an African achievement and that some cattle were probably domesticated in Africa, unlike sheep and goats whose domestication apparently resulted from Asiatic initiatives. It is in the context of African farming that most subsequent cultural changes in the continent must be seen.

One of the most important of these changes was the adoption of iron metallurgy, which in most of Africa took place from about the middle of the first millennium BC or somewhat earlier and greatly improved the efficiency of tools and weapons. Copper and copper-alloy metallurgy pre-dated iron metallurgy but was mainly practised in the lower and middle Nile Valley and North Africa. So great was the impact of the adoption of iron on both the means of production and the means of destruction during the last two millennia in Africa that archaeologists have tended to emphasize it and to overlook other matters. The period has been called 'the African Iron Age', terminology that is difficult to apply chronologically and that distracts attention from other important changes that were occurring in some African societies. It seems that over the last 5,000 years or more there was a rapid growth of interaction between human groups. This was probably brought about by a combination of population growth, increasing sedentism, ecological diversity, and an uneven distribution of resources. Certain animal and plant products, salt, copper, iron, and other commodities were increasingly exchanged between different population centres, and it was into such exchange networks that long-distance trade, both within and outside Africa, was eventually able to tap. At the local level, such intergroup dependence encouraged a complex interaction between individual settlements, so that some became larger and more important than others and in time came to control other settlements in their immediate region. At the same time there was increasing specialization and social stratification amongst the people living in the larger settlements. In certain instances, elite groups within hierarchical societies gained control of crucial resources, which became the basis of their political domination of the rest of the population in their region. It could have been in some such manner that there emerged in parts of Africa the cities and states that were the principal manifestations of social complexity and that form the subject of this book. These developments first took place in the lower and middle Nile Valley and in Africa north of the Sahara, but they also occurred in tropical Africa, particularly during the last two millennia. This book is an archaeologist's attempt to explain how and why this came to be the case.

In retrospect, many of the earlier attempts at such explanation now seem simplistic and even naïve, a range of theories from each of which its proponents claimed understanding could be gained. There was almost a competition to produce a theory that would explain everything. More recently this somewhat mechanistic, formulaic approach has been replaced by treating the subject as one aspect of cultural evolution, seen not as a step-like series of changes, as was once thought, but as a process varying in tempo and pattern from region to region and characterized by socioeconomic multicausality (Feinman and Manzanilla 2000). Nevertheless, some scholars considering the origins of cities and states as global phenomena still saw them as components of what they called 'the emergence of civilization', generally concentrating on West Asia, Pakistan–India, China, and Central and South America, with Egypt the only part of Africa given attention (Daniel 1968). The reason for this was the essentially nineteenth-century concept of 'civilization', which to Gordon Childe and many of his generation, principally trained in Greek and Roman classical history, implied the existence of writing (Childe 1957: 37). This was a Eurocentric view, in which civilization was defined by the extent to which other societies conformed to nineteenth- and early-twentieth-century European ideals. The use of the word 'civilization' in the title of this book is therefore intended to be provocative, to remind readers that Africa had its own 'civilizations'. However, after Childe the concept of civilization continued to attract prescriptive definition, although this became broader as time went on (e.g., Kluckhohn 1960: 400; Renfrew 1972: 11; Redman 1978: 218–20). In general it was thought that civilization implied cities, and vice versa, and this led to a debate about the definition of the word 'city', in which a list of ten criteria by Childe became influential (Childe 1950: 3, 9–16). The latter reflected the circumstances of city development and state formation in South-West Asia and, like Childe's definition of civilization, were of limited value in other parts of the world. As with the word 'civilization', subsequent attempts to define the term 'city' became increasingly generalized (e.g., Sjoberg 1960; Mumford 1961: 85; Redman 1978: 215–16). Nigerian geographer Akin Mabogunje reviewed 'the functional specialization theory of urbanization', pointing out that it was essential that functional specialization take place under three 'limiting conditions': the existence of a food surplus to feed the specialists, the existence of a small group of people able to exercise power over the food producers and ensure peaceful conditions, and the existence of traders and merchants to provide raw materials for the specialists (Mabogunje 1968: 35).

He defined urbanization as simply 'the process whereby human beings congregate in relatively large number at one particular spot of the earth's surface' (Mabogunje 1968: 33). The process of state formation, in his opinion, originated in the necessity to defend urban centres against external aggression, resulting in the extension of control over neighbouring cities (Mabogunje 1968: 37). However, by 1981 Adams would comment: 'Urbanism, to be sure, denotes no set of precise, well understood additional characteristics for societies so described' (R.McC. Adams 1981: 81).

Implicit in these attempts at definition was a concern with process, that is to say: how did cities develop, how did states emerge? It has been these questions that have increasingly attracted attention, resulting in a large literature. Investigations have concentrated on what has been called 'the rise of complex society', and there has been a tendency to separate the study of urbanization from that of state formation. Indeed, the rise of the state has been seen as central to the emergence of 'complex societies', which some anthropologists would prefer to call 'stratified societies' or 'pluralistic societies'. There has been much discussion of 'the anthropology of political evolution' (e.g., Claessen and Skalník 1978; Cohen and Service 1978; Claessen and van de Velde 1987; Eisenstadt et al. 1988; Claessen and Oosten 1996), but the emphasis has tended to be on theoretical considerations, and much of the evidence used has been drawn either from historical sources or from ethnographic and anthropological observations. For example, much attention had been given to the role of 'chiefdoms' and the ways in which they could have developed into states; Flannery (1999) drawing on ethnohistorical sources from Africa, Madagascar, Inner Asia, and Hawaii to examine the interaction of 'process' and 'agency' in such changes. Nevertheless, it has been difficult to relate such theories to archaeological evidence, although Jonathan Haas (1982) attempted to do this, and Roland Fletcher (1995) constructed a theory of urbanization on a similar basis. In addition, Trigger (2003), Maisels (2010), Lull and Micó (2011), and Smith (2012) have adopted a comparative approach in which more attention has been given to the archaeological aspects of complex societies.

Haas presented a state-formation theory that could be used in the interpretation of archaeological data. He defined a 'state' as being 'a society in which there is a centralized and specialized institution of government' (Haas 1982: 3) and examined the ways in which scholars have attempted to explain the emergence of such societies. He grouped these explanations into two schools of thought (Haas 1982: 15): the 'conflict' school (e.g., Fried 1967) and the 'integration' school (e.g., Service 1975). Instead, Haas suggested a theory 'introducing major integration elements into a broadened conflict model' (Haas 1982: 129). Examining the main theories for the emergence of state societies, he identified three groups (Haas 1982: 132–52): (1) warfare theories (e.g., Carneiro 1970); (2) trade theories, either interregional (e.g., Rathje 1971) or intraregional (e.g., Wright and Johnson 1975); and (3) an irrigation theory (Wittfogel 1957). Haas argued that in spite of differences between them, 'All the theories begin with stratification and outline alternate ways by which certain members of a society may gain differential access to basic resources'. He observed, 'This differential access is based on *control over the production or procurement* of the resources in question' (Haas 1982: 150–1; emphasis in original). It is that control, according to Haas, that gives rulers power. Subsequently, Flannery and Marcus (2012) have also emphasized the creation of inequality as an important factor in state formation. In addition, others have recognized the importance of power in the development of social complexity (e.g., Earle 1997; Maisels 2010). Haas understood power to be the capacity to oblige somebody else to do something that she or he would not otherwise do, through the application, threat, or promise of sanctions (Haas 1982: 157). He identified nine variables that could be used to measure power in social relationships and demonstrated how each of these could be recognized in the archaeological record (Haas 1982: 159–71). Redefining the word 'state' in terms of power, Haas called it 'a stratified society in which a governing body exercises control over the production or procurement of basic resources, and thus necessarily exercises coercive power over the remainder of the population' (Haas 1982: 172).

Although Haas attempted to relate some of the anthropological ideas about state formation to archaeological data, he made little mention of African states, drawing his archaeological evidence from Mesopotamia, China, Mesoamerica, and Peru. Like many anthropologists who have written about state formation theory, he restricted his discussion to what have been called 'pristine' states. These are states that arose so early or in such isolation that there can be no question of their being influenced by other states, as might have been the case with what have been called 'secondary' states. Thus, Haas ignored the archaeological evidence from African states, presumably because he considered them to be 'secondary' in origin, even excluding the early Egyptian state on this basis. It seems strange that so much theoretical work has gone into attempting to understand 'pristine' state formation when most states were inevitably 'secondary' in their origins. Barbara Price (1978: 161) commented on the limited theoretical treatment of the secondary state, and Renfrew referred to the idea of a division into 'pristine' and 'secondary' 'civilizations' as 'unacceptably diffusionist' (Renfrew 1983: 17). Renfrew thought that 'to understand the origins and development of any civilization', it is necessary to look at its local conditions: at subsistence, technology, social system, population pressures, ideology, and external trade. Yoffee (2005) also argued for a broader treatment of social change in the past. This is the approach adopted in this book, because although state formation theory and urbanization theory are important, it is also important to examine the archaeological evidence for the conditions that gave rise to states and cities, as Pauketat (2007) has insisted.

Anthropologists and historians have advanced various hypotheses to explain the development of states in Africa. Historian John Lonsdale reviewed the historiography of the subject (Lonsdale 1981) and identified the following hypotheses: (1) imposition by an autonomous will, (2) conquest, (3) demographic pressure, (4) a managerial basis of power, (5) long-distance trade, and (6) drought. These hypotheses were not seen as mutually exclusive; Lonsdale accepted that combinations of them might be used in an explanatory role in particular instances. Nevertheless, he stressed that most of these hypotheses originated at a time when there was relatively little known about African state formation. Lonsdale thought that three things had subsequently become apparent. First, state formation was a very slow process: 'frequently botched and started again', so that 'the decay and fall of kingdoms is as important a process as their rise'. Second, a great deal more had become known about the politics of state formation and state collapse (for the latter, Tainter 1988; Yoffee and Cowgill 1988). Power seems to have been decentralized in early kingdoms with their kings acting as mediators rather than autocrats. State emergence involved centralization of that power, and this was achieved by coercion, not by consensus. Third, it was more useful to explain the rise of particular states in terms of local politics, rather than to hypothesize about 'the idea of the state' and the diffusion of political ideas (Lonsdale 1981: 172–3).

Physical evidence is needed to test the theories concerning urbanization and state formation, but so limited is our knowledge of the later archaeology of Africa that ethnohistorical and historical evidence also need to be considered. The danger here is that we might 'allow the ethnographic present and the historically constructed past to exercise tyranny over our perception of past human behaviour' (Fletcher 1995: 212). Because of an uneven geographical distribution of excavations and other field researches, there have been relatively few general archaeological studies concerned with the origins and development of cities and states in Africa, and older contributions are of limited value. However, an early contribution to the general archaeological literature was Peter Garlake's *The Kingdoms of Africa* (Garlake 1978a), which was noteworthy for the author's insistence on the indigenous evolution of African states, although he also stressed the importance of external trade, whereby a small group could monopolize not the resources but the outlets by which they could be converted into a useful surplus.

Although it gave little attention to archaeological evidence, there was also Richard Hull's book *African Cities and Towns before the European Conquest* (1976). Relevant to the present discussion were parts of the book concerning the origins of cities and towns and their decline and disappearance. Hull identified five main urban types, assuming that major function explained origin but emphasizing that most cities and towns served a combination of such functions. The types were: spiritual and ceremonial centres, commercial centres, centres of governance, centres of refuge, and 'cities of vision' (Hull 1976: 120–1). Hull also outlined what he saw as the prerequisites for the growth of cities and towns in Africa: government had to be sufficiently developed to exert control over the agricultural surplus; leaders had to have enough power to demand labour from their people for the construction of public works; specialist craftsmen had to be present; and government had to have an ideological power base (Hull 1976: 2). For decline and disappearance, Hull suggested four main causes: environmental deterioration, collapse of political superstructure, revolt of peripheral cities against the mother city, and external military invasion (Hull 1976: 114–16).

Other publications relevant to the archaeology of cities and states in Africa include: Augustin Holl, *West African Early Towns* (2006); David Phillipson, *African Archaeology* (2005); Thurstan Shaw et al., *The Archaeology of Africa* (1993); and Joseph Vogel, *Encyclopedia of Precolonial Africa* (1997). Another source is *The Oxford Handbook of African Archaeology* (2013), edited by Peter Mitchell and Paul Lane. Chapter 48 in that book, by J. Cameron Monroe (2013: 703–22), entitled 'The archaeology of the precolonial state in Africa', provides a useful summary. Parts of *The Civilizations of Africa* by Christopher Ehret (2002) are also relevant, as are some of the papers in *African Archaeology* edited by Ann Brower Stahl (2005b). Furthermore, three essays of my own consider specific aspects of the subject (Connah 2000a; 2000b; 2008). In addition, there are historical studies: Roland Oliver, *The African Experience* (1993); John Iliffe, *Africans* (1995); John Reader, *Africa* (1997); and Anderson and Rathbone, *Africa's Urban Past* (2000).

When examining the archaeological evidence, a discrepancy becomes apparent. According to historical sources, there was a greater number of cities and states in Africa than the archaeological literature indicates. Fage and Verity's *An Atlas of African History* (1978) shows numerous cities and states in its maps of which little or nothing is known archaeologically. What about the early second-millennium AD state of Kanem east of Lake Chad, for instance, of which the capital Njimi has never been found? Or what about the sixteenth-century state of Kongo with its capital Mbanza Kongo, thought by Leo Africanus to have had a population of about 100,000 people (Africanus 1896: vol. 1, 73)? Virtually nothing is known about its archaeology, either.

These examples illustrate the two main reasons for the patchy state of arch-aeological knowledge on this subject. First, there is the problem of the archaeological visibility of the sites (Connah 2008). At the one extreme, a long-established, partly stone-built, commercial centre like Kilwa (Chittick 1974), and at the other extreme, a short-lived, grass-built, centre of governance like the Bugandan capital at Rubaga, visited by Henry Morton Stanley in 1875 (Stanley 1878: vol. 1, 199–202). The second of the main reasons for the patchy state of archaeological knowledge is the uneven distribution in space and time of archaeological field research in Africa. Comparatively large amounts of excav-ation and fieldwork have been carried out, for instance, on settlement sites of the last three millennia along the Sudanese Nile, but, in contrast, relatively little such work has been done, for example, on the Mozambique coast. These two problems of archaeological visibility and uneven field research frequently compound one another. Clearly, only the most intensive field investigations will reveal sites of low archaeological visibility.

A consequence of the patchy state of archaeological knowledge concerning cities and states in Africa is that any discussion of the relevant archaeological evidence might give a distorted picture. However, Chandler and Fox (1974) produced a series of maps of African cities at intervals between AD 1000 and 1850 mainly based on historical sources. Although the distribution of cities does not necessarily indicate the distribution of states, these maps do reflect the geographical distribution of cities and states indicated by the archaeological evidence. Thus they show that the main areas of urban development were: in the Maghreb of North Africa, along the lower Nile in Egypt, on the middle Nile in the Sudan, in West Africa along the southern edge of the Sahara, in the West African rainforest west of the lower Niger River, and on the Ethiopian Plateau. They also record urban centres on the East African coast, on the Zimbabwe Plateau, around the lower Congo, and in the Lake Victoria area. So the archaeological evidence does produce a geographical pattern comparable to that derived from historical and ethnohistorical evidence. It is this that has prompted the choice of subject matter for most of the substantive chapters of this book.

Some of the implicit assumptions in this book require examination. For instance, how are the terms 'city' and 'state' to be understood in this specific context? Some authors have written of 'cities' in Africa (Hull 1976) and 'kingdoms' (Garlake 1978a) or 'states' (Fage and Verity 1978). Others have accepted the existence of the West African 'empires' of Ghana, Mali, Songhay, and Kanem-Borno. The question is whether such terms accurately describe African realities or merely reflect the influence of European historiography. Studies of more recent African societies by anthropologists and ethnographers suggest that larger settlements in Africa occurred in a variety of forms, differing in character and scale, and that African polities tended to lack the autocratic, centralized, and bounded forms that the words 'kingdom' and 'empire' suggest. Perhaps the use of such terms resulted partly from a post-colonial reaction by scholars seeking to legitimize the African past in a global context, attempting to show that in certain respects Africa was like Europe. Indeed, they might have had some justification, for the cities and states of Medieval and Early Modern Europe were not always the autocratic, centralized, and bounded entities of popular Eurocentric imagination.

In an introductory essay to her edited book *Beyond Chiefdoms* (1999), Susan Keech McIntosh provided an important perspective on the subject of sociopolitical complexity in Africa. She pointed out: 'The initial establishment of supralocal organization in sub-Saharan Africa more likely took the form of a central ritual authority, lacking any significant political power or particular economic advantage' (S.K. McIntosh 1999: 23). She also remarked: 'It is quite common to find in African segmentary states a pattern of power counterpoised between a king and either associations (such as secret societies or cults with titled elders) and/or a council of lineage heads' (S.K. McIntosh 1999: 15). Other factors, such as religious affiliation, ethnic/linguistic identity, clan membership, age-grades, craft guilds, and trade obligations, can also play a part in limiting an African ruler's hierarchical authority implied by the term 'state'. Indeed, on the subject of urban origins, Roderick McIntosh argued that in some cases a heterarchical, horizontal sociopolitical structure existed, rather than a hierarchical, vertical one with control of surplus, visible stratification, and public monuments (R.J. McIntosh 1999; 2005). Also Ann Stahl questioned the progressivist and evolutionist assumptions in much that has been written about the appearance of aspects of social complexity, such as urbanism and states, in Africa. She recommended 'research strategies that can help us rethink how we perceive variability in time and space' (Stahl 1999: 46). Terms less loaded with meaning than 'city' and 'state' are needed for examples of uncertain character; 'large settlement' and 'polity' might be preferable. Roderick McIntosh observed: 'As archaeology matures we will look more inclusively at the full range of processes by which complex society emerged' (R.J. McIntosh 1999: 63).

One aspect of urban living, to which archaeologists need to give more attention, is sanitation. The informal disposal of human bodily waste becomes a serious problem as the density of settlements increases. Archaeological evidence of attempted solutions, in the form of latrines, drains, soakaways, and sometimes water supply, has been identified in some African regions and periods but is apparently absent from others. Inevitably, this raises the question of whether some excavators have failed to identify such evidence. Possibly the subject has been regarded by some scholars as not worth their attention, and yet the provision of such facilities, or the lack of them, is relevant to evaluating the technology of an urban society, as well as having significant social and health implications. Nevertheless, archaeological evidence for African sanitation has not yet received the attention afforded to that of Mohenjo-Daro, for example, in Pakistan (Jansen 1989).

The chapters that follow are a series of case studies, whose choice has been dictated by the availability of archaeological evidence as well as historical and ethnohistorical evidence. Chapters 2–11 examine the main areas of archaeological evidence by grouping that evidence both geographically and chronologically (Fig. 1.1). Thus, Chapter 2 discusses the earliest instance of African social complexity: the Pharaonic state and its settlements along the lower Nile. The later states and settlements of North Africa are then examined in Chapter 3. In previous editions of this book, these regions were excluded, although it was acknowledged that they influenced to varying extents the developments that took place in the Sudanese Nile Valley, the Ethiopian Plateau, and the West African savanna. The intention was to look at the cities and states of tropical Africa, because they were regarded as comprising a logically coherent group. In contrast, North Africa and Egypt have long had such diverse connections with the Mediterranean and South-West Asia that it seemed legitimate to exclude them from a study of the African evidence. This reflected a long-standing tendency for Africanist scholars to focus on what they called 'sub-Saharan Africa', conveniently beheading the continent in the process. More recently it has been realized that discussions should be set in a continent-wide, and even global, context. Peter Mitchell's book *African Connections: An Archaeological Perspective on Africa and the Wider World* (Mitchell 2005) has influenced this new orientation. Mitchell's book is a timely reminder that although connections between different societies are sometimes not represented in their material cultures, they might still be indicated by 'shared ideas and beliefs' (O'Connor and Reid 2003a: 3). The widespread dispersal of religious ideologies is a major example, but physical evidence for other aspects of culture such as the board game of mancala, played in both the Roman world and over much of Africa, is another example that is relevant here (Townshend 1979; de Voogt 2010).

However, most Africanist archaeologists have only limited knowledge of the archaeology of North Africa and Egypt, particularly of the latter with its enormous number of publications. Therefore, Chapters 2 and 3 in the present book are superficial compared with other chapters, but they have an essential role as contextual material. Moving on, Chapter 4 discusses the evidence from the middle Nile for the cities and states of Kerma, Napata, and Meroë, perhaps the first of such developments in tropical Africa, and also considers the evidence for the successor states of Christian Nubia. This is followed in

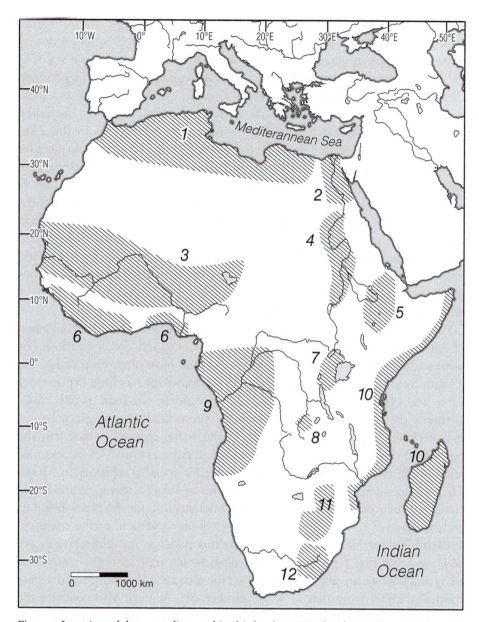

Fig. 1.1 Location of the areas discussed in this book. 1: North Africa (Chapter 3);
2: Lower Nile (Chapter 2); 3: West African savanna (Chapter 6); 4: Nubia (Chapter 4);
5: Ethiopian Highlands (Chapter 5); 6: West African rainforest (Chapter 7); 7: Interlacustrine
Region (Chapter 10); 8: Upemba Depression (Chapter 10); 9: The Far West of Central Africa
(Chapter 10); 10: East African coast and islands (Chapter 8); 11: Great Zimbabwe and
related sites (Chapter 9); 12: South African sites (Chapter 11). Drawn by Joe LeMonnier.

Chapter 5 by an examination of the evidence for Aksum and Christian Ethiopia. The scene is then changed to West Africa, and Chapters 6 and 7, respectively, look at what archaeology has to tell us of the cities and states of the West African savanna and of the West African rainforest and its fringes. Chapter 8 takes us across the continent again to examine the archaeological evidence for the cities of the East African coast and islands, including Madagascar. In contrast, Chapter 9 considers the evidence from the Zimbabwe Plateau and related areas in the interior, and Chapter 10 focuses on the Upemba Depression and the Interlacustrine Zone, in Central Africa, also discussing evidence from further west. Chapter 11, like Chapters 2 and 3, is new to this third edition. Both previous editions excluded the southern extremity of the continent, because the book was limited to *tropical* Africa. Chapter 11 considers the appearance of large settlements and centralized polities on the South African Highveld and in adjacent areas during the second millennium AD, particularly during its later part. Finally, Chapter 12 discusses possible common circumstances in the examples of social complexity that have been examined in the previous chapters.

The subject matter of this book is limited to the last five and a half millennia of Africa's past (Fig. 1.2) but prior to colonialism and decolonization. For some parts of Africa the last two millennia or so have often been called 'the African Iron Age', but such technoepochal terminology has little explanatory value and obstructs rather than aids understanding (Connah 1998b: 5–6). Certainly the period concerned was one of substantial technological change, but there were also profound economic and social changes, which it is the purpose of this book to investigate. This investigation consists of the examination of the relevant archaeological evidence for social complexity in Africa. That evidence consists of the material remains of larger settlements and of the culture of their occupants, together with inferences about the relationship of such settlements to the populations of their hinterlands and to the resources available in those hinterlands. In assessing this evidence, it is important to ask how we know that a particular archaeological site represents the remains of a city and how we are able to assume that the area around it constituted a state controlled either from that or from another city. We can also compare the picture that emerges from the archaeological evidence with the picture that can be reconstructed from ethnohistorical or historical evidence. At the very roots of our enquiry, however, are basic questions around which the whole discussion revolves: how and why did cities and states emerge in Africa? In particular, what factors led to their development in some parts of the continent but not in others? These questions allow us to assess, principally using archaeological evidence, both the theoretical explanations of anthropologists like Haas (1982) and the explanatory hypotheses advanced by

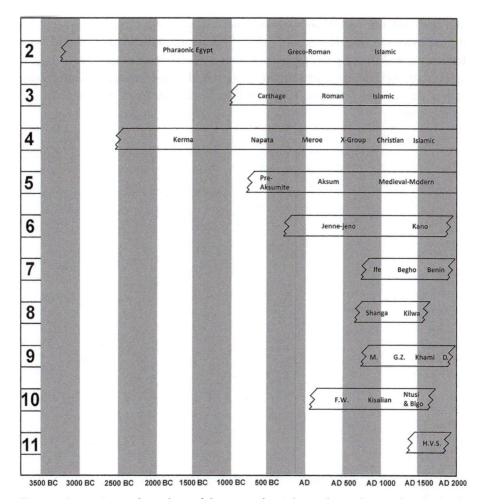

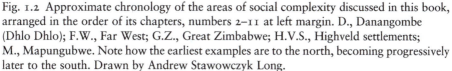

Fig. 1.2 Approximate chronology of the areas of social complexity discussed in this book, arranged in the order of its chapters, numbers 2–11 at left margin. D., Danangombe (Dhlo Dhlo); F.W., Far West; G.Z., Great Zimbabwe; H.V.S., Highveld settlements; M., Mapungubwe. Note how the earliest examples are to the north, becoming progressively later to the south. Drawn by Andrew Stawowczyk Long.

Africanist historians (Lonsdale 1981). In attempting such an assessment, the approach is based on that advocated by Renfrew (1983: 17), discussed above (p. 7). The archaeological evidence for each group of African cities and states is investigated from the point of view of geographical location, environmental conditions, subsistence, technology, social system, population pressures, ideology, and external trade. Whatever the weaknesses of the archaeological evidence for the emergence of cities and states in Africa, it can increase the time depth of our understanding of these processes and test

and flesh out our historical sources, where such sources exist. The archaeological evidence reveals a remarkable diversity of both urbanism and state
formation in Africa's past, suggesting that a world-wide reappraisal of these
aspects of social complexity might be required – a reappraisal that should
at last pay proper attention to the physical evidence from previous African
civilizations.

Chapter 2

Origins: social change on the lower Nile

The earliest example of social complexity in Africa was along the lower valley of the River Nile. Some of the first indications have been found at Hierakonpolis, on the west bank of the Nile in southern Egypt, where extensive habitation and cemetery sites date to the fourth millennium BC. This and other sites suggest that social changes were already taking place amongst the formerly dispersed agropastoral people of the region. Local elites were emerging, and by about 3000 BC there is evidence for the First Dynasty of Pharaonic rulers of 'Ancient Egypt'. This polity has long occupied a special place in Western consciousness, both scholarly and public. Pharaonic Egypt has been regarded as one of the great 'civilizations', as an almost mythical construct and treated as separate from the overall study of Africa's past. However, archaeologists are now considering Egypt in its African context, for example, O'Connor and Reid (2003b) and Exell (2011), but for a long time this was not done. It was insisted that Egypt during the last three millennia BC demanded extensive archaeological investigations, but until the middle of the twentieth century the rest of the continent was given far less attention. Consequently, the capacity for Egyptology to shed light on the processes leading to social complexity, in Africa and elsewhere, has sometimes been overlooked. This is unfortunate because the Egyptian evidence has great comparative value.

That evidence is exceptional in three ways. First, the climate and environment of the Nile Valley and its surrounding deserts have resulted in the survival of a range of organic materials rarely encountered in archaeological contexts elsewhere in Africa. Second, the monumental expression of social order by ancient Egyptians has left extensive physical evidence in the form of pyramids, tombs, temples, statues, and other structures that have dominated scholarly attention. Third, the development of writing, of which there was already an early form by about 3300 BC (Davies and Friedman 1999: 36–7; O'Connor 2011: 143–7), means that there are substantial documentary sources, particularly for later periods, as well as archaeological evidence. These factors have resulted in a massive quantity of data that has affected much of its interpretation. The Ancient Egyptians recorded their history in terms of the reigns and dynasties of their rulers, the latter numbered from one to thirty. This has been presented as a sequence lasting three millennia, a chronology originating from the work of a third-century BC Egyptian priest called Manetho. The sequence comprises the Early Dynastic Period, the Old

Kingdom, the Middle Kingdom, the New Kingdom, and the Late Period, the second and subsequent of these being separated from each other by three Intermediate Periods of sociopolitical instability (Baines and Malek 2000; Shaw 2000). This sequence provides the longest and most detailed historical account in any part of Africa but has tended to encourage a conservative approach to the archaeological study of Ancient Egypt.

In contrast, during recent years there have been attempts to look at the evidence more objectively and to ask either new questions of it or old questions in new ways. We have a relatively detailed picture for much of the time occupied by the mature Pharaonic state, characterized by periods of centralized power that alternated with periods of sociopolitical fragmentation, what Kent Flannery (after Henry Wright) called 'cycling' (Flannery 1999: 4–5). However, it is the earliest periods, generally referred to as the 'Predynastic', that have the greatest capacity to throw light on the processes that led to the emergence of social complexity in Egypt. Thus, Barry Kemp devoted a third of his book *Ancient Egypt: Anatomy of a Civilization* to the foundations of the state (Kemp 1991) and David Wengrow (2006) traced relevant social transformations from 10,000 to 2650 BC, ending his investigation near the point where studies of Ancient Egypt have often begun.

Geographical location and environmental factors

Without the River Nile, Ancient Egypt would have been desert. As now, in most places there was little rainfall, in some areas virtually none, with an average monthly maximum temperature in June and July of 34°C (for Cairo, at present) and high evapotranspiration. However, the Nile, one of the world's great rivers, was fed with water from the Ethiopian mountains and from deep in equatorial Africa. Once a year, usually without fail, it flooded a narrow strip of land on each side as well as other nearby low-lying areas. This not only saturated the ground but also left fertile silt lying on top. Each year, after the floodwaters had receded, highly productive agriculture flourished on the irrigated land each side of the Nile and in the Nile Delta where the river entered the Mediterranean Sea. The main crops were emmer wheat and barley, plus lentils, chickpeas, vegetables, fruit, sesame, and flax. Livestock included cattle, sheep, goats, pigs, pigeons, ducks, geese, and bees. During the Pharaonic period, as is still the case, Egypt was the gift of the Nile, and the Nile was the gift of Africa. The river supported agricultural production that yielded a large surplus, able to support a complex society with a dense population. It also abounded in fish, reeds that were used in construction and matting, and papyrus that provided writing materials. In addition, wild game beyond the valley margins remained a hunting resource for a long time. Furthermore, the Nile provided transportation from one end of this long narrow country to the other. With the prevailing wind blowing from the north and the river flowing from the south, boats could sail in one direction and drift or be rowed back. In this way bulky commodities and heavy raw materials could be moved and relatively easy communications could be maintained between different communities (Fig. 2.1).

With abundant food in most years, Ancient Egypt was a land of plenty with a good transportation system. Yet each side of the narrow occupied area, usually so close that it could be seen from the banks of the Nile itself, there was desert, appearing to shut off this land of plenty from the outside world. Also the Mediterranean Sea to the north and rocky cataracts in the Nile to the south seemed to enclose Egypt from those directions. However, Ancient Egyptians not only learnt to exploit the mineral and other resources of the surrounding deserts but also traded with their southern neighbours along the Nile in Nubia. In addition, trade was developed with people in the Levant and with others as far away as Mesopotamia with its emerging city-states. The Sinai Peninsula provided early contacts with those regions; by the late fourth millennium BC the domestication of the donkey and its use as a pack animal facilitated growing interaction with the southern Levant that acted as a funnel for commodities from further afield (Wengrow 2006: 36, 136). In the third millennium BC, maritime trade, particularly with Lebanon, became more important; Egypt was supplied with the timber that it lacked, mostly cedar that was used in boat construction (Wengrow 2006: 148). This combination of resources, from both the Nile Valley and further afield, continued to benefit Egypt for many centuries, in spite of changes. After the Pharaonic period, Egypt's geographical position and its environment remained advantageous, in turn under Persian, Ptolemaic, Roman, Byzantine, and Arab rule. To Imperial Rome it was an important source of grain; in the late first millennium BC Alexandria became one of the world's intellectual centres; by the early second millennium AD al-Fustat (under modern Cairo) was one of Africa's wealthiest cities; and Egypt has continued to provide a link between Africa and the Mediterranean, South-West Asia, the Red Sea, and the Indian Ocean. It was not for nothing that Napoleon sought to occupy it at the end of the eighteenth century AD or that Germany made it a strategic objective during World War II. Post-Pharaonic Egypt can contribute to an understanding of subsequent state and urban development in the rest of Africa, just as Pharaonic Egypt helps us to understand their origins.

Geographical and environmental advantages relevant to the Nile are discussed in greater detail in Chapter 4, on Nubia, although concerning the valley south of Egypt. However, there were also constraints on human occupation in both areas. In Egypt, a major problem was the very river that gave it life: not

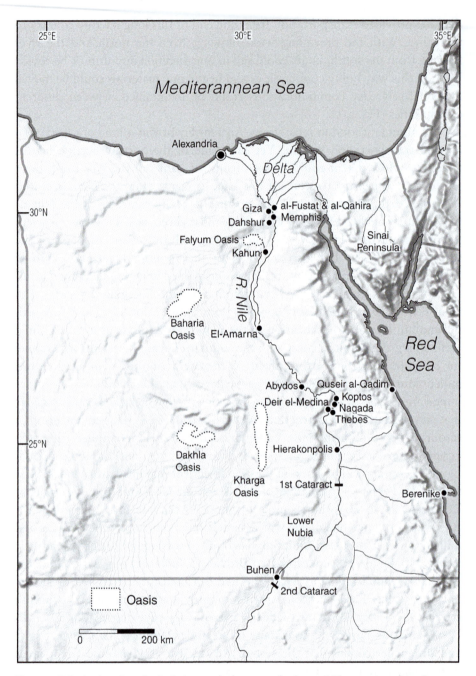

Fig. 2.1 Principal archaeological sites and places on the lower Nile mentioned in the text. Drawn by Joe LeMonnier.

only was it a perennial source of river-borne diseases but in some years its flood could fail and in other years be so high that settlements and farmland were swept away. Crops and livestock could be lost and famine could threaten. Such events resulted from short-term climatic oscillations, but changes over longer periods were of greater significance. Thus the increasingly dry conditions in much of the Sahara from about the fourth millennium BC (Hendrickx and Vermeersch 2000: 35) must have had an impact on the Egyptian Nile Valley, as people were forced out of the desert into its margins, including the Mediterranean coast to its north and the Sahel to its south. It is surely significant that it was at about this time that signs of social complexity appeared in Egypt, as its resources and those of its margins and oases attracted more and more people (Hassan 2002: 323).

Sources of information

Historical evidence

There is information on social and political organization in Egypt over the last six millennia, particularly for the Pharaonic period. Both documentary and archaeological sources throw light on the emergence and vicissitudes of the Ancient Egyptian state and on the character and role of its cities. A variety of written material exists, both in hieroglyphs used for formal purposes and in more rapidly written scripts such as hieratic and the later demotic (Baines and Malek 2000: 198–201). Much of this is on papyrus, which the dry environment has often preserved, but there are also many inscriptions on other materials, particularly stone. In conjunction with large numbers of painted and/or carved depictions, these written sources show how the Ancient Egyptians saw themselves and how they represented their past. Inevitably such evidence requires critical interpretation, and this has generated a vast amount of scholarship. Consequently, the development of writing in Ancient Egypt has provided us with a picture of past society unparalleled in the rest of Africa for that period. We have the names of real people and descriptions of actual events; we are also provided with a detailed chronology of impressive length.

Surviving documentation includes monumental and funerary inscriptions; administrative records; correspondence; religious and ritual material; astronomical, medical and mathematical texts; narrative fiction; poetry; and writing for everyday purposes. Collectively, these sources provide valuable information on the character of Pharaonic society; concerning the New Kingdom, for example, even the details of private life can be reconstructed (Meskell 2002). The documentary sources indicate an abundant agricultural surplus in most years, supporting a complex society with a dense population, amongst whom a substantial number of people appear to have been at least partly literate. There is written evidence for government officials, priests, craftsmen, artists, scribes, soldiers, merchants, and many others, as well as for the numerous farmers who produced the food. Documentation reveals a hierarchical state headed by an absolute monarch with both secular and sacred authority, the Pharaoh, and a government that became increasing bureaucratic as time passed. People lived in cities, towns, and villages and on estates. There was a complex religious ideology concerning both life and death; the central role of religion contributed to Ancient Egypt's long survival, by encouraging social and political cohesion in spite of periods of instability and collapse. A concept of right order produced a society that appears to have been conservative, although there were changes as time passed.

Archaeological evidence

Much can be learned from the extraordinary amount of archaeological evidence, particularly for Pharaonic Egypt. Famously, this includes massive public works such as pyramids, numerous temples, and statues and other stone sculptures of rulers and gods, often with associated texts. It has been suggested that the construction of the pyramids functioned as an 'economic engine' that drove the Pharaonic state. The sheer size of each of these monumental building projects involved the collection and redistribution of resources on a massive scale, in order to support the necessary workforce and specialists. Of the largest of the pyramids it has been claimed that, especially during the Old Kingdom, they served as 'a major catalyst for ... the development of Egypt as one of the world's first true states' (Lehner 1997: 9). Building on such a scale would have required complex organization efficiently directed, indicating the existence of a powerful centralized state. In addition to these monumental structures, there were many other tombs and burials whose level of sophistication reflected the hierarchical character of that state, as did the large number of informative wall paintings within some tombs. Inevitably, it has been pyramids, other tombs, and temples, often constructed in stone, and the numerous sculptures and paintings, which have attracted the greatest attention from archaeologists. As a result, the latter have usually been preoccupied with elites and state ritual, although there is now a growing interest in the rest of the Ancient Egyptian population. One consequence has been that until recently relatively little attention was given to the archaeology of Pharaonic settlements. Indeed, at one time it was thought that Ancient Egypt was a case of 'civilization without cities' (Wilson 1960), a belief now firmly rejected (Trigger 2003: 120). It was also presumed that most of the evidence for urbanization was buried beneath Nile sediments or covered by modern occupation and that excavation would be difficult because of ephemeral building materials, loose spatial organization, and royal residences that shifted periodically.

Nevertheless, there is archaeological evidence for the development of urbanism as well as for the emergence of the Egyptian state. Although the Predynastic period is principally known from burials, both the process of urbanization and the rise of the state can be traced in the character and location of the cemeteries (Wilkinson 1996: 86–8). In addition, there were villages clustered along the Nile, and by about 3500 BC there were large settlements at Hierakonpolis, Koptos, Naqada, and Abydos, all in Upper (southern) Egypt. These appear to have been sprawling, low-density settlements, in contrast to later walled, brick-built towns of higher population density. Subsequently, Ancient Egyptian towns and cities seem to have developed for various reasons: as administrative, cult, or craft centres; as military bases; or as a combination of several of these. Their ties with agriculture remained strong because it usually formed their main resource base. Inevitably, they competed with one another for assets, and during the Predynastic period this must have led to some centres and some individuals gaining more wealth and political power than others. By the late fourth millennium BC there were a number of such centres of power, controlling limited areas and headed by elite figures with both secular and sacred authority. It was out of their continuing and apparently violent rivalry that the Egyptian Dynastic state emerged about 3100 BC (Kemp 1991). An indication of this centralizing process is provided by the so-called Cities Palette (Kemp 1991: 50; Wengrow 2006: 209), a fragment of a stone cosmetic palette that appears to depict seven walled cities under attack, presumably by a locally powerful early ruler (Fig. 2.2). A similar representation of a city under attack is present on the Narmer Palette from Hierakonpolis; it also shows Narmer, wearing the crown of Lower Egypt, inspecting ten decapitated prisoners; on the other side of the palette, wearing the crown of Upper Egypt, he is about to strike a prisoner (Wengrow 2006: 42–3).

Archaeological investigations have provided information about the layout of Pharaonic cities and other settlements. An early example is the Old Kingdom mortuary-cult 'town', attached to the Valley Temple of King Sneferu of the Fourth Dynasty at Dahshur (Kemp 1991: 148). Possibly occupied by only a hundred people, already there are indications of planning in its layout. Indeed, the Middle Kingdom town of Kahun, also known as Lahun, attached to the pyramid of Senusret II, is evidence of orderly planning by central authority (Fig. 2.3) and has been estimated as capable of containing a population of about 5,000 (Kemp 1991: 149–57). Such state control is particularly evident in the case of the Middle Kingdom fortress of Buhen, just north of the Second Nile Cataract in Nubia, on what was then Pharaonic Egypt's southern frontier (Kemp 1991: 168–72). Although military considerations were clearly of primary importance in its plan, it was in effect a fortified town that probably had

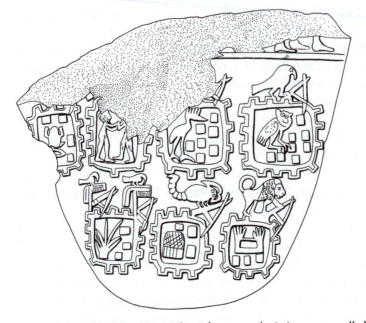

Fig. 2.2 One side of the 'Cities Palette' fragment, depicting seven walled towns under attack by animals symbolizing the monarchy and wielding hoes. It is presumed that the palette, which dates to about 3000 BC, celebrated victories in the expansion of the kingdom of Hierakonpolis and that it provides evidence for early state development on the lower Nile. From Kemp 1991: 50, fig. 16.

a large population (Fig. 2.4). More important, however, was the New King-dom city of El-Amarna, constructed for 'the heretic king' Akhenaten and named Akhetaten, for which population estimates vary between 20,000 and 50,000 (Kemp 1991: 269). This short-lived city has been extensively excavated over many years, providing information on both its layout and on the lives of its inhabitants (Fig. 2.5). The spread of house sizes indicates a society grading from poor to rich without any major gaps, the great gulf being between the residents as a whole and the ruler and his family (Kemp 1991: 298, 300). In contrast, layout details of the major cities of Memphis and Thebes are limited because of their lengthy occupation, although ironically the entire plan of the craftsmen's village of Deir el-Medina (Fig. 2.6), near Thebes, has been revealed by excavation (Meskell 2002: 42). However, the layout of the later city of Alexandria, during the Ptolemaic and Roman periods, is known (Lloyd 2000: 406). It demonstrates the continuity of urbanism in Egypt, as also do the even later Islamic cities of al-Fustat and al-Qahira (Fig. 2.7) from the seventh to twelfth century AD (Kubiak 1987; Raymond 2000).

Not only are the archaeological sites of Pharaonic and later Egypt informa-tive; they have also yielded enormous quantities of cultural material of a

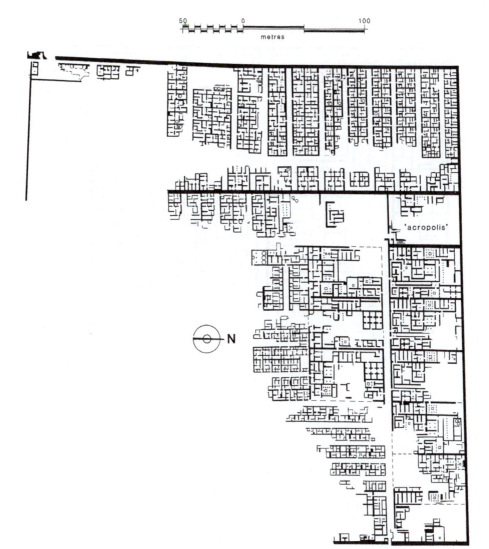

Fig. 2.3 Plan of the Middle Kingdom town of Kahun, of which part has been lost to cultivation. An early example of orderly planning by central authority, it was attached to the pyramid of Senusret II (c. 1842–1837 BC) to house the workmen who built the pyramid and the priests and others responsible for maintaining the cult of the dead king. After Kemp 1991: 150, fig. 53.

variety unmatched in many other parts of the world. This includes pottery, stone vessels, basketry, clothing, footwear, furniture, a great range of metal-work, tools, weapons, jewellery, cosmetic objects, children's toys, board games, symbolic and religious items, and many other artefacts. There are also the remains of boats, including one that is 43.3 metres (142 feet) long, dated to

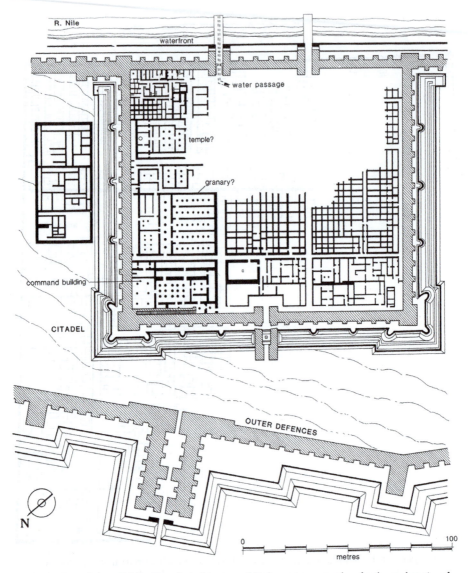

Fig. 2.4 Plan of the Middle Kingdom fortress of Buhen, an example of urban planning for the military. This was constructed by Senusret I (c. 1918–1875 BC) to protect Egypt's southern border. From Kemp 1991: 170, fig. 60.

slightly before 2500 BC, found in a pit adjacent to Khufu's pyramid at Giza (Lehner 1997: 119). Even earlier boats have been found in the boat-grave cemetery at Abydos, which has provided evidence of the world's oldest sewn planked hulls by the fourth millennium BC (Ward 2006). Such boats not only were used on the Nile but could also be dismantled for overland transport to the Red Sea, where they enabled participation in maritime trade.

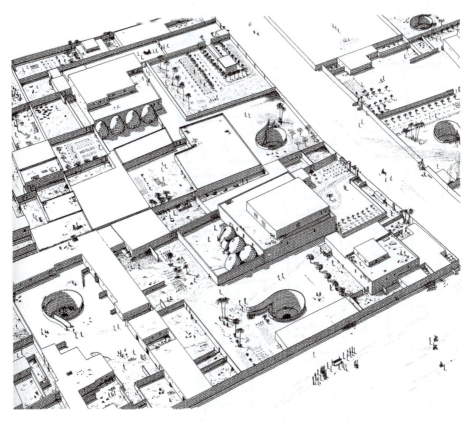

Fig. 2.5 Perspective reconstruction of part of a residential area in the New Kingdom city of El-Amarna. This was a new city, founded by Akhenaten (c. 1353–1336 BC) and abandoned soon after his death. It is one of the few Pharaonic Egyptian cities to have been extensively excavated. After Kemp 1991: 295, fig. 98.

In addition there are the remains of food and plants. This great range of evidence has survived because of the dry climate but also because of Pharaonic Egyptians' concern that their afterlife should be a continuation of their real life. Their tombs were frequently furnished with everything to achieve this; the Eighteenth Dynasty tomb of Tutankhamun is the most famous example. Amongst these items are models mainly of wood, which provide details of everyday life during some periods. These depict a wide range of individual activities, such as brewing beer, cooking, grinding grain, and milking a cow. They also show group activities, such as ploughing with oxen, butchering, workers in a granary, sailing and rowing boats, soldiers marching, and a cattle census being taken (Tooley 1995). Add to these a variety of other funerary and religious artefacts and it is apparent that a detailed picture of Pharaonic Egyptian life can be reconstructed, suggesting how much archaeological

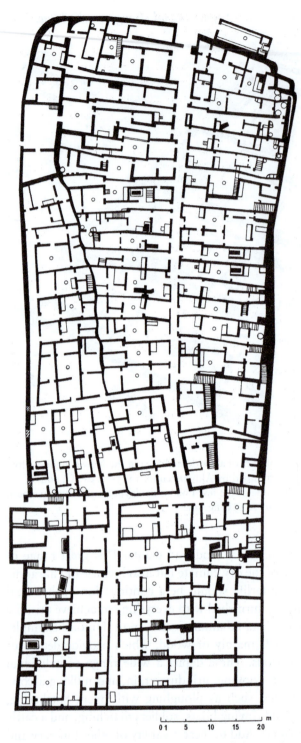

```
                              m
  0 1    5      10    15     20
```

Fig. 2.6 Plan of Deir el-Medina village near Thebes, in the Nineteenth and Twentieth Dynasties (c. 1292–1075 BC). This New Kingdom settlement housed scribes and workmen who constructed the royal tombs, and their families, close to the Valley of the Kings. The site has provided useful information about living conditions at the craftsman level of society. From Stead 1986: 8, fig. 6. *Egyptian life,* The Trustees of the British Museum, London.

Fig. 2.7 Plan of the Fatimid city of al-Qahira, founded in AD 969, showing three periods of city walls. This city was situated on the site of modern Cairo and excavations have shown that it was much larger than seen here. This plan is from a coloured original in which Gawhar's Walls were yellow and do not show here; they enclosed a smaller area than the later walls. Badr al-Gamali's Walls were red and can be seen mostly parallel to Salah ad-Din's Walls, which were in black. Circled numbers 1, 2, 3, and 4 are the locations of archaeological excavations conducted from 2001 to 2014. After Pradines 2015. Reproduced by permission of Stephane Pradines.

evidence must have been lost from many contemporary societies in other parts of Africa. However, in the case of Ancient Egypt, perhaps it is human remains that provide the most significant evidence, especially those preserved by mummification. Ideas about an existence after death resulted in great care being devoted to mummification and burial, for many lesser people as well as for rulers and elites (Spencer 1982). This preservation of human tissues now provides medical research with unique information on diseases from the third millennium BC to the first millennium AD (Lambert-Zazulak 2000). Even animals and birds were mummified at times, providing valuable research material for zoologists. The practice of human mummification continued into the Roman period, and by then a realistic portrait of the more wealthy deceased was set into the head of the mummy case, probably painted during the prime of life (Peacock 2000: 433).

Because of the importance of Ancient Egypt for understanding state emergence and the development of urbanism during the last few millennia BC, the above discussion concentrates on that period, reflecting the major emphasis in archaeological research and publication over many years. However, documentary and archaeological evidence from Egypt during the first and second millennium AD is also of significance to the study of increasing social complexity in some other parts of the African continent.

Subsistence economy

Mixed agriculture provided the base of the Ancient Egyptian economy and of the economies of periods succeeding it (Baines and Malek 2000: 190–2). The main crops were wheat and barley, but a variety of vegetables, fruit, and other plants including vines were also grown. Not only were the seasonally inundated banks and basins of the Nile Valley highly productive in most years, but large parts of the Nile Delta also contributed to a food surplus, of which grain was routinely stored in silos, some controlled by the state. Ox-drawn ploughs were in use (Fig. 2.8), as well as hoes, and the *shaduf*, a human-powered, pivoted, weighted beam, was used to raise water to extend irrigated areas. In later times water was also lifted by the *saqia*, an ox-driven waterwheel, but this does not seem to have been introduced until early in the second millennium AD. Although arable agriculture provided the most important part of subsistence, particularly in the form of grain, large numbers of cattle, sheep, goats, pigs, and poultry were raised. Nevertheless, it is significant that the staple diet for lower-status Egyptians consisted of bread and beer, the latter made from partially cooked barley bread mixed with water to produce a gruel or soup. This was not very alcoholic but it was highly nutritious, more of a food than a drink (Kemp 1991: 120). Cattle were milked and milk products contributed to

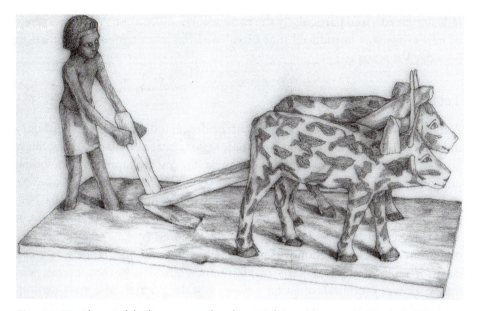

Fig. 2.8 Wooden model of a peasant ploughing with oxen, 43 centimetres long. From a Middle Kingdom (c. 1975–1640 BC) tomb. Drawn by John Pratt after Stead 1986, front cover. *Egyptian life,* The Trustees of the British Museum, London.

some diets, but for most people meat was probably limited and from small stock, beef being mainly eaten by the elite. Fish from the Nile seem to have been widely consumed, but hunting in the desert margins gradually became limited to elite sport (Baines and Malek 2000: 193).

Agricultural production depended on the labour of large numbers of peasant farmers and remained so until the late second millennium AD. It provided the bulk of the revenue that supported the Pharaonic Egyptian state and the later polities of the Nile Valley. In Ancient Egypt, apart from oxen for ploughing, donkeys to help with transport, and some mechanical assistance for raising water, it was human sweat that underpinned subsistence, provided by a rural population that was subjugated by a divine monarchy and a controlling bureaucracy. Although horses were introduced to Egypt as a result of the Hyksos invasion and swiftly adopted during the early Eighteenth Dynasty (Wilkinson 2011: 257), they seem to have been restricted to elite sport and to military use for pulling chariots. Camels, although thought to have been present earlier, became important only during the first millennium BC (Blench 2000: 316). Chickens appear to have been introduced to Egypt by the second millennium BC (Dueppen 2011: 145), but the general impression of Pharaonic agriculture is one of conservatism. It seems that the subsistence economy of Ancient Egypt consisted of a highly productive arable and pastoral agriculture, whose very strength discouraged innovation. It was not until the first

31

millennium AD, and particularly the early second millennium AD, that a range of new crops was introduced that broadened Egyptian agricultural practices (van der Veen 2011: 231).

Technology

Both documentary and archaeological evidence indicate an extraordinary diversity of technical skill in the Pharaonic state (Lucas and Harris 1962; Shaw 2012). Extractive industries were amongst the most important, including quarrying for building stone, some of it very hard (Lehner 1997: 206–7), and mining for gold, copper, and semi-precious stones. Boats on the Nile and sledges on land were used to transport quarried stone (Lehner 1997: 202–5), often in large and heavy pieces, to building sites, where the quality of masonry and construction was generally high. In addition, stone was much used for sculptures, particularly of pharaohs, gods, and historic events, and fine work was produced, often on a massive scale. Inscription-cutters demonstrated their ability on many of the buildings, monuments, and sculptures. Mud bricks were made and used, especially in less important buildings. There was a very wide range of manufacturing (Stead 1986: 36–45; Baines and Malek 2000: 194), including metals, wood, pottery, textiles, boat-building, salt, jewellery, paint and varnish, papyrus and ink, glass (mainly during the New Kingdom), and many other materials. Surveying, engineering, and architectural skills were highly developed, as were the mathematical and astronomical knowledge that underpinned them (Lehner 1997: 212–14). Medical knowledge was present (Majno 1975: 69–140) and an ability to write facilitated both intellectual and practical endeavours, although the extent of literacy amongst society as a whole is uncertain (Baines 1983: 584). In addition, the technology of warfare was given considerable attention; in the second millennium BC, for instance, the Egyptian use of the horse-drawn chariot in battle was highly effective, as were bows and arrows for many centuries (Baines and Malek 2000: 202–3). Some domestic industries were organized on a semi-industrialized scale (Baines and Malek 2000: 195), such as bread and beer making, butchering, wine making, the production of honey, and the manufacture of cosmetics.

The range of technology in Egypt seems to have increased from the first millennium BC onwards, including a greater use of iron in a metallurgy previously based on copper and later on bronze. Nevertheless, the diversity of technology that existed during the main periods of the Pharaonic state is most impressive. Clearly, functional specialization had attained a remarkable level, well able to support a complex society of both primary producers and urbanites that was normally controlled by a powerful, centralized, autocratic,

Fig. 2.9 Two of the Giza pyramids: Menkaure's in the foreground, Khafre's in the distance. Fourth Dynasty (c. 2520–2472 BC). Photograph by author, 1984.

and bounded state. What is most remarkable, however, is that this apparent technological sophistication actually depended on simple technology. Industries seem to have had relatively little mechanical assistance; for example, during earlier periods even wheeled vehicles were unknown. Instead, technology relied heavily on manual skill and sweated labourers whose willingness must at times have been doubtful. It is also apparent that an intellectual capacity for problem solving enabled many tasks to be successfully accomplished that might otherwise have been impossible. The Giza pyramids are still impressive even today (Fig. 2.9), although they were the product of what, in modern terms, was a limited technology. They are notable examples of achievement by sheer human endeavour. Like the subsistence economy of Pharaonic Egypt, however, so successful was its technology that conservatism became deeply ingrained (but see Shaw 2012), and it is arguable that Ancient Egypt ultimately failed to keep pace with the changing world around it.

Social system

Pharaonic Egypt was an autocratic society in which the ultimate source of power was a ruler with both sacred and secular authority (Wilkinson 2011). Supporting that authority was a large priesthood, a literate bureaucracy, and an eventually professional army, all three of which gained increasing influence within the state as time went on. During the three millennia that the Ancient Egyptian state existed, there were periods of political weakness and even of disintegration, but there were also periods when the central government was strong and when the state extended its control into adjacent territories in Nubia and the Levant. The Egyptian population was stratified into a hierarchy headed by the ruler and his family, with an elite consisting of priests, government officials, and army officers. Below them were craftsmen practising a wide range of skills, merchants who contributed importantly to the economy, and soldiers who later were professionals. At the bottom of society was a very large peasant class, mostly of subsistence farmers who supplied the state with food, in the form of taxes, and provided corvée labour on government mining, quarrying, and construction projects (Meskell 2002: 13). Government could demand such labour in lieu of taxes, because in theory all land belonged not to the farmers but to the pharaoh, although in practice much of it was actually the property of temples or of members of the elite. In addition, there were slaves, seemingly captives from foreign wars. Wilkinson (2011: 364) has painted a grim picture of life for the bulk of the Egyptian population, with a lifespan of about thirty-five years (Meskell 2002: 13 gives thirty-six years), afflicted by diseases, and kept 'in a state of permanent penury' by an oppressive government and upper class who expended enormous resources on making sure that they themselves lived and died luxuriously. It is hardly surprising that desperate peasants, determined to have a share of the country's undoubted wealth, robbed many royal and elite tombs during the course of the state's existence.

During the eighteenth century AD, Jean-Jacques Rousseau wrote about what he called 'the social contract', an unwritten agreement between government and the governed that benefitted both (Rousseau 1966). In Pharaonic Egypt, this contract depended on the people's fundamental beliefs in a range of gods with whom the pharaoh could commune on behalf of the country as a whole. This, it was believed, would ensure that the Nile flooded at the right time and to the right level and that there was peace and stability within the country. In return, particularly the lower classes laboured to do the pharaoh's will. Through the long course of Ancient Egyptian history, this situation varied considerably, but it is apparent that slowly the contract failed. Droughts, famines, succession problems, instances of weak leadership, political infighting, and external attack all contributed to this failure, as did the poor treatment of many ordinary Egyptians by the state. Usually overtaxed and often underfed, any resistance by the lower classes to the state was likely to be met with violence: beatings, imprisonment, even death were the tools of a repressive system. As Maisels (2010: 173) has written: 'State formation in Egypt was clearly a product of violence', and violence was often a major element in ensuring the state's continuity. The Ancient Egyptian passion for written records has provided ample evidence that for the majority this was not the golden age that some have subsequently thought it. Yet those same records provide exceptions: although primogeniture within the royal family theoretically determined Pharaonic succession, nevertheless some pharaohs had humble origins and achieved power partly by personal ability; there were even instances when women governed in their own right and others where they were highly influential within the state.

Overall, it is astonishing that the Pharaonic state survived so long and was so frequently able to remake itself after periods of failure. It was based on a society characterized by extreme inequality; particularly during its later periods it seems that its frequently corrupt and violent government neither knew nor cared about the plight of many of its people. There must always be a question of whether such a society can endure, but in the case of Ancient Egypt it managed to do so for a very long time.

Population pressures

For Pharaonic Egypt, Kemp (1991: 10) stated that by the time of the late New Kingdom the total population 'had probably not exceeded 4 to 5 million'. In Roman Egypt, for which documentation is much better, Peacock (2000: 444) estimated a total of 4.75 million, of which 1.75 million lived in towns. These figures are modest by modern standards, but living conditions were very different from those of the modern world. Given the limited cultivatable land in the Nile Valley, although augmented by that in the Nile Delta, and given a limited agricultural technology, it is possible that Ancient Egypt did near its maximum carrying capacity in years of low Nile levels when famine threatened. Nevertheless, it is apparent that compared with neighbouring regions in most years it offered both a bountiful environment and a strong economy that attracted migrants. The Asiatic Hyksos, the so-called Sea Peoples, Libyans, Persians, Greeks, Romans, and Arabs were amongst these. Eventually, migrant inflow led to both political change and ethnic change and very likely caused population pressure. Indeed, at a much earlier date, the origins of the Pharaonic state might be seen as partly the consequence of an increasingly crowded upper Nile Valley, as climatic deterioration drove in people from the fringing deserts (Hassan 2002: 323). Lehner (1997: 7) gives an estimated population for Egypt when the Giza pyramids were built, in the third millennium BC, of 1.6 million, compared with 58 million in AD 1995. He is of the opinion that Khufu's pyramid could have been built by teams of 25,000 men, each team working three-month stints for twenty years (1997: 224). That such workforces could have existed is indicative of a sizeable population. Another indication that this was probably the case for much of Ancient Egypt's history is the treatment of those who transgressed: this was a totalitarian state very ready to use violence on its population, even death when thought appropriate. Life, it appears, was cheap, suggesting that the population was thought sufficiently large to accommodate such measures of control. Furthermore, an indication that life was expendable is the incidence of human sacrifice at an early date, particularly in the late fourth to early third millennium BC (Bard 2000: 71). Overall, it seems likely that population pressure was a characteristic of Ancient Egypt, given its limited area, but that relatively high productivity counterbalanced this in years when the Nile inundation was normal.

Ideology

Ancient Egyptian ideology centred on the unifying role of an absolute ruler, the pharaoh, as opposed to the chaos that could result from political and social division. It was the divine ruler's obligation to see that the Egyptian concept of right order prevailed. So strongly held were these ideas that even during periods of internal dissension or external threat, as Wilkinson (2011: 405) has stated, 'the sheer weight and antiquity of Pharaonic beliefs had a tendency to win through in the end'. These beliefs involved numerous gods and goddesses with a variety of functions, some of the deities local, some venerated throughout the country. Ra, Amun, Horus, Osiris, and Isis were amongst the more important, but there was great complexity in religious ideas, which also changed as time went on (Baines and Malek 2000: 212–14). Large numbers of temples and their priests ensured that appropriate religious ceremonies were observed, in the process gradually becoming a powerful element in state infrastructure. Thus religious ideology played a major role in the functioning of the Pharaonic state, as is evident from the virtual revolution that occurred when Amenhotep IV, Akhenaten, attempted to change the state religion during the later fourteenth century BC (Wilkinson 2011: 279–300). The power of tradition was such that, after his death, his successors speedily reverted to previous practices. Ancient Egyptian ideology was more than religion, however; there was also a fundamental conviction that Egypt was the world, that it was superior, different from the inferior places and peoples who lay beyond the deserts to east and west, beyond the Nile cataracts to the south, and beyond the sea to the north. As Egypt came to play a greater commercial and political role in the region around it, this idea inevitably weakened. Although lip service continued to be paid to long-held traditions, the desecration and plundering of the tombs of their predecessors by some later rulers (Wilkinson 2011: 395–7) was indicative of a cynicism that would eventually contribute to the dissolution of the Pharaonic state. That state had depended on a powerful ideological base; when its constituent beliefs failed, so did the state.

External trade

Pharaonic Egypt's location in a major alluvial valley, watered by the annual inundation of the Nile, provided food and some resources but lacked other raw materials, particularly minerals. However, as already discussed (p. 19), Egypt's geographical position enabled it to obtain these by trade or intimidation from Nubia to its south and from the eastern Mediterranean and South-West Asia to its north. Its commercial activities also extended into the surrounding deserts and, by transporting dismantled boats across the desert (Ward 2006), also along the Red Sea perhaps as far as the region of modern Eritrea. The Nile provided access deep into the African interior, with both waterborne transportation and overland routes that cut across some of the bends in the river. Gold, ivory, ebony, animals and animal skins, incense, and other African exotica were the main attractions to the Egyptians. Sinai gave land access to the Levant, and Egyptian shipping enabled heavy commodities to be transported relatively easily by sea. Wood, copper, possibly tin, silver, precious stones, wine, and oil were obtained, in exchange for gold, linen, grain, and, particularly in later periods, even papyrus (Baines and Malek 2000: 20). Trade connections also introduced to Egypt new elements of material culture, especially during the Second Intermediate Period, such as bronze, new crops, the horse and chariot, composite bows, and new musical instruments. Although Ancient Egypt could provide many essentials, nevertheless trade with surrounding regions was vital to its economy; the increasing importance to Egypt of access to the resources of those regions partly explains its imperial ambitions during the New Kingdom. Pharaonic Egypt's decline as an international power during later periods occurred at the same time as a decline in its international trade.

Ancient Egypt was a nonmonetary economy; coinage was adopted only in the late fifth century BC, when the Athenian currency was introduced as the monetary standard (Wilkinson 2011: 452–3). Therefore, for most of its earlier history, commercial transactions in Egypt used barter but, as Kemp (1991: 248, 250) explains, this was not as crude as it might seem. It depended on a system in which everything 'had a value, expressed in various units which coincided with quantities of certain commodities'. This might appear an inefficient method of exchange, but it was clearly adequate because it survived for a long time. However, by Ptolemaic, Roman, and Islamic times a more complex economic system had developed, which supported a more extensive external trade.

Light has been shed on this by archaeological investigations at the Ptolemaic and Roman port of Berenike (Fig. 2.10), of the third century BC to fifth century AD, on the Egyptian Red Sea coast (Cappers 2006; Sidebotham and

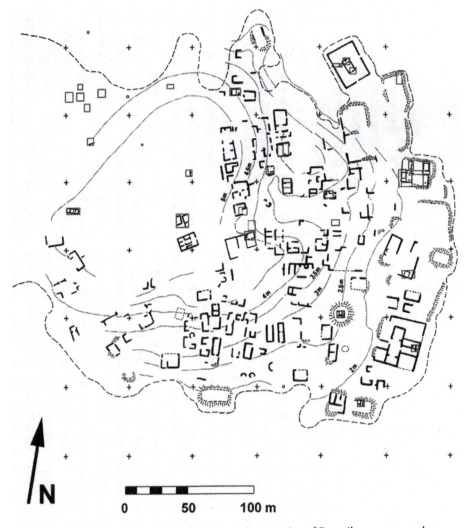

Fig. 2.10 Plan of the main part of the Graeco-Roman city of Berenike, a port on the Egyptian Red Sea coast. Darker features are building remains, lighter rectangles are excavation cuttings. Contours are at 0.5-metre intervals. After Cappers 2006: 52, fig. 4.3. Reproduced with permission of the Cotsen Institute of Archaeology, University of California, Los Angeles.

Wendrich 2007). Archaeological evidence from the Roman (first to third centuries AD) and Islamic (eleventh to fifteenth centuries AD) ports at Quseir al-Qadim on the same coast is also highly informative (van der Veen 2011). Situated in a coastal desert, to which food had to be transported from the Nile Valley and water from possibly as far, the extremely dry conditions at these sites have preserved a wide range of archaeological materials, including botanical remains. From Quseir al-Qadim the latter included ninety-five plants important to the economy, providing direct evidence of long-distance seaborne commerce and of the introduction of South and South-East Asian crops into Egypt and neighbouring areas. Like Berenike, Quseir al-Qadim was a transit hub, situated at the Red Sea end of the shortest land route to the River Nile, down which imports were passed to Alexandria and on to the Mediterranean world and Western Europe. During the Roman period, black pepper from India was the most important of the traded commodities, and contemporary authors confirm its frequent use in Rome. It continued to be important in Islamic times, but the evidence from Quseir al-Qadim shows that many other spices were also handled by then, including ginger, turmeric, cardamom, fagara (a medicinal fruit from China or the Indian subcontinent), and betel nut. In addition, the evidence for introduced crops amongst the remains from Islamic Quseir al-Qadim include citron, rice, cotton, lime, banana, aubergine, sugar cane, and taro. Huge potential profits from the Indian Ocean trade were a major reason for the existence of these ports, although the risks involved were substantial. In Islamic times there was also the added incentive of an ability to supply food, sourced from the Nile Valley, to pilgrims going to or returning from Mecca across the Red Sea. Other archaeological evidence from Quseir al-Qadim includes Roman ship-rigging artefacts of wood and fragments of Islamic ship timbers, two of the former being of teak, which is likely to have come from India. Furthermore, participation in the Indian Ocean commerce during Islamic times is indicated by the presence of Indian resist-dye textiles, Chinese celadon, and Thai ceramics. In addition, details of that commerce during both periods are available from documentary evidence. As indicated by the botanical evidence, Egypt appears to have developed substantial trading contacts with both South and South-East Asia by Roman and Islamic times (Fig. 2.11). Indeed, maritime trade on the Red Sea and beyond was probably already active at an earlier date. At the end of the seventh century BC, the Saite ruler Nekau II (of the Twenty-sixth Dynasty) had started to dig a canal between the Nile and the Red Sea, which the Persian king Darius I completed in 497 BC. Subsequently, it seems to have silted up, but this first attempt at a Suez Canal indicates how important the Red Sea trade must already have been to Egypt (Wilkinson 2011: 451).

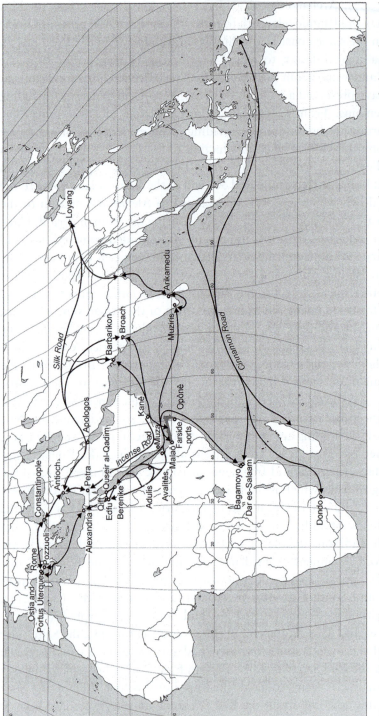

Fig. 2.11 Main trade routes during the Roman period in the Indian Ocean and related regions. This map indicates the extent to which Northeast and East Africa were in contact with other parts of the world. It is an important reminder that even the Africa of two millennia ago should not be considered in isolation. From Cappers 2006: 12, fig. 1.1. Reproduced with permission of the Cotsen Institute of Archaeology, University of California, Los Angeles.

Conclusion

The archaeology of the Egyptian Nile Valley has frequently been studied divorced from the rest of Africa (Exell 2011). Similarly, the archaeology of the rest of Africa has usually been perceived as isolated from that of the lower Nile. This situation can impede an understanding of state formation and the emergence of urbanism in Africa as a whole. An opportunity is lost, not only to investigate the earliest example of these processes in Africa, but also to trace their vicissitudes over the course of many centuries. Pharaonic Egypt and subsequent polities are richly documented by both historical and archaeological sources. They show how, in the long term, states and cities can emerge, flourish, dwindle, collapse, and form again, in a sequence that can recur as political, economic, and social conditions change and as cultures and ideas change. These complicated processes are easier to trace in the Egyptian past than in that of much of the rest of Africa, where the available evidence is often limited and restricted to shorter periods. To write about 'the rise and fall of Ancient Egypt' (Wilkinson 2011) is surely to oversimplify a situation in which such complex societies do not actually 'fall' but change into something different as the world around them changes. In the case of Ancient Egypt, it is apparent that religious beliefs and cultural practices were so strongly held that they limited the capacity for change until the country came, in turn, under Persian, Ptolemaic, Roman, and Arab control. It is a fitting reminder that culture is dynamic, not static, and that people who actively try to 'preserve' their culture are in the end imperilling their future, a danger that still exists in the modern world.

The succession of polities in the lower Nile Valley also permits an analysis of the circumstances in which they developed, disintegrated, and formed again. The major factor in the case of Egypt seems to have been its strong agricultural base, capable of producing surplus food not only for local consumption but also for export to surrounding, less fortunate lands. A second factor was the extraordinarily versatile technology that is so richly documented in the archaeological evidence. Although limited by its dependence on manual energy and skill, with little mechanical input, its achievements are amongst the most impressive examples of functional specialization from the premodern age. To this should be added the third factor, a social system that provided an enduring element within the state and its settlements. Ancient Egypt was a dictatorship, a totalitarian state based on a stratified society in which the individual did what he or she was told, at the risk of physical punishment or even death. It seems likely that this situation was partly the product of the fourth factor, population pressure particularly during periods of low Nile level. Labour and life were cheap; the former could be expended extravagantly on public works of monumental scale, and loss of the latter was part of the price of political and social stability and order. Of fundamental importance for the continued survival of such an autocratic society was the fifth factor: a powerful state religion. In a situation where the ruler communed with the gods, or was even perceived as one of them, to disobey was not only treason, it was also sacrilege. Religious belief was only one element, however, although probably the most important, in an ideology that insisted that everything was for the best as it was and that it was vital that it continue. Literacy and education appear to have been socially limited, and for the mass of the population it was vital to *believe* that the sun would rise tomorrow and that the river would flood at the right season and to a desirable level. Lastly, the sixth factor is that of external trade: it is clear that this was of great importance to Ancient Egypt. It provided raw materials not available in Egypt itself and, along with highly productive agriculture, formed a major part of the Egyptian economy.

This analysis of the circumstances of states and cities in the lower Nile Valley provides a template for understanding comparable phenomena in other parts of Africa. It also serves as a reminder that Africa was never isolated in the past and should not be studied as if it was. Egypt was a part of Africa, as it still is, and was positioned 'at the bridge between Africa and Asia, the tropics and the temperate zone' (Baines and Malek 2000: 20). It is vital to understand the implications of this if one is to understand Ancient Egypt. Equally, it is vital to understand Ancient Egypt if one is to understand Ancient Africa.

Chapter 3

The Mediterranean frontier: North Africa

North Africa is situated between the Sahara Desert and the Mediterranean Sea, between an inhospitable environment discouraging travel and one facilitating extensive maritime contacts. Consequently, it has long tended to look to the north rather than to the south, constituting a frontier zone for the rest of the African continent. Excluding the lower Nile Valley, North Africa's habitable coast to the east is so narrow that in places the desert reaches the sea, but the coast broadens in the west into cultivable plains and still further west there are mountains separating it from the desert. Climatically, North Africa belongs with the Mediterranean, with hot dry summers and mild winters when most of the modest rainfall occurs. Culturally, the region has been a meeting place for people from the Levant, Greece, Rome, Europe, and Arabia and the indigenous Libyans. As a result, North Africa has played a role in the history of Europe as well as in that of Africa. The Mediterranean has been the link, providing relatively easy movement for traders and migrants and a frequent focus for armed conflict. Commencing early in the first millennium BC, a series of colonial and indigenous settlements developed that included urban communities and indications of state development. These were technologically sophisticated societies, at least partly literate, that constituted early examples of African social complexity, not as early as its development in the Nile Valley but still preceding that of most of the rest of Africa. As such, North Africa was eventually to stimulate changes in other parts of the continent, particularly in the Sahel beyond the Sahara and in adjacent regions.

Geographical location and environmental factors

North Africa extends from the lower Nile Valley to the Atlantic coast of Morocco. In terms of modern political geography, it includes western Egypt, Libya, Tunisia, Algeria, and Morocco. In Egypt and Libya the settled zone is mainly restricted to the coast by the Sahara, but in Tunisia, Algeria, and Morocco a variety of different environments, including those of the Atlas Mountains that rise to more than 4,000 metres, have provided greater opportunities for human settlement. Extending almost 3,700 kilometres from east to west, the geographical and environmental diversity of the region is striking. Average monthly temperatures in coastal Tripoli range from 14°C in January to 28°C in August but can be much higher in the desert and its margins.

Indeed, a temperature of 58°C, recorded in 1922 at El Azizia in north-west Libya, has been claimed to be the highest in the world. In contrast, winter frosts can occur inland and the highest of the Atlas Mountains are snowcapped. Rainfall also varies wildly, from as much as 1,200 millimetres a year in the coastal mountains of the west to as little as 200 millimetres in the semi-desert that forms the southern limit of most human occupation. In addition, rainfall is unreliable in many areas and evapotranspiration high. Consequently, water availability is a problem in much of the region; irrigation is often necessary; and extensive areas are of limited use. Nevertheless, parts of North Africa have long supported a highly productive agriculture; depending on local conditions, different areas have grown a variety of crops. Pastoralism has also been important, particularly in the mountains and the semi-desert. Furthermore, much of the Mediterranean coast is well provided with harbours, and fishing has been another important source of food. Although North Africa has its share of human diseases, its varied environments have long been generally conducive to settlement, as repeated colonial immigration has demonstrated.

Any consideration of the geography and environment of North Africa must include the Mediterranean Sea, as well as the lands that form its southern shore (Fig. 3.1). As the largest inland sea in the world, the Mediterranean has long been a means of contact between people, particularly those of its coasts. This has been made possible by its winds and currents and frequently calm or relatively calm seas. Although violent storms can occur, refuge in a safe harbour is often possible. Early seafarers with limited maritime technology and navigational knowledge could sail much of the Mediterranean without losing sight of land (Aubet 2001: 169). Currents and winds also influenced the selection of sailing routes, for which the islands of Cyprus, Malta, Sicily, Sardinia, Ibiza, and the south-eastern coast of Spain provided ports-of-call (Aubet 2001: 182–5). In addition, the geographical configuration of the Mediterranean coasts meant that Greece and Italy, with Sicily, were within relatively easy reach of North Africa. Furthermore, the Straits of Gibraltar gave access to the Atlantic coasts of Morocco and south-western Spain; a minimum of 14 kilometres of sea separated North Africa from the Iberian Peninsula; and people could walk from the coast of the Levant to Egypt.

Sources of information

Historical evidence

A substantial amount of historical documentation exists for the last three millennia in North Africa. The societies responsible for the emergence of urbanization and the development of states in this region were all literate

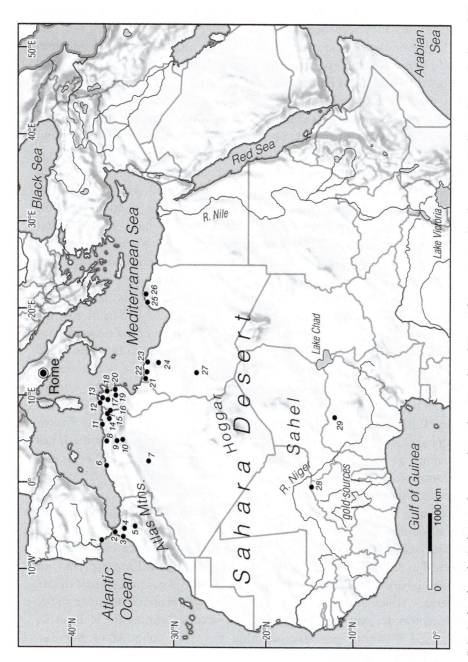

Fig. 3.1 Principal archaeological sites, places, and people in North and West Africa mentioned in the text. 1, Gadir; 2, Qsar es-Seghir and Tangier; 3, Lixus; 4, Al-Basra; 5, Fez; 6, Algiers; 7, Mzâb; 8, Djemila; 9, Thamugadi; 10, Timgad; 11, Hippo Regius; 12, Utica; 13, Carthage (Tunis); 14, Bulla Regia; 15, Althiburos; 16, Thugga; 17, Kairouan; 18, Kerkouane; 19, El Djem; 20, Mahdiyya; 21, Sabratha; 22, Oea (Tripoli); 23, Lepcis Magna; 24, Ghirza; 25, Ptolemais; 26, Cyrene; 27, Garamantes (Old Jarma); 28, Kissi; 29, Durbi Takusheyi. Drawn by Joe LeMonnier.

45

to some extent, and also Greek, Roman, and other writers recorded the activities of North African communities. External observers were sometimes prejudiced or poorly informed, and some documentary materials was written after the events they recorded, based on earlier sources that have not survived. However, inscriptions principally on stone and coins are also informative and often well dated, particularly for the Roman period.

It appears to have been Phoenician seafarers and traders, from the coast of what is now Lebanon, who inaugurated significant social change in North Africa. By the end of the second millennium BC their activities had extended throughout the length of the Mediterranean and they had founded trading colonies at Gadir, on the Atlantic coast of south-west Spain, and at Lixus, on the Atlantic coast of Morocco. Their principal motivation seems to have been the acquisition of metals, particularly silver, copper, gold, and tin, for all of which there was a substantial demand in South-West Asia. In addition, political and population pressures in their homeland could have initiated what became a widespread diaspora. As time went on, they also founded colonies in other places, including Malta, Sicily, Sardinia, Ibiza, southern Spain, and along the North African coast, selecting locations suitable as staging points on their long voyages and as potential trading centres. Utica, in Tunisia, was perhaps the earliest African colony; nearby Carthage was founded in 814 or 813 BC (Aubet 2001: 159–65). Subsequently, Carthage was to become a major urbanized state, whose rivalry with the rising power of Rome led to the three Punic Wars of the third and second centuries BC, culminating in the destruction of Carthage (Hoyos 2010). This was one of the major conflicts of the Ancient World and received attention from a number of Greek and Roman writers, but surviving Carthaginian written sources are limited. Nevertheless, the Phoenician alphabet, in which the Carthaginian language, Punic, was written, has been claimed as ancestral to the later alphabets of the Western World, and Punic continued to be written during the Roman period in North Africa and survived in a spoken form even longer (Lancel 1995).

A little later than Carthage was the Greek colony of Cyrene, according to tradition founded in 631 BC, which became one of the principal cities of the Hellenistic world and gave its name to the Roman province of Cyrenaica, established in 74 BC. This city developed further during the Roman period but appears to have declined after an earthquake in AD 365. The Cyrenaican city of Ptolemais, which also had Greek origins and was probably founded in the seventh century BC, survived longer and was occupied during the Hellenistic, Roman, and Byzantine periods, and after the Arab conquest of AD 643 (Kraeling 1962; Kenrick 2013).

Following the destruction of Carthage, North Africa was gradually absorbed into the growing Roman Empire, although it was not until the early third century AD that the Roman occupation of North Africa was completed. Documentary sources are numerous but patchy, mainly because North Africa was on the edge of the Empire and attracted relatively little attention from Roman historians. The spread of Christianity during the Late Roman period led to an increase in written sources, although those by Bishop Augustine of Hippo Regius and others tended to be dominated by religious issues (Sears 2011). Overall, the documentary sources show a Roman North Africa that consisted of numerous towns and cities, together with associated areas of rural settlements, estates, and farms. A productive agriculture developed from Carthaginian times, with a surplus of grain and some other commodities being exported. Silphium, an indigenous strong-smelling plant now extinct that was used in Greece and Rome for culinary and medicinal purposes, was also exported, as was *garum,* a sauce that was made from the entrails of salted fish and considered a great delicacy. Particularly productive was the region that now forms the northern part of Tunisia. South-west of Carthage, rebuilt during the Roman period, was an extensive wheat-growing district, and the grain shipments to Rome from here and other parts of North Africa became extremely important. The Roman army, in the form of the Third Augustan Legion, provided security, particularly along the vulnerable southern frontier. For four centuries or more North Africa became an integral part of a huge area with similar political institutions, economic and social organization, and culture. At least officially there was even a common language, in the form of Latin, although Punic and Libyan languages and cultures survived.

Gradual changes occurred in North Africa during the course of the late third, fourth, and early fifth centuries AD, particularly associated with the growing importance of Christianity (Sears 2007). Then, from AD 429 to 533 the Vandals, a Germanic warrior group, gradually occupied North Africa, leading to some socioeconomic decline but mainly replacing the ruling elite, with little change for the indigenous people (Clover 1993). Nevertheless, the Vandal invasion was 'the beginning of the end of Roman Africa' (Mattingly 1994: 215). Byzantine rule from Constantinople replaced that of the Vandals during the sixth century AD but appears to have been tenuous, as is apparent from the relative ease with which the Arabs overran North Africa during the seventh century (Christides 2000; Kenrick 2009: 6–8; Kaegi 2010).

There are numerous written sources for Islamic North Africa, in Arabic, Greek, and Latin, but many of them are of later date than the periods they describe (Christides 2000: 71–7). In some ways Islamic North Africa was the successor to Roman North Africa, although cities became less important than rural areas, which were characterized by a fragmented society of

Libyan tribes. However, some cities survived and some new ones were built, such as a capital for what was now called Ifriqiyah, a city that was founded in AD 670 at Qayrawan (Kairouan) in central Tunisia. Islamic society also adopted the Roman culture of public baths, which had flourished in Roman North Africa but was largely abandoned in Medieval Western Europe (Yegül 2010). Furthermore, during the Fatimid period in North Africa and Egypt in the tenth to twelfth centuries AD, art and architecture attained some of the highest standards in the Islamic world (Bloom 2007). It was as traders, however, that the inhabitants of Islamic North Africa made their greatest contribution to African history. During the Roman period there had been trade with people in the Sahara; the Garamantes of the Fezzan, who occupied oases south of Tripoli, participated in this, and there is growing evidence of its importance (Wilson 2012). It was this trade that enabled Garamantian urban growth and incipient state development in the hostile environment of the central Sahara during the late first millennium BC and early first millennium AD (Mattingly 2013; Mattingly and Sterry 2013). Furthermore, it was the *foggara* irrigation of the Garamantian settlements that, in turn, made those trading activities possible. Nevertheless, the extent to which such trade penetrated the desert to the south of the Fezzan is uncertain (Mattingly 2011); it appears to have consisted mainly of relay exchange, rather than exchange across the breadth of the desert. It was North African Arab traders who eventually conquered trans-Saharan travel by the use of camels as pack animals (Bulliet 1975). Capable of carrying loads of 150 to 200 kilograms each (Gauthier-Pilters and Dagg 1981: 110), they can cover 30 to 40 kilometres a day and can voluntarily go without water for up to 10 days and for longer if browsing on plants with a high water content or in cooler weather (Wilson 1984: 151, 173). They can eat thorny plants that other animals avoid and have large soft feet adapted to walking on soft sand, although liable to injury on stony surfaces. The main problem with camels is that they are susceptible to trypanosomiasis, not usually spread by tsetse flies as with other domestic animals but by other biting flies (Wilson 1984: 122–7). The single-humped camel was probably domesticated in southern Arabia, where desert Arabs learnt how to overcome problems of management. Introduced to Roman North Africa, they were used to pull ploughs and carts, but by the fourth to sixth century AD camel caravans were in use, as indicated in a stone carving from a tomb at Ghirza, in Tripolitania (Mattingly 1994: plates 59 and 61). Able to cover long distances in the desert, Islamic North Africans were to have a major impact on the peoples south of the Sahara, spreading their religion and influencing the development of trade and urbanization.

Archaeological evidence

There is plentiful archaeological evidence for the state and urban developments in North Africa that are recorded in historical sources. In spite of its destruction and later rebuilding by the Romans, the outline of the city of Carthage during the pre-Roman period is known. Excavation has uncovered housing as early as the eighth to seventh centuries BC and evidence of metalworking, dye production, and the making of fine pottery (Aubet 2001: 218–26, figure 48). The latest phase of the Punic city, in the second century BC, was carefully planned, with streets crossing at right angles and stone houses of several storeys. Shops and workplaces seem to have been mixed with domestic accommodation, and buildings were provided with washrooms and had cisterns and pipes for the supply of water and soakaways and other pipes for waste water and sanitation (Lancel 1995: 152–72).

Early cemeteries have also been investigated; their grave goods included gold jewellery and items of ivory thought to have been carved in Carthage as early as the seventh century BC (Lancel 1995: 70–6). Particular attention has been given to the *tophet*, a cemetery reserved for the burial of infant cremations from about 700 to 146 BC. This yielded more than 20,000 urns, the earlier ones containing the remains of foetuses and premature or newborn (probably stillborn) babies and later ones those of infants up to three years old. There has been debate over claims by some hostile ancient writers that child sacrifice was practised in Carthage and at other Phoenician sites, and some archaeologists have thought that the *tophet* burials at Carthage and elsewhere are evidence of this. However, it is possible that the *tophet* was merely a burial place reserved for very young children, who were not buried in cemeteries with adults. Death from natural causes has seemed the most likely explanation, in a society that probably had a high infant mortality, particularly in an urban environment where the very young would have been the most vulnerable to infection (Aubet 2001: 250–6). Nevertheless, argument on this subject has continued (Smith et al. 2011; Schwartz et al. 2012; Smith et al. 2013; Xella et al. 2013).

Because of the role of Carthage in maritime trade and as a sea power, with its location commanding the narrowest part of the Mediterranean between North Africa and Sicily, its two interconnected harbours are particularly interesting. Enclosed from the sea and entered by a narrow channel, they consisted of an outer commercial harbour and an inner military one. Excavation has shown that the inner harbour, which was circular, was first constructed in the late third or early second century BC, although subsequently rebuilt during the Roman period. On an island in the centre of the Punic inner harbour was a circular stone building that provided covered storage for at least 30 warships, and up to 140 others could have been berthed around the perimeter of the harbour (Hurst 1979; Lancel 1995: 176–8).

Carthage was the most important of pre-Roman Punic and Numidian cities in the western part of North Africa. Thugga and Kerkouane (Fig. 3.2), both in northern Tunisia, are other examples of pre-Roman urbanism. Also important

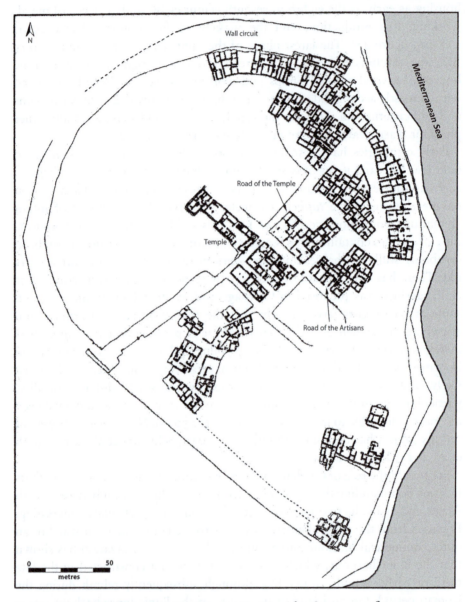

Fig. 3.2 Plan of the Punic city of Kerkouane, Tunisia. After Sears 2011: fig. 1.5. Redrawn by Andrew Stawowczyk Long.

is Althiburos, in western Tunisia, where survey and excavation has thrown valuable light on Numidian settlement during the first millennium BC (Sanmarti et al. 2012). Furthermore, the cities of Sabratha, Oea, and Lepcis Magna, which became important during the Roman period, had Punic origins. Sears (2011: 13–30) has stressed both the development of urbanization and the emergence of states before the extension of Roman control over North Africa began in the second century BC. Nevertheless, it was the incorporation of North Africa into the Roman Empire that resulted in the most substantial archaeological evidence of both urbanization and centralized state authority in North Africa (Sears 2011: 32, map 2, 121, map 5). The physical remains are amongst the most impressive to have survived above ground from the Roman world. This is because Roman North Africa was one of the wealthiest and most populated parts of the Empire; following political and economic decline during the subsequent Vandal and Byzantine periods, population densities in Islamic North Africa were lower and urban centres either shrank or were abandoned. This situation contrasts with places that continued to be important urban centres, such as Carthage, which has remained occupied since Roman times and is now part of Tunis, and Oea, which lies under the modern city of Tripoli.

The archaeological record for Roman North Africa provides a remarkable picture of both urban and rural life during a period of more than 400 years. In conjunction with the documentary record and with inscriptions and coinage, it is possible to reconstruct much of the history of the region. Numerous urban centres existed, particularly in parts of Tunisia and Algeria, ranging from large to small, as well as country villas, farms, frontier defences such as forts, and roads. Collectively, these sites provide abundant evidence for a state infrastructure that was complex, sophisticated, and prosperous. Its essentials also survived for a remarkably long time, even when in apparent decline during the late Roman, Vandal, and Byzantine periods. Most buildings were constructed in stone, often in fine masonry; principal city streets were paved and provided with drainage systems. Of central importance in each Roman city was the forum, as a meeting place, often with a basilica where courts took place and a curia where the town council met. In addition, cities seem to have competed with one another in their construction of monumental public buildings. These usually included temples, an amphitheatre for spectacles and public punishments (the one at El Djem, in Tunisia, could seat 30,000 people), a theatre for dramatic performances, one or more monumental arches, and, for a few cities, a circus for chariot races. As time went on, they also included public baths (such as the Large South Baths at Timgad, in Algeria, Fig. 3.3), the usage of which became a major part of Roman culture in North Africa as elsewhere in the Empire (Yegül 2010).

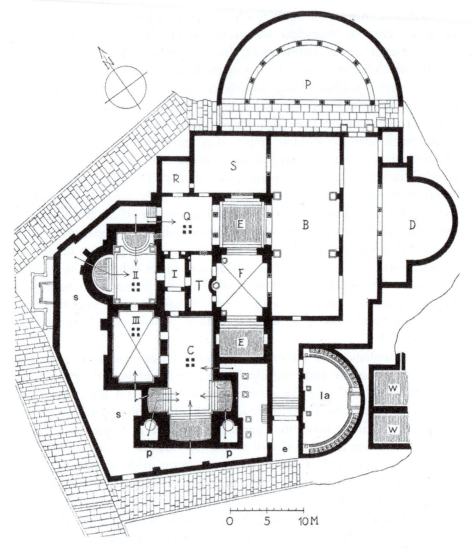

Fig. 3.3 Plan of the Large South Baths at Timgad, Algeria. From Yegül 2010: fig. 59, after Krencker, D. et al. 1929.

To supply the baths with water and to meet other requirements in urban centres, aquaducts were also constructed, sometimes bringing water from considerable distances. In addition, there were statues of gods or civic leaders, marketplaces and shops, and, in coastal cities, harbours. The imperial government was the ultimate authority, controlling security, taxation, the administration of law, and other matters of importance, but many of the decisions about urban planning seem to have been made by the individual cities. This was in spite of a tendency to adopt general Roman models, such as orthogonal layouts in which streets met at right angles. Most often it was members of a city's administrative or commercial elite, or the city itself, that financed monumental building projects. This was a means of establishing prestige within the urban community; in order to ensure that such generosity was not forgotten, it was often recorded in inscriptions, in Latin and Punic, which provide information about urban history. Another source of such history is the cemeteries or necropoleis located on the edges of many cities, with some of the burials marked by monumental tombs with inscriptions.

Many public and private buildings display evidence of prosperity, such as fine carving, richly decorated mosaic pavements, or wall paintings, often informative on a variety of subjects. Matters of more personal concern were also attended to. In the Seaward Baths at Sabratha, there is a hexagonal communal latrine with seats placed over a drain around three sides of the marble-faced room and with a channel in front of the seats providing clean water for washing oneself (Kenrick 2009: 58, figure 18). Latrines were often associated with bath buildings because both needed water; the Large Baths at Djemila, in Algeria, for instance, featured a facility that could accommodate twenty-two to twenty-four people (Yegül 2010: 142). Similar comforts were probably present in private houses also; in a villa at Bulla Regia, in Tunisia, for example, is a two-hole latrine in a small closet with a decorative mosaic floor (Manton 1988: 125–6: illustration 72). This subject needs to be seen in the context of sanitation in the Roman world as a whole, for which Scobie (1986) has provided a detailed study. In North Africa every effort seems to have been made by the elite to make life pleasant for themselves, and even less fortunate people benefitted to some extent from the thriving economy.

There was variety in the layout of North African Roman cities and also changes that occurred over the centuries. In earlier times they often lacked city walls, which were added at a later date, indicating changes in security. One of the most impressive cities was Sabratha, a large, affluent city on the coast of Libya (Fig. 3.4), with a layout contrasting, for example, with Thamugadi, a small inland city in Algeria (Fig. 3.5). There were also changes to North African cities caused by the adoption of Christianity; Late Roman Carthage, for instance, had sixteen known churches within and outside its walls. Subsequently, Vandal occupation of North Africa for a century seems to have contributed little to the archaeological record, although the following Byzantine period did see a small revival of cities and the construction of new city walls, the restoration of old churches, and the building of new ones (Kenrick 2009: 7–8).

The invasion of North Africa by Muslim Arabs in the seventh century introduced a different culture to the region. Although it became less urbanized than it had been during the Roman period, new capitals were built at Kairouan

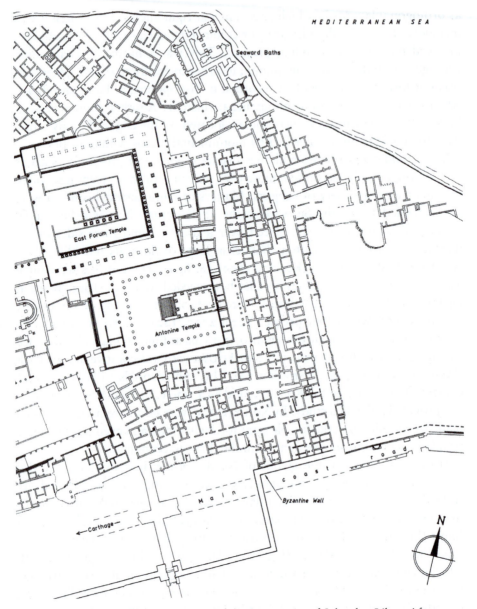

Fig. 3.4 Plan of part of the central area of the Roman city of Sabratha, Libya. After Kenrick 1986: fig. 123.

in the late seventh century and at Mahdiyya in the early tenth century, both in Tunisia. In addition, new state structures emerged from the confusion that followed the invasion, the most significant being controlled by the Aghlabid dynasty during the ninth century and by the Fatimids during the tenth to

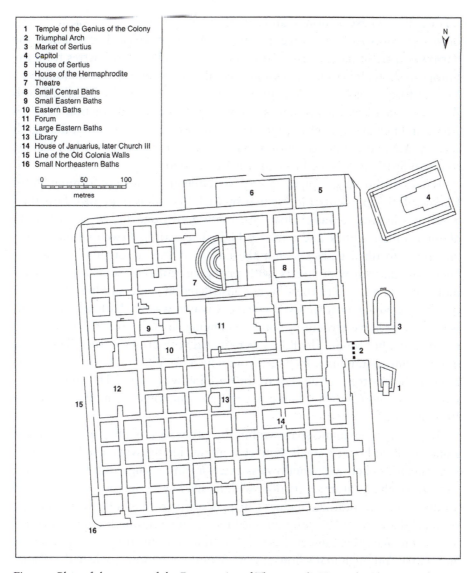

1 Temple of the Genius of the Colony
2 Triumphal Arch
3 Market of Sertius
4 Capitol
5 House of Sertius
6 House of the Hermaphrodite
7 Theatre
8 Small Central Baths
9 Small Eastern Baths
10 Eastern Baths
11 Forum
12 Large Eastern Baths
13 Library
14 House of Januarius, later Church III
15 Line of the Old Colonia Walls
16 Small Northeastern Baths

Fig. 3.5 Plan of the centre of the Roman city of Thamugadi (Timgad), Algeria, in the third century AD. From Sears 2007: fig. 14.

twelfth centuries. The latter period was one of outstanding cultural achievement (Bloom 2007), but, as with subsequent periods in the region, it has not received much archaeological attention. Principal cities included Fez, Tangier, Algiers, Tunis, Kairouan, and Tripoli, but continuing occupation has made their archaeological investigation difficult. From the eleventh century there were also the remarkable cities of Mzâb, in the harsh Algerian Sahara, each constituting a separate city-state (Jaabiri and Yahia 2000).

For a detailed excavation of an Islamic city, it is necessary to look at the site of the small city of Qsar es-Seghir, on the Moroccan coast. Located near the narrowest part of the Straits of Gibraltar, it was only 22 kilometres from the European shore. It was, in succession, a conduit for people and commodities, a frontier fortress, and a colonial outpost. Occupied in turn by Muslim North Africans and Christian Portuguese, it was the scene of interaction between Africa and Europe. The settlement seems to have originated in about the eighth century AD and continued until about the fourteenth century when Islamic southern Spain approached its end (Redman 1986).

Qsar es-Seghir was a planned city, its circular layout conforming to an Islamic ideal supposedly represented by early Baghdad (Fig. 3.6). Less than 3 hectares in area, it was enclosed by a mortared stone and fired-brick wall, about 1.8 metres thick and 8 metres high. The wall had twenty-nine towers and three fortified gates. Within the city wall was a roughly rectangular layout of relatively wide streets, with a congregational mosque, a public bath building, and a market. These were constructed in stone and fired brick; the building of which most survived when excavated was the bath building. This was an impressive structure, with a changing area, a cold room, a warm room, and a hot room. The floors were paved with bricks or tiles. There was also a room containing a furnace, from which hot air circulated beneath the floor of the hot room. Adjacent to the building was a well. The complex is a reminder of how much Islamic society had inherited from the preceding Roman world.

Much of the remaining space within the city wall was filled with houses of stone and fired brick; a small number were outside the wall. The houses were rectangular in plan, with windowless exteriors and a single entrance from the street through a bent-axis corridor. Within each house, the rooms were ranged around a central court and included living/sleeping rooms, a kitchen, a storage space, and a latrine. The latter emptied into an underground drain, which fed into a drainage system under the middle of the adjacent street; each house also had a well. Although many houses were of only one storey, some had a second storey reached by an internal stairway. Material culture at Qsar es-Seghir was simple: most of the pottery was wheel-made but undecorated, sometimes with a clear lead glaze on the interior. Much of it was probably locally produced, but there were also decorated ceramics that were mostly imported from elsewhere in North Africa and from Islamic Spain. Iron was used for weapons, tools, and nails, and items of personal adornment were made of bronze or brass, sometimes coated in silver or gold. Bone and ivory were made use of and glass vessels were used but rare. A few Islamic coins of gold, silver, and copper were also found. Some people seemed wealthier than others but not to any great extent. Partly this might be because of Islamic restraint in display but

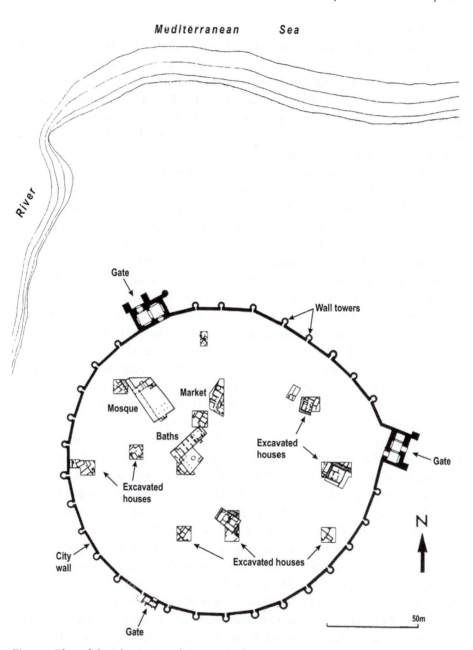

Fig. 3.6 Plan of the Islamic city of Qsar es-Seghir, Morocco. After Redman, 1986: fig. 3.2.

more likely it is because Qsar es-Seghir was a small city of workers and traders, with a maximum population of only 1,200 to 1,300 inhabitants.

Islamic Qasr es-Seghir came to a violent end in the fifteenth century, when a Portuguese army, equipped with cannon, attacked it. Renamed Alcacer Ceguer, the city became part of a Portuguese expansion into northwest Africa that eventually included Tangier and several ports along the Atlantic coast. As such it was a fortress city, with modernized fortifications, a garrison of soldiers, and a population that was predominantly male. Eventually, the greater profitability of its more distant overseas interests led Portugal to abandon North Africa. After ninety-two years the Portuguese left Qsar es-Seghir, first destroying many of its buildings and some of its fortifications to discourage reuse of the site, which was never reoccupied.

The Portuguese city was different from the preceding Islamic one. Although it retained the circular plan, its defensive walls were reduced in height and broadened at the base, as well as surrounded by a deep ditch. Five bastions were also built, three of them around the former city gates; the one closest to the sea became a fortified citadel. These modifications were designed to make the city more easily defended against cannon fire and to enable the efficient use of cannons and firearms against attackers. The street layout seems to have remained much as it had been but with more open spaces at the ends or intersections of streets, most of which were paved with cobbles. The mosque was turned into a church and subsequently rebuilt. The old market disappeared and the public bath building became a prison or arsenal. The houses in the Portuguese city also differed from the Islamic ones, although in many cases the earlier buildings were reused. Their plan was usually linear, with rooms that were increasingly private as one moved away from the largest one, to which an often decorative front door gave access. Many houses were also the location of commercial activities and were not as well finished internally as the Muslim houses had been. Although still built mainly of stone, they lacked the latrines and drains of the earlier houses; fewer houses had their own wells, as public wells in the city were also used. Many houses were subdivided as time went on, probably because of a growing population, which might have reached about 1,000 people. The Portuguese occupants seem to have had more personal possessions than their predecessors. Most of the pottery was imported from across the Straits of Gibraltar, much of it glazed tableware, and later there was even some Chinese porcelain. There were many metal objects, mainly of iron, as well as numerous items of personal adornment of bronze, silver, and gold. Glass vessels and bracelets were common and coins were more numerous than they had been during the Islamic period. Collectively, the evidence suggested a three-tier hierarchy, consisting of a large number of people of relatively modest means, a small number who were rather wealthier, and just one who was richer than anyone else, reflecting a typical military community.

The pre-fifteenth-century archaeological evidence from Qsar es-Seghir provides an important example of North African Islamic urbanism. It should be considered together with other Islamic urban sites in Morocco, such as

Al-Basra, to the south of Qsar es-Seghir. This was the site of another walled city, mainly occupied in the ninth and tenth centuries AD but abandoned by about the thirteenth century (Redman 1983; Benco 2004). Al-Basra has also been set in its regional context in a study of the political economy and settlement systems of northern Morocco (Ennahid 2002).

Subsistence economy

During the last three millennia the people of North Africa have mainly depended on mixed agriculture to exploit the variety of environments in the region, including desert, where the oasis cultivation in the Fezzan was particularly impressive (Mattingly 2011; 2013; Mattingly and Sterry 2013). Different areas have been important for cereal cultivation, particularly wheat and barley, or for the production of olive oil, wine, dates, fruit, vegetables, and honey. Cattle, sheep, and goat pastoralism have also contributed to subsistence, particularly in the mountains and the semi-desert. Limiting factors of water stress and high temperatures have often been ameliorated by irrigation, so that during some periods North Africa became a major exporter of food. In addition, access to a long coastline has enabled fishing to contribute significantly to human subsistence. Inevitably, subsistence in the region varied throughout the long period considered in this chapter, fluctuating with economic conditions and the level of security. However, Punic, Greek, Roman, Vandal, Byzantine, and Arab colonists saw North Africa as a food source capable of generating considerable wealth, as well as supporting its own people. The latter peaked at perhaps 3 million inhabitants late in the second or in the third century AD, although the number is thought to have fallen by the seventh century (Kaegi: 2010: 64). However, during the first and second centuries AD, North African grain exports fed Rome, the capital of the Empire, providing enough for eight months of each year, some half a million tons (Manton 1988: 108). In addition, agricultural exports included massive quantities of olive oil, but also wine and other commodities. Significantly, a second-century AD coin of Hadrian depicts a personification of Africa holding a cornucopia in one hand, a symbol of plenty consisting of a goat's horn overflowing with flowers, fruit, and corn. In the other hand the figure holds a scorpion, suggesting perhaps an acceptance of the counterbalancing constraints of the African environment (Fig. 3.7).

Technology

Throughout the relevant time there was a sophisticated level of technology in North Africa, comparable to that of the contemporary Mediterranean world in general. There is abundant evidence of skilled craftsmanship in stone, wood,

59

Fig. 3.7 Silver denarius of Hadrian commemorating his visit to Africa in AD 130–131. On the reverse is a personification of Africa wearing an elephant skin head-dress and holding a cornucopia and a scorpion. 'Africa' at this time consisted of the Roman province of Africa Proconsularis, approximately equivalent to modern northern Tunisia and northeastern Algeria. From Manton 1988: fig. 14.

ferrous and nonferrous metal, pottery, and other materials. Building of both domestic and public structures frequently attained high standards, particularly during the Roman and Islamic periods, and boat construction was already well developed in the Punic period, with both warships and merchant vessels playing an important role in Carthaginian history. Engineering was also competent, as evidenced by the harbours at Carthage in the final centuries BC and by the aqueducts and other facilities for water supply during the Roman period. Similarly, the harbour and lighthouse at Roman Lepcis Magna (Sears 2011: 37, figure 2.1) are evidence of a capacity to plan and complete large construction projects. Also in the Punic and Roman periods, urban drainage and sanitation were attended to, and in Roman North Africa both urban and rural road building were important. In addition, there are indications of urban planning in most periods. Dye and *garum* were manufactured and olive-oil production was organized on a semi-industrial scale, as indicated by the remains of stone olive-presses (Fig. 3.8) and by large numbers of amphora used in the transport of oil or wine. However, perhaps the most impressive of the surviving evidence for technological expertise in Roman North Africa is the work of stonemasons and sculptors and the makers of mosaic pavements, the latter depicting scenes from daily life as well as mythology (Dunbabin 1978). Punic flooring included what the Romans called *pavimentum Punicum*, made up of terracotta fragments set in mortar (Hoyos 2010: 85, 221), perhaps the inspiration for the later but different potsherd

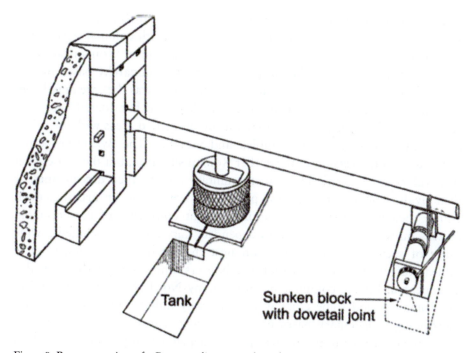

Fig. 3.8 Reconstruction of a Roman olive-press, based on remains at Hinshir Sidi Hamdan, southeast of Tripoli. From Kenrick 2009: Fig. 77.

pavements of West Africa (p. 198). Another Carthaginian innovation was the threshing-cart, known to the Romans as the *plostellum Punicum* (Hoyos 2010: 221), and it appears that Punic agriculture, which included the use of the plough, was generally sophisticated. Wheeled vehicles were in use until the third century AD, when they were mainly replaced by camel transport; the Carthaginians had horse-drawn chariots and in Roman North Africa carts were pulled by horses, oxen, or camels, as also were ploughs (Bulliet 1975: 17, 137–40). Finally, North African states from the first millennium BC to the second millennium AD minted their own coinage.

Social system

North African society remained hierarchical during the many centuries discussed in this chapter, although the character of its social structures varied through time. For the Carthaginians and the Hellenized people of Cyrene, mercantile success and consequent wealth were often the basis of political power and entry to a governing elite consisting of privileged families. In Roman North Africa the situation was similar, but its leaders were subject to the superior authority and fiscal control of imperial Rome. Nevertheless, social integration of Punic and other local people with colonial settlers and their descendants makes it difficult to decide the extent of 'Romanization' in North Africa. During the Vandal period there was monarchy based mainly on oppression of the population, and much the same was the case in indigenous states and tribal areas during the overall period considered here. The relationship of mobile pastoral tribes outside the settled areas with the urban and rural communities was complex and variable. The Byzantine period restored a diluted version of the earlier Roman situation, but the subsequent Arab rulers were essentially successful military leaders, their descendants, or their rivals. Common to all these periods, however, was an urban element within society, fluctuating in importance but consisting of cosmopolitan citizens on whom the ruling elites depended. City-dwellers included a wide range of socioeconomic groups, amongst them religious leaders, traders, skilled craftsmen, artisans, servants, labourers, and slaves. There was also an educated, literate component within many North African cities, and in the Roman period some cities were essentially military in their character, functioning as legionary bases or as settlements for army veterans. Urban government, at least in the Roman period, depended on populism as well as legal sanctions, as indicated by the number of public baths, amphitheatres, theatres, circuses, temples, and other facilities that were constructed for the benefit of citizens. However, North African cities have to be considered in the context of the rural economies that supported them. The greatest numbers of cities were situated in the agriculturally most productive regions, and each city had a close relationship with its surrounding countryside. Many of the urban elite owned country estates, which are particularly well known from the Roman period. Agricultural wealth was based on the labour of a large population of rural workers, who included slaves and who were at the bottom of the social pyramid.

Population pressures

North Africa has been called 'the wealthiest region of the western half of the [Roman] empire in the first few centuries [AD]' (Kaegi 2010: 65). This contrasts with the relatively impoverished and thinly populated condition of many areas observed by visitors in the late second millennium, leading some to suggest climatic deterioration as an explanation. This is now thought not to have been the case; instead, it appears to have been skilled land management, particularly of water in marginal areas, that underpinned past agricultural success, most notably during the Roman period. In contrast, many subsequent Arab settlers seem to have been more interested in pastoralism in the semi-desert interior than in the cities and farmlands of the coastal regions (Kenrick 2009: 10). Although North Africa was a land of urban centres in Carthaginian, Roman, and later times, it is the number of Roman cities and towns, their density in more fertile areas, and their presence even in drier areas that is most impressive. Northern Tunisia and northeast Algeria had the greatest density, but urban centres also occurred from the Atlantic coast to Tripolitania, the latter supporting two of the best-known cities, Sabratha (Kenrick 1986) and Lepcis Magna. Subsequently, cities appear to have become less numerous but the rural settlements that supported them continued to be important. Statistics are absent but it seems likely that the overall population declined after the third century AD. At its peak, there must have been considerable pressure on land, especially the more productive land near cities. Such land generated a great deal of wealth, particularly on large agricultural estates that were often the property of absentee landowners and worked by slaves. There is abundant archaeological evidence for this wealth in cities such as El Djem, in present-day Tunisia. Crowded housing in the excavated portions of some cities, particularly in the later Roman period, suggests population pressure also existed in urban environments, especially among citizens of lower socioeconomic status. Furthermore, beyond the settled areas, at the margins of the desert, there must also have been population pressures, with attempts to control the seasonal movements of pastoralists by frontier forts, fortlets, and strategically located barriers. In addition, during the later Roman and subsequent periods, many farms were fortified, indicating insecurity probably brought on by competition for resources. Considering the marginal constraints of North Africa, located between the sea and the desert and limited further by mountains to the west, it seems probable that population pressures did exist at times.

Ideology

Religious beliefs were important throughout the communities of North Africa during the periods considered. They varied with ethnic, cultural, linguistic, and ideological identity. Carthaginian religion, with its origins in the Levant, had its own distinctive deities, comprising a very large number of gods and goddesses of whom the goddess Tanit and the god Baal seem to have been the most significant. Hostile Greek and Roman writers were critical of Carthaginian beliefs, particularly regarding child sacrifice, concerning which the evidence remains ambiguous. It is nevertheless clear that their religion was of major importance to the Carthaginians for the well-being of their state in both peace and war. In contrast, the Greek colony of Cyrene reverenced traditional Greek deities and others of the Hellenized world. Similarly, the Roman colonists honoured Roman gods, although there was also a broadminded acceptance of cults from other places, such as Isis and Serapis from Egypt and Mithras from Persia. However, it was the state cult of the Emperor (Fig. 3.9) that was most important: 'It kept the peoples of the Empire together and sacrifices and libations had to be observed as homage before official functions and other important occasions' (Manton 1988: 128). This is testimony to the central importance of religious ideology in the maintenance and extension of state authority. It is significant that North African Christian martyrs, in the third and early fourth centuries AD, were persecuted because of their refusal to sacrifice to the Emperor; it was their disloyalty to the state rather than their religious belief that was judged criminal. Nevertheless, by the fourth century Christianity had practically taken over North Africa, where it appears to have

Fig. 3.9 Marble portrait head of Septimius Severus, from Djemila, Algeria. Images of this sort must have been important in the cult of the Emperor, particularly in the case of this emperor, who was a North African, born in Lepcis Magna. From Manton 1988: plate 13.

spread more quickly than it did in other parts of the Empire, and early in the century it was accepted by the Emperor Constantine as the state religion. Its divisive influence continued, however, with bitter and often violent disputes amongst Christians between Catholics and Donatists and with the later Vandal attempts to impose Arianism. The social and political tensions that resulted inevitably contributed to the ultimate collapse of Roman North Africa. Continuing dissension amongst Christians weakened even the sixth-century Byzantine reassertion of state control. The success of the Arab invasion of North Africa during the seventh century seems to have owed as much to the cohesion of their Islamic faith as to their military superiority, and Christianity appears to have collapsed rapidly. However, in its turn, Islam also became divided by conflicts and schisms, especially those between the Shia and Sunni sects. The story of religious ideology in North Africa shows how such beliefs can contribute authority and cohesion to a state or, equally, cause dissension that leads to state disintegration.

External trade

With its long Mediterranean coastline providing seaborne access to some of the most remarkable urban and state developments of the last three millennia, external trade was of great importance to North Africa for much of this time (Fulford 1989). Indeed, external contact must have had great antiquity, as indicated by ivory from African savanna elephants that reached southern Portugal by the first half of the third millennium BC (Schuhmacher et al. 2009). The very foundation of Carthage and other Phoenician settlements in the late second to early first millennium BC was the product of a wide trading network. An important part of this comprised the Mediterranean and Atlantic coasts of southern Spain and northwest Africa (Serrano 2011: 21). It is apparent that both Carthage and the later Roman colonies owed much of their economic success to their export capacity, particularly of agricultural products. Grain and olive oil appear to have been the largest exports, but wine, *garum*, and other commodities were also traded. In addition, wild animals were sent from Africa to Roman amphitheatres, as attested archaeologically by a late third-century AD Sicilian mosaic showing an elephant being loaded onto a ship (Manton 1988: 40). Exported animals also included lions, leopards, hippopotami, rhinoceros, giraffes, and even zebras; some of these must have come from the African interior. Slaves were another important export; it has been estimated that between 250,000 and 400,000 new slaves were required each year to maintain the slave workforce of the Roman state. Amongst these were Africans, many of them probably supplied by the Garamantes of the Fezzan to Mediterranean traders (Fentress 2011: 66, 68). Ivory, from both elephant tusks and hippopotamus teeth, was another important export, as were various African exotica, such as animal skins and semi-precious stones. Previously, Carthaginian trade had also included decorated ostrich-egg shells (Lancel 1995: 218–20) and similar commodities. Furthermore, it is possible that North African merchants were already handling West African gold in the fourth century AD, considerably earlier than was previously thought (Garrard 1982; MacDonald 2011).

This raises the question of Saharan trade prior to its major development beginning late in the first millennium AD. This has often been dismissed as unlikely because Roman material, for instance, appears not to have penetrated south of the desert, in contrast to the way that it reached far beyond other frontiers of the Roman Empire. However, there are indications that interchange over short distances could have taken some commodities across the Sahara in both directions, perhaps in a relay of exchange along the trade routes. With doubtful exceptions, Roman coins do not seem to have reached south of the desert, but it is unlikely that they would have been acceptable in societies unfamiliar with their use and possible that any remaining there would have been melted down for their metal content. From a later date, Arabic coins are similarly rare south of the Sahara in spite of the substantial trade that is known to have developed by then. Nevertheless, Roman trade goods did reach the Garamantes, in the Fezzan (Mattingly 2011: 54–5), and the Tomb of Abalessa, in the Hoggar. In addition, carnelian and glass beads and woollen textile fragments from burials at Kissi, in Burkina Faso, as well as the first appearance of donkeys, horses, camels, and chickens south of the desert, are further indications of pre-Islamic trans-Saharan contact (MacDonald 2011: 76).

It seems likely, therefore, that North African exports to or across the Sahara already included two commodities that were later to become of importance – beads and textiles – but there were also fine ceramics and other prestige goods. As for the main imports of the Roman cities and rural estates of North Africa itself, they must have comprised a wide range of consumer goods from the Mediterranean world, many of them appropriate to the affluent lifestyles of the elite. Similarly, the later Arab settlements absorbed substantial imports, although mainly from the Islamic world. Throughout the long period reviewed in this chapter external trade was clearly well developed. The resulting 'connectivity', defined as 'the frequency and velocity of connections between cities or regions' (Dowler 2011: 2), has been of the greatest importance in the influence of North Africa on its surrounding regions and that of the surrounding regions on North Africa. As a frontier, North Africa has contributed both to the Mediterranean world and to the African world to its south, in the latter case particularly during the Islamic period, as shown for example by the

Fig. 3.10 Arabic inscription and frieze on copper-alloy bowl from a fifteenth- to sixteenth-century burial at Durbi Takusheyi, northern Nigeria. Haase 2011: fig. 2, p.103. Drawing by Michael Ober, Römisch-Germanisches Zentralmuseum (RGZM). Reproduced by permission of Detlef Gronenborn, RGZM).

Arabic inscription (Fig. 3.10) on a copper-alloy bowl from a fifteenth- to sixteenth-century AD burial at Durbi Takusheyi, in northern Nigeria (Haase 2011; Gronenborn et al. 2012). Indeed, North African Islamic trade also penetrated far to the north, so that two Barbary lions reached the Royal Menagerie of England during the thirteenth to fifteenth centuries AD, as shown by their skulls that were excavated from the moat of the Tower of London (Barnett et al. 2008).

Conclusion

The influence of the states and cities of North Africa on other parts of the continent has sometimes been overlooked. Scholars who were specialists in North African history and archaeology have regarded Africa south of the Sahara as not their concern; those who studied the regions south of the desert have usually had little knowledge of lands to its north. Nevertheless, it has long been acknowledged that the Islamic societies of North Africa had a profound effect on many people in the West African savanna, particularly during the second millennium AD. Traders and others from across the Sahara stimulated commercial activity, the emergence and growth of cities and states, the spread of the Islamic religion, and the adoption of limited literacy. Gold, ivory, slaves, and spices travelled north with the camel caravans; salt, copper alloys, beads, cowries, textiles, and other manufactured products travelled south.

What is less clear is whether such trade existed before the advent of the Arabs in North Africa, even if only on a much smaller scale. The accepted view has been that it did not or was virtually nonexistent. Gradually, however, this is being challenged, and there are indications that there was increasing trans-Saharan contact at least by North Africa's late Roman period. Possibly this had existed even in Carthaginian times, but relevant evidence is very limited. Nevertheless, the notion of the Sahara as an impassable barrier does need to be reassessed; given the moister climate of the Early Holocene there must have been a long-established mobility within this enormous region and in its margins before the subsequent development of drier conditions.

Nor was the Mediterranean a frontier in any exclusive sense; rather, it was a vibrant interactive zone that brought North Africa into continual contact with people to its north, including Greece, Rome, and southern Spain, and to its east, including Egypt and the Levant. With a variety of highly productive agricultural environments, sophisticated technology, organized social hierarchies, functional specialization, a substantial population, a series of religious ideologies to legitimize the sociopolitical status quo, and a substantial export potential, North Africa has often been a major attraction to outsiders. Clearly, the Phoenicians thought so, and the Greeks, Romans, Vandals, Byzantines, and Arabs. Of the people who exploited its benefits, it was surely the Vandals, from central Europt, whose presence was most remarkable. As a frontier, North Africa seems to have been highly permeable.

Chapter 4
Sudanic genesis: Nubia

Other than Pharaonic Egypt, some of the earliest evidence for urbanization and state formation in Africa was along the middle Nile, in the region called Nubia. One of the best-known examples was Meroë, located about 200 kilometres north-east of the modern city of Khartoum, in Sudan. Mentioned as early as the fifth century BC by Herodotus (Powell 1949: vol. 1, 121), its antecedents lay in Napata and Kerma, the latter dating back to before 2000 BC, and it was succeeded by the kingdoms of Christian Nubia, which survived until the early second millennium AD, and by Islamic states that existed until recent times (Welsby 1996; 2002; Edwards 2004; 2007; UCL 2013).

At the beginning of the twentieth century, scholars attributed such developments to the influence in turn of Pharaonic, Ptolemaic, Roman, Byzantine, and Islamic Egypt, located to the north of the area. Later the emphasis was changed to one that stressed the indigenous character of Nubian achievements but acknowledged the contributions made to them by northern cultures. William Adams, the author of a 1977 monograph on the archaeology of this area, described Nubia as '*the* transition zone, between the civilized world and Africa' and entitled his book *Nubia: Corridor to Africa*. According to Adams, the importance of this narrow corridor through the barren land of Nubia arose from the fact that it was for long the only dependable route across the great barrier of the Sahara Desert, a major road into the heart of Africa. The African interior contained resources much coveted by the outside world – gold, ivory, and slaves – but also other mineral, animal, and vegetable products (Adams 1984: 40). These could be tapped via the Nubian corridor. However, with the development of Red Sea shipping from the first millennium BC onwards, and of trans-Saharan camel caravans during the first millennium AD, the middle Nile Valley gradually lost its significance as a major world trade route. That role was finally destroyed by the expansion of maritime trade around Africa's coasts in the sixteenth and seventeenth centuries AD.

Both archaeological and documentary evidence support the idea of Adams' trade corridor, and the growth of cities and states was centred on it. This suggests that this part of Africa can provide us with an example of trade as a major stimulus towards the development of social complexity. Perhaps so, but these developments took place at the interface of considerable cultural contact, of which trade was only one element, as Adams indeed stressed. People are very likely to meet one another in corridors.

Corridors, however, usually lead somewhere, and archaeologists have debated the extent to which the culture of the inhabitants of the middle Nile Valley might have influenced the rest of Africa. At one extreme, Sayce thought that 'Meroë ... must have been the Birmingham of ancient Africa' (Sayce 1911: 55). At the other extreme, Trigger (1969) complained about 'the myth of Meroë' and Shinnie (1967: 167) pointed out that 'not a single object of certain Meroitic origin has been found away from the Nile to the west'. Indeed, in the first edition of this book (Connah 1987) it was suggested that the Nubian corridor was a cultural cul-de-sac, an interpretation also advanced by Alexander (1988). However, such a view implies only a passive role for Nubia, suggesting that it was a mere receiver of cultural influences rather than also an initiator of cultural changes. It also reflects a former research emphasis on Lower Nubia, the narrow, desert-enclosed part of the Nile Valley north of the Second Cataract, and the relatively little attention given to the valley further south and its rainfed wadis and savannas. As Edwards (1996: 5) put it: 'Meroe, and indeed Kerma before it, should be seen as the early examples of a long and enduring tradition of Sudanic kingdoms.' Edwards subsequently expanded this view in his 2004 book *The Nubian Past*, and similarly Fuller (2003: 183) stressed the 'distinctive Sudanic system of power' in Meroitic society. Whatever the external influences, Nubia should be seen as a Sudanic genesis of social complexity.

Geographical location and environmental factors

The Nile is a very long river that runs from the Lake Region of East Africa to the Mediterranean Sea, passing through a number of contrasting environments, some of which are amongst the driest in Africa. Because it flows through so much arid country for much of its length, the river and its narrow valley have played an important role in human history. Ancient Egypt was, as Herodotus called it, 'the gift of the river' (Powell 1949: vol. 1, 111) but if this was true of the lower Nile, it was also partly true of the middle Nile, the subject of this chapter. This is the land of the Nile cataracts impeding navigation, a series of rocky, swift rapids. Most of the cataracts are conventionally numbered from one to six: the First Cataract just south of Aswan, in southern Egypt; the Sixth Cataract a little north of Khartoum in the Sudan. It is this long and narrow strip that for the last 2,000 years or so has been known as 'Nubia' (O'Connor 1993: xii), although the location of its southern limits has varied. In this discussion, the 'middle Nile' will be that part of the Nile Valley between Sennar on the Blue Nile south of Khartoum, and the First Cataract at Aswan, in the north (Fig. 4.1). However, in addition to the river valley, it is essential to consider the land to its east and west, particularly in southern Nubia, which does receive a little seasonal rain.

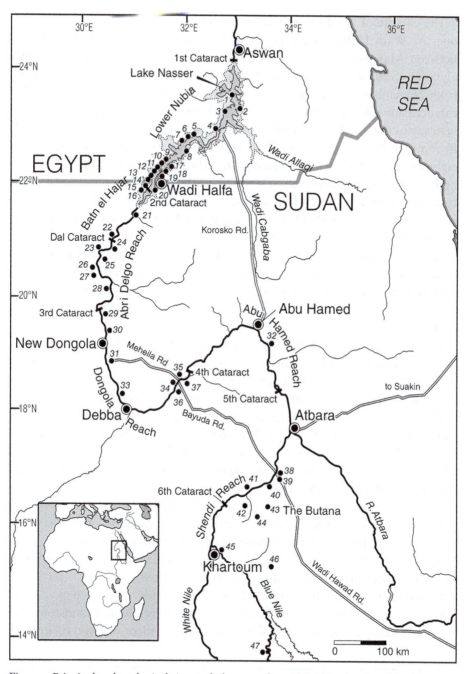

Fig. 4.1 Principal archaeological sites and places on the middle Nile mentioned in the text. (Some place-name spellings vary.) 1, Kalabsha; 2, Sabaqura; 3, Ikhmindi; 4, Maharraqa; 5, Sheikh Daoud; 6, Karanog; 7, Aniba; 8, Qasr Ibrim; 9, Arminna West; 10, Tamit; 11, Abu Simbel; 12, Ballana; 13, Faras; 14, Debeira West; 15, Buhen; 16, Kasanarti; 17, Jebel Adda; 18, Qustul; 19, Debeira East; 20, Meinarti; 21, Duweishat; 22, Kulubnarti; 23, Amara;

The climate of the more northerly parts of the middle Nile is an extreme one. At Wadi Halfa, in the northern Sudan, the mean daily temperature between May and September is about 32°C, but the temperature nearly always exceeds 38°C during the day and may reach above 49°C. However, from November to March it is comparatively mild, with temperatures that can occasionally drop almost to freezing. Between Aswan and Dongola, that is to say in the northern half of the middle Nile region, it almost never rains. In contrast, the southern half of the region has a well-defined wet season of eight to ten weeks, in July and August, although the actual rainfall is very limited, increasing from north to south from about 25 millimetres at Dongola to about 180 millimetres at Khartoum. Another climatic factor of importance is wind, which blows steadily from the north for the whole year, resulting in considerable accumulation of desert sand, particularly on the west bank of the Nile, where it has constantly encroached on both settlements and fields. However, with the exception of the reverse bend between Abu Hamed and Debba, it has also made upstream navigation possible on the river, just as the direction of the current has facilitated downstream navigation (Adams 1977: 33–5).

The vegetation of the middle Nile region varies from total desert in the north to acacia desert scrub in the south (Andrews 1948: 34). The most important part of the environment, however, is the River Nile itself, rising more than 3,000 kilometres to the south and bringing to Nubia both the water and soil that are necessary to sustain human settlement. Most vegetation maps are of too small a scale to show details of the vegetation of the long river littoral, so narrow that in places it is a mere few hundred metres wide or is absent. However, date palms (*Phoenix dactylifera*) are common, really domesticated trees but so numerous that they look like part of the natural vegetation. Other trees also grow along the river littoral, the most important being the dom palm (*Hyphaena thebaica*), various acacias, and the tamarisk. Most of the rest of the vegetation consists of cultivated plants, but halfa grass grows wherever it can find moisture, and when the river is low a fringe of papyrus reed can be found in some places at the water's edge (Adams 1977: 37–8).

Environments vary along the Nubian Nile because of its geology. From Khartoum to Aswan, the river flows alternately over Nubian sandstone and basement complex (mostly granite). As a result, there are six geographic

---

Caption for Fig. 4.1 (*cont.*) 24, Ferka; 25, Sai; 26, Seddenga; 27, Soleb; 28, Sesebi; 29, Kerma and Pnubs; 30, Argo; 31, Kawa; 32, Kurgus; 33, Old Dongola; 34, El Kurru; 35, Jebel Barkal; 36, Sanam; 37, Nuri (sites 34–7 constitute Napata); 38, Meroë; 39, Hamadab; 40, Shendi; 41, el Hobagi; 42, Wad ben Naqa; 43, Musawwaret es-Sufra; 44, Naqa; 45, Soba; 46, Jebel Qeili; 47, Sennar. After Adams 1977 with additions. Drawn by Joe LeMonnier.

subdivisions of the middle Nile (Adams 1977: 21–33), their boundaries mostly consisting of the main cataracts of the river where it crosses from one geological formation to another (Fig. 4.1). In general, sandstone areas have supported farming settlements but granite areas have not. To the south there is semi-desert grassland beyond the river littoral and therefore pastoralism. Within the Shendi Reach, the furthest south, lay the heartland of the Meroitic state, including the city of Meroë itself. To the north of the Shendi Reach lies the Abu Hamed Reach, a region of barren granite with low productivity, which extends to the Fourth Cataract and seems never to have been an important area for settlement. Between the Fourth Cataract and the Third Cataract lies the Dongola Reach, with potentially cultivable land on both sides of the river. This reach saw the earliest developments of complex society on the middle Nile: both Kerma and Napata were situated there. From the Third Cataract to the (unnumbered) Dal Cataract is the Abri-Delgo Reach, important during the Egyptian (New Kingdom) colonial expansion, in the second half of the second millennium BC. Further north is the Batn el Hajar, a name meaning 'belly of rock', appropriate for this bare granite landscape, extending from the Dal Cataract to the Second Cataract. Last of the geographic subdivisions is Lower Nubia, stretching from the Second Cataract to the First Cataract. Now almost totally submerged beneath Lake Nasser (in Egypt; its southern part, in Sudan, is called Lake Nubia), it was formerly moderately prosperous. In spite of the virtual absence of rainfall, archaeological evidence suggests that at times this was a significant area of settlement and that its proximity to Egypt gave it an important role as a cultural contact zone.

In the middle Nile region, cultivation of seasonally inundated or irrigated land, in recent times, produced sorghum, barley, beans, tobacco, lentils, peas, watermelons, maize, some wheat, and other plants. Animal husbandry was important, mainly involving cattle, sheep, goats, and donkeys. Chickens, pigeons, ducks, and dogs were kept, but horses and pigs were rare (Trigger 1965: 19–22; Adams 1977: 54). Little of the native fauna seems to have survived to later historical times, although fish remained an important resource. At first a primary source of ivory, ostrich eggs and feathers, skins, and even live animals for the Egyptian trade, Lower Nubia in particular gradually became merely a pipeline through which these passed on their way north.

A longer-lasting Nubian resource consisted of minerals, including copper, fine-grained igneous rocks, and, most important, gold. Gold was scarce but occurred widely, particularly in the desert to the east of the Nile Valley. Another resource of importance throughout most of the history of the region was slaves. Even with this commodity, however, as time went on Nubia became the pipeline rather than the source. It seems that the indigenous resources of Nubia were less important than those that it obtained from further south (Adams 1977: 41–3).

A constraint on human settlement in the middle Nile was the level of the river itself, whose height in the flood season could be too low for irrigation or so high that floodwater swept away both settlements and cultivable alluvium. There were also long-term fluctuations in the average level of the Nile, such as Adams (1977: 242) hypothesized to explain the apparent virtual abandonment of Lower Nubia during the first millennium BC. This region, he claimed, was reoccupied only at the beginning of the first millennium AD, with the advent of the *saqia*, the ox-driven water wheel, which could raise irrigation water to greater heights than were possible with the man-powered *shaduf* – although subsequently it appeared that the abandonment might have been overstated and the *saqia* not introduced until about the fourth century AD (Edwards 1996: 80–1, 91; Welsby 1996: 156; Edwards 2004: 202–4). Another constraining factor was the availability of arable land, of which three sorts existed: *seluka* land, *saqia* and *shaduf* land, and basin land (Trigger 1965: 19–21). *Seluka* land was situated on the floodplain and was inundated each year when the river was high. When the level fell, the land could produce a crop without further watering, and its exploitation was therefore an example of 'recessional cultivation', which is discussed elsewhere (p. 153). In contrast, *saqia* and *shaduf* land consisted of relatively small areas that had to be watered mechanically but could be cropped almost continuously. Basin land, although of importance in Egypt, was more limited in Nubia, and consisted of land lying in natural depressions adjacent to the river, into which floodwater overflowed or was channelled by a canal.

The life-giving waters of the Nile brought suffering to the inhabitants of Nubia also. Schistosomiasis, a water-borne disease that is common in much of tropical Africa and is caused by a blood fluke that lives in freshwater snails, is prevalent in the Nile Valley. The fluke gains entry to the human bloodstream usually through breaks in the skin and then attacks the liver and other organs. Another affliction associated with water is onchocerciasis, or river blindness, caused by filarial worms transmitted by the minute fly *Simulium damnosum* (Manson-Bahr and Apted 1982: 166). Malaria, tuberculosis, and trachoma are other diseases along the middle Nile (Adams 1977: 40–1).

A further constraint on settlement has been the depredations of human beings themselves. The middle Nile Valley has suffered numerous military invasions from its north, and the nomadic pastoralists of the adjacent deserts have repeatedly harassed the sedentary farmers along the river, particularly after desert nomads adopted the camel; evidence from Qasr Ibrim indicates that it was in the Nile Valley by the early first millennium BC (Rowley-Conwy 1988). Nevertheless, it seems that desert pastoralism was so important to the riverine economy (Edwards 1996; 2004) that it was essential for people within the valley to control or coexist with those from outside it. This must have been a strong incentive to more powerful political organization and to greater social complexity.

Sources of information

Historical evidence

Understanding of early cities and states in the middle Nile region is based on historical documentation and archaeological data. Except for the Islamic period of the second millennium AD, the timespan is too great for oral tradition to contribute. Adams (1977: 66–70) identified six groups of historical sources.

The first consists of Egyptian texts in hieroglyphic and hieratic. These cover the period from the first half of the third millennium BC to near the end of the second millennium BC, but contain little about Nubia. The second group comprises Nubian hieroglyphic texts of the Napatan period, from the eighth to about the fourth century BC. Written by Egyptian scribes in the Egyptian language and in hieroglyphics, these also contain little about Nubia and throw no light on contemporary Nubian language. Consequently, when in later times Nubians developed their own Meroitic alphabet, they left texts that are difficult to understand because their language bears no recognizable relationship to any other language (Welsby 1996: 190; Edwards 2004: 176–9). Used from about the second century BC to about the fourth century AD, Meroitic writing can be read, but the language of the writing cannot be fully understood (e.g., Trigger 1973). The third group of historical sources are writings by classical authors. One of the earliest was Herodotus, who visited Egypt in the fifth century BC. Other classical writers also contributed information on Nubia, but these Greek and Latin texts are the view of the outsider, written from hearsay evidence. Knowledge of the region appears to have been limited: the Nile Mosaic at Palestrina near Rome, of the late second century BC, shows 'the landscape of lower Nubia combined with the fauna of upper Nubia' (Meyboom 1995: 50). The fourth group, that of ecclesiastical histories, is also limited in value. Several church historians wrote about the conversion of Nubia in the sixth century AD to Christianity, but their accounts conflict depending on their doctrine. Also, the information that they give is mainly concerned with the first century of Christian Nubia, because subsequently the Arab conquest of Egypt cut off contact with the rest of Christendom. The fifth group consists of Arab sources. The most important is the fourteenth-century geographer al-Maqrizi, whose writing also preserves part of a tenth-century first-hand account of Nubia. Again, these sources represent the views of outsiders and they are confined to the first half of the second millennium AD. The sixth group is records by European travellers in the Early Modern period. Their value is limited for the sixteenth and seventeenth centuries, but several eighteenth-century travellers wrote about Nubia; much of this material belongs to the nineteenth century.

Thus there are nearly 5,000 years of historical documentation for the middle Nile. The documentation has three weaknesses: first, the further up the Nile one goes, the less informative it is; second, the texts provide only an intermittent recorded history; third, most of the documentation was written by visitors to Nubia, attempting to understand what they saw or were told.

Archaeological evidence

In such circumstances archaeological evidence has a vital role to play, although studies of ancient Nubia have suffered from historical bias. Archaeological research commenced at the beginning of the twentieth century with the work of Reisner, Firth, Griffith, Garstang, and Wellcome, to be followed until 1958 by others (Adams 1977: 78–80), but there was a tendency for excavations to be tomb, temple, and palace–oriented and for much of the detailed information never to reach publication. Only with the international archaeological campaign of the 1960s, made necessary by the construction of the Aswan High Dam and the creation of Lake Nasser/Nubia (Hassan 2007), did there develop both an interest in the excavation of settlement sites and a substantial archaeological literature.

Some of the earliest archaeological sites relevant to the origins of cities and states in the middle Nile region are Egyptian rather than Nubian. They represent two main periods of colonial expansion, first during the Pharaonic Middle Kingdom, and second during the New Kingdom. The first of these expansions belonged mainly to the Egyptian Twelfth Dynasty of the first quarter of the second millennium BC and resulted in the construction of a series of forts in Lower Nubia, most of them clustered around the Second Cataract (Adams 1977: 175–83; Edwards 2004: 91–4). Buhen is the best known of those that have been excavated. It consisted of a series of mud-brick fortifications built on a massive scale, enclosing a small town (Emery 1965: 149). This was not the first Egyptian town at Buhen, for during the Fourth and Fifth Dynasties of the Old Kingdom, around the middle of the third millennium BC, there was already a sizeable town surrounded by a stone wall (Adams 1977: 170–4). It has been assumed that the Middle Kingdom forts were constructed in order to protect Egypt's southern frontier, but Adams suggested that they were primarily intended to protect and control the commerce of the Nile Valley (Adams 1984).

During the Pharaonic Second Intermediate Period, which lasted from the end of the first quarter of the second millennium BC to the middle of that millennium, Egyptian political control of Lower Nubia seems to have weakened and the Second Cataract forts might have been abandoned. However, the New Kingdom, of the second half of the second millennium BC, saw a new colonial initiative by Egypt that extended Egypt's dominion further up the Nile than ever before, or indeed ever again until the conquests of Mohammed Ali early in the nineteenth century AD.

Egyptian authority was established to at least the Third Cataract, and evidence of the most southerly Egyptian presence is provided by inscriptions at Kurgus, between the Fourth and Fifth Cataracts (Edwards 2004: 105). The Middle Kingdom forts were restored, and new fortified towns were built in the Abri-Delgo Reach and in the Dongola Reach. In time, the military character of Egyptian settlement diminished and the building of temples replaced that of fortresses. During the period as a whole, however, colonial settlements of importance grew up particularly in the Abri-Delgo Reach and included such towns as Sai, Amara, Soleb, Seddenga, and Sesebi (Delgo). Further south, in the Dongola Reach, there was less Egyptian colonization but towns developed at both Kawa and Napata, possibly to control the Meheila Road, a desert route that cut across the great bend of the Nile in this region. Most remarkable of the New Kingdom temples in Nubia is that of Abu Simbel in Lower Nubia, but another of importance was constructed far to the south at Jebel Barkal, where the Temple of Amon, founded by the Egyptian Pharaoh Rameses II, later became the ideological centre of the indigenous Napatan state. New Kingdom colonization of the northern parts of the middle Nile terminated towards the end of the second millennium BC, probably because of growing political problems in Egypt. The colonial domination of parts of Nubia by Egypt was over, but its consequences for the people of Nubia were to be long-lasting (Adams 1977: 217–45).

Egyptian involvement in Nubia had already elicited an indigenous Nubian response by the Second Intermediate Period. It was at this time, about the middle of the second millennium BC, that the Nubian kingdom of Kerma was at the climax of its development in the period known as the Classic Kerma. Prior to that, its emergence can be traced back for about 1,500 years through the Middle Kerma and the Early Kerma to its indigenous origins in the Pre-Kerma before 3000 BC (Bonnet 1990; 1992). That its roots included a substantial pastoralist element is apparent from the sheep and cattle remains with some of the Kerma burials, and MacDonald (1998) suggested that the sociopolitical changes indicated by the Kerma evidence originated in what he termed the 'Mobile Elites', of the African savanna and Saharan margins, from 4000 BC onwards. Nevertheless, Kerma reached its high point at a time of

Egyptian weakness during the Second Intermediate Period, when the Second Cataract forts might have been abandoned, and it disappeared at the time of Egypt's colonial expansion during the New Kingdom.

Although there was dense Kerma settlement as far south as the Kawa region (Smith 2003: 88), the most important archaeological evidence comes from Kerma itself, a complex of sites situated on the east bank of the Nile at the northern end of the Dongola Reach, one of the more fertile regions of the middle Nile. Excavations at Kerma by G.A. Reisner, in 1913–16, concentrated on an extensive cemetery containing several thousand graves (Reisner 1923). A number of these were covered by burial mounds, or 'tumuli', as the excavator called them. Of these tumuli, eight were unusually large, the largest being about 91 metres in diameter. Like the smaller examples they contained burial chambers, but in the case of the three largest the body of the mound had an internal structure of mud-brick walls. Part of this structure consisted of a corridor running across the mound, with other walls at right angles to it. In the main chamber, the principal burial lay upon a bed, accompanied by weapons and personal possessions. Other human bodies, whose attitudes suggested that they had been sacrificed, took up the rest of the space. A far larger number of sacrifices lay in the transverse corridor, and later subsidiary burials, some also accompanied by human sacrifices, had been inserted in many places between the walls. In Tumulus X, where the main chamber had been long ago robbed, Reisner found 322 sacrifices in the sacrificial corridor, and estimated that there had originally been as many as 400 before disturbance by tomb robbers (Reisner 1923: Parts I–III, 312). Such evidence suggests a highly centralized political authority, and it seems justifiable to claim Kerma as the earliest state in tropical Africa.

Excavations by Charles Bonnet more recently have shed additional light on Kerma (Bonnet 1990; 1992; 1997; Bonnet and Valbelle 2014). A greater chronological range of burials has now been examined, and because the dry climate has preserved bone, leather, hair, and feathers, a remarkably detailed picture of Kerma society can be reconstructed. For instance, a life expectancy of thirty-one years has been calculated for those who died naturally, although those who were sacrificed were generally younger than this, and some individuals lived until they were eighty years old. In addition, the remains of an extensive and long-lasting settlement have now been uncovered (Fig. 4.2). Mainly of rectangular houses of mud-brick or wood, this has provided evidence of an elaborate system of fortification consisting of a mud wall with projecting rectangular towers and a ditch. As time passed there were substantial changes in the plans and layout of structures within the settlement, and both stone and fired brick were used in the defences. Overall, it seems that this early urban development grew up around a sanctuary that evolved through time into a

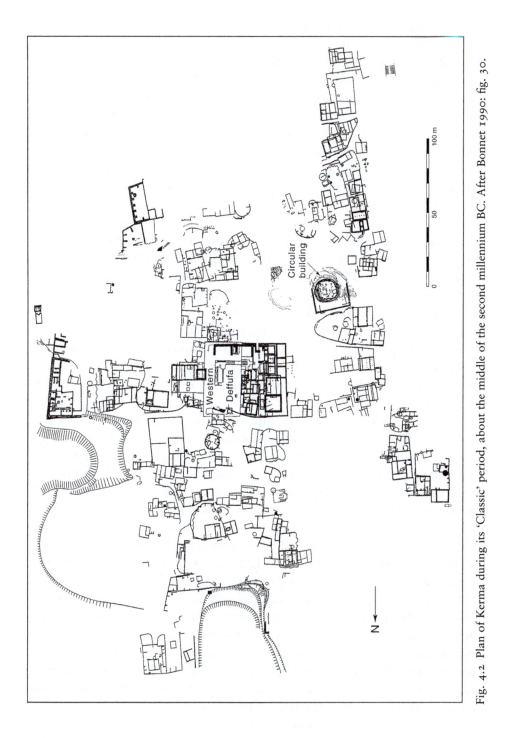

Fig. 4.2 Plan of Kerma during its 'Classic' period, about the middle of the second millennium BC. After Bonnet 1990: fig. 30.

Western
Deffufa

Circular
building

100 m

50

0

N

79

massive mud-brick temple, known as the Western Deffufa. This is a solid rectangular mass of mud-brick, measuring about 27 by 52 metres at the base and originally probably far exceeding the height of 19 metres that has survived to modern times (Reisner 1923: Parts I–III, 21–40). The structure has no internal chambers, only the remains of a narrow, winding stair that must have led to its top. Excavations by Bonnet, however, have shown that it was not originally a solid structure but a temple with interior chambers that were later filled with brickwork, while at least twelve phases have been distinguished in its masonry (Bonnet 1992: 613–14). A similar but smaller structure, known as the Eastern Deffufa, is situated in the cemetery about 4 kilometres to the east of the settlement and appears to have been an outsized mortuary chapel (Reisner 1923: Parts I–III, 122–34). Attached to one side of the Western Deffufa was a building from which Reisner excavated more than 500 mud sealings of Egyptian type, which had been affixed to various containers. There were in addition many fragments of items of Egyptian manufacture and assorted raw materials. This led Adams (1984: 51) to suggest that this was a trading depot, but the discovery by Bonnet of a bronze workshop in the same place, and the argument of Lacovara (1991) that some of the Egyptian material was in the process of being recycled, makes it more likely that this was merely an activity area.

Bonnet's excavations have also shown that by the first half of the second millennium BC the Kerma settlement contained a very large circular building of wood and mud-brick that was at least 10 metres high, probably with a conical roof. Clearly an elite structure, its apparent similarity to much later audience chambers recorded ethnohistorically in other parts of the continent emphasizes the African character of the Kerma development. It contrasts with a rectangular residential or administrative building and with an Egyptian-style temple, both dating towards the end of the Kerma sequence and located a kilometre away (Bonnet 1992). By this time the Egyptian New Kingdom might have taken control of the area, but it seems that prior to this Kerma had already attained urban status and become the capital of tropical Africa's first identifiable state. David O'Connor had no doubt about this, referring to Kerma as 'the earliest city in Africa outside of Egypt' and concluding that 'the social complexity and the advanced degree of political centralization evoked in the city and cemetery of Kerma would seem to be those of a state, not a complex chiefdom' (O'Connor 1993: 50, 55). An indication of the demographic processes involved in the formation of this early city and state has been provided by stable isotope analysis of human skeletal material from Kerma burials, suggesting that a significant portion of the population might have originated elsewhere (Thompson et al. 2008).

The extent of Egyptian influence in Kerma has become doubtful. For instance, Bourriau (1991: 135–6) has shown that whereas Kerma pottery that occurs in Egypt during the Eighteenth Dynasty is 'tableware or cooking pottery', indicating the presence of Nubians, the Egyptian pottery found at Kerma in the Classic Kerma period consists of 'jars for the storage and transport of commodities' that are not 'sufficient evidence for the presence of Egyptians'.

New Kingdom colonization apparently brought Kerma to an end, but when that in turn declined, the next indigenous Nubian development was that of Napata, a kingdom that arose on the Dongola Reach during the ninth century BC (Shinnie 1996: 95–105; Welsby 1996; Edwards 2004: 112–40). This kingdom, usually known as the Kingdom of Kush, was focused until the fourth century BC on an area extending downstream from the Fourth Cataract for a distance of 24 kilometres. It is the whole of this district that is referred to as Napata, and it includes major cemetery sites at El Kurru (Dunham 1950) and Nuri (Dunham 1955), a cemetery and temple sites at Jebel Barkal, and a cemetery, temple, and town site at Sanam (Griffith 1922). After the fourth century BC, the political focus of Kush seems to have moved south to Meroë on the Shendi Reach of the Nile, although the relationship of Napata and Meroë is still not fully understood. Napata seems to have had its origins in the power vacuum left by the end of Egyptian colonial domination towards the close of the second millennium BC (Morkot 2003). As already mentioned (p. 77), Egyptian New Kingdom colonization had led to the growth of a town at Napata and to the construction of a temple of Amon at Jebel Barkal. With the end of Egyptian control, it seems that power fell into the hands of local rulers who, with the sanction of the priests of Jebel Barkal, went on to control much of Nubia and, in the eighth and seventh centuries BC, Egypt itself which they ruled as the Twenty-fifth Dynasty (Bonnet and Valbelle 2006). Subsequently, Napata became of less importance, but its culture seems to have remained imitative of that of Pharaonic Egypt, although displaying Nubian characteristics. Significantly, Napata was still important to the later rulers of Kush, located at Meroë, who continued to be crowned there and to build temples there. Indeed, it is possible that some of the latest Napatan burials were of rulers whose capital had already been transferred to Meroë.

Archaeological evidence for the Napatan state is mainly limited to the sites already mentioned. The cemeteries at El Kurru, Jebel Barkal, and Nuri have been interpreted as 'royal' cemeteries, and it is from El Kurru and Nuri, excavated early in the twentieth century by Reisner, that much of our information comes. All three cemeteries are characterized by tombs covered by small, steep-sided pyramids, almost certainly inspired by New Kingdom examples such as those at Aniba in Lower Nubia (Shinnie 1996: 100), and mummification was practised. In addition, temples at Jebel Barkal and Sanam have been excavated, and in a number of other places there are the remains of temples constructed by Taharqa, one of the Nubian rulers of Egypt (Fig. 4.3). Nevertheless, there is little known about Napatan settlement sites, in spite of what appears to have been a large town at Sanam, which might have been the principal population centre of Napata. Thus, although hieroglyphic inscriptions from excavated tombs have enabled a substantial reconstruction of the Napatan dynastic sequence (Welsby 1996: 207–9), we have relatively little information about the social and economic organization of the people that these rulers governed. Adams (1977: 293) was of the opinion that this was not a 'complex, urbanized society', but Kendall (1991) has since identified a Napatan palace building at Jebel Barkal; it is also possible that there was a walled town at El Kurru (Welsby 1996: 148). Furthermore, Napata was at the terminus both of the Bayuda Road, the land route to Meroë, and of the Meheila Road, the land route to Kawa and Argo, which possibly, with Seddenga further to the north, were also Napatan settlements of importance. Napata, it would appear, must have been a major staging point in the trade of the middle Nile (Edwards 2004: 139).

As Napata declined, Meroë rose to prominence, and in its case there is abundant archaeological evidence suggesting both urbanization and state development. Meroë seems to have been of particular importance during the first century AD, but it probably extended from before the fourth century BC to about the fourth century AD. Excavations at the site of Meroë itself have indeed indicated that its earliest building level could have belonged to the eighth century BC or perhaps even earlier (Török 1997: Part I, 15–20). Like Napata, Meroë seems to have been a Nubian response to the world to its north. For Napata, it was Pharaonic Egypt that was an important cultural influence; for Meroë, it was Ptolemaic Egypt, which was part of the wider Hellenistic world.

Archaeological evidence for the Meroitic period includes the remains of large settlements, of which Meroë itself is the most important. Situated on the east bank of the Nile, some 200 kilometres downstream from modern Khartoum, Meroë has suffered a chequered archaeological history. Forgotten until its rediscovery at the end of the eighteenth century AD, parts of the site were 'ransacked' by Ferlini in the 1830s (Adams 1977: 295), and early in the twentieth century parts were excavated at separate times by Budge, Garstang, and Reisner. Only Reisner's work was conducted in an adequate fashion, and even his excavations had to be published posthumously by Dows Dunham. The extensive excavations by Garstang were unscientific and remained largely unpublished, until Török rescued them eighty-three years later (Török 1997). At the time only the first season's work was described in detail (Garstang et al. 1911). Limited excavations by Peter Shinnie during the 1960s and 1970s remain the only archaeological investigations at Meroë carried out and

Fig. 4.3 Upper part of a stone statue of Taharqa, excavated from a cache of statues at the Egyptian town of Pnubs, near Kerma. Seventh century BC. According to Adams 1977: 248, Taharqa 'is the only Nubian to be mentioned by name in the Bible' (2 Kings XIX, 9). After Bonnet and Valbelle 2006: 122.

published in a scientific fashion. Shinnie also summarized what was then known about Meroë and related sites (Shinnie 1967) and later followed this with a more general study (Shinnie 1996). Welsby (1996) and Edwards (2004: 141–81) provided other syntheses.

The site of Meroë (Fig. 4.4) covers an area roughly 0.75 kilometre by 1 kilometre (for plans, mostly variants of the same originals, see Shinnie 1967: 76; 1996: 107; Adams 1977: 299, 314; Bradley 1982: 164; Welsby 1996: 149; Török 1997: Part II, figs. 1–3; Edwards 2004: 146). Within the settlement was a large, stone-walled precinct, roughly rectangular in shape, in which lay a labyrinth of buildings, mostly of monumental character. Many of these buildings, which were usually of mud-brick, often with an external facing of fired brick, were excavated by Garstang, who interpreted the area as the residence of the rulers of Meroë, calling it the 'Royal City'. Its buildings were believed to include palaces, audience chambers, stores, and domestic quarters for the palace staff; many of them seem to have been of two storeys (Török 1997: Part I, 36). There was also a small temple, in front of which was found a bronze head of Augustus, of Roman manufacture (Shinnie 1967: plate 28). Perhaps the most remarkable feature of the Royal City, however, was its so-called Roman Bath. This consisted of a large brick-lined tank with water channels leading into it from the Nile. At first interpreted as a swimming bath (Shinnie 1967: 79), it was later suggested that it was a water sanctuary associated with Nile floodwater festivals (Török 1992: 117; Welsby 1996: 122–3).

Outside the Royal City, much of the rest of the site is covered by two extensive occupation mounds, and it is possible that Meroë originated as a settlement split between three alluvial islands in a braided channel of the Nile, the course of the river having since changed (Bradley 1982). The south mound remains unexcavated, and the only investigations of the north mound were test excavations by Shinnie. These revealed remains of mud-brick structures serving industrial, domestic, and public functions, as well as furnace remains that indicated both iron smelting and iron smithing (Bradley 1982; Shinnie and Kense 1982). Other than this, little is known of ordinary buildings, although Shinnie (1967: 77) described 'many mounds covered with red [fired] brick fragments' and mentioned 'six large mounds of slag and other debris of iron smelting' on the edges of the site. The significance of these mounds of slag has long been discussed. Some idea of their size can be gained from a railway cutting made through one of them for the line from Khartoum to Atbara. Possibly this was the mound into which Arkell excavated an unpublished trial trench in 1940, recording that it consisted of 'solid slag and debris from iron smelting from top to bottom' (Shinnie and Kense 1982: 18).

The site of Meroë also has the remains of a number of temples, and, in contrast with the scant attention given to the residential and industrial areas,

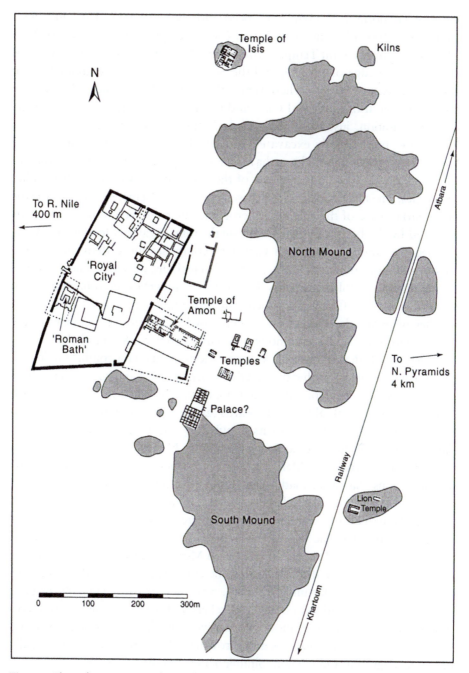

Fig. 4.4 Plan of Meroë, in Sudan. After Shinnie 1967: fig. 19; Welsby 1996: fig. 66; and Török 1997: Part II, fig. 1.

the more important of these have been entirely excavated. They include a temple of Amon, adjacent to the Royal City; a temple of Isis, on the northern edge of the site; the Lion Temple, which stands on top of one of the slag heaps on the eastern edge of the site; and the Sun Temple, which is situated about 1 kilometre east of the site. There is also the Shrine of Apis, located about 2.5 kilometres south of the Royal City, and several lesser temples within the site itself. In addition, just to the east of the settlement site lie three cemeteries which have been entirely excavated and which were found to contain many hundreds of graves, thought to have been occupied by common citizens of Meroë. Some 3 to 4 kilometres east of the main site, however, lie three other cemeteries. The most important of these is the North Cemetery, which was the main burial place of the rulers of Meroë and their immediate relatives, characterized by the best preserved of the small stone pyramids for which Meroë has become famous. The South Cemetery comprises more than 200 graves, most containing common citizens, but it also includes mastabas and pyramids belonging both to rulers and (it is thought) to members of the ruling family. In contrast, the West Cemetery, which contains about 500 graves, including a number of pyramids, seems to have been for less important members of the royal family and also for commoners (Shinnie 1967: 75–87; Hinkel 2000).

It is regrettable that archaeologists have concentrated on the tomb, temple, and palace aspect of Meroë, rather than on the settlement itself and its apparent urban status. At its peak it might have had a population of 20,000 to 25,000 people (Grzymski 1984: 289), although Edwards (2004: 147) thought it 'quite impossible even to estimate the size of its population' and suggested that its 'urban character' had still 'to be clearly demonstrated'. Nevertheless, an emphasis on monumental structures at Meroë has produced both inscriptions and artistic representations that have made contributions to our knowledge of Meroitic society and history. In particular, we know the names and approximate dates of most of the rulers of Meroë, even though there is still some uncertainty about the details of this dynastic sequence (Shinnie 1967: 58–61; Adams 1977: 251–2; Welsby 1996: 207–9). The inscriptions are in Meroitic, however, rendered either in hieroglyphs or in the distinctive Meroitic cursive alphabet, and because this language cannot be fully understood (p. 75), they can be read only in part. Luckily, the temple and pyramid-chapel reliefs and the small number of pieces of sculpture in-the-round are more informative: depicting gods, rulers (male and female), and vanquished enemies and throwing light on royal dress and regalia and on iconography and religion (Shinnie 1967: 101–9).

Although little is known of the housing of ordinary people at Meroë itself, excavations at the site of Hamadab, some 3 kilometres to the south, have revealed an apparently large nucleated Meroitic settlement of more than 15 hectares (Fig. 4.5). There seems little doubt of the urban character of this

Fig. 4.5 Meroitic 'Upper Town' of Hamadab, near Meroë. Representing the originally walled core of the urban settlement, founded probably in the last century BC. Reproduced by permission of Pawel Wolf, cf. fig. 2 Wolf et al. 2014. Drawing by Nicole Salamanek (Beuth Hochschule for Applied Sciences Berlin / Geomedia Lab) / Hamadab Archaeological Project (Qatar-Sudan Archaeological Project).

site, and several potentially similar large sites are known to the south and north of Meroë (Edwards 2004: 147–8; Wolf et al. 2014).

There are many other sites along the middle Nile which both culturally and chronologically can be described as 'Meroitic'. Perhaps the most important of these are situated in the western part of the 'Island of Meroë', a name applied to the area known as the Butana, in the triangle formed by the confluence of the rivers Atbara and Nile. Two of these sites are particularly significant: Naqa and Musawwarat es-Sufra (Shinnie 1967: 87–95; Adams 1977: 318–21; Edwards 2004: 150–3). At Naqa there are remains of a town nearly as extensive as those of Meroë itself, and there are at least seven stone temples, several possible palaces, and two large cemeteries. One of the temples, the Lion Temple of Natakamani and Amanitere, has remarkable exterior reliefs depicting the first-century AD king and queen and the lion god Apedemak. The reliefs on the two pylons of this temple are an explicit statement of autocratic authority, showing both king and queen brandishing weapons whilst grasping their vanquished foes by the hair. In contrast, the site of Musawwarat es-Sufra is something of a mystery, consisting principally of a cluster of monumental stone buildings, of which the largest, the Great Enclosure, has no Nubian or Egyptian parallel. It included a temple, with a remarkable irrigated garden, perhaps a palace, and apparently a religious pilgrimage centre (Welsby 1996: 143–6; Wolf 1997; Wenig 2001; Edwards 2004: 153).

Another site in the Meroë area is Wad ben Naqa on the east bank of the Nile, where there is evidence of a considerable town. Excavations there have revealed the remains of a large, square building of at least two storeys, which has been interpreted as a Meroitic palace, apparently similar to others at Meroë, Jebel Barkal, and Naqa. It was built of mud-brick, its exterior walls faced with fired brick and plastered with white stucco. Only the lower floor survived, consisting mainly of long, narrow rooms that were probably vaulted storerooms, supporting more important rooms in the storey above. Nevertheless, the building is an indication of the development of centralized authority in the Meroitic state (Vercoutter 1962; Adams 1977: 322–3).

Other evidence of Meroitic settlement has been found as far south as Sennar, far up the Blue Nile, and as far north as Maharraqa, in Lower Nubia, a distance of more than 1,100 kilometres (Edwards 1989; 1996). Settlement on the middle Nile was discontinuous, being concentrated along those stretches of the river that were economically more viable. Adams (1977: 302) identified three main areas of Meroitic culture: the Southern Province, containing Meroë itself; the Napatan Province; and the Lower Nubian Province. The Southern Province, which may be regarded as the Meroitic homeland, was connected to the Napatan Province not by the barren Abu Hamed Reach of the Nile but by the Bayuda Road, an important desert route that bypassed both the Fifth and Fourth Cataracts and the contrary winds of this part of the Nile. In the Napatan Province there was Meroitic activity at Jebel Barkal, Sanam, Kawa, and Argo and (further north) at Seddenga, but the development of the Korosko

Road – a desert route leaving the Nile at Abu Hamed that rejoined it far downstream in Lower Nubia – cut this area off from the mainstream of commerce, so that the Napatan Province became something of a cultural and economic backwater. It is possible that the introduction of the camel, probably in the early first millennium BC (Rowley-Conwy 1988), was one of the factors that eventually brought about this change (Adams 1977: 304–5). North of the Napatan Province lay the barren Batn el Hajar, but beyond that was the Lower Nubian Province where substantial Meroitic settlement has been claimed (Adams 1977: 345–81). As already explained (p. 74), it was an area thought to have been virtually uninhabited for some centuries, until resettlement in the second and third centuries AD as a result of the introduction of the *saqia*, the ox-driven water wheel, but this view has been challenged (Edwards 2004: 202–3). The evidence of both cemeteries and occupation sites indicates that Meroitic settlement in Lower Nubia was characterized not by large settlements with monumental buildings, as in the southern provinces, but by a nearly continuous line of farming villages along the Nile, together with a few relatively small administrative centres. Qasr Ibrim, Jebel Adda, and Faras were amongst the latter, all of them walled settlements. Karanog appears to have been another important centre, but it consisted of a scattered collection of houses without a surrounding wall. Amongst these, however, were two large mud-brick buildings, each apparently of three storeys, that are thought to have been successive palaces of local governors, although their dating remains problematic (Woolley 1911; O'Connor 1993: 100–1). Apparent cultural differences between the Meroitic north and south prompted Adams to conclude that in Lower Nubia there had been a secularization of government and that control of trade had passed into private hands, allowing a widespread development of material prosperity (Adams 1974; 1976). Subsequently, however, this interpretation was questioned and it was suggested that the settlement of Lower Nubia might not have been as dense as was thought (Edwards 1996: 50–2).

The Meroitic state seems to have faded away in the fourth century AD, significantly at a time when substantial changes were taking place in the Mediterranean world to the north. Some Meroitic urban centres were abandoned and long-distance trade declined, but the elite burials in the mounds of el Hobagi, 70 kilometres south-west of Meroë, suggest continuity of Meroitic traditions along with a re-emergence of older ones (Lenoble and Sharif 1992; Edwards 1996: 92–3; Welsby 1996: 202; Edwards 2004: 191–3). Other indications of a successor state have been found in Lower Nubia, where the 'X-Group', called by Adams the 'Ballana Culture' (1977: 392) and treated by Edwards (2004: 182–211) as one of several 'post-Meroitic transitions', suggests the development of an absolute monarchy during the fifth and sixth centuries AD. The X-Group was first recognized from scattered burial evidence, but subsequently a number of village sites were identified, as well as larger settlements at Jebel Adda and Qasr Ibrim; excavations at this latter site suggested that it was a manufacturing centre at this time (Adams 1982: 27–8; Alexander 1988: 81–2). In addition, the extensively excavated settlement of Meinarti, just north of the Second Cataract, was also occupied in both the Late Meroitic and X-Group periods (Adams 2000; 2001; 2002).

Nevertheless, the X-Group is best known from the remarkable burials of Ballana and Qustul, situated a little upstream of Jebel Adda. These were excavated by Walter Emery in the early 1930s and produced evidence of a concentration of wealth and autocratic power in the hands of a few individuals, thought to be kings (Emery 1938; 1948). There were 122 tombs at Ballana on the west bank of the Nile and 61 at Qustul on the east bank. All 183 of these tombs were excavated, and the size of the structures and richness of contents of perhaps 40 of them might suggest that they contained 'royal' burials. Typically, these larger tombs consisted of a series of brick chambers, constructed at the bottom of a large pit, which was entered by means of a ramp cut into the hard alluvium. The chambers were roofed with barrel vaulting and in front of them there was often a small open court into which the entrance ramp opened. After the burials and offerings had been placed inside the chambers, in the court and at the bottom of the ramp, both the pit and the ramp were filled with earth and a large earthen mound was raised over them. At Ballana the largest of these mounds measured 77 metres in diameter and 12 metres in height. It was the contents of these tombs that were most impressive, however. The 'king' was buried with his 'queen' and with his servants, horses, camels, donkeys, dogs, sheep, and cows. Also included were furniture, food and drink, cooking utensils, jewels, weapons, tools, and personal possessions.

Many of these tombs had been ransacked by tomb-robbers in the past but some survived intact. One of the more remarkable was Tomb 95 at Ballana (Fig. 4.6). Animal burials lay at the bottom of the entrance ramp, beyond which were three sealed burial chambers. Inside the first chamber was the skeleton of the 'king', who had been laid, wearing his silver crown and other finery, on a wooden bier from which he had been displaced soon after burial by the collapse of the chamber roof. Also in the chamber were the skeletons of his 'queen', wearing a silver crown, and of a male servant and a cow. Weapons and other personal possessions lay in other parts of the chamber. In an adjacent chamber were the skeletons of six additional servants, two of them children, accompanied by more weapons and by lamps, iron ingots, pottery wine jars, drinking cups, and other things. Most of the third chamber was packed with more pottery wine jars and drinking cups and with them were numerous bronze cups, a bronze flagon and pan, a stone bowl, a large vessel of green glass, several scarabs, and a small gold ingot (Emery 1938: vol. 1, 135–41).

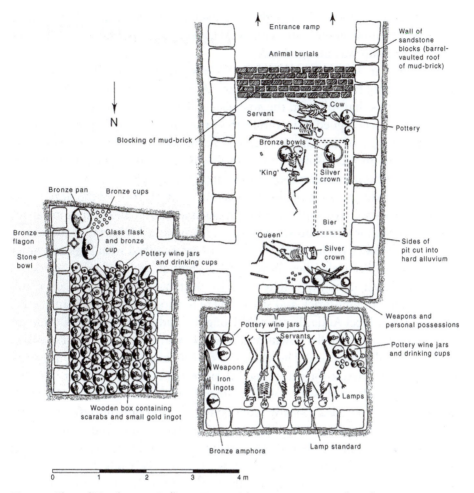

Fig. 4.6 Plan of Tomb 95 at Ballana, Egypt. After Emery 1938: vol. 1, fig. 68.

The animals buried in the tombs at Ballana and Qustul had been pole-axed, and it was presumed that the human beings, other than the main burial in each tomb, had met their deaths either by the cutting of their throats or by strangulation. The combination of monumental tomb, wealth, and human sacrifice for the burial of crowned individuals is surely indicative of absolute monarchy in Lower Nubia during the time to which the X-Group belongs.

Reisner, who first identified the X-Group, thought that it represented an invasion of a new people. There is, however, increasing evidence that this culture evolved within the Nile Valley, where both settlement and burial evidence suggest that it was a direct successor culture to the Meroitic state, with similar subsistence strategies and with characteristics comparable to those indicated by the el Hobagi burials far to the south (Welsby 1996: 204–5;

Edwards 2004: 206–7). Then, with the conversion of the people of the middle Nile to Christianity in the sixth century AD, a new period of state development and urbanization was inaugurated.

The Christian kingdoms of Nubia (Welsby 2002) existed from the sixth century to about the fourteenth century AD. They developed out of Pre-Christian states that followed the so-called collapse of the Meroitic state, but Fuller (2014) has argued that, rather than resulting from collapse, they were the consequence of increasing regional economic independence. This was supported by an increasing cultivation of summer crops, such as *Sorghum bicolor* and *Pennisetum glaucum*, and winter crops, such as wheat and barley, in each case made possible by the third-century introduction of the *saqia*. Also important was the growing of cash crops such as cotton and grapes in Lower Nubia. The major Christian states were Nobadia and Makuria, to the north, and Alodia (Alwa), to the south; Nobadia became unified with Makuria at an early date. Collectively they have left substantial archaeological evidence (Edwards 2004: 212–55). There are, for instance, the remains of many churches built of mud-brick and stone. There is also evidence of urban centres at Qasr Ibrim, Jebel Adda, Faras, Old Dongola, and Soba, as well as evidence elsewhere of many smaller towns and villages, fortresses, monasteries, industrial sites, and cemeteries. The churches of Medieval Nubia have attracted archaeological interest for many years (Clarke 1912), but it was not until the 1960s that much work was done on other Christian sites. Study of church architecture has revealed a steady reduction in size and pretentiousness as time went on, reflecting the gradual decline of Christian Nubia and of its Monophysite, Coptic church. Nevertheless, many of the buildings were impressive structures with stone columns, masonry piers, and brick vaults (Adams 2009). Most important are the episcopal cathedrals at Qasr Ibrim, Faras, and Old Dongola and a possible cathedral at Jebel Adda (Adams 1977: 473–8). The insides of many churches were originally decorated with brightly coloured wall paintings. Only fragmentary remains of these were known until the 1960s, when excavations revealed well-preserved paintings in three churches, of which those discovered in Faras cathedral were quite remarkable. This building (Vantini 1970) had been abandoned after it filled with blown sand during the heyday of Nubian Christianity. Within it were numerous large paintings depicting biblical scenes and individuals, as well as Nubian kings, bishops, and eparchs (high-ranking government officials), most identified by name.

The archaeological remnants of the churches of Nubia indicate the existence of organized religion and secular authority as separate but interacting entities, each needing the protection of the other. Under their joint umbrella, the society of the middle Nile developed its commercial activities to a high level and became, at least in the northern part of the region, probably more densely urbanized than in earlier periods. Unfortunately, archaeological excavation of the major urban centres has not been extensive; both Faras and Jebel Adda, for instance, were lost beneath Lake Nasser before much could be done. Work continued at Qasr Ibrim, however, which was occupied throughout the Christian period and which survived as an island at the edge of Lake Nasser, although later 'almost totally destroyed' by the lake (Edwards 2004: 159–60). Excavations there demonstrated that the Early Christian period (c. 500 to c. 800 AD) displayed a remarkable continuity from X-Group times, with many of the same houses remaining in use and manufacturing activities continuing on a large scale. Only the conversion of Meroitic temples to churches and the building of a cathedral and of a monastery mark the introduction of Christianity. During the Classic Christian period, however, from c. 800 to c. 1200 AD, the city seems to have become primarily a pilgrimage centre, with most of its housing being cleared to provide a large open plaza. Nevertheless, during the Late Christian period (c. 1200 to c. 1500 AD) the site was again fortified and once more became crowded with houses, regaining its commercial importance and (according to excavated manuscript material) also becoming an administrative centre (Adams 1982: 28–30; Alexander 1988). Excavations of settlements dating from AD 1000 onwards have also been conducted at Kulubnarti, near the Dal Cataract, providing further information on the Christian periods and shedding light on subsequent Islamic occupation (Adams 2011).

The standard of living for the more affluent during the Christian period has been indicated by excavations at the site of Old Dongola, far to the south, the capital city of the kingdom of Makuria (e.g., Godlewski and Medeksza 1987). A heated bathroom with piped hot water and painted decorations was found in one supposed house (Jakobielski 1982), and fragments of pottery toilet seats were also recovered (Godlewski 1991: 92–3, 97). Even further to the south, the site of Soba, the capital of the kingdom of Alodia, has also been partly excavated and has revealed rectangular palatial buildings and churches of mud-brick, fired brick, and stone, as well as both rectangular and circular (wooden) domestic structures and many burials. Its radiocarbon chronology is from the fifth to the eleventh or twelfth century AD (Welsby and Daniels 1991; Welsby 1998; 2002; Edwards 2004: 221–3). In addition, some of the smaller settlements in Nubia have been excavated, such as Arminna West (Weeks 1967) and Debeira West (Shinnie and Shinnie 1978), both of which were referred to as 'towns' by their excavators, although Adams (1977: 488) thought that such settlements, although 'densely urbanized', numbered only 200 to 400 inhabitants. Indeed, the packed houses of Arminna West (Fig. 4.7) suggest an urban environment. Many houses in these settlements attempted to deal with one of the problems of such crowding by providing 'inside' latrines (Adams 1977: 491). Usually these would have required night-soil

94

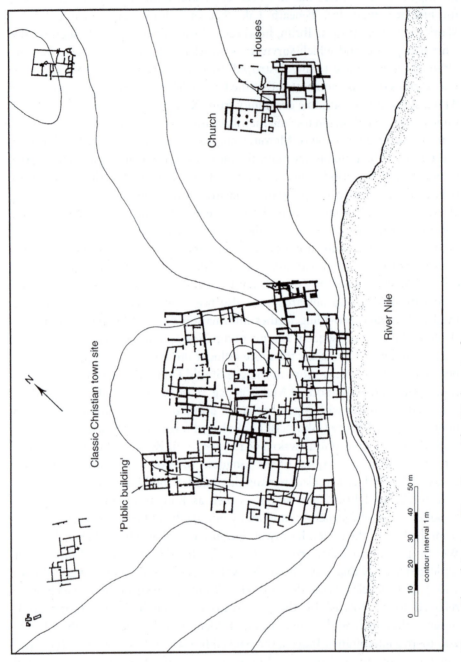

Classic Christian town site

N

'Public building'

Church

Houses

River Nile

0   10   20   30   40   50 m

contour interval 1 m

Fig. 4.7 Plan of Arminna West, Egypt. After Weeks 1967: fig. 1.

carriers, but at Debeira West there were some latrines that discharged into individual, vaulted soakaways that were filled with ash and potsherds (Shinnie and Shinnie 1978: 106).

Although some Christian Nubian settlements lacked fortifications, suggesting peace and stability at times, there were nevertheless many such structures built over the centuries. In the Early Christian period there were fortified sites at Faras, Sabaqura, Sheikh Daud, Ikhmindi, Kalabsha, and Qasr Ibrim, all in Lower Nubia, presumably responding to military threats from Egypt. Subsequently, fortified settlements, forts, and even castles existed in many other parts of the middle Nile, probably because of raiders from the adjoining deserts and dynastic and civil conflicts, as well as the need to protect trade. By the Late Christian period fortified settlements were common, concentrated particularly in the Batn el Hajar, in which poor and isolated region many people seem to have sought refuge (Welsby 2002: 129–36). In particular, between Faras and Ferka, near the Dal Cataract, two-storey 'castle-houses' were constructed, with restricted external access, hidden storage crypts, and latrine facilities (Fig. 4.8), obviously designed to provide refuge in times of danger (Adams 1994). Christian Nubian polities were, in fact, disintegrating into a society of peasant farmers gathered around the castles of local rulers. The Christian Church was also in decline, and Arabs from the desert were moving into the region of the middle Nile. With the gradual Arabization and

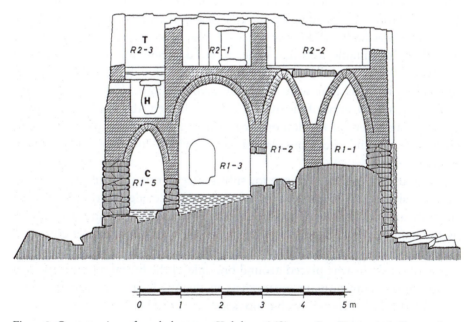

Fig. 4.8 Cross-section of castle-house at Kulubnarti (Site 21-S-2, House A1). C, cesspit; H, secret crypt; T, toilet chamber. After Adams 1994: fig. 11b.

Islamization that overtook the area by about the fourteenth century AD, numerous sheikhdoms based on the tribe replaced central government. However, eventually a series of loose confederations appeared, the largest and longest-lasting of which was the Fung kingdom of Sennar, which survived from the sixteenth century to the early nineteenth century AD (Elzein 2004). Furthermore, the settlement of Qasr Ibrim, whose occupation dates back to perhaps 1500 BC, was not abandoned until the early nineteenth century AD, epitomizing the continuity of urban and state traditions in the middle Nile region (Adams 1977: 508–636; Alexander 1995). Although those traditions seem to have had little influence on the rest of tropical Africa (Shinnie 1989; Alexander 1993a), this impression needs some qualification. First, archaeologically diagnostic artefacts, such as Meroitic and Christian decorated pottery, are unlikely to have penetrated to economically peripheral areas of the African savannas, and therefore influences from the Nile Valley might be difficult to recognize. Second, during the early Islamic periods large settlements and associated polities did appear in Darfur (west of the Nile) at Uri and Ain Farah, east of the Nile along the Red Sea coast at Badi' and 'Aidhab, and inland at 'Allaqi (Elzein 2004: 35–42).

Subsistence economy

The development of cities and states in the middle Nile region was supported by mixed farming, depending on the cultivation of cereals and vegetables and on animal husbandry (Edwards 2004). A major factor must have been the availability of suitable soils that either received seasonal floodwater or could be irrigated mechanically. All the developments that have been discussed took place in areas that were relatively favoured agriculturally. Of the six geographic subdivisions of the middle Nile, the barren Abu Hamed Reach and Batn el Hajar were of less importance, while the remainder, particularly the Shendi Reach and the Dongola Reach, were the locations of important developments.

Direct archaeological evidence for subsistence during the periods that have been considered is not plentiful. However, there is evidence from Kerma for the cultivation of barley and for the herding of cattle, sheep, and goats, as well as for hunting, fishing, and the keeping of dogs and donkeys. Sacrifices of sheep and goats were a consistent feature of Kerma burial, and in many cases a row of ox skulls was placed around one side of the burial mounds (Bonnet 1990; 1992). Transhumant pastoralists in the Wadi Hariq, 400 kilometres west of the Nile, known archaeologically as the Handessi Horizon, were contemporary with Kerma and possibly contributed to its subsistence base (Jesse et al. 2004). All this suggests an early importance of animal husbandry in Nubia; later evidence, from Meroitic times, reinforces this impression. A bronze bowl (Fig. 4.9) from Tomb G187 at Karanog in Lower Nubia, for instance, is decorated with an engraved scene showing a cow being milked and another cow suckling a calf, whilst other calves have been tied to a tree. Milk is being presented to a woman seated before a corn-stalk hut, the apex of which is decorated with an ostrich egg; the hut is similar to some made in

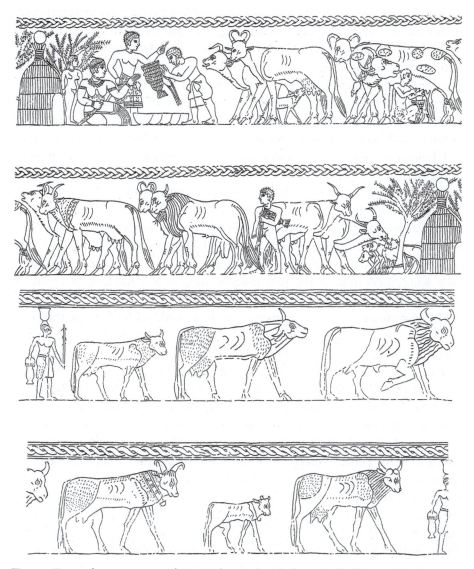

Fig. 4.9 Pastoral scenes engraved on two bronze bowls from Tomb G187 at Karanog, Egypt. The two at the top are on one bowl and the bottom two on another. From Woolley and Randall-MacIver 1910: vol. 4, plates 27 and 28.

parts of the African savanna until recent times. This bowl is actually one of two, the other (Fig. 4.9) showing a bull, four cows, and a calf, as well as a herdsman (Woolley and Randall-MacIver 1910: vol. 3, 39, 59–61, vol. 4, plates 26–8). To these rural scenes can be added the fact that the quantities of bones of cattle, sheep, and goats excavated from Meroë, and the ages of the animals from which they came, indicate that meat as well as milk was important (Carter and Foley 1980). Indeed, it has been suggested that the archaeological sites of the Butana region near Meroë reflect its exploitation by semi-nomadic pastoralists, demonstrating the significant role of pastoralism in the Meroitic subsistence economy. Adams (1981) was unconvinced of the latter, stressing the role of cultivation, and in the drier northern Meroitic provinces it does seem likely that the cultivation of either naturally or mechanically irrigated land provided the greater part of the subsistence base. Evidence for the growing of sorghum has come from Meroë, Musawwarat es-Sufra, and Naqa, and of barley from early levels at Meroë (Edwards 1996: 22). Evidence from Qasr Ibrim shows that barley, emmer wheat, and common millet were at first important, but that the 'summer crops' of sorghum, cotton, durum wheat, bread wheat, bulrush millet, termis bean, and sesame were introduced during the first five centuries AD, about the time that the *saqia* was being adopted in the area (Rowley-Conwy 1991). Sorghum seems to have become especially important, and a relief on a granite boulder at Jebel Qeili, in the southern Butana, depicts the sun god apparently presenting the Meroitic King Sherkarer, of the first century AD, with a number of heads of sorghum (Shinnie 1967: 51, 96).

The subsistence economy seems to have remained much the same throughout Christian and Islamic times (Welsby 2002: 183–9). At Soba, far to the south, for instance, the excavated cereal remains were dominated by sorghum and bulrush millet during Early and Classic Christian times (van der Veen 1991: 266); at Qasr Ibrim, sorghum, barley, wheat, and pulses were the major plant foods during the Late and Terminal Christian periods (Adams 1996: 100) and during the Islamic period. In addition, a variety of fruits and vegetables had probably long been important. The New Kingdom paintings in the tomb of Djehuty-hetep at Debeira, in Lower Nubia, depicted workers harvesting dates and dom-palm fruit (Säve-Söderbergh 1960: 38–40). The Christian deposits at Soba produced evidence of grapes, figs, dates, dom palm, African fan palm, and Christ's thorn; those at Debeira West, castor oil, dates, cucumber, (African) groundnuts, and dom palm (Shinnie and Shinnie 1978: 107); and from late in the same period at Qasr Ibrim came castor bean, watermelon, onion, garlic, and probably cucumber.

Nevertheless, Edwards (1989; 1996; 2004) questioned the assumption that cultivation in the Nile Valley was the main subsistence base and stressed the probable importance of rainfed agriculture along wadi beds and on other suitable alluvial soils, particularly (citing Ahmed 1984) in southern Nubia. Edwards also emphasized the important and continuing input from pastoralism, of which the number of domestic animals buried in X-Group tombs at Ballana and Qustul remind us. So too might the bones of sheep, goats, cattle, and pigs, as well as goat droppings, at the Christian site of Debeira West (Shinnie and Shinnie 1978: 107), and the bones of sheep, goats, pigs, cattle, horses, donkeys, and camels, and sheep, goat, horse, donkey, and camel dung, in the Late and Terminal Christian deposits at Qasr Ibrim (Adams 1996: 101). For Islamic times Qasr Ibrim continues to be informative, showing sheep, goats, and cattle to be common. That domestic animals were so important even in the rainless north of Nubia might seem difficult to believe, but in 1963 a livestock census, along the Sudanese stretch of the Nile Valley subsequently flooded by Lake Nubia, reported 2,831 cattle, 19,335 sheep, 34,146 goats, 86 horses, 3,415 donkeys, 608 camels, and large numbers of chickens, pigeons, and ducks, in an area which had just over 50,000 people (Adams 1977: 54). To the south, with seasonal grazing available away from the river, pastoralism must have been even more important.

Nubia's subsistence economy supported both a sedentary population along the thin ribbon of the Nile, concentrating in places with water and fertile silt and in rainfed wadis, and a more mobile population, dispersed through the savanna lands of the south. In addition, mechanical means of irrigation further increased the agricultural viability of parts of the region.

Technology

Abundant direct archaeological evidence throws light on the technology of the middle Nile during the periods under review (Welsby 1996; 2002; Edwards 2004). At times this part of Africa reached a high level of technological sophistication. There is, however, a problem in interpreting such evidence: how much of this technological achievement is attributable to indigenous endeavour and how much to exotic sources, be they imports or the presence of expatriate craftsmen? Because of the repeated cultural contact along the middle Nile, these are difficult questions to answer. Nevertheless, when evaluating the contribution of technology to social complexity, it is important to attempt to separate the indigenous and the foreign import.

Perhaps the most outstanding aspects of middle Nile technology were building and construction. Ashlar masonry, coarser types of stonework, fired brick, and mud-brick were all handled with skill to produce structures that were often complex. Foreign influence is evident in much of this, from the Temple of Amon at Jebel Barkal to the pyramids of Napata and Meroë or the churches of Christian Nubia, all of which are examples of buildings of alien inspiration, if not of foreign construction. Nevertheless, most of these structures have distinctively Nubian characteristics. The *deffufa*s and tombs of Kerma and the tombs of Ballana and Qustul were, indeed, indigenous in design and execution. So also was the unique Great Enclosure at Musawwarat es-Sufra. Clearly, Nubians expended considerable energy on building, although many of their less important structures were probably of grass and wood. Such examples as the Meroitic palace at Wad ben Naqa, the cities and towns of Meroitic and Christian Nubia, or the water-storage *hafir*s of the dry areas east and south-east of Meroë are eloquent of effort as well as of building and engineering skills. Furthermore, the heated bathroom of the supposed house at Old Dongola (p. 93) and the latrines in Christian Nubian houses (Adams 2001: 53–4, plates 17e and 20e; Welsby 2002: 170–2) demonstrate a concern for comfort and convenience, not just for monumental structures.

Associated with building were a number of other skills, such as quarrying, stone-dressing, mud-brick making, brick-firing, carpentry, sculpture, wall painting, and inscription cutting. A knowledge of surveying and architectural design would also have been necessary; on the wall of one of the pyramid chapels at Meroë is an architect's elevation drawing at a scale of 1:10 that appears to have been done during the construction of one of the other pyramids in the cemetery (Welsby 1996: 134–5; Hinkel 2000: 19). The question of foreign influence and sometimes even foreign execution inevitably arises in such matters, but, again, the end products usually had a local input. For much of the time under discussion the people of the middle Nile were at least partly literate and during the Meroitic period even developed their own unique alphabet. Moreover, the frequency of graffiti and other inscribed material at Nubian sites indicates that in some periods literacy was fairly widespread.

Another important aspect of Nubian technology was the extraction and manufacturing of metal, especially of iron. It is clear that many items of bronze, silver, or gold were imported, but the furnace remains and substantial quantities of iron slag at Meroë suggest that there at least an extensive iron-working industry flourished. Further evidence of this is provided by the range of iron weapons and tools recovered from Meroitic sites, including spears, arrowheads, hoe blades, adzes, axes, shears, and tweezers (Shinnie 1967: 162–5). Mounds of iron slag, probably of a similar date, have also been reported from Kerma, Kawa, and Argo (Shinnie 1967: 182), and the iron objects from the Ballana and Qustul tombs indicate that iron-working skills remained at a high level even after the decline of the Meroitic state. Another metal for which Nubia was an important source was gold, much of which came from the desert east of the Nile, north of the Fifth Cataract

(Vercoutter 1959: 129). Particularly during the New Kingdom period, this area seems to have been one of Egypt's main suppliers, as paintings in the Theban tomb of Huy appear to indicate (O'Connor 1993: 63).

In addition, manufacturing along the middle Nile produced pottery, textiles, leatherwork, woodwork, basketry, and wine. Fine pottery had been made during the Kerma period, but exceptionally high-quality wares were produced during Meroitic, X-Group and Christian times. These were wheel-made, well fired, and often had painted decoration. It is apparent that they were fired in special kilns of brick, of which a number have been excavated at Debeira East that date from late X-Group and Early Christian times (Adams 1977: 402–3). Other kilns have been uncovered at Faras, dating from the Early and Classic Christian periods (Adams 1961; 1977: 496, 498), and kilns are also known from Meroitic contexts at Meroë and Musawwarat es-Sufra and from the Christian period at Old Dongola.

Textile production seems to have been important, largely because cotton was grown in the area at least by Meroitic times, but textiles found in Meroitic, X-Group, and Christian tombs at Ballana and Qustul during the 1960s included cotton, linen, and animal fibre from either goats, sheep, or camels (Thurman 1979: 36). Clearly, leather working depended on the widespread animal husbandry, and basketry was based on palm fibres and grasses that were widely available. Only wood working remains difficult to understand in the environment of this region, but there is plentiful direct evidence for it in both X-Group and Christian deposits at Qasr Ibrim (Adams 1982: 28–9). As for the wine, a number of supposed wine presses have been found in Lower Nubia; although the environment was not really suitable for vine cultivation, it seems that wine was produced locally whenever the supply of the superior Egyptian product was interrupted.

Some items in Meroitic, X-Group, and Christian sites suggest imported technologies. Such items as glassware, lamps, furniture, and jewellery of gold or silver set with semi-precious stones mostly represent status symbols that were not part of Nubian technology. There were also some aspects of Nubian technology that resulted from technology transfer. Amongst these was mechanical irrigation. The *shaduf* and the *saqia* were most important for the development of human societies on the middle Nile. Equally important was transportation technology, enabling the commerce of the region to exist. The oldest aspect of this was the sailing boat, in use on the Nile throughout the period under discussion. It was, however, the development of desert transportation systems, particularly that involving the camel, that seems to have had the greatest impact on the commercial life of this region. These aspects of irrigation and transportation emphasize the importance of technology to social development on the middle Nile.

Social system

Monumental tombs at Kerma, Napata, Meroë, and Ballana and Qustul, in their scale, construction, and contents, show the presence of absolute monarchy at various times. The divinity and/or autocracy of such rulers is demonstrated by the practice of human sacrifice at Kerma, and at Ballana and Qustul, and by the sculptured reliefs of some Meroitic buildings. Some of the latter are supplemented by inscriptions, which unfortunately we cannot fully understand. Meroitic monarchy gave women an important role; indeed, sometimes they governed in their own right. Absolute monarchy is also suggested by the existence of large and elaborate domestic buildings interpreted as palaces, of which those at Meroë, Wad ben Naqa, and Jebel Barkal are perhaps the most convincing. In addition, numerous temples represent ideologies in which both spiritual and secular powers were intertwined. Indeed, not only is the archaeological record eloquent of the emergence of absolute authority, but it also chronicles its dissolution, as indicated by the numerous fortified buildings of Late Christian and Islamic times.

At the other end of the social scale, the archaeological evidence shows us a numerous labouring class that presumably consisted, during most periods, of both free peasants and slaves. Their presence is indicated not only by the clusters of small houses in many settlements and the numerous 'poorer' graves in cemeteries but also by the monumental constructions such as temples, tombs, and burial mounds that were the achievement as much of their labour as of the authority of their rulers. The relationship of this lowest level of society, to both the rulers and their associated elite, is on occasion starkly demonstrated by the sacrifice of such lesser human beings at the burial of those to whom they were subservient, as was the case at Kerma and at Ballana and Qustul.

Archaeological evidence for the development of trade and manufacturing, particularly in the Meroitic and Christian periods, would suggest that at times there must have been a middle section in this stratified society, made up of merchant-entrepreneurs and some skilled craftsmen, as well as various government officials and holders of temple or church appointments. Some burials at Kerma, Napata, and Meroë seem to belong neither to the elite nor to the peasantry. Meroitic houses included both 'de luxe' and 'humbler' structures (Adams 1977: 357–8).

Archaeological evidence also indicates the development of functional specialization. Cross-cutting much of the social hierarchy but sometimes contributing to its differentiation, there emerged a variety of specialized occupations. By Meroitic and Christian times, for instance, there were specialist potters making high-quality wheel-formed wares, as distinct from traditional potters, who continued to turn out rougher, hand-built pottery. In addition, there must have been iron smelters, blacksmiths, and perhaps other metal workers; spinners and weavers; builders, who would have included both masons and brick makers; leather workers; carpenters and joiners; basket makers; and boatmen. There would also have been scribes, artists (both sculptors and painters), priests and temple and church officials, some soldiers, and merchants.

A level of social complexity conducive to both urbanization and state formation would appear to have been reached during several periods along the middle Nile. However, the social systems discussed were as much symptomatic as causative of the development of cities and states. It is necessary to look further if this development is to be explained.

Population pressures

The people of the middle Nile were agriculturalists who lived in dry savanna to the south and in a desert to the north. They were able to do this because of the existence of the river, which provided water and a base from which, particularly in the south, they could exploit the seasonal grazing and rainfed cultivation of the surrounding areas. However, cultivable land and accessible pasture were limited; indeed, in some areas they were absent. Yet, where present, they had the potential to yield a surplus and to support population growth. The problem was that if the population grew, there was nowhere to go: there was only a finite amount of land that could be exploited by the means available. As a result, the settlement of the region was restricted to a long, narrow, frequently broken strip of viable agricultural land, with some isolated more fortunate areas, and to adjacent areas that could support transhumant pastoralism or rainfed cultivation. Theoretically, therefore, the middle Nile constituted a classic example of environmentally induced population pressure.

Although limited, there are some archaeological indications of population pressures during certain periods. For instance, the distribution of archaeological sites in Lower Nubia seems particularly dense for later Meroitic and Christian times. Although Edwards (1996: 80) stated that the Meroitic population was actually small, it seems that this rainless area did support a surprisingly large number of people. Similarly, the existence of Meroitic sites in the dry western Butana, away from the Nile but along wadis that could provide seasonal cultivation, suggests that the population of that area found it necessary to exploit available resources to the limit. It is even possible that the crowding of houses within some Meroitic and Christian settlements was partly caused by a desire to conserve adjacent cultivable land.

The most obvious way that the carrying capacity of the region could be improved was by increasing the available cultivable land, and the only way to do this was to introduce better irrigation technology. Two such improvements took place during the periods under review. The first was the introduction of the *shaduf*, an idea imported from Egypt probably during the New Kingdom. Possibly it encouraged the growing population of that time that was calculated by Trigger (1965: 156–66). The second was the *saqia*, again a foreign idea, adopted in Nubia in about the fourth century AD during the X-Group period (Edwards 1996: 80–1, 91). In conjunction with the new 'summer crops' introduced around this time (p. 92, 98), it is likely that the improved irrigation that resulted did lead to an increase in population; indeed, the adoption of the *saqia* and the new crops would suggest that population pressure caused their adoption.

Edwards (1994: 9) argued that in the Meroitic state, as generally in the Sudanic savannas: 'The availability of labour and the means of controlling it, rather than land, tended to be a major determinant of production'. Nevertheless, it is possible that finite resources of productive land did result in population pressures along the middle Nile, pressures that would have been accentuated by fluctuations in river level and rainfall that caused periodic famines. It seems that cultivable land and accessible grazing could indeed have been scarce resources at times. Control of them might have provided a power base for an emerging elite and, therefore, might have been a contributory factor in the growth of cities and states. Indeed, the control of both labour and land could have been important.

Ideology

Tombs, temples, and churches have much to tell us about the beliefs of those who built them. Their designs, sculptural and graphic decorations, and inscriptions indicate that Nubia was often a borrower and adapter of foreign faiths. Until about the middle of the first millennium AD it was the gods of Pharaonic Egypt that dominated Nubia; indeed, their veneration survived longer on the middle Nile than in Egypt itself. The most important of these seem to have been Isis and Amon; worship of the latter became a state cult for both Napata and Meroë, with their rulers often taking the name of Amon as part of their throne names, for example, Tenutamon and Natakamani. From about the middle of the first millennium AD to almost the middle of the second millennium, Christianity became the dominant faith, to be replaced, in turn, by Islam. Nevertheless, all these faiths developed their own Nubian characteristics, and there were also at times separate indigenous beliefs. This is indicated by the human sacrifices at Kerma and at Ballana and Qustul, and also by the worship of Apedemak, the lion god of Meroë, who seems to have resulted from Egyptian-Meroitic syncretism (Zabkar 1975).

The archaeological evidence suggests that these ideologies contributed to the development of states and cities. Prior to the arrival of Christianity on the middle Nile, the religious beliefs of Nubia were characterized by an integration of secular and spiritual authority, as frequently the case in Africa. The ruler became the personification of the god, a notion that sometimes manifests itself archaeologically in monumental tombs and temples, which were an expression of both human and divine authority. This provided legitimization for the rule of an absolute monarch, who could literally claim a divine mandate. The power base of a ruler was strengthened because it was both physical and spiritual. The state developments of Kerma, Napata, Meroë, and the X-Group all benefitted from this ideological contribution. With the advent of Christianity, the ruler was no longer a god, even though divinely sanctioned. Human and divine authority were separate, and 'royal' tombs disappeared from the archaeological record. However, this did not necessarily mean any loss of authority by the temporal ruler who, as the Faras paintings show, could still call on ideological support from a Church that was in turn protected. As a result, the Christian states of Nubia were ruled by both Crown and Cross: the one claiming authority over people's bodies, the other over their souls (Adams 1977).

The role of ideology in the process of urbanization was different. The construction of an important temple or church at a particular place sometimes led to the development of a settlement at that place or to increased growth of a settlement. In this way, some cities came into existence as religious ceremonial centres or became more important because they assumed such a role. Nubian cities also had a more general symbolic role, irrespective of whether religion, administration, or commerce was the main activity; each city conferred political and ideological legitimacy on the regime that controlled it.

External trade

As discussed at the beginning of this chapter (p. 69), Nubia was a major trade corridor into the heart of Africa for South-West Asia and the Mediterranean. Moving north were gold and other minerals, ivory, slaves, and a range of African exotica; going south was a variety of manufactured goods, including many luxuries. It was an example of characteristic exchange between the developed and underdeveloped world: manufactures for raw materials.

Archaeological evidence for this trade is abundant, although it tells us little about some aspects. Least well represented in the archaeological record are the commodities that were traded north to Egypt, but there is some evidence. For example, diorite quarries in the Nubian desert west of Abu Simbel were being exploited during the Egyptian Old Kingdom and Middle Kingdom. This rock was favoured for statues and stelae in Egypt at this time and apparently was transported as far as Giza, near modern Cairo, a distance along the Nile of more than 1,200 kilometres (Adams 1977: 169–70). Similarly, copper-smelting furnaces have been found in the Old Kingdom town investigated at Buhen (Adams 1977: 170–4), and numerous gold mines, which were producing by Middle Kingdom times, are known in the desert east of the Second Cataract area and in the Batn el Hajar (Vercoutter 1959). Archaeological evidence suggests that all these activities were at first in Egyptian hands, and, initially at least, their output was probably only for Egyptian use. Evidence for the trade in ivory is less easy to find, but in the Napatan town of Sanam one room of a possible storehouse had part of its floor covered with tusks (Griffith 1922: 117, plate LIIIb). In addition, ivory tusks were found in one of the storerooms in the palace at Wad ben Naqa (Vercoutter 1962: plate XXb). Almost invisible in the archaeological record, however, is the trade in slaves, which was probably of importance for much of the time considered (Alexander 2001). The people sacrificed at Kerma or Ballana and Qustul, for instance, were not necessarily slaves, although they might have been. It could be significant, nevertheless, that the relief at Jebel Qeili and those on the pylons of the Lion Temple at Naqa show live rather than dead captives; they were worth more alive. As for the tropical exotica that were traded north, Egyptian documentary and archaeological sources provide details; amongst other things, they seem to have included ostrich eggs and feathers, various skins from wild animals, live wild animals, ebony, semi-precious stones, and incense. A painting in the mid-second-millennium BC tomb of Rekhmire at Thebes shows such a range of goods (Kendall 1997: 9). It seems likely that the commodities sought by Egyptians were collected at trading stations during the Egyptian Old and Middle Kingdoms, and the Second Cataract forts might have had such a role during the latter period. Egyptian control of trade is also probable following the New Kingdom expansion into Nubia, but in the Kerma, Napatan, Meroitic, and later periods there must have been indigenous control.

There is better archaeological evidence for the commodities that were traded south into Nubia, although it has problems. Outstanding amongst these imports was a range of manufactured items that, although often common in their places of origin, seem frequently to have been prized as status symbols in Nubia and therefore buried in the more important graves. Indeed, the possession of such 'prestige goods' and the distribution of some of them to elite supporters could have contributed significantly to the power base of Nubian rulers (Edwards 1994: 11–12). Sometimes these objects can be attributed on the basis of style to their places of origin, although more commonly their foreign manufacture has merely been assumed because of the technology by which they have been produced. Perhaps the most impressive, by reason of its fragility and the distances that it nevertheless travelled, is the glassware that has been found in Meroitic, X-Group, and Christian Nubian contexts. Shinnie (1967: plates 82–4) illustrated two glass vessels from Meroitic graves at Faras in Lower Nubia and one from Meroë itself, but the most impressive Meroitic collection of glass is perhaps that excavated from tombs at Seddenga on the Abri-Delgo Reach of the middle Nile (Leclant 1973; Wildung 1997: 364–8). In addition to glassware, fine metalwork and jewellery seem also to have figured amongst the imports to Nubia. For example, a silver gilt goblet, probably of Roman origin, was found at Meroë (Shinnie 1967: plates 78–81), and a gold ring, also from Meroë, was inscribed in Greek (Shinnie 1967: plate 61). From various Meroitic contexts have also come an assortment of bronze lamps, bowls, beakers, bottles, and vases, whilst the X-Group tombs of Ballana and Qustul produced metal goods and other manufactures that seem to have originated in Byzantine Egypt. Some objects might even have been loot from Nubian raids into Egypt, such as the bronze head that was found buried in front of one of the temples at Meroë and that probably came from a statue of the Roman Emperor Augustus (Shinnie 1967: plate 28). However, the most common imports in Meroitic Nubia, according to the archaeological record, were beads of glass or stone, so common indeed that Adams (1977: 373) suggested that they might have been used as a medium of exchange.

In addition to the durable manufactures that were traded into Nubia, the imported goods also included some consumables that have not usually survived in archaeological deposits. Some of the Meroitic glass vessels, for instance, are of shapes used elsewhere for containing unguents and oils, and it is likely that they were imported for their contents rather than for themselves (Shinnie 1967: 130–1). Similarly, some of the imported Graeco-Roman pottery that appears alongside indigenous wares in Meroitic contexts could have arrived in Nubia as containers for consumables. An Egyptian Old Kingdom text, for example, mentions the Nubians' fondness for Egyptian honey (Adams 1984: 41), and the Egyptian amphorae that are found in Nubian sites of Meroitic, X-Group, and Early Christian date seem to have been imported full of either olive oil or wine. There must also have been other imported commodities that have left little archaeological evidence, such as some of the fine textiles that have been recovered from Meroitic, X-Group, and Christian tombs at Ballana and Qustul (Thurman 1979).

Other archaeological evidence that throws light on the organization of Nubian trade is the location of some of the major urban sites. All of the cities that survived for any length of time seem to have been at places where the export commodities of the African interior could be collected at the riverbank, ready for shipment to Egypt. As time went on and trade networks expanded ever further into the interior, so these places appeared successively further up the Nile: first there was Buhen, then Kerma, then Napata, then Meroë, and finally there were Shendi, Soba, and Sennar. Some of these places, and indeed others also, grew particularly important because they were situated at a point where a major land route reached the Nile. Thus, Meroë and Napata stood at the southern and northern end, respectively, of the Bayuda Road, which cut off the great bend of the Nile containing the Fourth and Fifth Cataracts. In turn, Napata and Kawa stood at each end of the Meheila Road, which cut off the next great bend of the river further downstream. These routes were only part, however, of those that seem to have existed by Meroitic times, including the Korosko Road, which cut off the whole of the Nile bend that contained the Second, Third, and Fourth Cataracts; the Wadi Hawad Road, which led south-east from Meroë to Aksum; and another route that led north-east from the Atbara–Nile confluence to the Red Sea port of Suakin (Adams 1977). The location of urban centres and the existence of these land routes suggest two things: first, that the external trade of the Nile might have played an important role in urban growth; second, that such trade was only part of a vast network of regional trading links. Archaeological evidence from the Gash Delta in eastern Sudan (Fig. 5.1, p. 113) suggests contact with Kerma and the possibility that the area between the Gash and Baraka Valleys was the location of the Land of Punt, whose trade with New Kingdom Egypt was recorded in a carving at Deir el Bahari. These are indications of how extensive that network might have been (Fattovich 1991; Mitchell 2005: 78–80).

Until we have more archaeological evidence for regional trading systems in this part of Africa, it is probably premature to assess the actual contribution that *external* trade made to the development of cities and states on the middle Nile. Nevertheless, it could be argued that trade in general provided a major causative factor for these developments and that if there had been no trade centred on the Nile, then there would have been little social development there. However, external trade was only one aspect of long-continued cultural interaction between the middle Nile and the world to its north; significantly, one that is more susceptible to archaeological study than some others.

Conclusion

Considering its environment, Nubia would seem to have been an unlikely place for the development of states and the appearance of cities. Yet not only did these things happen, they happened here earlier than anywhere else in tropical Africa. It is little wonder that a common explanation has been to regard such developments as 'secondary' in character, resulting directly from contact with Egypt. An examination of the archaeological evidence reveals a more complex situation, in which exotic influences undoubtedly played a role but where important contributions and initial development came from within, so that the resultant social complexity had its own distinctive Nubian characteristics.

First, Nubia was partly a gift of the Nile, just as Egypt was completely so. Water and silt from the Nile allowed the development of a sound subsistence base that in some favoured areas was capable of producing a surplus, especially where seasonal grazing and rainfed cultivation were possible near the river. It is noticeable that all of the major sociocultural developments discussed in this chapter were located on more favoured parts of the river and not in the less productive areas. The more southerly regions of Nubia, with greater rainfall and access to seasonal grazing for savanna pastoralists, were especially fortunate. Second, Nubian technology, although often influenced by foreign ideas and products, was able to extend the cultivated land and to intensify its exploitation by means of mechanical irrigation. It was also able to provide both land and water transportation systems that could overcome the communication problems of a population strung out along many hundreds of kilometres of river.

It seems likely that cultivable land and accessible grazing became scarce resources, providing a power base for those who controlled both those resources and the people necessary for their exploitation. Limited resources, particularly during periods of climatic stress and growing populations, encouraged people to gather in urban aggregations, with their potential for surplus storage. Social stratification followed, with society divided between the rulers and the ruled, and with an increasingly sophisticated technology stimulating the development of functional specialization and social differentiation. However, it was trading and exchange activities, and the general cultural interaction of which they were a part, that became the catalyst for major social and political developments in Nubia. In particular, Nubian rulers acquired prestige goods that confirmed their superior status and gave them the means of ensuring the support of other members of the elite. It is likely that the middle Nile had long been part of an extensive regional trading system, but from Egyptian Old Kingdom times onwards the demand of the developed world to the north for raw materials and tropical exotica created a major interest in external trade. Nubia became both a pipeline of supply and a successful entrepôt, profiting not so much from its own products but from those that it handled on their way north or on their way south. The origins of Kerma can already be discerned at this time. Subsequently, Egypt controlled this trade itself, extending its authority into Nubia both in Middle Kingdom and, more extensively, in New Kingdom times. When Egypt's grip weakened, indigenous control quickly reasserted itself, first with Kerma and eventually with the states of Napata and Meroë, as well as those of later times. The earlier of these polities might have been only tentative, but by Meroitic times we find evidence of a highly complex, stratified society. It is, however, apparent from archaeological evidence that all of these autocratic regimes sought to strengthen and legitimize their control by sheltering behind powerful religious ideologies, of which in turn contributed to the growth of urban centres. The foreign origin of most of those religions indicates the considerable contribution made to Nubian developments by cultural contacts with the north, but even with religion there was a strong indigenous input.

The emergence of social complexity on the middle Nile may thus be seen as the result of a complex interaction between local and exotic factors but an interaction in which indigenous people made their own decisions. As Shinnie (1967: 169) wrote of the best known of these polities: 'Meroë was an African civilization, firmly based on African soil, and developed by an African population.' Indeed, the roots of Meroitic achievement can be traced back to Kerma in the middle of the second millennium BC, and the cultural origins of Kerma appear to have been contemporary with those of Pharaonic Egypt. Rather than continuing to see the development of social complexity in Nubia as secondary to that of Egypt, we should perhaps begin to regard them as parallel and interacting African achievements.

Chapter 5

Isolation: the Ethiopian and Eritrean Highlands

For many observers it has been the isolation of this region, particularly that of the central highlands of Ethiopia and Eritrea, that has made the greatest impression. The core of the region is a great block of mountains, everywhere more than 1,000 metres in height, that reaches a general level of 2,300 metres and in places exceeds 4,200 metres above sea level. One could not imagine a less likely setting for state emergence and urbanization. Nevertheless, in the modern countries of Ethiopia and Eritrea there is evidence for such developments during the first few centuries AD, and indications of their origins during the first millennium BC (D.W. Phillipson 2009a; 2009c; 2012). Not only are these dates early for the attainment of social complexity in tropical Africa, but these achievements were highly sophisticated. Almost 2,000 years ago, the state of Aksum boasted urban centres; its own form of writing; coinage in gold, silver, and bronze; masonry buildings of a distinctive architectural style; unique monuments that indicate quarrying and engineering skills; extensive trading contacts both within and outside Africa; and a significant role in international politics. Indeed, Aksum seems to have been one of the first states to adopt Christianity (D.W. Phillipson 1998: 145 note 1). However, the antecedents of Aksumite culture can be discerned as early as the eighth century BC in the period formerly known as the Pre-Aksumite. Large settlements existed at Yeha, in Ethiopia, and at Matara and Sembel, in Eritrea, the last one of these belonging to the possibly earlier Ona Culture (Schmidt and Curtis 2001; Schmidt et al. 2008; Curtis 2009; Fattovich 2009; Schmidt 2009). In some places inscriptions appeared and there was sophisticated stone masonry, sculpture, and metallurgy, although stone artefacts were also still used. Furthermore, there were contacts with South Arabia and to a lesser extent with the Nile Valley. Far from being isolated, Ethiopia and Eritrea appear to have formed, at times, an important zone for cultural integration. For Edward Ullendorff (1960: 23) the region was 'a bridge between Africa and Asia'.

After the rise of Islam in the seventh century AD, Ethiopia did become increasingly isolated, leading the eighteenth-century historian Gibbon to make his famous exaggerated remark that: 'Encompassed on all sides by the enemies of their religion, the Aethiopians slept near a thousand years, forgetful of the world by whom they were forgotten' (Gibbon 1952: Vol. 2, 159–60). However, the Ethiopians' successful survival through those centuries can hardly be likened to sleep; for some form of Ethiopian state did survive down to modern times, albeit one of a mostly nonurban type. The Christian Church of Ethiopia also survived, leaving as a legacy of those centuries some of the most remarkable ecclesiastical architecture in the world. Clearly, apparent isolation has had benefits.

Geographical location and environmental factors

The northern end of the East African Rift Valley divides the mountains of Ethiopia and Eritrea into two parts (Fig. 5.1). The highlands to the north and west of this valley form the heartland of old Ethiopia, formerly called Abyssinia. This huge area of mountains is roughly triangular; its northern end lies close to the western shore of the Red Sea and is now part of Eritrea. Compared with the dry, hot plains on both the African and the South Arabian side of the Red Sea, the Ethiopian and Eritrean Highlands offer relatively attractive environments. As a result, cultural contact and even movement of people might be expected from an early date. It was apparently from such interaction that social complexity first developed in the northern Ethiopian and Eritrean Highlands.

Proximity to the Red Sea had other consequences. For the ancient world, as for the modern world, the Red Sea comprised a major shipping route, which connected the Mediterranean with the trade of the Indian Ocean. Ethiopia and Eritrea, able to tap the resources of the African interior, had direct access to this major route, and this was an important contributory element in the rise of the Aksumite state.

The highlands consist of basalts and other lavas overlying sandstones and limestones. Most of the region is tilted to the west and therefore drains into the Nile, particularly into the upper Blue Nile, which issues from Lake Tana. The drainage pattern has cut deeply into the landscape, carving spectacular gorges, often hundreds of metres deep, which break up the surface of the high plateau. Parts of the original high plateau have been so eroded that very little level country remains, except in the form of flat-topped *ambas*, isolated hills with precipitous sides (Buxton 1970: 18–20).

The most important environmental factor in the Ethiopian and Eritrean Highlands is altitude. Within about 250 kilometres of each other lie the hot dusty salt flats of the Danakil Desert and the cool heights of the Semien Mountains, which sometimes experience heavy snow falls (Buxton 1970: 18). Altitude is thus a major determinant of both climate and vegetation. Ethiopians recognize three main climatic zones: *dega*, which is land above 2,400 metres with an average temperature of 16°C; *woina dega*, which is land between 1,800 and 2,400 metres with an average temperature of 22°C; and

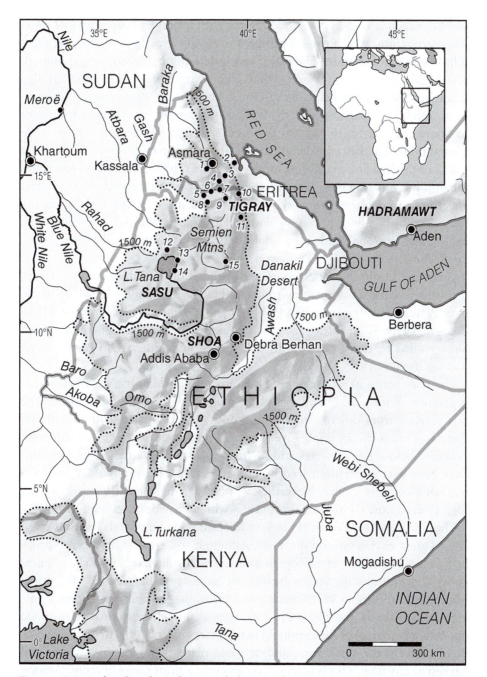

Fig. 5.1 Principal archaeological sites and places in the Ethiopian and Eritrean Highlands mentioned in the text. 1, Sembel; 2, Adulis; 3, Kohaito; 4, Matara; 5, Aksum; 6, Yeha; 7, Debra Damo; 8, Haoulti Melazo; 9, Maqaber Ga'ewa; 10, Addi Galamo; 11, Quiha; 12, Gondar; 13, Gouzara; 14, Lalibela Cave; 15, Lalibela. Based on Ullendorf 1960. Drawn by Joe LeMonnier.

kwolla, which is land below 1,800 metres with average temperatures of 26°C and higher. However, although temperatures vary greatly with altitude, there is little seasonal variation. The major factor determining seasonality is rainfall. The highlands occasion a somewhat greater rainfall than is usual at this latitude in Africa, but because the rain is brought by winds from the south-west, rainfall is heaviest and the wet season longest in the south-western highlands; the far north has less rain and a shorter wet season. The average annual rainfall in the central highlands is about 1,000 millimetres. The nearby plains of the Red Sea coast, now mostly in Eritrea, have a comparatively slight rainfall, but this occurs in January and February when the highlands are dry, and the coastal plains are at their hottest and driest at the time when the heaviest rain is falling in the highlands. Pastoralists and agriculturalists can exploit this seasonal and altitudinal variation in rainfall (Ullendorff 1960: 26–8; Buxton 1970: 20–1; Phillipson 1998: 11–15).

Given the height and open character of much of the Ethiopian Highlands, exposure to wind is another environmental factor of significance. Much of the high plateau is sufficiently windswept for this to affect its utilization. Thus Buxton (1970: 60) recorded that the population of the Debra Berhan area in Shoa tended to cluster in and around the gorges, rather than on the open plateau itself.

The wide range of altitude and climate is responsible for a great variety of vegetation. Within the boundaries of the modern states of Ethiopia and Eritrea this extends from desert scrub to rainforest, but even within the highlands there was originally an impressive range. Temperate forests of *Podocarpus* sp. occurred below 2,200 metres and of *Juniperus* sp. above that level, but both have been extensively destroyed by human activity, leaving most of the high plateau bleak and empty. Nevertheless, much of the vegetation cover of the high plateau now consists of short grass, which provides excellent grazing.

The considerable altitudinal range of the Ethiopian Highlands has thus given rise to great environmental diversity. Although soil erosion has been a problem, some 27 percent of Ethiopian and Eritrean soils have been classified as good agricultural soils and a further 13 percent as fairly good (Ethiopian Mapping Authority 1988: 8). Such a combination – a variety of environments and the availability of fertile soils – has enabled agriculture to provide the most important resources of the region. In many places it is possible to obtain two or three crops in the same year, and in some places it is possible to sow and harvest at any time. This is achieved by growing a great range of crops. Among cereals, for instance, teff, wheat, barley, sorghum, and finger millet can all be grown, although it is teff that is most commonly grown in areas of middle and higher altitude. Ethiopia also produces a remarkable selection of vegetables and many types of fruit. Other agricultural products of importance comprise maize and *ensete* (in the high rainfall areas of the south-west), coffee, cotton, *chat* (a narcotic), *nug* (a source of oil), various medicinal plants, and sugar-cane. Agriculture also includes large numbers of livestock, particularly cattle (for milk and meat), hair sheep (rather than wool sheep), and goats. Working animals have included oxen for pulling ploughs – a use unique in tropical Africa – horses, asses, and mules, the last important for carrying loads in the broken landscape. Additional useful animals include chickens, dogs, and bees; civet cats also are kept and the civet collected for use in perfume (Ullendorff 1960: 28–30; Pankhurst 1961: 200–19; Finneran 2007: 67–77).

The native fauna of the Ethiopian and Eritrean Highlands provided other resources. Not only could fishing and hunting supplement diet, but valuable trade goods could be obtained from many wild animals, such as elephants, rhinoceros, crocodiles, lions, leopards, giraffes, and zebras. Resources of significance also included minerals, of which gold and iron ore seem to have been the most important, but copper, silver, lead, and tin could be found (Pankhurst 1961: 224–9; Phillipson 2000: vol. 2, 470, 473). In addition the region produced good building stone; timber became scarce only in more recent centuries. Finally, human life, as so often in tropical Africa, provided an important resource in the form of slaves. It has been estimated that between 1800 and 1850 about 1,250,000 slaves were exported. Numbers for earlier periods are unknown, but the trade could still have been of significance (Alexander 2001). Overall, as with Nubia, the nonagricultural resources of Ethiopia consisted in the main of commodities sought after in the ancient Mediterranean world.

The environment of the Ethiopian and Eritrean Highlands was clearly an attractive one for human settlement. Nevertheless, constraints did exist. The first is that extensive areas of the highlands were too rocky, too exposed, or too high to have much agricultural value. In addition, much of the landscape was so rough and so obstructed by gorges and other natural features that communication remained difficult until modern times. A second constraint is that historical sources show that Ethiopia was not as healthy as it seems. Thus Pankhurst (1961: 238–47) showed that the highlands have suffered from occasional epidemics of great severity. Some of these cannot now be identified, but it is apparent that smallpox, cholera, influenza, and bubonic plague were amongst them. Dysentery, leprosy, eye diseases, guinea worm, and elephantiasis are also mentioned amongst diseases found in Ethiopia; in the lowlands malaria and other fevers were a serious problem. In the highlands themselves, tapeworm was prevalent, largely because of the practice of eating raw meat, but this affliction has been customarily treated with indifference because of the existence of the *kosso* tree, whose flowers produce a drug that is highly effective in expelling these intestinal worms. Perhaps the most serious constraint in the highlands, however, has been the periodic recurrence of famine, recorded as early as the ninth century and still a major concern in modern times (Pankhurst 1961: 230–7). Famines could result from crop failure, brought on by inadequate or even excessive rainfall, or by unusually low temperatures. They could also result from crop destruction caused by swarms of mice, troops of monkeys, or (most serious of all) massive invasions of locusts. Serious as some of these constraints might appear, however, the greater number were episodic, so that overall they seem to have had little inhibiting effect on the growth of social complexity in the Ethiopian and Eritrean Highlands.

Sources of information

Historical evidence

Oral traditional, historical, and archaeological sources all throw light on the development of urbanization and state emergence in this region (D.W. Phillipson 2009a: 1–2). Least valuable of them is oral tradition, which attempts to explain the past with fantastic stories, and the Aksumite period is somewhat beyond its range. Nevertheless, the most famous of Ethiopian oral traditions, that concerning the visit of the Queen of Sheba to Solomon and the consequent birth of the founder of the Ethiopian royal house (Buxton 1970: 34), does provide some support for the Semitic contribution to Ethiopia indicated by other sources (Munro-Hay 1991: 9–16).

Historical sources are more important and are of four types. First are references to Ethiopia by ancient foreign writers (Finneran 2007: 16–24). For example, Pliny the Younger (about AD 77) mentioned Adulis (Munro-Hay 1991: 17), and the *Periplus of the Erythraean Sea*, also of the first century AD, mentions Adulis, Koloè (possibly Kohaito or Matara), and Aksum (Kobishchanov 1979: 41; Anfray 1981: 363). Classical sources indicate a powerful Aksumite kingdom that was able to conquer parts of South Arabia in the sixth century AD and, before that, was already partly urbanized and exporting ivory, rhinoceros horn, tortoiseshell, and obsidian through Adulis (Anfray 1981: 363).

The second type of historical sources consists of inscriptions on stone found in Aksumite or earlier contexts (Phillipson 2009c: 265–8) and inscriptions and representations on Aksumite coins. Unlike Meroitic inscriptions, those from Aksumite and earlier times can be read, being written in Ge'ez (the old Ethiopian language), in Sabaean (South Arabian), or sometimes in Greek. The inscribed stones provide information about military exploits, such as King Ezana's apparent expedition to Meroë in the fourth century AD and

King Kaleb's campaigns in South Arabia in the sixth century AD (Munro-Hay 1991: 228, 230). In addition they tell us the names and titles of some of the rulers of Aksum, as do the coins that might record as many as twenty-four different Aksumite kings (Pankhurst 1961: 401). The coins are also informative in other ways, recording, for instance, the fourth-century acceptance of Christianity, by replacing the pagan crescent and disc with the cross (see Fig. 5.9).

Few of these inscriptions are later than the fourth century, and probably none is later than the ninth (Buxton 1970: 119). The Aksumite kingdom disappeared sometime between the seventh and the tenth century AD (Munro-Hay 1991: 93–4; Negussie 1994: 27–9). Its capital moved to an unidentified location in eastern Tigray (D.W. Phillipson 2009a: 9), and there followed some centuries for which there is little historical source material. It is not until the end of the fifteenth century that there is again a substantial body of external sources, and these constitute the third type of historical data (Munro-Hay 1991:19–25; Finneran 2007: 24–6). These writings, by European visitors, throw a great deal of light on Ethiopian society from the sixteenth century onwards. Amongst these accounts, those by the Portuguese Francisco Alvares, relating to 1520–6, and by the Scotsman James Bruce, relating to 1768–73, stand out as remarkable (Pankhurst 1961: 100).

The fourth type of historical sources consists of writings by Ethiopians themselves. The oldest surviving manuscripts date from the thirteenth century, but the greater part of Ethiopian writing was on religious subjects and provides little information on secular matters. However, royal chronicles were also written from the fourteenth century onwards, and these form the principal source for later Ethiopian history (Buxton 1970: 129; Taddesse 1972; Marcus 2002).

Archaeological evidence

The investigation and publication of the abundant archaeological evidence has sometimes been deficient. Excavation has concentrated on sites with Aksumite masonry structures, and publication has tended to be descriptive and preliminary, rather than concerned with analysis and synthesis. Michels, in Kobishchanov's book (1979: 1–34), emphasized the importance of the pioneering work of the German Aksum expedition of 1906 and of research by the Ethiopian Institute of Archaeology from the 1950s to the early 1970s. Subsequently, however, political events in Ethiopia prevented further archaeological fieldwork until the beginning of the 1990s. The resumption of such work, particularly by David Phillipson, added substantially to knowledge of ancient Aksum (D.W. Phillipson 1994; 2000; 2012). At about the same time, several publications appeared which made the results of earlier research more accessible (Munro-Hay 1989; 1991; Anfray 1990; Phillipson 1997; 1998).

Relevant Ethiopian archaeological evidence was formerly divided into three main periods: Pre-Aksumite, Aksumite, and Medieval–Modern Ethiopian. Approximately, these periods represented the eighth century BC to the first century AD, the first century AD to the seventh to tenth centuries AD, and the seventh to tenth centuries AD to the present. It is the first two of these that are of greatest importance for this chapter, and it is these periods that have attracted most archaeological attention. Francis Anfray, who was responsible for much of the excavation in Ethiopia during the 1960s and early 1970s, divided the Pre-Aksumite into a South Arabian period, lasting from the fifth to the fourth century BC, and an Intermediate period, lasting from the third century BC to the first century AD. He saw the Aksumite period as continuing until the ninth century AD; Michels also argued for a long chronology (Anfray 1968: 355–8; Michels 2005). Fattovich (1990: 14–15) suggested a start for the Pre-Aksumite possibly as early as the tenth century BC. He thought that its origins lay in developments in social complexity beginning in the third millennium BC with the Gash Group in the Eritrean-Sudanese lowlands, developments that shifted to the Eritrean-Ethiopian Highlands early in the first millennium BC (Fattovich 2010). In contrast, Munro-Hay (1991), considering only the Aksumite period and drawing on his studies of Aksumite coinage, preferred a short chronology. This consisted of six phases commencing in the first century AD and terminating in the early seventh century, with the later seventh to the twelfth centuries placed in a Post-Aksumite period. Furthermore, a comparison of the stratigraphic evidence from Aksum and Matara led Negussie (1994) to conclude that (for the Aksumite period) a long chronology was indicated for Aksum itself but only a short one for Matara, possibly reflecting the greater importance of eastern Tigray, the location of the latter site, towards the end of the first millennium AD (D.W. Phillipson 2009a: 9). Subsequently, D.W. Phillipson (2009c) and Fattovich (2009) suggested the abandonment of the term 'Pre-Aksumite' and its subdivisions. A more realistic timetable might consist of merely recognizing contrasting periods in the first millennium BC, the first millennium AD, and the second millennium AD. Most recently Bard et al. (2014) have identified five phases of development at Aksum, based on their Bieta Giyorgis excavations, from the fourth century BC to possibly the ninth century AD. Archaeological research in Eritrea (Schmidt and Curtis 2001; Schmidt 2009; Curtis 2009; Schmidt et al. 2008) and in South Arabia (Finneran 2007: 111–13) now allows this evidence to be seen in a regional and chronological context.

The best-known Ethiopian site of the first millennium BC is Yeha (Buxton 1970: 36–7; Anfray 1972b; 1990: 26–7; Michels, in Kobishchanov 1979:

10–12; de Contenson 1981; Fattovich 1990; 2009; D.W. Phillipson 2012). Situated in the northern end of the highlands where the Aksumite state was to develop, this place has the remains of a temple (Fig. 5.2) built of ashlar sandstone masonry set on a stepped base. Parts of this ruin still stand to a height of about 9 metres, and it is now thought to date from the seventh or sixth century BC and to have similarities to contemporary South Arabian buildings. According to Fattovich (1990: 4), the Yeha temple was originally at least 13 metres in height and approximately 19 by 15 metres in area; the size and quality of masonry are very impressive. It is perhaps older than

Fig. 5.2 Inside the temple at Yeha, Ethiopia, dating from the seventh or sixth century BC. Parts of this ruin are 9 metres in height. Photograph by author, 1996.

the Parthenon in Athens and implies a highly organized society. Yeha has also produced a number of inscriptions that are written in a South Arabian language and in a South Arabian script. There is, in addition, a cemetery of subterranean tombs and the site of a stone building which excavation has shown was destroyed by fire and subsequently replaced by a new building. Anfray, who excavated a part of this latter structure, which is known as Grat-Be'al-Guebri, was of the opinion that it was a palace. Yeha also seems to have other occupation deposits and may possibly have been an early urban centre. Iron was already in use, and amongst the bronze objects recovered from Yeha are thirteen 'identity marks', consisting of openwork geometrical or animal designs which often incorporate alphabetical characters (Anfray 1990: 25–7; Fattovich 2009: 281). These have been regarded as personal seals, and their impressions have been found on pottery. The larger ones might have been animal brands (three illustrated in Buxton 1970: 37 are 8 to 11 centimetres long), possibly for paint branding sheep because bronze would seem unsuitable for fire branding. Paint consisting of red ochre and water could have been used.

The South Arabian influence seen at Yeha is also apparent in the two localities of Haoulti-Melazo, situated in the same general area as Yeha, where several sites have produced so-called Pre-Aksumite material. This includes fragments of dressed stone with South Arabian inscriptions, two limestone statues of seated female figures, and a sophisticated limestone throne decorated with low-relief carving. There is symbolism associated with the moon god, Almouqah, apparently venerated in the northern part of Ethiopia as well as in South Arabia. The statues are comparable to one of similar date from Addi Galamo, found with other things including a broken altar showing the crescent and disc of Almouqah. Similar material is also known from Maqaber Ga'ewa (de Contenson 1962; van Beek 1967; Michels, in Kobishchanov 1979: 12–13; de Contenson 1981; Fattovich 1990; 2009; D.W. Phillipson 2012: 28–9).

So-called Pre-Aksumite material was recorded from numerous sites, extending from northern Eritrea into Tigray (Fattovich 1990: 3). Many of these sites are between Aksum and Yeha, having been identified during a surface survey by Michels (2005), and there appears to have been cultural continuity in north-east Tigray (D'Andrea et al. 2008). The earliest 'Pre-Aksumite' culture was influenced by South Arabia, but from the beginning Pre-Aksumite culture showed originality and gradually developed characteristics of its own, while those of South Arabia faded. In particular, the language and script used for inscriptions grew less like the South Arabian from which it had originated and more like Ge'ez, the ancestor of the Eritrean and Ethiopian languages Tigré, Tigrinya, and Amharic. South Arabian influence seems to have been from the kingdom of Saba, which appears to have originated as early as the late second millennium BC (Finneran 2007: 113). Inscriptions in Sabaean have suggested the existence of a state known as D'mt by the mid-first millennium BC, located in Tigray and adjacent parts of Eritrea. This development has been associated with modest urban growth at least at Yeha and Matara. Disintegration is thought to have followed during the last two or three centuries BC, however, and it is difficult to relate the sociopolitical situation to that of the subsequent Aksumite period (Fattovich 1990). D.W. Phillipson (2009c: 266–8) questioned the evidence for the D'mt state, and Fattovich (2009: 287) had similar doubts.

Nevertheless, it is probable that Aksumite society did develop from the cultures of the first millennium BC in its region. This earlier archaeological evidence could represent the origins of urbanization and state formation, stimulated in part by South Arabian influences, but Aksumite evidence indicates a society in which these processes had reached a mature stage. Some suggestion of continuity between the two has been provided by excavations on Bieta Giyorgis, a hill 1 kilometre to the north-west of Aksum. These have revealed a sequence covering the mid- and late first millennium BC, overlain by early Aksumite deposits (Bard et al. 1997). Subsequently, they have also provided a revised overall chronology for the Aksum area (Bard et al. 2014).

The most thoroughly researched of the Aksumite sites is Aksum itself (D.W. Phillipson 1994; 1997; 1998; 2000; 2003; 2012). It is famous for its stelae, tall, thin, standing stones of which the largest have been carved to represent multistoreyed buildings, although many stelae are small and undecorated. Similar standing stones are also known at other Aksumite sites, but none of them with such enormous proportions or such careful finishing and decoration as some of those in the main stelae group at Aksum. One of the larger ones (Stela 3) of that group remained standing and consists of a single block of granite 21 metres high (plus about 3 metres underground), carved to represent nine storeys, with a false door at its base (Fig. 5.3). The fallen pieces of a taller one (Stela 2, about 28 metres long and carved to represent ten storeys) were taken to Rome in 1937 and erected there, although it was reerected at Aksum in 2008 following its return to Ethiopia. The largest of all, however (Stela 1), lies broken on the ground at Aksum and was nearly 33 metres in length, being carved to represent twelve storeys (on counting storeys, see Buxton and Matthews 1974: 57). D.W. Phillipson (1994: 192) described this monster stela as 'a strong candidate for consideration as the largest single monolith which humans have ever proceeded to erect'. Indeed, van Beek (1967: 117) suggested that perhaps it fell while being erected, and archaeological evidence has since supported this interpretation (Phillipson 2000: 161–4, 252–4). More than 140 stelae are known from four main groups in Aksum, although most are far smaller than those just described. In addition,

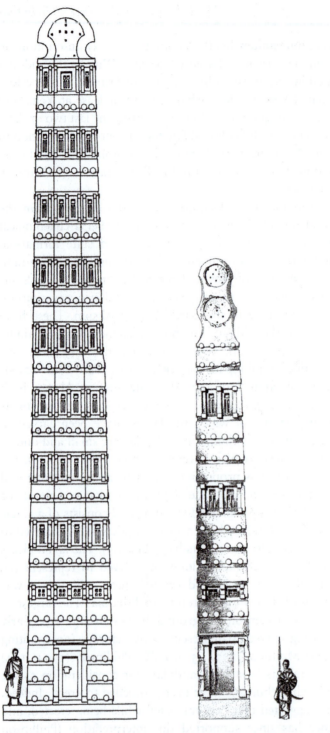

Fig. 5.3 Stelae 3 and 6 at Aksum, Ethiopia. Stela 3, which has continued to stand, is the third largest of the storeyed stelae and Stela 6 the smallest. Stela 3 after Krencker 1913: Tafel VI, as reproduced in D.W. Phillipson 1997: fig. 30; Stela 6 after Krencker 1913: Tafel II as reproduced in Phillipson 1997: fig. 13. Stela 3 is 20.57 metres high, above ground level. Stela 6 is 15.22 metres long. Reproduced by permission of David Phillipson.

more than 100 stelae (possibly up to 300), both Pre-Aksumite and early Aksumite in date, are thought to have existed at the Ona Enda Aboi Zague site on the northern side of Bieta Giyorgis hill (Bard and Fattovich 1993: 17).

Excavations amongst the main stelae group at Aksum have addressed the question of their purpose and the problem of their date. Work by Chittick (Munro-Hay 1989) and Phillipson (2000) revealed extensive, subterranean, multichambered Aksumite tombs, so it is apparent that the area was a cemetery. The largest stela appears to have been intended to mark two monumental underground tombs: a stone-built 'Mausoleum' to its west, more than 16 metres long and with ten side-chambers, and a possibly similar structure to its east that has been only partly investigated and that might never have been completed. As already stated, it seems that this giant stela fell and broke during the process of erection. Only 2.8 metres (8.5 percent) of its 33-metre length was intended to be set into the ground, and there is no sign of base plates such as were fitted to the other large stelae after erection, so it is possible that the Mausoleum was never actually used for burial (or was later heavily robbed). This stela probably represents the last of a series of storeyed stelae, each having been taller than its immediate predecessor until the inevitable disaster occurred. Significantly, no attempt seems to have been made to clear up the debris or to replace the stela, suggesting that the project might have been abandoned. Phillipson (2000: 164) dated this event to the fourth century AD, and Munro-Hay (1991: 68) put it at approximately AD 400. Broadly coinciding with the official adoption of Christianity at Aksum by King Ezana, which Munro-Hay (1991: 78) estimated at around AD 333, it might have been this ideological change that led to the project's abandonment. Certainly, the form of elite tombs changed at this time; the nearby 'Tomb of the False Door', discovered and named by Chittick in the early 1970s, consists of a subterranean granite-built chamber covered by a squat surface structure which appears to have been intended to represent a temple or palace. Lacking an associated stela but retaining a carving of a door similar to those on the storeyed stelae, it appears that this represents an early stage in the Christianizing of the burial tradition, dating to the late fourth or early fifth century AD (Phillipson 2000: 427). A little to the north of Aksum lie twin subterranean tombs traditionally attributed to the sixth-century kings Kaleb and Gabra Maskal, which appear to mark a further stage in this process (Phillipson 2000: 427, 431).

Other than the largest stela, it is often difficult to associate these standing stones with specific tombs and in many cases impossible, but it seems they were primarily intended as tomb markers. It appears that the area of the main stelae group at Aksum was used for burial from at least the first or second century AD. A series of platforms was gradually built up, on what originally must have been a gentle slope. Stelae were erected on these platforms, beneath which were subterranean tombs. This process continued for so long that a number of stelae of rougher, earlier type were actually buried upright by later deposits, and some of the later carved stelae had their lower parts covered (Munro-Hay 1989: 330). In addition to the tombs already mentioned, the main stelae area contained several shaft tombs and an extensive rock-cut tomb called the 'Tomb of the Brick Arches', which was discovered and named by Chittick. Probably dating to the fourth century AD (Phillipson 2000: 128–32), this tomb had not suffered as much from robbers as most of the others investigated, and excavations within it by both Chittick and D.W. Phillipson produced substantial amounts of important cultural material. More difficult to understand is the curious structure known as the Nefas Mawcha, which is adjacent to the main stelae group and seems also to have been a tomb. It consisted of a giant granite slab, 17.3 metres long, 6.5 metres wide, and 1.1 to 1.7 metres in thickness, which rested on supporting slabs and walls. This enormous slab weighs about 360 tonnes, and its supporting structure collapsed in antiquity when the slab was struck by the largest of the stelae (Stela 1) as it fell, weighing as it did some 517 tonnes (Phillipson 1994: 192, 197). The Nefas Mawcha must, therefore, pre-date the fall of the largest stela; Munro-Hay (1989: 120) suggested that it belongs to the third century AD. Probably it was intended to be covered by rubble and soil, although it was apparently unfinished when it was wrecked by the falling stela (Phillipson 2000: 481).

Ancient tombs also exist in other parts of Aksum, usually associated with stelae. To the south-east of the city, for instance, is the large rock-cut tomb known as the 'Tomb of King Bazen', so completely robbed that it is undatable but traditionally attributed to the legendary King Bazen, who was supposed to have been contemporary with the birth of Christ (Munro-Hay 1991: 13). More informative, however, is the so-called Gudit Stelae Field, with 594 large stones, most of which were probably stelae. Situated just outside Aksum to its south-west, this seems to have been a cemetery for 'middle-class' Aksumites, rather than for the rulers and the elite for whom the other tombs were constructed (Ayele 1996: 614; Phillipson 2000: 225–8). Nevertheless, modest though Gudit Stelae Field tomb 'GT II' was, Chittick's excavations of 1974 recovered early third-century glassware of high quality, in spite of the depredations of tomb robbers (Munro-Hay 1989: 143–6, 190–1). Ayele's excavations of 1994, 1995, and 1996 suggested that the area was used for nonelite burials from the mid-second to the mid-fourth centuries and possibly for much of the first five centuries AD.

In addition to stelae and tombs at Aksum, there are a number of stone platforms that have been interpreted as the bases of thrones. Such thrones seem to have been important in Aksumite culture: one existed at the site of Matara; they are mentioned in two inscriptions of King Ezana; and in the sixth century Cosmas Indicopleustes saw one close to a stela at Adulis. Ezana's inscriptions also say that he erected metal statues, and although none of these has been found, a stone slab was discovered in Aksum at the beginning of the twentieth century that had hollowed-out footprints 92 centimetres long. If this slab was the plinth for a statue, as has been claimed, then the statue must have been enormous (Anfray 1981: 372; Phillipson 1998: 30; 2012: 136).

Aksum is also notable for the discovery of several Greek, South Arabian, and Ge'ez stone-cut inscriptions mostly of the fourth-century King Ezana, in whose reign Christianity appears to have been adopted (Pankhurst 1961: 28–30; Munro-Hay 1991: 224–9; D.W. Phillipson 2012: 57–63). It is rare that African archaeological evidence can speak to us so directly: 'I will rule the people', claims Ezana, 'with righteousness and justice, and will not oppress them' (Pankhurst 1961: 30).

Furthermore, Aksum has produced some remarkable residential building evidence. At the beginning of the twentieth century, the German Aksum expedition excavated three multiroomed structures of monumental scale, which were provisionally identified as palaces. These are known, respectively, by the names Enda Mika'el, Enda Semon, and Ta'akha Mariam (Phillipson 1997: 93–120). An attempt was made by the German expedition to produce architectural reconstructions of these buildings. The result for the central part of Enda Mika'el was a castle-like structure of four square towers, standing four storeys high on a stepped base. In the case of Ta'akha Mariam the reconstruction was even more impressive, producing a huge complex of court-yards, towers, and connecting buildings, which measured overall 80 by 120 metres and was of two storeys and, in places, three storeys (Buxton 1970: 93; Michels, in Kobishchanov 1979: 6; Phillipson 1998: 84–6). Reconsideration of the evidence led Buxton and Matthews (1974: 55, figs. 6–8) to suggest that Enda Mika'el was of only three storeys and of a somewhat different design, but their reconstruction still indicated the former existence of an impressive structure.

These buildings, in common with other major Aksumite buildings, were of a distinctive architectural style (Buxton 1970: 91–102; Buxton and Matthews 1974). They were built on a massive masonry podium with stepped sides, a feature of Pre-Aksumite and South Arabian origin that must have increased a building's apparent height. They were also built with a characteristic indented plan, both the podium and the wall surfaces being alternately recessed and projecting, a design that must have given the buildings an appearance of great strength. The upper storeys were apparently of mud-mortared rubble reinforced with timber, a type of construction that left the ends of some timbers projecting from the walls at the corners of windows and doors and at intervals along the wall surfaces. This constructional method is known from excavated archaeological evidence (Munro-Hay 1989: 138, plate 8.8), from its representation on the largest stelae (Buxton and Matthews 1974), and from the tenth- or eleventh-century church of Debra Damo, studied by the German Aksum expedition and by Matthews and Mordini (1959) and now dated by D.W. Phillipson (2009b: 63) to the 'third quarter of the first millennium AD'. Matthews was even able to attempt reconstructions of Aksumite interiors (Buxton 1970: 94–5; Buxton and Matthews 1974: figs. 12, 18, 28). However, Anfray (1981: 370) questioned whether the walls of such structures would have been strong enough to support more than two storeys. Nevertheless, he pointed out that in the sixth century AD Cosmas Indicopleustes wrote that in Ethiopia he saw a 'royal dwelling with four towers'. Whatever the details, it seems that these monumental residential structures were attempting to appear of great height; even two storeys, set on a solid masonry base, would have the appearance of a three-storey building. In fact, Anfrey has demonstrated that they were imposing buildings, with his excavation of the so-called Dongur Mansion, on the western side of Aksum. Excavated in 1966–8, this was a forty-room complex occupying approximately 3,000 square metres, with remains still standing in places to a height of 5 metres. Stone-built, it comprised a central structure and a series of interior courtyards that created separate blocks of rooms (Fig. 5.4). It was thought by its excavator to date to about the seventh century AD. Rather smaller than Ta'akha Mariam, Anfray interpreted it as a villa of a member of the elite, not a royal palace (Anfray 1968: 360–3; 1972a: plate 1 for plan; 1981: 365–6; 1990: 97, 100–3; Michels, in Kobishchanov 1979: 7–8). With its many rooms and courtyards, the Dongur Mansion could have housed numerous retainers, craftsmen, servants, and slaves, as well as an elite extended family. It might also have provided storage for agricultural produce and trade goods. Indeed, Munro-Hay (1991: 49) suggested that this and similar complexes might have been village centres surrounding landlords' houses.

Excavations elsewhere in and around Aksum indicated the existence of other stone buildings, some of which were for nonelite occupants. D Site at Kidane Mehret consisted of the remains of a peasant settlement of the eighth to fifth century BC, followed by a long hiatus in occupation and then a Late Aksumite settlement of the sixth to eighth century AD. This site was situated about a kilometre north of Aksum, apparently separate from the city, and appeared to have been a farming village. Similarly, K Site in Maleke Aksum indicated the presence of nonelite occupants but within Aksum itself. They appeared to have been involved in industrial and craft activities during the fifth and sixth centuries AD (Phillipson 2000: 372–9, 417–18). It seems likely that Aksum

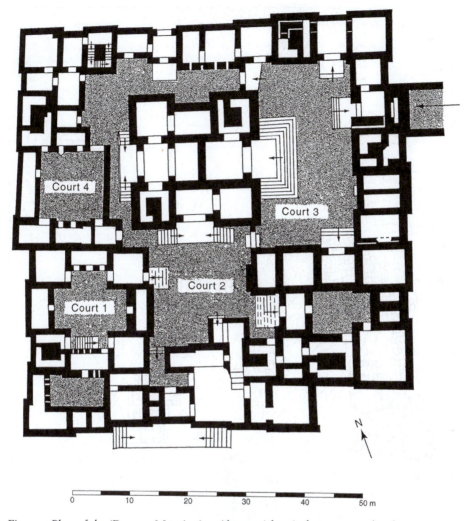

Fig. 5.4 Plan of the 'Dongur Mansion' at Aksum. After Anfray 1972a: planche 1.

was an extensive city during the first millennium AD, and excavations by Chittick at the base of the hill behind the main stelae group showed the impact of the city on its immediate environment. An erosional cycle was indicated and the hillside is now largely rocky, with little soil, suggesting that the eventual decline of the city might have been linked to environmental deterioration caused by a high population density.

Amongst other Aksumite sites, Matara (Fig. 5.5) is one of the most extensively investigated, although poorly published. Now in Eritrea, it lies about halfway between the Aksumite port of Adulis and the capital Aksum and is likely to have been a place of economic and political significance. The site

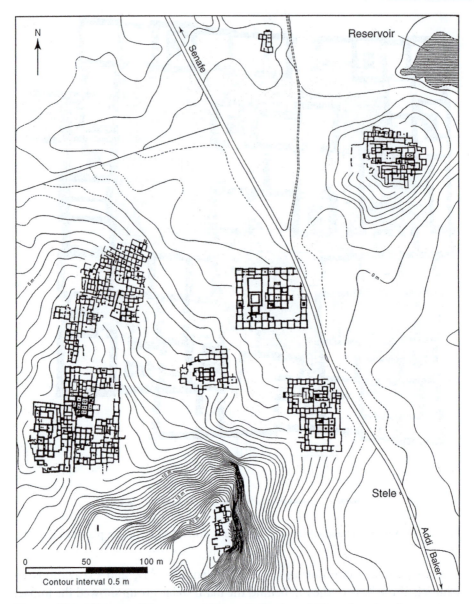

Fig. 5.5 Plan of Matara, Eritrea, providing an indication of Aksumite urban layout. After Anfray 1974: fig. 7.

occupies about 20 hectares, and deposits up to 5 metres deep contain evidence of two main phases of occupation: first in about 500 to 300 BC and then (after a long abandonment) an Aksumite period of about AD 700. Anfray excavated tombs, churches, and residential buildings, and amongst the latter were both elite houses and ordinary dwellings. Mound B yielded a large, multiroomed mansion; three other similar 'villas' were uncovered. In addition, however, there were houses of only two or three rooms and others that were intermediate in size between these and the villas, suggesting a social hierarchy. Some of the residents of Matara must have had considerable wealth, because a remarkable hoard of goldwork of Roman and Byzantine origin was found. In addition, some material sophistication is suggested by the presence of a piped water supply, provided by fitting the bodies of amphorae one within the other, which served the baptistery of the principal church discovered. The excavations at Matara also provided an important indication of Aksumite urban layout (Anfray 1967; 1974; 1981: 367–8; Michels, in Kobishchanov 1979: 14–16).

There are other Aksumite urban sites at Adulis, on the coast, and at Kohaito, north of Matara, both now in Eritrea. The remains of stone buildings of Aksumite style have been excavated at Adulis, and artefacts of both Aksumite and Mediterranean origin have been found there, indicating its role in long-distance trade (Paribeni 1907; Anfray 1974; Peacock and Blue 2007). Subsequent excavations have revealed an important chronological sequence relevant to the southern Red Sea region and the Horn of Africa (Zazzaro et al. 2014). Kohaito, like Matara sometimes thought to be the Koloè mentioned in the *Periplus of the Erythraean Sea* (p. 116), has not been excavated but is best known for a dam, built of carefully fitted blocks of stone, that is 67 metres long and about 3 metres high (Anfray 1981: 368). This dam was designed to form a reservoir of water; Pankhurst (1961: 24) called it 'one of the greatest engineering feats of the Aksumites'. Another Aksumite site is at Gobedra Hill, about 4 kilometres west of Aksum, where there are quarries from which came the granite used for the dressed stones of local Aksumite buildings and for some of the stelae. There are also traces of a road by which such material was transported to Aksum (Phillipson 2000: 229–51). In addition, de Contenson excavated a late Aksumite stone structure at Ouchatei Golo nearby, suggesting that it was a Christian church, and undressed stelae were found in its vicinity (de Contenson 1961; Michels, in Kobishchanov 1979: 10; D.W. Phillipson 1994: 192; 1998: 92; 2012: 91).

Far more Aksumite sites are known than have been excavated or published in detail. Anfray (1973: 21) provided a site distribution map, which showed that the nuclear area of the Aksumite state must have been located around Aksum and Adulis. He also proposed a distinction between an eastern and a western Aksumite province, the archaeological record suggesting that the eastern province was more prosperous but that the western was the centre of political power. However, it has been suggested that this centre moved east in Late Aksumite times, with a new capital at a location not yet identified (D.W. Phillipson 2009a: 9). In addition, Michels conducted a stratified random sampling of archaeological evidence in 40 percent of a 500-square-kilometre area, in the Aksum–Yeha region. About 260 sites were discovered, ranging from single compounds to large towns and including temples, stelae fields, tombs, and workshops. The survey suggested that much evidence still remained to be located in other areas but shed some light on Aksumite political organization, demonstrating that the fertile soil of the Aksumite Plain had been a factor in the development of that organization (Michels, in Kobishchanov 1979: 22–4; Michels 2005).

Chronological problems (p. 118) make it difficult to date the end of the Aksumite period. Significantly, the issue of coinage ceased early in the seventh century, and subsequently there seem to have been few imports or stone buildings. It appears that the economic and political base of the Aksumite state was seriously weakened by the extension of Arab control over the Red Sea trade route. Plague, drought, and environmental deterioration might also have contributed to Aksumite decline. According to legend, an Agau chieftainess called Gudit from further south destroyed the Aksumite state late in the tenth century AD. As a result of this or other problems, the political centre of gravity moved south from eastern Tigray, where numerous ancient churches suggest it was located by this time (D.W. Phillipson 2009b: 51–74, 87–107), to the Lalibela area, in Lasta (Buxton 1970: 44; Munro-Hay 1991). An Ethiopian state survived, but during the earlier part of the second millennium AD it seems to have lost its previous urban character, its rulers now leading a semi-nomadic life in a succession of camps, which Pankhurst (1979) called 'moving capitals'. Such a camp might consist of as many as 100,000 people; continual movements seem to have been necessitated by the rapid exhaustion in any one area of food and firewood. The sites of these transient settlements have a comparatively low archaeological visibility and have had little attention from archaeologists, although this is changing (Finneran 2009; 2012). The visible archaeological evidence for the period from the sixth to the fourteenth centuries AD has been dominated by ecclesiastical structures, for not only did Christianity survive and flourish but it also provided a stable element in Ethiopian society. Some remarkable 'built' churches from this period have been studied, including Debra Damo, already mentioned. Rock-hewn churches are more numerous, however, having survived more readily. These have a long history, but the most remarkable of them are at Lalibela. There are others in Tigray Province and scattered across the Ethiopian Highlands, providing evidence of technical skill and of an ability to marshal the material resources implied by these vast undertakings. The church of Beta Giyorgis (St George) at Lalibela, for instance, is a complex and sophisticated 'building' entirely carved, inside and out, from one gigantic block of stone (10.6 metres high) that had first to be isolated in a huge quarry pit (Fig. 5.6). Past studies of the Lalibela

Fig. 5.6 Beta Giyorgis, one of the Lalibela rock-hewn churches, Ethiopia. It is located within a pit quarried into bedrock. From D.W. Phillipson 1998: plate 10. Reproduced by permission of David Phillipson.

churches have tended to be architectural or art-historical, but there are now indications that archaeological structural analysis and excavation of associated deposits will provide new information about their chronology (Fauvelle-Aymar et al. 2010). Published accounts of Ethiopian rock-hewn churches include those of Buxton (1971), Gerster (1970), Plant (1985), and D.W. Phillipson (2009b).

In the latter half of the second millennium AD 'static capitals', as Pankhurst (1979) called them, tended to replace the frequently moved camps, although even these were shifted periodically or used only seasonally. Beginning in the late sixteenth and early seventeenth century there grew up a practice of constructing stone castles, which formed the nuclei of capitals. It was one of these castles that was studied at Gouzara by Annequin (1965), but the most successful of the castle-based capitals was that at Gondar (Fig. 5.7), north of Lake Tana (Finneran 2007: 259–63), where no less than twenty successive emperors made their capital prior to the nineteenth century. Right down to modern times, Aksum, much reduced in size, continued to be important as a religious centre. It is popularly believed by Ethiopians that the true Ark of the Covenant is kept there, and such emperors as were able to do so went there for their coronation (Pankhurst 1979: 4–6). This typifies the continuity often claimed to be characteristic of Ethiopian culture (Phillipson 2004). Archaeological evidence supports the idea of such continuity: some

Fig. 5.7 The seventeenth-century castle of Emperor Fasiladas, Gondar, Ethiopia, in the 1860s. From von Heuglin 1874.

ecclesiastical buildings make use of Aksumite ruins as foundations, such as the 'Old Cathedral' of Maryam Tsion at Aksum, and many built and rock-hewn churches have Aksumite architectural features (D.W. Phillipson 2009b). However, until recently archaeologists paid little attention to the last thousand years of Ethiopia's past.

Subsistence economy

Until D.W. Phillipson's excavations of the 1990s little archaeological attention was given to economic evidence. Nevertheless, Kobishchanov was able to reconstruct the Aksumite subsistence base from inscriptions and other historical sources. According to him, both terracing and irrigation were practised and ox-drawn ploughs were in use. Wheat and other cereals were grown, viticulture existed, and large herds of cattle, sheep, and goats were kept, as well as asses and mules. He also claimed that elephants had been domesticated but were reserved for use by the royal court (Kobish[ch]anov 1981: 383).

Subsequently, D.W. Phillipson was able to confirm much of this picture with archaeological evidence. Excavation of the D Site at Kidane Mehret revealed a farming village of the sixth to eighth century AD, a kilometre to the north of Aksum. This site produced plant remains including wheat, barley, teff, oats, a range of pulses, grape, gourd, noog (*nug*), linseed, cotton, and brassica (Phillipson 2000: 366). Animal bones indicated that cattle were the most common livestock, followed by sheep and goats. Chicken and equid (perhaps donkey) were present (Phillipson 2000: 369). There is also evidence of earlier subsistence from the D Site at Kidane Mehret, where deposits of the eighth to fifth centuries BC contained botanical and faunal remains almost comparable to those of the Aksumite period at this site (Phillipson 2000: 364, 369). In addition, a substantial quantity of ivory, found within the Tomb of the Brick Arches, indicates the exploitation of elephants (Phillipson 2000: 116–25). The importance of cattle is further apparent from several animal-model basins of pottery found in Aksum, each with a pair of yoked oxen of a shorthorn, humpless breed (Munro-Hay 1989a: 240, 256–7; Phillipson 2000: 63–4). Additional archaeological evidence for subsistence comes from the hill of Bieta Giyorgis, where excavations at the Ona Nagast settlement site yielded cattle and sheep and/or goat bones, as well as evidence of wheat, barley, teff, lentils, and grapes, from a context described as 'Middle Aksumite' (Bard et al. 1997: 395). Subsequent detailed study of the Bieta Giyorgis faunal remains provided evidence from around 700 BC to AD 1200 that confirms the dominance of cattle, both *Bos taurus* and *Bos indicus*, which were intensively exploited for meat, milk, and traction, as well as confirming the presence of domestic sheep and goats (Chaix 2013). Domesticated livestock seem to have played an important role in the economy. Witness, for instance, the inscriptions of Ezana, recording 31,957 head of cattle, 51,050 sheep, and 827 'beasts of burden'; figures remarkable not only for their size but also for an exactitude that suggests that they might have been the result of counting rather than guesswork (Munro-Hay 1991: 227–8).

Evidence of Pre-Aksumite subsistence also includes bronze sickles found at Yeha and Haoulti; pottery models of cattle at the latter site, sometimes wearing yokes; and grindstones found at various sites (Michels, in Kobishchanov 1979: 14; de Contenson 1981: 356–7; Anfray 1990: 47). Examination of grindstone material and wear has suggested a change from milling husked grains during the Pre-Aksumite period to that of free-threshing wheat by late Aksumite times (L. Phillipson 2012). Evidence of agriculture during the first millennium BC also came from the excavation by Joanne Dombrowski of Lalibela Cave, east of Lake Tana, which produced cultivated barley, chickpeas, and some unspecified legumes, together with bones tentatively identified as cattle and small stock, associated with stone artefacts. Indeed, it seems that agriculture developed at an earlier date than this in Ethiopia. Christopher Ehret used linguistic evidence to argue that it originated as much as 7,000 or more years ago. Some archaeological evidence supporting this claim is the tentative identification of domesticated cattle during the sixth millennium BC at Quiha rock shelter (Barnett 1999). In addition, Ethiopian and Eritrean rock paintings depict cattle and herdsmen, fat-tailed sheep, and even a man with an ox-drawn plough, but these are undated.

Clearly, by the beginning of the first millennium AD a strong subsistence base had been developed, consisting of broad-based, mixed agriculture. It seems likely that wheat and barley played a particularly important part: Munro-Hay (1991: 185–6) commented on the frequent depiction of ears of wheat or barley framing the royal bust on Aksumite coins, and D.W. Phillipson concluded that it is specifically emmer wheat that is represented. Pottery resembling the modern trays on which *injera* (the flat bread made from teff) is prepared appears only in the late Aksumite period (Munro-Hay 1989: 308, 311). This would suggest that this small and hardy cereal, which will grow at higher altitudes than wheat and barley and which now forms an important part of diet in the highlands, was not of such significance in Aksumite times. It is important to stress again the significance of the high fertility of the Aksumite Plain. On the basis of local farmers' opinions, Michels classified its soil as good to excellent, supporting a full range of cereal crops on land that relies on seasonal rains. In short, the heartland of the Aksumite state lay in an area that was advantaged so far as cereal cultivation was concerned, and which almost certainly was capable of producing a storable surplus.

Technology

Ethiopian and Eritrean archaeological evidence is highly informative on the technology of the periods under discussion. As with the middle Nile, there exists some difficulty in discriminating between things made in Ethiopia or Eritrea by local craftsmen and those imported from elsewhere or made locally by expatriate craftsmen (p. 99). Nevertheless, the technology of the Aksumite period, in particular, ranks amongst the most sophisticated to be found in precolonial tropical Africa.

First, some Aksumite sites have provided evidence of remarkable engineering skills. To quarry, transport, and attempt to erect such a monolith as the largest of the stelae at Aksum must have required theoretical knowledge, practical skill, and good organization. Furthermore, the giant granite slab of the Nefas Mawcha and substantial numbers of other stelae, although smaller, also imply the existence of considerable engineering ability (Phillipson 2000: 229–66). This ability could be directed to practical as well as ceremonial purposes. The dam at Kohaito and the Mai Shum reservoir at Aksum (Butzer 1981: 479) suggest that such expertise was applied to the task of water storage, although this was not for irrigation, as claimed from historical sources (Sulas et al. 2009). So far as archaeological evidence is concerned, it was in quarrying, carving, and manipulating masses of stone that the Aksumites evinced their main engineering ability. These skills had a long history, from the cutting of subterranean tombs during the first millennium BC to the quarrying of rock-hewn churches during the second millennium AD.

Aksumite archaeological evidence can throw a good deal of light on that expertise (Phillipson 1994; 2000: 229–66). Granite quarries to the west of Aksum have rows of slots that were cut for the insertion of either iron or wooden wedges, the latter probably tightly driven while dry and then soaked with water, so that their expansion split away the large pieces of stone needed for stelae and other purposes. Indeed, some of the stelae still standing at Aksum have traces of these slots, which were not completely removed by the percussive stone dressing employed to finish their surfaces. The extent of such finishing seems to have varied greatly, no doubt depending on the importance of the client and the cost of the job, but the Aksumite masons were capable of very high quality work. The storeyed stelae, for instance, have dressed surfaces that are both smooth and attractive, with the north face of the one that remained standing (Stela 3) faintly showing the bands of careful tooling that were necessary to achieve this. Furthermore, indented parts of the decoration on the largest stela have their edges undercut, so that when lit by the sun the resulting shadows enhanced the relief. Even with the hardened iron tools that must have been employed, it would have required an extraordinary combination of skill and patience to produce such results in a material like granite (although most of the stone called 'granite' at Aksum is technically syenite, which is softer). In contrast, the archaeological evidence also suggests that Aksumite knowledge of mechanics was sometimes deficient. With only 8.5 percent of the total length of the largest stela intended to go into the ground, it would appear that the centre of gravity either had not been calculated or had been calculated incorrectly. It is little wonder that it probably fell during the course of erection (Phillipson 2000: 161), although architect Ruth Plant (1985: 22) raised the possibility that an earthquake could have been responsible.

People in the highlands excelled in building construction, from the first millennium BC to the second millennium AD. Using mud-mortared stonework, reinforced with timber, to construct stepped and indented walls, strengthened at the corners with dry-laid ashlar masonry, the Aksumites constructed monumental elite residences of two or three storeys. It is possible that the architecture of these buildings was influenced by Roman style, conveyed perhaps via Syria, with which early Christian Ethiopia had connections (Michels, in Kobishchanov 1979: 27), but whatever the source of the style the workmanship was distinctively Aksumite. Building skills also extended to tombs, temples, early churches, and other structures. In addition to employing stone and timber, Aksumite builders learned both to manufacture and to use fired bricks, and the construction of brick arches and of brick barrel vaulting were both understood. Lime mortar and lime render were also used – although rarely, perhaps because of the quantity of wood needed to burn the limestone (Munro-Hay 1989: 162–3). Concerning ordinary domestic buildings, the small number of excavated stone houses (Anfray 1974: 756, figure 7; Phillipson 2000: 372–9) are supplemented by both Aksumite and earlier pottery models. These came from Haoulti and from Aksum (Munro-Hay 1989: 288; 1991: 254) and depict both rectangular and round structures.

Other skills were associated with building construction. These included stone sculpture and inscription cutting. Because the latter used, at one time or another, both South Arabian and Greek characters, it seems likely that a foreign hand or a foreign-trained hand was sometimes present. Nevertheless, the gradual ascendancy of Ge'ez would suggest that even this work was eventually done by Aksumites. Also associated with building were fine wall paintings, which were a feature of the interiors of many Ethiopian churches. Here again, the debt to foreign influences was great, but the style that developed was distinctly Ethiopian (Buxton 1970: 136). The origins of Ethiopian wall painting are not really known, but probably the churches of Christian Aksum were already decorated in this way (Phillipson 1998: 136).

Although metallurgy seems to have developed early in Ethiopia and Eritrea and to have achieved a high level of quality, there is evidence of stone-using people at Gobedra, near Aksum, during the first millennium BC and during the same time at Lalibela Cave, east of Lake Tana. At other sites near Aksum, there is similar evidence from the second millennium BC at Anqqer Baahti, and from as far back as the tenth millennium BC at Baahti Nebait (Phillipson 2000: 22–6, 504). However, the use of stone artefacts continued into Aksumite times at both Aksum and other sites. Research by Laurel Phillipson has shown how such artefacts were still used in the first millennium BC and until late in the first millennium AD, providing a cheap and readily available means of shaping wood, finishing pottery, preparing hides, manufacturing leather clothing, and producing parchment, as well as sometimes carving ivory (L. Phillipson 2009a; 2009b; 2013a; 2013b; Phillipson and Sulas 2005).

Nevertheless, by the seventh or sixth century BC a partly literate urban culture using bronze and iron was present at Yeha. This could have been the result of influences from southern Arabia, where iron had been in use from about 1000 BC, but it is possible that the use of copper had already reached northern Ethiopia from the Nile Valley. Whatever the case, by the late first millennium BC, a range of iron and bronze artefacts was in use. During the Aksumite period metal craftsmanship excelled both in the number of techniques employed and in the variety and the quality of its products, which were made in gold, silver, copper, bronze, and iron (Munro-Hay 1989: 210–34; D.W. Phillipson 2012: 165–9). Among the more remarkable achievements was the use of mercury gilding, to inlay gold on selected areas of silver and bronze coins (Munro-Hay 1991: 177, 188). Admittedly some of the metalwork might have been imported from elsewhere, but mineral resources were such (p. 115) that iron must have been mined and smelted in Ethiopia, as perhaps some other metals were. As for gold, supposedly one of Ethiopia's exports, it could probably have been obtained by panning superficial alluvial sources rather than by mining.

Archaeological evidence from Aksumite sites also indicates other manufacturing skills. Again the difficulty is to untangle the imported items from the locally produced. Most pottery was made locally and was at times remarkably sophisticated considering that it was formed without the use of a wheel, but a small amount came from the Mediterranean world, particularly from northern Egypt, probably as containers for wine or olive oil (Munro-Hay 1989: 235–316). Leather working appears to have been practised (Munro-Hay 1989: 321), and it is surmised that textile production was important, although textiles of foreign origin were also in use. Carving of high quality was done in ivory (Phillipson 2000; 2012); bone was worked (Munro-Hay 1989: 321–2); and civet was probably produced (von Endt 1978). The depiction of vines and grapes on third-century AD ivory carvings found in the Tomb of the Brick Arches; the recovery of grape seeds from the Kidane Mehret site, north of Aksum; and the existence of several rock-cut tanks at Adi Tsehafi, north-west of Aksum, which might have been wine presses, suggest that wine making was also practised (D.W. Phillipson 1997: 162–5; 1998: 59–60; 2012: 116–17). From historical and ethnohistorical sources, it seems that salt was probably obtained from the Danakil Desert, but there is no archaeological evidence for this. Coins were struck in Ethiopia during Aksumite times for at least 350 years, although some coins were imported (D.W. Phillipson 2012: 181–93). Finally, there were numerous luxury goods: jewellery, glass, and fine metal-work, for instance, which were of foreign origin. Nevertheless, although most of the surprisingly large amount of glass found in Aksum seems to have come from the eastern part of the Roman Empire or beyond, the characteristics of some pieces (Fig. 5.8) suggest that they were made at Aksum (Munro-Hay 1989: 208–9). It now appears that fragmented glass from imports was remelted and worked in a variety of ways (D.W. Phillipson 2012: 162–5).

Social system

Ethiopian and Eritrean archaeological evidence suggests that at least by Aksumite times there was a considerable degree of social complexity. Society appears to have been a stratified one. At the top was an absolute monarch, frequently depicted on Aksumite coins wearing a crown and sometimes shown seated on a throne (Fig. 5.9). Some of the inscriptions on the coins suggest that these rulers were, nevertheless, concerned about popular opinion; for example, 'May this be pleasing in the countryside' (D.W. Phillipson 2012: 188) and 'Joy be to the peoples' (Buxton 1970: 39) lack the usual tone of autocracy. However, monarchical government, whatever its exact character, is indicated also by other archaeological evidence. Thus, at least some of the monumental, multiroomed, residential buildings must have been royal palaces. In addition, there are monumental tombs that must have been for royal burials and those of other leading members of society. Other sorts of monumental structures also hint at the existence of a monarchical state: temples in earlier periods, churches in later ones, and the storeyed stelae at Aksum. One thing is common to many of these structures: they are large. According to historian Kobish[ch]anov (1981: 394), this 'mania for the gigantic' was intended 'to instil awe-inspiring admiration for the greatness and strength of the potentate to whom the monuments were dedicated'. However, not all the fine mansions or the large tombs might have been intended for royalty; they seem too numerous for that. Certainly, stelae of small or medium size are too common for such a conclusion. In addition, the distribution of luxury goods, many obtainable

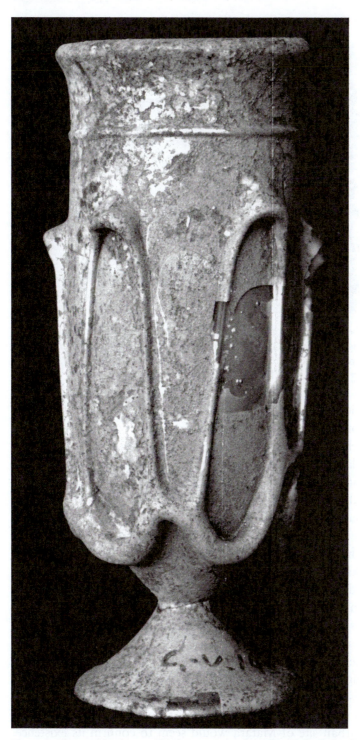

Fig. 5.8 Glass goblet from a third-century tomb in the Gudit Stelae Field, Aksum (height 125 millimetres). Probably a local manufacture imitating an Alexandrian product. From D.W. Phillipson 2012: fig. 60. Reproduced by permission of David Phillipson.

Fig. 5.9 Ge'ez-inscribed Aksumite copper coin of King Armah (sixth to seventh centuries AD), showing the king crowned and throned holding a Christian processional cross, with another cross on the reverse, its centre gilded. Diameter 20 millimetres. From D.W. Phillipson 2012: fig. 75. Reproduced by permission of David Phillipson.

only from trade with the outside world, is too widespread. It seems that there was not only a monarch but also an elite section of society.

Equally, the archaeological evidence suggests the existence of numerous peasants and/or slaves. The existence of the latter might be assumed from the long survival of slavery in Ethiopia, condoned as it was even by Ethiopian Christianity (Pankhurst 1961: 372–3). In a burial excavated at Matara the body apparently had worn iron shackles but might have been a criminal rather than a slave. However, it seems likely that slaves were one of the exports of the Aksumite state. Whatever the status of the sweating humanity that would have toiled on such tasks as moving and raising the stelae, large labour forces must have been involved. Constructional work on the scale frequently achieved in Aksumite times implies a numerous and an obedient labour force. If the modern world was built on machines, the ancient world was built on human backs. Indeed, the necessarily agricultural basis of Aksumite society, and that of earlier and later times, would require the existence of a large peasant class, which during times of war would also have provided the bulk of the fighting men. As is often the case, such a class is not so well represented in the archaeological record as that of the elite, but the smallest houses of those excavated in the urban site of Matara would seem to confirm its existence. Furthermore, the large number of small rooms surrounding the central structure at such elite residences as the Dongur Mansion would suggest that many of the lowest class lived in some sort of client relationship to society's more privileged people. Most, however, were probably scattered through the countryside in villages and hamlets, such as those located in the survey by Michels (2005).

Intermediate-sized houses excavated at Matara would indicate that there were also people who belonged to neither the elite nor the peasantry, at least in Aksumite times. Phillipson (2000: 374) provided some confirmation of this, interpreting the Late Aksumite D Site at Kidane Mehret, just to the north of Aksum, as representing 'a middle-rank settlement' with 'a status well above that of a peasant farmstead'. In addition, the burials of the Gudit Stelae Field, placed in modest tombs that were nevertheless marked by medium-sized to small stelae and in at least one case contained high-quality grave goods, have been interpreted as those of 'middle-class' Aksumites (p. 124). It might be expected that such a class would include government officials, scribes, priests of temple or church, middle-ranking members of the army, merchants, and perhaps some of the more skilled craftsmen. Amongst such a class there would probably be some foreigners, permitted to live in Ethiopia because of their special skills.

The archaeological evidence also suggests functional specialization. In Aksumite times, as well as rulers, government officials, and peasant farmers, there were expert builders, including masons, brickmakers, carpenters, and joiners. In addition, there must have been miners, quarrymen, iron smelters, blacksmiths, other metal workers, potters, ivory carvers, workers of leather, makers of stone artefacts, and transporters of goods. One would expect merchants, artists, scribes, coiners, some professional soldiers, and temple or church officials. Many of these specialists must have been urban dwellers, living in towns and cities that apparently did not need protection by surrounding walls, a lack that led D.W. Phillipson (2012: 119) to question their urban status. However, we know little of the layout of these settlements, although Anfray (1974: fig. 7) threw some light on that of Matara (Fig. 5.5), and Michels outlined the probable changing form of the city of Aksum during the first millennium AD.

Population pressures

The Ethiopian and Eritrean Highlands were attractive to human settlement, providing climatic conditions and soils conducive to cereal–plough agriculture and stock raising. Although large areas of the highlands were too rocky or too exposed, this was offset by the benefits of the great altitudinal range. This gave diversity to the subsistence base, apparently leading to a growth in population during the Aksumite period and probably to localized population pressures that must have contributed to increasing social complexity.

The antecedents of Aksum during the first millennium BC were indigenous, although absorbing some influences from South Arabia. These developments and the subsequent Aksumite state were in a part of the highlands that in recent times has had less rainfall and a shorter wet season than areas to the south. The Aksumite region was probably prone to drought-induced famine, and during the second millennium AD Ethiopia's centre of gravity was considerably further south. It is possible that the north-eastern highlands, with a growing agricultural and urban population, suffered from recurrent episodes of population pressure caused by drought and other crises, such as crop destruction by locusts. In those circumstances, considerable power would be placed in the hands of those who controlled the most productive agricultural land. Furthermore, the long-term effects of tree clearance, cultivation, and periodic drought could have caused the destruction of some agricultural land by erosion, another factor that could place pressure on subsistence agriculturalists.

Using geoarchaeological evidence, Karl Butzer suggested that Aksumite culture flourished at a time of better spring rains than at present, and declined when land pressure and erratic rainfall caused soil destruction during the seventh and eighth centuries (Butzer 1981: 471). Bard et al. (2000: 80–1) supported this interpretation, identifying a humid episode from the mid-first millennium BC to the mid-first millennium AD during which agricultural activity was intensified to sustain a state-level urban society. Consequently, demographic pressure increased, reaching a peak in the mid-first millennium AD and causing progressive soil degradation that led to environmental deterioration by the seventh and eighth centuries AD and famine in the ninth century. Thus population increase stimulated by favourable climatic conditions could have come under great pressure when conditions became less favourable. Significantly, ecological degradation does seem to have become a problem in some areas. Evidence excavated by Chittick at Aksum suggested serious erosion of a hillside following tree clearance and cultivation (p. 127).

According to D.W. Phillipson, population growth in the Aksum area eventually led to environmental collapse and depopulation, to which a sixth-century outbreak of bubonic plague might have contributed (D.W. Phillipson 2012: 206–7, 209). The consequent decline was probably one of the causes of a shift in the centre of the Aksumite state to north-eastern Tigray after the sixth century. Indeed, it seems that resources were unequally distributed in north-eastern Ethiopia and Eritrea and that some areas were under greater settlement pressure than others. Partial confirmation of this is provided by the settlement-pattern survey undertaken by Michels in the Aksum area (p. 129–30). This stratified random sampling survey demonstrated a growth in the population of Aksum during the period AD 450–750 to a total estimated at 39,603, followed by a decline in the succeeding period of AD 750–850 and population collapse after 850 AD (Michels 2005). Moreover, according to D.W. Phillipson (2012: 120), Michel's figure for Aksum's maximum population was significantly underestimated. A growing population could have contributed to the emergence of the city and state of Aksum, just as its decline contributed to their collapse.

Ideology

Archaeological evidence from Ethiopia and Eritrea indicates that religion played an important role in the emergence of the Aksumite state and in the continued existence of its successors. The evidence also suggests that religion contributed to the process of urbanization before and during Aksumite times and to the eventual reappearance of urban living in the second half of the second millennium AD. At first, religion consisted of a complex polytheism probably of South Arabian origin. From the fourth century AD onwards, for both the later Aksumites and subsequent Ethiopians, the principal religion has been Christianity of a distinctive Ethiopian type (Phillipson 1998; Finneran 2002: 120–47). Ullendorff (1960: 97) called Ethiopian Christianity 'the most profound expression of the national existence of the Ethiopians', and it is possible that the beliefs that pre-dated it had a similar significance.

The most obvious indication of the role of religion consists of the numerous and impressive remains of temples and churches. The temple of Yeha was so well built that after more than 2,500 years its ruins still stand to a height of about 9 metres; the churches of Ethiopia are the most important surviving structures of their period. The direction of resources into such buildings must have been in the hands of the ruler and the elite, who no doubt expected in return an ideological legitimization of their position.

That such a legitimization was claimed by the monarchical Aksumite state is indicated on the coins that were minted. The earlier ones showed the crescent and disc, representing the moon and sun of earlier beliefs; the later ones included the cross (Fig. 5.9), among the earliest coins of any country to do so, according to Buxton (1970: 40). The stone-cut inscriptions of Ezana also demonstrate the support that the monarchy sought from religion, calling first on pre-Christian deities and subsequently on the Christian god.

In addition there are the stelae, particularly the larger stelae at Aksum that seem to have been grave markers for royal burials (D.W. Phillipson 1994; 2000; 2012). As such, they appear to have had a religious role as well as being symbols of state authority. Groups of holes at the tops of the storeyed stelae (Fig. 5.3) have been thought to indicate the fixing of religious symbols to the stone. These symbols were probably of metal, but none survives. Consequently there has been debate as to whether the symbols consisted of the crescent and disc or the Christian cross (e.g., van Beek 1967: 118, 121). D.W. Phillipson has shown that these stelae are, in fact, pre-Christian in date, and indeed a stela at Matara does have a crescent and disc carved at its top. The more important of these monuments must have played a significant role in reinforcing the power of the state.

Perhaps less obvious is the contribution that religion made to urbanization. The temple at Yeha and the tombs and stelae at Aksum suggest that these urban developments were religious centres as well as commercial and administrative ones. Certainly it was as a religious and a ceremonial centre that Aksum survived into modern times, so that Bent (1893) could call it 'the sacred city of the Ethiopians'. Also, in Ethiopia during much of the second millennium AD it was religion that maintained the few static settlements: Lalibela might have been principally a religious centre but its archaeological remains imply that there must have been many people living in its vicinity. When urban centres appeared again in the second half of the second millennium AD, the Church still played an important role: Gondar, for example, is said to have had no less than forty-four churches (Pankhurst 1979: 5). Clearly, something more than religious fervour was involved; there were the politics of propitiating a powerful clergy and there was prestige for the ruler and supporting elite.

External trade

Aksum had trading contacts with the Roman provinces of the eastern Mediterranean and with Egypt, Nubia, South Arabia, the Persian Gulf, India, and Sri Lanka (Phillipson 1998: 69). Kobishchanov (1979: 175) used both historical and archaeological sources to put together an impressive list of goods imported into the Aksumite kingdom. They consisted of iron and nonferrous metals, and artefacts made of them; articles of precious metals; glass and ceramic items; fabrics and clothing; wine and sugarcane; vegetable oils; aromatic substances; and spices. From historical sources, Kobishchanov (1979: 172) also reconstructed the exports of Aksum. They comprised ivory, gold, obsidian, emeralds, aromatic substances, rhinoceros horn, hippopotamus teeth and hide, tortoiseshell, slaves, monkeys, and other live animals. These details suggest that Aksumite external trade was extensive and, like the Nubian trade of the middle Nile, basically involved the exchange of raw materials and African exotica for manufactured and luxury articles. It seems unlikely that trade prior to the rise of Aksum was so widespread, and it is apparent that post-Aksumite Ethiopia suffered from a comparative trading isolation. It is tempting, therefore, to conclude that the Aksumite state was a product of the international trade of its day. If Nubia was the corridor to

Africa, as Adams thought (Chapter 4), then it might be claimed that for a time Aksum, through its port of Adulis, was a front door to the continent. Indeed, it has been suggested that the rise of Adulis damaged the Nile Valley trade and contributed to the decline of Meroë after the first century AD.

As regards the commodities that were imported and exported, archaeology is both informative and disappointing. As is the case with Nubia, exports are not well represented in the archaeological record. However, an elephant tusk was found at Adulis (Anfray 1981: 377), and the Tomb of the Brick Arches at Aksum has yielded evidence not only for Aksumite involvement in the ivory trade but also for fine craftsmanship in its utilization (Phillipson 2000). It seems that Aksum became 'a major supplier of ivory' to the Mediterranean world (D.W. Phillipson 2012: 196). Furthermore, occasional gold artefacts from excavations in Aksum (Munro-Hay 1989: 210) and the finding of more Aksumite gold coins in South Arabia than in Ethiopia itself (Munro-Hay 1991: 183) are indications of a trade in gold. The problem is that many of the other commodities exported would either not have survived or would need to be identified as of Aksumite origin in the country to which they were traded. Archaeological evidence for imports is much better, although durables tend to survive and consumables do not. In addition, soil and climatic conditions in the Ethiopian and Eritrean Highlands are not as conducive to the preservation of organic materials as they are in the middle Nile Valley. As a result, most of the evidence for imports consists of artefacts of metal, ceramic, and glass. For example, Aksum and Adulis have produced Byzantine bronze artefacts, and from Matara has come a Byzantine bronze lamp, two Byzantine gold crosses, a necklace of Roman silver coins of the second to third centuries AD, and a bronze lamp of South Arabian origin depicting a dog catching an ibex (Kobishchanov 1979: 173–4). Even more remarkable is the hoard of 104 Indian coins of third-century date that were found at Debra Damo (Munro-Hay 1982: 111). Examples of ceramic and glass imports are more numerous. Aksum, for instance, has yielded amphorae of Mediterranean origin, pottery imitative of Roman fine ware, and glass ointment flasks of Roman and Egyptian manufacture (Kobishchanov 1979: 173). Such imports as wine and oil, however, which must have been inside some of these pottery and glass containers, have left no trace. Even textiles, which were probably imported in significant quantities, are represented only by occasional discoveries such as that of silk fabrics at Debra Damo, which originated from Coptic, Mesopotamian, and Islamic Egyptian sources of sixth- to twelfth-century AD date (Kobishchanov 1979: 174).

Some confirmation of the importance of Aksumite external trade is offered by several other pieces of evidence. Thus, Aksum was the first state in tropical Africa to mint its own coinage, which was produced in gold, silver, and bronze. It is noticeable that the Aksumite monetary system was similar to the Byzantine system in weight, standard, and form (Kobish[ch]anov 1981: 386) and that many of its coins, particularly the gold ones, were inscribed in Greek, not Ge'ez (Munro-Hay 1991: 180–95). Therefore, it would seem likely that coins were introduced because of Aksum's participation in an international trade that was accustomed to such a means of exchange. The earliest Aksumite coins belong to the third century AD, the latest to the seventh century (Munro-Hay 1991: 67–8), and it is surely significant that they ceased to be issued at a time when Aksum's external trading interests were in decline. Nevertheless, of the several thousand coins that are known, 90 percent have been found in northern Ethiopia itself and consist mainly of bronze coins. A few bronze coins have also been found in Egypt, Meroë, Israel, and Aqaba, but most of the gold coins have come from South Arabia and, less certainly, from India (Kobish-chanov 1979: 184; Munro-Hay 1991: 184; Phillipson 1998: 69). It would appear that the coinage of Aksum had a rather limited circulation, although foreign coins were imported into Aksum from South Arabian, Roman, and Indian sources.

A further indication of the importance of external trade to Aksum is the geographical location of this state. Situated in the extreme north-eastern part of the Ethiopian and Eritrean Highlands, it was in an advantageous position to take part in the Red Sea trade. It was sitting at the side of one of the major sea routes of the ancient world and had easy contact with Arabia across the Red Sea (Pankhurst 2004). Just as the coinage died when Aksum was excluded from these routes, so too did the Aksumite state fade away. Indeed, during the second millennium AD the political and cultural centre of Ethiopia was located far to the south. By then the need was not for access to the Red Sea but for isolation from Ethiopia's enemies.

The geographical location of Aksum in relation to the network of trade routes within this part of Africa provides still more evidence for the role of external trade in the development of this state and of its cities. According to the *Periplus of the Erythraean Sea*, the journey from Adulis to Koloè (either Kohaito or Matara) took three days, and the journey from Adulis to Aksum took eight, as it apparently still did at the beginning of the twentieth century (Kobishchanov 1979: 185). By the standards of ancient trade routes this was a brief journey, and this route from Adulis to Aksum was, in fact, merely the beginning of a route that led from the Red Sea to the Nile Valley, ending near Meroë. Another route ran north-west from Aksum to the Aswan region, across the Nubian Desert, a journey which took thirty days according to Cosmas Indicopleustes. Yet another route ran south from Aksum to Lake Tana and Sasu, the latter reputedly a source of Aksumite gold. According to Cosmas Indicopleustes this journey took fifty days. Branches from this route led, respectively, to Shoa and into the region of the African Horn (Kobishchanov 1979: 185–6). Thus Aksum was at the centre of a web of regional trade routes (Sernicola and Phillipson 2011) that tapped the resources of the African interior and injected some of them into the Red Sea trade.

Conclusion

Ethiopian and Eritrean isolation was relative to the circumstances of the surrounding world. The Aksumite state of the first millennium AD was able to benefit from its participation in regional and international trade and for a time ruled parts of southern Arabia; the Ethiopian state of much of the second millennium AD was able to isolate itself from hostile neighbours. Situated, as it were, on the roof of the world, ancient Ethiopians could join or reject that world as they wished. Thus can be explained the paradox of a people who have spent much of their history forgotten by the rest of humanity but who were, nevertheless, the creators of one of the earliest states and some of the earliest cities in tropical Africa.

It can be argued, therefore, that the geographical location of Ethiopia and Eritrea and their mountainous environment played a basic role in these developments. In particular, the diversity of well-established agriculture made possible by the great altitudinal range and influences from South Arabia during the first millennium BC provided a foundation for what followed. It is significant that the growth of social complexity during the last few centuries BC and the first few centuries AD took place in that part of the Ethiopian and Eritrean plateau most accessible from the Red Sea coast. However, compared with the surrounding lowlands, the highlands were healthier, had better soils, and a greater range of agricultural adaptations, providing a fertile seedbed for social change. In particular, the heartland of the Aksumite state lay in an area with a strong agricultural resource base in cereals, other crops, and livestock. This appears to have triggered localized increases in population and in population density during a relatively favourable climatic period early in the first millennium AD. In such a situation and given likely rainfall variability, episodes of stress brought on by periodic drought-induced famine would have created temporary population pressures, which could be exploited by those with access to land that was more productive. Such land was probably a limited resource, the control of which could have provided a power base for an emerging elite. Archaeological evidence indicates that by Aksumite times there had developed a partly urbanized stratified society consisting of monarch, surrounding elite, 'middle class', and peasant/slave class. It also suggests a fair degree of functional specialization with a sophisticated technological base. Furthermore, it is clear that the social order was confirmed and legitimized by religious dogma. Even the change from pre-Christian to Christian beliefs may be seen as a reinforcement of the prevailing social system, in which control of people must have been as important as control of productive land.

To all this must be added the impact of external trade, particularly the export of ivory, a highly valued commodity in much of the ancient world. Such trade was not in itself a cause of social complexity but, nevertheless, was a contributory factor of some importance. It is clear that the apogee of the Aksumite state and cities was coterminous with Aksum's involvement in the Red Sea trade, but it is equally apparent that the state of Ethiopia, if not its cities, was able to survive many centuries of comparative isolation from international trade during the second millennium AD. However, the Red Sea trade, conducted by Aksum through its port of Adulis, was actually part of a widespread network of trade that Aksum had developed throughout much of north-east Africa. Thus Aksum profited from the role of entrepôt, acquiring wealth and prestige from commodities mostly obtained from others. If Ethiopia and Eritrea appear to have been isolated, this was clearly an isolation that had its benefits.

Chapter 6

Opportunity and constraint: the West African savanna

In May 2012 the United Nations estimated that 18 million people in the Sahel region of West Africa were suffering from food shortages caused by drought and conflict and that nearly 1.5 million children were near starvation. The Sahel was defined broadly, although technically it is only the driest of the savanna zones south of the Sahara Desert. Nevertheless, how could it be that one of the areas of early urbanization and state formation considered in this book is situated within this apparently disastrous zone? Clearly, its occupants did not always face the bleak situation that now exists. Particularly this seems to have been the case immediately bordering the southern edge of the Sahara, which was the setting for important social and political developments during the first and second millennia AD. Some historical sources indicate conditions that were far from bleak. For example, in the early sixteenth century Leo Africanus said of Jenné, situated in the Inland Niger Delta on the edge of the Sahel zone: 'This place exceedingly aboundeth with barlie, rice, cattell, fishes, and cotton' (Africanus 1896: vol. 3, 822). This description was by an outsider, for Leo Africanus came from North Africa, but a local scholar, al-Sa'di, writing in about 1655, wrote: 'This city is large, flourishing and prosperous; it is rich, blessed and favoured by the Almighty ... The area around Jenné is fertile and well populated; with numerous markets held there on all the days of the week' (al-Sa'di 1964: 22–4). Although it was pointed out that al-Sa'di might have been biased in favour of Jenné (McIntosh and McIntosh 1980: vol. 1, 49), Bovill (1968: 135) thought that this was a 'convincing tribute'. Thus, it seems from historical sources, oral tradition, and archaeological data as if the West African savanna was in the past a zone that offered opportunities as well as constraints to the people who lived there.

Geographical location and environmental factors

Throughout the history of the human race in Africa, the most important ecosystem in the continent has probably been the savanna. Rich in faunal and floral resources, by the Holocene attractive for both cereal agriculture and livestock rearing, it offered conditions of relatively easy movement in which natural resources and manufactured products could be readily exchanged. The most extensive area of savanna in Africa consists of a broad zone that stretches from the Atlantic Ocean to the Gulf of Aden. This chapter is concerned with the western part of that zone, the savanna lands to the west of Lake Chad.

The West African savanna consists of grassland with varying densities of trees and shrubs, situated between the tropical rainforest to the south and the Sahara Desert to the north. In the past the Sahara formed what Bovill (1968: 1) called 'one of the world's greatest barriers to human movement', although, as Bovill showed, trade repeatedly breached that barrier. Beyond lay the lands of the Mediterranean, heart of the Roman and of the Medieval world, with contacts deep into Eurasia. To the south was the tropical rainforest and beyond that only the Atlantic Ocean, bordering a coast that until the middle of the second millennium AD was to remain isolated from the rest of the world. This is in contrast to the East African coast, discussed in Chapter 8, where external contact is known to have been present for some 2,000 years. Much of the coast of West Africa is uninviting when approached from the sea: natural harbours are relatively few and most of the coast is fringed by mangrove swamps or exposed surf-pounded beaches or is backed by inhospitable desert. The real problem, however, is that south of Morocco, along the Saharan coast, the prevailing winds are always from the north. Given the technology of the ships of the ancient and Medieval worlds, it was possible to sail south but impossible to return (Mauny 1978: 292–3). As a result, Cape Bojador at about latitude 26° north remained effectively the furthest south to which outside ships were able to penetrate until towards the middle of the fifteenth century AD. It was only at that time that circumstances changed, because of the adoption of the lateen sail and of the stern-post rudder by seafarers of the western Mediterranean and Atlantic seaboard, which enabled ships to sail into the wind as well as with the wind. Bovill also emphasized the importance of the discovery that it was possible to return from the West African coast, not by fighting contrary winds along the coast but by striking west into the Atlantic to pick up winds blowing from the south and west. This discovery, discussed by Crosby (1986: 112–14), occurred about 1440 and was made possible, Bovill suggested, by the Portuguese adoption of the caravel, a vessel that was much more manoeuvrable than earlier ships (Bovill 1968: 115). The caravel had both lateen sails and a stern-post rudder.

If the ocean could remain a barrier for so long, it is perhaps surprising that so formidable a barrier as the Sahara Desert should have been successfully breached by trade at least eight centuries earlier. The fact that it was has often been explained as the result of another cultural innovation: the introduction to Africa of the domesticated camel as a mode of transport over long distances through arid regions (Bulliet 1975). It will be argued below that the 'ship of the desert', as the camel has been called, did not inaugurate trans-Saharan trade but, in the hands of people who knew how best to utilize its peculiar physiology, it undoubtedly led to a very substantial development of that trade. The camel seems to have been brought into use in the Sahara during the first few centuries AD, coming originally from Arabia, although it appears to have been known in Egypt for many centuries previously (Rowley-Conwy 1988). It was not until after the seventh century AD, however, that the coming of the Arabs to North Africa brought about the development of trans-Saharan commerce based on the use of camel transport (Mauny 1978: 286–92).

It would be a mistake, however, to think of the West African savanna as merely a uniform zone, isolated to varying degrees through time by the desert, the forest, and the ocean. Rather, it was a world of its own and a highly complex world, richly endowed with resources. Indeed, the West African savanna consists of a parallel series of different environmental zones, running roughly from west to east and forming a part of a greater series of such zones extending from south to north across West Africa. These zones have usually been characterized in terms of vegetation differences; one of the best-known attempts to do this was the map produced by Keay (1959). Thus a hypothetical traveller, journeying north from the Nigerian coast, could traverse in less than 1,500 kilometres a whole range of environments, from coastal mangrove swamp to true desert (Fig. 6.1). On the way she or he would pass through tropical rainforest, forest–savanna mosaic, relatively moist woodlands and savanna, relatively dry woodlands and savanna, wooded steppe, and subdesert steppe. The close proximity of these different environments must have had an important influence on the development of human culture in West Africa. Because of the range of ecozones and ecotones that they presented, there was both the necessity and the occasion for the exchange of raw materials and products across environmental boundaries. Each environment possessed some resources but lacked others. Thus salt was available in the desert and along the coast but was relatively difficult to obtain in the savanna, where for cereal agriculturalists it was a physiological necessity (Alexander 1993b). Thus the forest was deficient in meat but the savanna supported very large numbers of domestic animals, particularly cattle (Buchanan and Pugh 1955: 120–3). There are many other examples, but the important point is that the complexity of the West African environment provided conditions conducive to the development of a complex network of regional trade. Within that network the West African savanna, relatively easy to traverse, played an essential part. It is likely that such trading activity was almost as old as West African food production, and, indeed, its remoter origins must have been even earlier.

Consider the main resources that would probably have been available in the West African savanna 2000 to 3000 years ago. Foremost of these would have been agricultural products: cereals such as sorghum, millet, fonio, and African rice; several indigenous yams; vegetable oils such as those

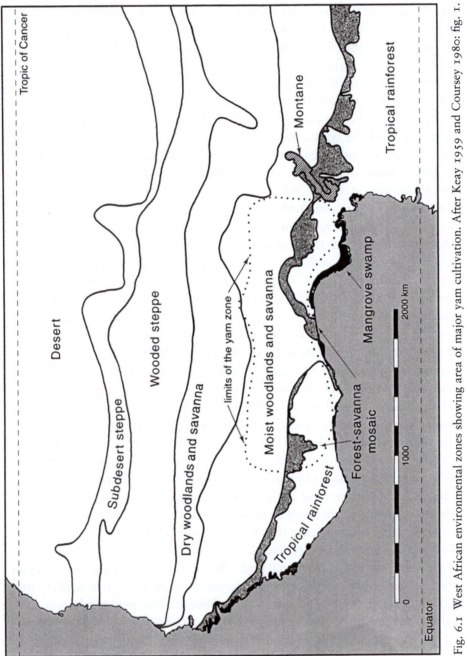

Fig. 6.1 West African environmental zones showing area of major yam cultivation. After Keay 1959 and Coursey 1980: fig. 1.

obtained from the shea-butter tree and the oil palm; two African groundnuts; cowpeas; black beniseed; and other things (Harris 1976: 329–32). There would also have been meat, dairy products, and hides and skins from the numerous cattle, sheep, and goats. Furthermore, food supplies could have been supplemented by hunting wild animals and by fishing; such 'wild' resources could in addition have provided ivory. Moreover, a number of wild plants and trees could have contributed to human sustenance, particularly in times when cultivated crops failed, while at all times botanical sources would have been able to supply a wide range of useful raw materials, for baskets, canoes, medicines, roofing, and many other purposes (Dalziel 1937; Casey 1998). Important inorganic materials would have been available in the West African savanna, as well: in particular, iron ore, alluvial gold, rocks suitable for making grindstones, good building earths, and potting clays. Last, a relatively high population density would have provided a resource in itself that could have been exploited: the slave trade has a history in West Africa which goes further back than the advent of Europeans on the Guinea Coast (Alexander 2001).

Nevertheless, the West African savanna was a zone of constraints as well as opportunities. Foremost of these constraints was water availability. The rainfall is markedly seasonal, the amount less and the wet season shorter the further north one goes. Also the temperature increases as one goes north, leading to a greater loss of surface water to evaporation, so that much of the northern parts of the savanna consist for most of the year of a virtually waterless landscape. Although drinking water for both domestic animals and human beings is usually available by digging wells of varying depths, in such conditions the margins of perennial rivers and lakes assume an especial attraction for agriculturalists. It is in such areas that 'floodwater farming' in its various forms has been of great importance. Such farming techniques – of which 'recessional cultivation' (the cultivation of naturally watered areas as floodwaters recede) is probably the most common – were one of the principal ways of intensifying African agricultural systems. Such techniques seem to have underlain the growth of social complexity in the Egyptian Nile Valley, and in West Africa they existed (and still exist) both in the Inland Niger Delta in Mali (Harlan and Pasquereau 1969) and around the southern edge of Lake Chad (Connah 1985), as well as probably in other places. Nevertheless, there is a second environmental constraint in the West African savanna that sometimes discourages human settlement around the very bodies of water that attract it. Of the major diseases found in the savanna that can seriously damage human or animal health, sleeping-sickness and animal trypanosomiasis, malaria, schistosomiasis, filariasis, river blindness, and a range of intestinal parasites are associated in one way or another with water. Clearly the West

African savanna was no earthly paradise but did offer considerable opportunities to human groups that could adapt to its constraints.

Significantly, this interplay of opportunities and constraints was not static through time, because even over the last 3,000 years there have been variations in the West African climate which have had profound effects on human societies in the savanna. Although conditions in West Africa were becoming steadily drier from about 4,500 years ago, Brooks (1998) identified an arid period between about 300 BC and about AD 300, a period of increased rainfall from about AD 300 to about 1100, another dry period from about 1100 to about 1500, another period of increased rainfall from about 1500 to about 1630, and yet another dry period from about 1630 to about 1860. Dating these periods is uncertain, and in addition there have been frequent shorter fluctuations in rainfall, resulting in droughts similar to those of recent decades and sometimes more severe (Shanahan et al. 2009). Within the savanna, economic and social responses to these changes have tended to be characterized by stability and growth during moister periods, and instability and decline during drier periods. This is to claim not that climate has been deterministic, but that it has been one of the factors that have shaped the complex dynamic relationship of people and environment.

Sources of information

Historical evidence

Until late in the twentieth century, knowledge of the precolonial cities and states of the West African savanna was mainly based on historical sources. Some of these originated as oral traditions, but many of them consist of documentation, usually in Arabic and mainly written by outsiders who at best had only visited the area. The principal of these were al-Masudi, ibn Hawqal, al-Bakri, al-Idrisi, Yaqut, al-Umari, ibn Battuta, ibn Khaldun, Leo Africanus, al-Maqrizi, ibn Said, al-Sa'di, and ibn Fartua. Collectively they throw light on the period roughly from the tenth century AD to the seventeenth century. Similar sources also provide brief references to the West African savanna back to the eighth century AD. Drawing on all these and other sources (including the writings of mainly nineteenth-century European travellers, such as Park, Denham, Clapperton, Caillié, and Barth), modern historians have been able to reconstruct, in varying degrees of detail, the history of the most important states of this area over the last 1,200 years or so. For example, Nehemiah Levtzion (1973) examined the old states of Ghana and Mali, and John Hunwick (1971) those of Songhai, Borno, and Hausaland. In fact, there exists an extensive literature on the history of the regions that were known as the

Western and Central Sudan. It is the character of the sources on which that literature is based, however, that for a long time determined the standard explanation of the development of cities and states in the West African savanna. That explanation was most clearly stated by Levtzion:

> *Sahil* is the Arabic word for 'shore', which is well understood if the desert is compared to a sea of sand, and the camel to a ship. Hence, the towns which developed in the Sahel ... may be regarded as ports. These towns became both commercial entrepôts and political centres. Those who held authority in these strategic centres endeavoured to extend it in order to achieve effective control over the trade. Thus trade stimulated a higher level of political organization, while the emergence of extensive states accorded more security to trade. Political developments in the Western Sudan, throughout its history, are related to the changing patterns of intercontinental and trans-Saharan trade routes. (Levtzion 1973: 10)

In other words, cities and states in this zone developed as a result of external stimulus, in the form of long-distance trade. In addition, this view usually emphasized the role of Islam in these developments. Such an explanation might be expected, of course, if sources are limited to post-eighth-century AD documents written by people of Islamic culture, who mostly belonged to lands beyond the Sahara. As a view of the later developments in the West African savanna, it is no doubt sound, but does it adequately explain the origins of these developments? Fortunately, there is another source of information that has neither the chronological limitations of the historical sources nor their possible prejudices: this consists of archaeological evidence, a source that deserves more attention than formerly (Fig. 6.2).

Archaeological evidence

The archaeology of the West African savanna is still limited by insufficient fieldwork and excavation. Furthermore, much of the earlier work was technically inadequate and publication was often poor or absent. There was also a tendency to adopt research strategies designed to throw more light on historically known sites. Mauny (1961) synthesized this earlier work, but so little was known about the archaeology of the area that in 1979 McIntosh and McIntosh (1979: 227) called the three millennia preceding the earliest historical documentation the 'silent millennia'. Similarly, Mauny himself used the phrase 'les siècles obscurs' (the obscure centuries) in the title of a book about the interface of history and archaeology in tropical Africa (Mauny 1970).

Nevertheless, archaeological research in the West African savanna is now throwing new light on the origins of cities and states in this area. Perhaps the

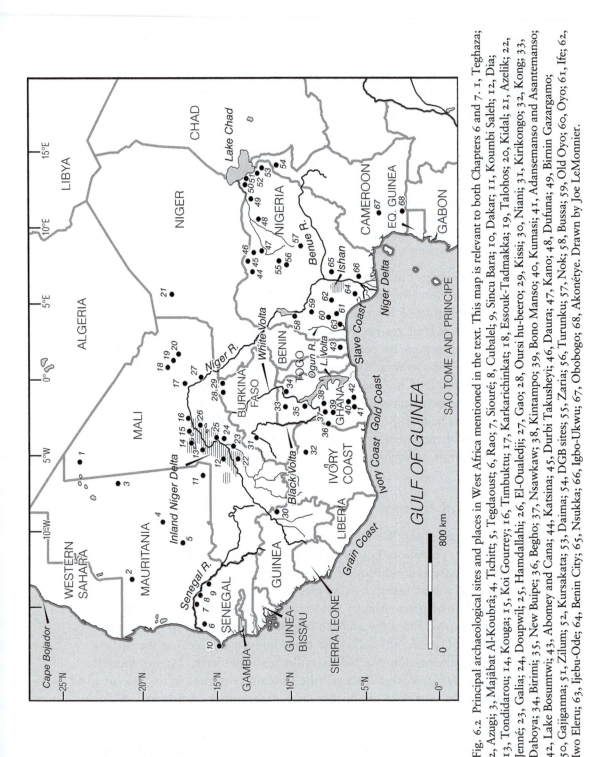

Fig. 6.2 Principal archaeological sites and places in West Africa mentioned in the text. This map is relevant to both Chapters 6 and 7. 1, Teghaza; 2, Azugi; 3, Majâbat Al-Koubrâ; 4, Tichitt; 5, Tegdaoust; 6, Rao; 7, Siouré; 8, Cubalel; 9, Sincu Bara; 10, Dakar; 11, Koumbi Saleh; 12, Dia; 13, Tondidarou; 14, Kouga; 15, Koi Gourrey; 16, Timbuktu; 17, Karkarichinkat; 18, Essouk-Tadmakka; 19, Talohos; 20, Kidal; 21, Azelik; 22, Jenné; 23, Galia; 24, Doupwil; 25, Hamdallahi; 26, El-Oualedji; 27, Gao; 28, Oursi hu-beero; 29, Kissi; 30, Niani; 31, Kirikongo; 32, Kong; 33, Daboya; 34, Birimi; 35, New Buipe; 36, Begho; 37, Nsawkaw; 38, Kintampo; 39, Bono Manso; 40, Kumasi; 41, Adansemanso and Asantemanso; 42, Lake Bosumtwi; 43, Abomey and Cana; 44, Katsina; 45, Durbi Takusheyi; 46, Daura; 47, Kano; 48, Dufuna; 49, Birnin Gazargamo; 50, Gajiganna; 51, Zilum; 52, Kursakata; 53, Daima; 54, DGB sites; 55, Zaria; 56, Turunku; 57, Nok; 58, Bussa; 59, Old Oyo; 60, Oyo; 61, Ife; 62, Iwo Eleru; 63, Ijebu-Ode; 64, Benin City; 65, Nsukka; 66, Igbo-Ukwu; 67, Obobogo; 68, Akonétye. Drawn by Joe LeMonnier.

earliest sign of complex societies in semi-arid West Africa is the appearance, from about 4000 BC, of what MacDonald (1998) termed 'Mobile Elites', based on transitory accumulations of pastoral wealth and power. This development is represented in the archaeological record by evidence for cattle herding, the making of valued objects in polished stone, and the construction of mounds – some for burial and others for the ritual disposal of objects belonging to the deceased. MacDonald suggested that, in favourable regions, additional climatic or cultural stimuli resulted in these Mobile Elites developing into semi-sedentary chiefdoms by about 1500 BC. One of these, he claims, was in the Dhar Tichitt-Walata area, in south-eastern Mauritania, where Holl (1985) studied a large series of drystone-built settlement sites dating from about 4,000 to about 2,000 years ago, which are strung out along more than 100 kilometres of sandstone cliffs. Towards the end of their occupation these sites formed a settlement hierarchy of four ranks: seventy-two hamlets with less than twenty compounds each, twelve small villages with twenty to fifty compounds each, five large villages with 120 to 198 compounds each, and one regional center, Dakhlet el Atrous I, measuring 92.75 hectares with 590 compounds, which could be described as a city. The communities in these settlements practised mixed farming based on grain cultivation (particularly bulrush millet: *Pennisetum* sp.) and the herding of cattle, sheep, and goats. They also exploited wild grains and fruits, fished in the freshwater lakes that then existed, and hunted a range of wild animals. Climatic deterioration almost certainly played a part in concentrating population into this area. It also eventually led to the abandonment of the settlements and their survival as archaeological sites, providing us with some of the earliest indications of developing social complexity in the West African savanna and the adjacent Sahara (Fig. 6.3).

The ideas of MacDonald and Holl challenged previous ideas about the processes and timing of social change in West Africa. Perhaps the greatest challenge, however, came from the work of Susan and Roderick McIntosh in the late 1970s and early 1980s on the settlement mounds of the Inland Niger Delta of Mali (McIntosh and McIntosh 1980; McIntosh 1995; McIntosh 1998; 2005). By combining regional surface investigations with excavations at the sites of Jenné-jeno, Hambarketolo, and Kaniana, the McIntoshs were able to trace the emergence of urbanism in this area, from its apparent origins in about the third century BC to the foundation in the early second millennium AD of the nearby historical city of Jenné. At Jenné-jeno the settlement had grown to at least 12 hectares by about the first century AD and reached its maximum extent of 33 hectares by about the ninth century (Fig. 6.4). At this latter stage it consisted of a packed mass of compounds, containing both round and rectangular mud houses, that was surrounded by a

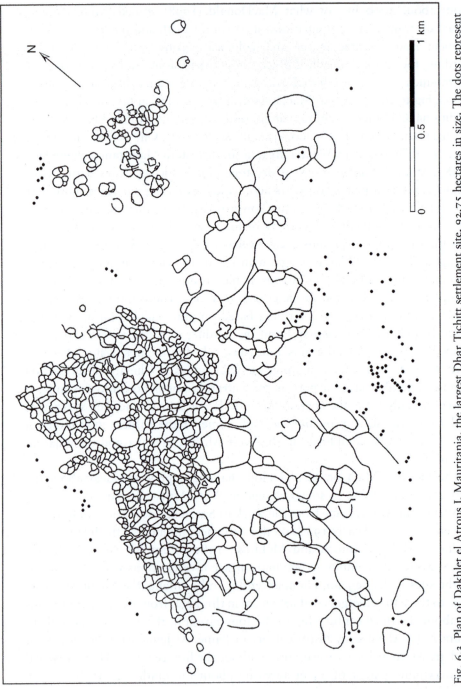

Fig. 6.3 Plan of Dakhlet el Atrous I, Mauritania, the largest Dhar Tichitt settlement site, 92.75 hectares in size. The dots represent tumuli, and the enclosures are stone compound and corral walls, not houses. After MacDonald 1998: fig. 4.5.

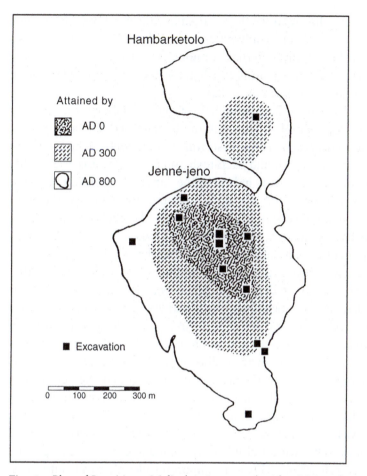

Fig. 6.4 Plan of Jenné-jeno, Mali, showing growth. After McIntosh 1995: fig. 10.3.

mud-brick city wall some 2 kilometres long. Its population has been estimated at between 4,800 and 12,800, and if the adjacent site of Hambarketolo is included, along with twenty-five other contemporary satellite sites
clustered around Jenné-jeno within a 1-kilometre radius, a population of
10,000 to 26,700 is possible. Although such a high density might have been
exceptional, this is only a relatively small part of the Inland Niger Delta,
suggesting that there was an overall population buildup in the area from late
in the first millennium BC to early in the second millennium AD. Excavated
evidence from Jenné-jeno suggests that the economic base for this development consisted of mixed farming on the seasonally inundated floodplain and
its margins, particularly involving rice and cattle, but it is apparent that
fishing, hunting, and the gathering of wild plant food were also important.

In addition, both metallurgy and other craftsmanship were well developed, and Jenné-jeno participated in a trading network with a radius of at least 350 kilometres. Yet so far as any external stimulus is concerned, such as that suggested by Levtzion, 'Jenné-jeno is too big, too early, and too far south' (McIntosh and McIntosh 1980: vol. 2, 448).

Although the evidence from Jenné-jeno has established a convincing case for the indigenous development of urbanism in the Inland Niger Delta, it has not demonstrated the existence there of a stratified sociopolitical hierarchy or centralized authority (McIntosh and McIntosh 1993a), unless it is argued that the construction of the city wall indicates the latter. As a result, the site provides little information about the origins of state formation in the West African savanna. Possibly we should reexamine our theoretical assumptions, as the McIntoshs have suggested, but the amount of excavation that has been done is still very small considering the size and number of the sites involved. This is a characteristic problem of urban archaeology, although one that systematic multiple coring of deposits might eventually overcome to some extent. Nevertheless, the homogeneity of material culture over a considerable area of the Middle Niger, the existence of a three-tier settlement hierarchy in the Jenné-jeno area, and a positive correlation of site size with surface artefact diversity on sites within a 4-kilometre radius of Jenné-jeno suggest that at its maximum development the city might indeed have formed the centre of a sociopolitical or economic development larger than its own immediate urban environment (McIntosh 1995: 410). However, R.J. McIntosh (2005: 187) has argued that this was not a hierarchy but 'a highly complex society organized horizontally, a heterarchy, with multiple overlapping and competing agencies of resistance to centralization'. This is an important idea that calls into question the traditional ideas of urban hierarchical evolution, for both Africa and some other parts of the world.

Archaeological field research in other parts of the Middle Niger and adjacent regions has shown that past urban development was no isolated phenomenon. In the Timbuktu region, for instance, surface and excavated evidence indicate settlement growth in the first millennium AD, although followed by decline caused by increasing aridity (Post Park 2010). The same seems to have occurred in the Méma region to the west of the Inland Niger Delta (Togola 2008), and probably also in the Lakes Region of the Middle Niger (McIntosh 1994: 178). However, Gao Ancien, on the Niger to the east of Timbuktu, revealed a sequence of archaeological deposits from the sixth or seventh century AD to the fifteenth or sixteenth century (Insoll 1996a: 41). Subsequent work, at both Gao Ancien and the nearby site of Gao Saney (Sané on p. 180), indicated occupation beginning in the seventh or eighth century and produced substantial evidence for long-distance trade in glass beads and copper during the eighth to tenth centuries (Cissé et al. 2013).

More than 1,000 kilometres to the north-west, the Middle Senegal Valley has presented a different picture from that of the Middle Niger. Although this is also a floodplain initially colonized about 2,000 years ago, which has a large number of clustered settlement mounds, most Middle Senegal Valley sites remained small, and the excavated evidence from Cubalel and Siouré indicates a small-scale society that changed little throughout the first millennium AD. Only at the end of that millennium did major changes in scale and complexity take place, at the same time as a sudden expansion of trading contacts, changes that led to the emergence of the so-called Takrur Empire at the beginning of the second millennium AD. It has been suggested that this contrast in the organization of society, on the Middle Niger and the Middle Senegal, resulted from differences in the distribution of land-forms. Evenly distributed subsistence opportunities on the Middle Senegal favoured an even distribution of population in small groups, whereas on the Middle Niger a very uneven distribution of such opportunities encouraged more specialization. Jenné-jeno and a number of other settlements, such as Kalifa Gallou (40 hectares), Dia (50 hectares), Toladie (85 hectares), and Soy (110 hectares), grew up as urban centres because of their unusually advantageous positions (McIntosh et al. 1992; McIntosh 1994: 178–9). An apparent exception in the Middle Senegal Valley is the site of Sincu Bara, of the first millennium AD, 67 hectares in extent with occupation deposits up to 3 metres in depth but lacking obvious mounds (McIntosh and Bocoum 2000).

The success of the McIntoshs' research stems at least in part from their early realization that:

> the most effective way to investigate the appearance and development of the pre-colonial town in West Africa is not to excavate only the town site, but to document and explain the evolution of the settlement hierarchy of which the town is the summit. (McIntosh and McIntosh 1980: vol. 2, 346)

Instead, much of the field research by other archaeologists, particularly the older work, has tended to focus on the sites of cities or towns which can, with varying degrees of certainty, be identified in the historical sources (Fig. 6.2). For instance, important excavations have been conducted at Tegdaoust, in the Mauritanian desert, of which the main site is 12 hectares in size. Work over many years revealed multiple phases of occupation, much of it the remains of stone buildings provided with facilities including wells, hearths, and latrines (Fig. 6.5). The earliest phase was preurban, and the entire occupation is thought to extend from the seventh to the sixteenth century AD (Holl 2006

summarizes earlier publications). The site has been identified with the historically known town of Awdaghost, which was a desert port-of-trade on one of
the trans-Saharan routes. The excavated evidence indicates that Tegdaoust
became a flourishing Islamic town, heavily involved with trade beyond the
desert. In contrast, the site of Niani, in Guinea, is of uncertain significance.
Its excavator claimed it to have been the capital of the old state of Mali,
but excavations did not reveal the wealth of Arab imports that might have
been expected (Filipowiak 1969). Other writers suggested that the real
capital was much further to the north-east; Conrad (1994) argued that its
location changed more than once. The radiocarbon dates for Niani are from
the sixth to the tenth centuries AD and suggest a reoccupation in about the
sixteenth and seventeenth centuries (Calvocoressi and David 1979: 15–16, 23;
Sutton 1982: 306, 311). The gap in these dates further reduces the likelihood
that this was the capital of the state of Mali at the height of its power in the
fourteenth century, although Holl (2006: 2–3) appears to think that it could
have been.

However, the site of Koumbi Saleh, in Mauritania, is thought by most
scholars to have been the capital city of the old state of Ghana. Excavations
have been conducted there on a number of occasions, some of the earliest
being those of Thomassey and Mauny (1951; 1956). This site, of 49 hectares
with stone buildings of several storeys and extensive cemeteries, is clearly of
great importance. Although Thomassey and Mauny failed to explore its
lower occupation levels, excavations by Robert and Robert (1972) and later
by Berthier have remedied that omission. There are now radiocarbon dates
for the site extending from the ninth to the fifteenth century AD (Berthier
1997: 102; Holl 2006: 13). The problem with Koumbi Saleh is that in the
eleventh century al-Bakri described it as consisting of two towns: an Islamic
town and a royal town (Levtzion 1973: 22–3). Unfortunately, it seems that it
is the Islamic town that has been excavated; evidence for indigenous origins
would be more likely to be found in the native town than in the strangers'
town.

An important excavation of an early West African urban complex was
conducted in 2005 at the site of Essouk-Tadmakka, in Mali (Nixon 2009).
This was a major Saharan trading town at a place first mentioned by Ibn
Hawqal in the tenth century AD. Its main site covers 50 hectares, and excavation at the EKA location in its centre revealed horizontally stratified deposits
6.5 metres in depth, containing the remains of both dry-stone and *pisé* structures dating from the middle of the first millennium AD to c. 1400. Excavation
at this location and at EKB and EKC shed light on the changing scale of trade
over time, in particular providing unprecedented eighth- and ninth-century AD
evidence for extensive trade. The investigations were also informative about

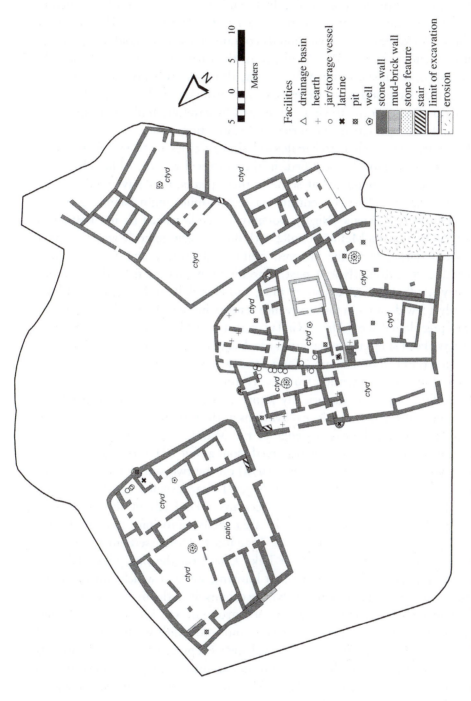

Facilities

△ drainage basin
+ hearth
○ jar/storage vessel
✶ latrine
⊠ pit
⊙ well
▮ stone wall
▮ mud-brick wall
▮ stone feature
▨ stair
▯ limit of excavation
░ erosion

Meters
5 0 5 10

N

Fig. 6.5 Plan of Building Sequence 6, eleventh century AD, at Tegdaoust, Mauritania. This shows the site in its most developed stage. After Holl 2006, fig. 13.

the character of the Saharan trade, the town being advantageously situated in the Sahel, on the route from North Africa to the Niger Bend. The discovery in the EKA excavation of coin moulds containing traces of gold, dated to the ninth to tenth century AD, is evidence of the early development of the gold trade and of the first coins in West Africa, although probably these were only blanks that were subsequently minted in North Africa (Nixon et al. 2011). Social conditions in the town are indicated by carefully built living spaces in EKA and also by a latrine pit in the EKB excavation.

There are many other archaeological sites of cities or towns that can be identified, or tentatively identified, in the historical record. Although excavations have been conducted at some of these places, they have tended to be limited in scale and to concentrate on second-millennium Islamic deposits. Examples include Azelik (Niger), possibly Takedda visited by ibn Battuta in 1353 (McIntosh and McIntosh 1984: 85); Birnin Gazargamo (Nigeria), capital of Borno dating from the fifteenth century AD (Bivar and Shinnie 1962; Connah 1981); Kong (Ivory Coast), a trading town dating from the sixteenth century AD (Sutton 1982: 306–7, 311); and Hamdallahi (Mali), which lasted for only a few decades in the nineteenth century but has been called the biggest city of precolonial West Africa (Gallay et al. 1990; Mayor 1996). Other places that have been subject to excavation are Azugi, in Mauritania, and Marandet, in Niger (Holl 2006). Kano, Zaria, and Katsina in Nigeria have not yet attracted significant attention from excavators.

In addition to those historically known, there are numerous other large settlement sites. For example, excavations at the settlement mound of Tongo Maaré Diabal, on the eastern edge of the Middle Niger area, have shown that this 9-hectare 'town' was occupied from about AD 200 to about 1200. Also, work by Bedaux and others (1978) on the two settlement mounds of Doupwil and Galia in the Inland Niger Delta revealed settlements that were first occupied in the eleventh century AD. Each of the latter sites were probably about 8 hectares in area, before erosion, compared with the approximately 12 hectares of Tegdaoust. Other settlement mounds of importance are those south of Lake Chad, on the *firki* clay plains of north-east Nigeria (Daima is the best known), some of which constitute the remains of quite large settlements whose origins lie in the first millennium BC (Connah 1981). These are only part of a group of 822 known mounds that also extend across northern Cameroon and into south-western Chad (Holl 1996: 581). Although many of the settlements represented by these mounds were probably too small to be considered urban, they are nevertheless relevant to an investigation of West African urban origins in the context of a McIntosh regional settlement hierarchy. In northern Cameroon, for instance, Holl (1996: 589) suggested a settlement hierarchy of at least three levels: 'open mounds of different but generally small size; walled sites, former village chiefdoms and later district centres; and finally paramount central settlements'. Examples of the central settlements were from 7 to more than 20 hectares in area, and probably represent the origins of the walled cities and small states that were historically recorded in this region from the sixteenth to the nineteenth century AD (Gronenborn 2001). Also indicative of sociopolitical change in the same region are the sixteen so-called DGB sites in the Mandara Mountains of northern Cameroon. These remarkable dry-stone structures, consisting of platforms, terraces, and other features, appear to date from about the fifteenth century AD, are mostly less than 4 hectares in size, and remain of uncertain function. Nevertheless, their construction required substantial labour and skill that suggest growing social complexity (MacEachern and David 2013).

Enclosing settlements with walls of stone or earth, with banks and ditches, or merely with timber palisades or naturally grown vegetation seems to have been widespread in Africa over the last 3,000 to 4,000 years (Connah 2000a; 2000b) but became particularly common in West Africa during the second millennium AD. Probably this resulted from increased competition for resources, as populations expanded or environmental conditions deteriorated. In the West African savanna many towns and cities sought to protect themselves in this way, especially with the increasing use of horses in warfare from the thirteenth or fourteenth century onwards. By about the ninth century, however, Jenné-jeno was already walled. Much earlier is the evidence of a fortified settlement at Zilum, in north-east Nigeria, in the middle of the first millennium BC (Fig. 6.6). This was a settlement of 12 hectares, with an estimated population of 1,750 to 2,500. A combination of magnetic survey and excavation revealed the details of this site, a reminder of how much might be learned if a similar methodology was used at other large settlement sites (Magnavita et al. 2006).

Although primarily a protective strategy, almost certainly the enclosing of large settlements had other functions as well: it assisted in the governance of the inhabitants, made taxation and control of trade easier, clearly distinguished city-dwellers from outsiders, and imparted prestige to rulers. It has also provided archaeologists with important physical evidence. The surviving remains of these enclosures should have encoded in them information about many aspects of the societies that constructed them. Archaeological investigation of those remains might be able to throw light on the size and shape of a former settlement and on changes through time in that size and shape, as well as on numerous other matters. Appropriate research strategies include mapping of city enclosures, giving attention to location, layout, and structural sequence, and the excavation of sections through the remains of such

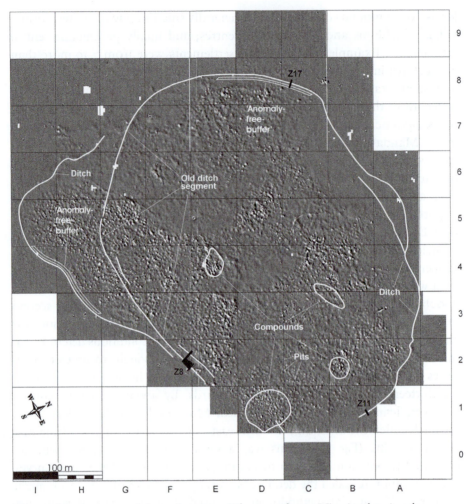

Fig. 6.6 Magnetogram of the settlement at Zilum, north-east Nigeria, showing the enclosing ditch and other features. The 'anomaly-free-buffer' is probably the location of a vanished bank or wall. Z8, Z11, and Z17 indicate test excavations of the ditch. From Magnavita et al. 2006, fig. 5. Reproduced by permission of Africa Magna Verlag, Frankfurt am Main.

structures and especially through the accumulated silt of any accompanying ditch or ditches. However, relatively little such work has been done, and the evidence is fast disappearing (Connah 2000a).

An example that has been investigated to some extent is the formerly massive city wall of Kano in the north of Nigeria, apparently constructed of both mud-bricks and dumped earth. In the mid-1820s Captain Hugh Clapperton recorded it as about 24 kilometres in length, with fifteen entry gates and with heights of more than 9 metres and a dry ditch on both the inner and outer sides (Denham et al. 1826, Clapperton's Narrative, 50). In 1885 Paul Staudinger claimed the wall to be 'probably twenty metres high' (Staudinger 1889, trans. Moody 1990: vol. 1, 210), and Frederick Lugard, faced with the task of storming the wall in 1902, admitted: 'I have never seen, nor even imagined, anything like it in Africa' (Lugard 1903: 28). It is therefore fortunate that we do have a surface archaeological study of the remains of the wall as they were in the mid-1960s, in which they were assessed in the context of the oral and documentary record (Fig. 6.7). This study, by H.L.B. Moody, identified three phases of growth in the Kano wall system: in the eleventh to twelfth century AD, the late fifteenth century, and the seventeenth century, a sequence documenting the growing size and importance of the city (Moody n.d. [1970]). Sadly, there have been few attempts to emulate this work, at least so far as accessible publications indicate, although the 6-square-kilometre walled site of Turunku, near Zaria in northern Nigeria, has been the subject of a preliminary study (Effah-Gyamfi 1986). The seriousness of this omission may be judged from the fact that in 1904 Lugard reported that there were forty walled cities within a 48-kilometre radius of Kano alone (Moody n.d. [1970]: 18). Clearly, field survey and excavation of the precolonial city and town walls of the West African savanna have the potential to add significantly to our understanding of the origins and development of urbanization in the region.

In addition to settlement sites, there are numerous burial sites that can provide information about the growth of social complexity in the West African savanna. Best known of these are tumuli, or burial mounds, which are found particularly in Mali but also occur as far west as the coast of Senegal and as far east as the extreme north of Nigeria. McIntosh and McIntosh (1980: vol. 1, 31–6) distinguished three types of burial mound in Mali: stone tumuli, in the Sahara; earthen tumuli, in the dry savanna to the west and east of the Inland Niger Delta; and tumuli covering rock-cut tombs, in the wooded savanna. It is the earthen tumuli, dating principally to the late first and early second millennium, which have provided the most relevant evidence for our inquiry. Both the size of these tumuli and the grave goods buried with the dead indicate differences in social status. Indeed, some of the larger earthen tumuli appear to have been remarkable structures. Thus some of them had their outer layers of clay baked rock-hard by numerous small fires that were lit on the mound surface. An example of such a tumulus is the 15- to 18-metre-high mound of Koi Gourrey (also known as Killi) in Mali (Desplagnes 1903), where two individuals had been buried with varied grave goods and with twenty-five to thirty other people, presumably sacrifices. Equally impressive was the tumulus of El-Oualedji, also in Mali, which was 12 metres high and contained a

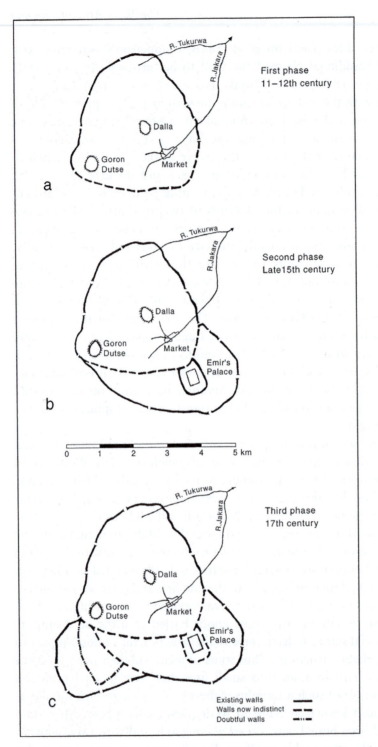

Fig. 6.7 Plans of the Kano city walls, Nigeria, from a survey in the mid-1960s, identifying three phases of growth (a, b, and c). After Moody n.d. [1970]: 39–41.

wooden funerary chamber, in which two individuals had been buried with accompanying objects (Desplagnes 1951; R. J. McIntosh 1998: 224–7). These, and perhaps a small number of other tumuli, indicate burial rites of the sort recorded by al-Bakri in the middle of the eleventh century for the kings of the state of Ghana:

> When the king dies, they build a huge dome of wood over the burial place. Then they bring him on a bed lightly covered, and put him inside the dome. At his side they place his ornaments, his arms and the vessels from which he used to eat and drink, filled with food and beverages. They bring in those men who used to serve his food and drink. Then they close the door of the dome and cover it with mats and other materials. People gather and pile earth over it until it becomes like a large mound. Then they dig a ditch around it so that it can be reached only from one place. (al-Bakri, as quoted by Levtzion 1973: 25–6)

Indications of the age of these large earthen tumuli are provided by radiocarbon dates: the early eleventh century AD for El-Oualedji (McIntosh and McIntosh 1986: 428, 439); the tenth to eleventh century for a tumulus at Kouga, in Mali (McIntosh and McIntosh 1980: vol. 1, 31); the eighth to the eleventh century for three tumuli at Toyla, Tissalaten, and Kawinza, in the Lakes Region of the Inland Niger Delta (McIntosh and McIntosh 1986: 428–9, 439); and the seventh century for tumuli associated with the Tondidarou standing stones, in Mali (Saliège et al. 1980; McIntosh and McIntosh 1986: 428, 439). It has been suggested that some of the grave goods from these mounds reflect 'the increasing wealth and power of groups controlling the flow of trade goods along the Middle Niger'. Possibly this increasing social stratification, plus the development of iron production in the Lakes Region and in the adjacent Méma region and the urban growth of Jenné-jeno, were all related in some way to the consolidation of the Empire of Ghana.

Perhaps the most impressive burial evidence comes from a number of tumuli in the Rao region of north-west Senegal, north-east of Dakar. These mounds yielded a remarkable collection of grave goods, including jewellery of silver and gold; one item of gold is a decorated disc of exceptional workmanship, 184 millimetres in diameter and 191 grams in weight. There were also an iron sword, beads, and objects of copper (of which two were Moroccan lidded bowls). These finds have been dated to a period for the northern Senegalese tumuli from the tenth century AD, continuing into the second millennium (Joire 1955; McIntosh and McIntosh 1993b: 104). It is thought that there were until recently more than 10,000 tumuli in Senegal, and collective inhumations often with rich grave furnishings have been found in a number of them (McIntosh and McIntosh 1993b: 75). The southern tumuli have been dated to approximately AD 700 to 1000, possibly earlier than those to the north but later than the earliest of the numerous megalithic sites, with which they overlap in time and space (McIntosh and McIntosh 1993b: 104–5). Found in both Senegambia and Mali, these arrangements of standing stones, in Senegambia apparently with associated burials and evidence of human sacrifice (Gallay et al. 1982), have proved difficult to date, but radiocarbon and pottery analysis suggest that they belong principally to the second half of the first millennium AD and the first half of the second (Gallay 2010). Collectively, the wealthy burials and monumental funerary structures of Senegal suggest increasing social differentiation by people who were in touch with both the gold-producing areas to their south and the Arab markets of the Mediterranean world to the north. Perhaps this is an archaeological expression of state emergence, in this case of the so-called Empire of Takrur (p. 161) or of some related polity.

Far to the south-east, between Katsina and Daura in northern Nigeria, the tumuli of Durbi Takusheyi also provide evidence of an elite, in this area relating to the emerging Hausa city-states of the fourteenth to sixteenth centuries AD (Griffeth 2000). Excavation of three of the at least eight mounds at this site revealed a single burial in each. Copper, bronze, brass, iron, silver alloy, and gold grave goods accompanied these, as well as cowries, glass beads, carnelian beads, ivory bracelets, and the remains of textiles (Fig. 6.8). The copper/copper alloy items included bracelets and anklets, buckets, and other items including bowls, one of which is inscribed in Arabic (p. 67) and indicates trading contacts with North Africa or further afield (Fig. 3.10). Two of the buried individuals are presumed to have been interred in a seated position and were possibly male; the third was accompanied by two earrings, a pendant, two rings, and other jewellery, all of gold, which suggest the deceased was female. Overall, the Durbi Takusheyi burials are important evidence of an hierarchical state with wide trading connections (Gronenborn 2011: 70–107; Gronenborn et al. 2012).

All the tumuli discussed above appear to represent non-Islamic burial practices, but such practices seem to have been varied; not only was there inhumation in tumuli, but some small earthen tumuli west of the Inland Niger Delta contained cremations in pottery urns. Indeed, the usual burial rite in the Inland Niger Delta seems to have been inhumation in large pottery urns (McIntosh and McIntosh 1980: vol. 1, 36–7). Other non-Islamic burial practices are also recorded archaeologically from the last three millennia in the West African savanna. However, although many of these are probably pre-Islamic in date, some could be later than the introduction of Islam to the area, which was certainly in progress by the eleventh century AD. This is because the replacement of previous practices by Islamic rites is likely to have been a gradual process, rather than an abrupt change.

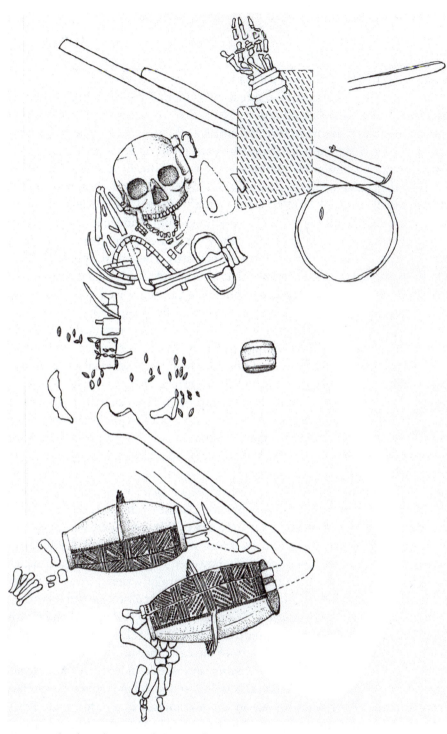

Fig. 6.8 Elite burial in Tumulus 5, Durbi Takusheyi, northern Nigeria, probably of the fourteenth century AD. The grave goods included two massive copper-alloy anklets, ingots of brass, other metal items, ivory bracelets, and cowrie and glass beads. The burial had probably been in a seated position from which it had subsequently collapsed. Drawing by Vera Kassühlke, Römisch-Germanisches Zentralmuseum (RGZM). Reproduced by permission of Detlef Gronenborn (RGZM).

Subsistence economy

Livestock husbandry and cereal cultivation seem to have been firmly established in the West African savanna by the first millennium BC (Klee and Zach 1999; MacDonald and MacDonald 1999; Neumann 1999). For example, there is evidence for domesticated cattle and small stock, as well as for both domesticated and wild *Pennisetum* sp. (bulrush [pearl] millet) at Karkarichinkat (Mali) in the second millennium BC (Smith 1992: 73–4). Also, *Pennisetum* was being grown by the beginning of the first millennium BC at Dhar Tichitt, in Mauritania, as part of a mixed farming strategy that included the herding of cattle, sheep, and goats (Munson 1976). Furthermore, from Jenné-jeno there is direct evidence for the cultivation of *Oryza glaberrima* (African rice), *Pennisetum*, and sorghum from about the third century BC onwards. These were apparently part of a diversified subsistence economy that also included substantial amounts of *Brachiaria ramosa*, a wild millet, and other wild cereals, as well as domesticated cattle, sheep or goats, and hunting and fishing. The occupation of Jenné-jeno lasted until about the fourteenth century AD; the economy remained remarkably stable throughout this period of approximately 1,600 years, although hunting became less important and the breed of cattle changed (MacDonald 1995: 313). This stability was despite climatic and demographic changes (McIntosh 1994: 172–3; 1995: 377–9). The strength of the subsistence base may be judged from the growth of this settlement, from at least 12 hectares by the beginning of the first millennium AD to a maximum of about 33 hectares towards the end of that millennium (Fig. 6.4). Indeed, the distribution of archaeological sites on the floodplain near Jenné-jeno indicates that towards the end of the first millennium the population density of the Inland Niger Delta was probably greater than at present. This was at a time when the climate of this area seems to have been wetter than usual, so that to a large extent this could explain the greater population density (McIntosh and McIntosh 1980: vol. 2, 428; R. J. McIntosh 2005: 84). Another factor of importance, however, might have been the practice of recessional cultivation (the cultivation of naturally watered areas as floodwaters recede), probably for growing rice. Recessional cultivation can constitute a form of agricultural intensification (Connah 1985), so perhaps urban growth in the Inland Niger Delta was supported by one of the relatively rare examples of African intensive agriculture. Whatever the case, the subsistence economy of the area seems to have been particularly successful. Indeed, the McIntoshs suggest that it was the agricultural surplus of the Inland Niger Delta that provided much of the food for urban centres situated in less fortunate areas such as Timbuktu, Gao, and places further afield. In such movement of foodstuffs, canoe transport on the Niger River seems to have played a major role (McIntosh and McIntosh 1980: vol. 2, 448–50).

Cultivation was already practised by about 1000 BC both in the Chad basin and in northern Burkina Faso. The settlement mound of Kursakata, in the Nigerian part of the former area, has produced grains of cultivated *Pennisetum glaucum* from the period between about 800 BC and about AD 100, and domesticated cattle and sheep or goats were present at the two settlement mounds of Gajiganna by about 1000 BC (Breunig et al. 1996; Neumann et al. 1996; Klee and Zach 1999). Significantly, the Chad basin is another area where recessional cultivation could have given the inhabitants an advantage, and it seems likely that most cases of increasing social complexity in the West African savanna had an agricultural base that was exceptional in some way, and therefore had the potential to produce a surplus. Probably this was frequently in the form of grain, which could be stored or transported. This meant that the surplus produce of more fortunate regions could support urban centres situated on trade routes at the edge of the desert. It also meant that specialists could be supported within those urban centres. Climatic and environmental deterioration might by the twenty-first century have rendered the West African savanna less agriculturally viable than it was a thousand years ago. The McIntoshs' evidence for this in the Inland Niger Delta is not the only evidence. A drop in the level of Lake Chad during the last millennium indicates that such deterioration might have been general in the West African savanna (Brunk and Gronenborn 2004), in spite of a relatively wetter period in about the seventeenth century.

The excavation of Oursi hu-beero, a house complex in northern Burkina Faso belonging to the eleventh century AD, has provided a remarkable insight into the details of a Sahelian subsistence economy (Petit et al. 2011). Pearl millet (*Pennisetum glaucum*), cowpea (*Vigna unguiculata*), and Bambara groundnut (*Vigna subterranea*) were the main cultivated plant foods, but *Sorghum bicolor* and *Hibiscus* sp. were also consumed, as were a range of wild plants and tree products. Domesticated animals included cattle, sheep, and goats, and dogs were eaten. Chicken were kept and also horses or donkeys. Fishing, hunting, and collecting molluscs contributed additional animal protein; a wide variety of fauna was eaten including monitor lizards, crocodiles, lesser pouched rats, hares, and antelopes. The use of such diverse food resources seems to have been typical of the drier savanna, as a strategy to minimise the risk of starvation, and has continued into modern times.

Technology

Iron technology emerged in West Africa no later than the middle of the first millennium BC (Pole 2010). Copper was also being smelted by a similar date (McIntosh 1994: 173–5; Woodhouse 1998). Evidence from Jenné-jeno indicates that the occupants of the settlement mounds in the Inland Niger Delta were using iron from the time of their arrival late in the first millennium BC, in spite of the nearest iron ore being 50 kilometres away (McIntosh and McIntosh 1986: 427; McIntosh 1995: 380). In addition, the builders of the tumuli and of the megaliths discussed above seem to have been iron users. Although the condition of excavated iron is often poor, it is clear that the metal was being used for a variety of purposes by the first millennium AD, ranging from weapons and tools to bracelets and other jewellery (e.g., Fabre 2009: figure 4). There is also evidence that these were indigenous products, in the form of furnace remains, slag, and other indications that smelting and black-smithing were widespread (e.g., Holl 2009). Indeed, iron production in the Méma region of Mali in the late first millennium and early second millennium AD was on too great a scale for local requirements only (Håland 1980). Similarly, in the Middle Senegal Valley the remains of some 60,000 iron-smelting furnaces have been counted, in only a 15-kilometre portion of the Mauritanian bank of the river, suggesting substantial iron production in the first half of the second millennium AD.

Judging by evidence from Jenné-jeno, copper was also reaching the Inland Niger Delta by the middle of the first millennium AD, and crucible and mould fragments as well as artefacts indicate that both it and bronze were being worked at Jenné-jeno by late in the same millennium, with brass introduced from the north at the end of that millennium (McIntosh 1995: 385). The early-second-millennium AD tumulus of Koi Gourrey (Killi) produced copper and bronze items, some of which appear to have been made by the lost-wax casting technique, as was also the case with two massive copper-alloy anklets (Fig. 6.8) in the probably fourteenth-century AD Tumulus 5 burial at Durbi Takusheyi (Desplagnes 1903: 165; Gronenborn et al. 2012). In addition, Bedaux and others (1978) excavated a mould for lost-wax casting from a context dated to the end of the eleventh and the beginning of the twelfth century, at the settlement mound of Doupwil in the Inland Niger Delta. Thus it seems likely that items of copper and copper alloys were manufactured locally, although the requisite metals were perhaps mined and smelted elsewhere.

Of less certain origin are the occasional items of silver and even gold jewellery recovered from some of the tumulus burials, the most remarkable being the gold disc from Rao (p. 169). Gold, although mentioned often in the historical sources, is rare in the archaeological record, as might be expected in view of its value. Nevertheless, an undated hoard of gold and silver excavated at Tegdaoust included five gold ingots as well as gold jewellery (Robert 1970), and crucibles with traces of copper and gold, from the same site, possibly belong to the eighth century AD. In addition, excavations at Jenné-jeno produced a gold earring from a ninth century AD context (McIntosh 1995: 390); the probably fourteenth-century AD Tumulus 7 at Durbi Takusheyi contained gold jewellery (Gronenborn et al. 2012); and coin moulds dated to the ninth to tenth century AD containing traces of gold were found at Essouk-Tadmakka (Nixon et al. 2011).

There must have been miners, particularly of gold, but with the exception of Kiéthéga (1983), archaeology has little to tell us of their techniques. This is in spite of the general location of the gold deposits being known and in spite of ethnohistorical observations of traditional gold-mining methods in West Africa. There might also have been specialist builders, because mud architecture dates from the early to middle first millennium AD at Tongo Maaré Diabal and Jenné-jeno, and from a similar date at Daima in north-east Nigeria. Later in the same millennium at sites in the Inland Niger Delta, mud-bricks rather than coursed mud (*pisé*) were used for building, and occasionally fired bricks were employed (McIntosh and McIntosh 1980: vol. 1, 188–92; Connah 1981: 147–9; McIntosh 1995: 364–5). A change from coursed mud to mud-brick also occurred at Kirikongo, in Burkina Faso, about AD 700 (Dueppen 2012: 275). Furthermore, in both the Inland Niger Delta and the Chad basin potsherd pavements were made late in the first millennium AD (Connah 1981; McIntosh 1995). In areas with suitable geology, building in stone was also practised, as at Dhar Tichitt, Tegdaoust, Koumbi Saleh, and Essouk-Tadmakka. In addition, some of the larger megalithic structures and tumuli suggest the presence of people specialized in the necessary construction techniques.

Concerning other crafts, pottery making had reached an impressive technical level by the beginning of the first millennium AD. Although handmade, like most traditional African pottery, it was generally thin-walled, symmetrically shaped in many forms, and well fired. It was usually painstakingly decorated, often with impressions and sometimes, in parts of the northern savanna, with painted patterns. Pottery figurines of both animals and humans were also made, particularly in the Chad basin and the Inland Niger Delta, those of the latter area demonstrating considerable artistic skill late in the first millennium and early in the second millennium AD. In addition, from this period at Jenné-jeno there were even pottery drainpipes, further demonstrating the versatility of fired-clay technology (Connah 1981; McIntosh 1995: 368–9). This was part of a tradition of ceramic craftsmanship in the West African savanna, of which the mainly first-millennium BC terracottas from Nok in northern Nigeria are perhaps the most remarkable examples (Boullier et al. 2002–3).

The production of textiles, as indicated by the archaeological occurrence of spindle whorls, might not have developed until the end of the first millennium AD, by which time the spinning and weaving of cotton was probably becoming established. Textile remains from Tongo Maaré Diabal have been dated to the second half of the first millennium AD, and woollen textiles from burials at Kissi in Burkina Faso have been dated mainly to the middle of that millennium, although it is uncertain whether they were produced locally or imported (Magnavita 2008). Previously, clothing was probably of leather and, with the long-standing traditions of livestock husbandry in the area, it is reasonable to suppose that the working of hides and skins had a long history. Other crafts that must also have been established for many centuries would have included wood working, bone working, basketry, and mat making. Although archaeological evidence for these activities can be limited, the 8000-year-old dugout canoe from Dufuna in north-eastern Nigeria, Africa's oldest boat, emphasizes the antiquity of both wood-working skills and water transportation in the West African savanna (Breunig 1996). Equally, the bone tools from the first-millennium BC deposits at Daima and the mat impressions sometimes used as a pottery decoration in the part of Nigeria south of Lake Chad serve as reminders of some of the other, less visible crafts (Connah 1981; Sterner 2012).

Social system

It is difficult to determine social organization from the available archaeological evidence in the West African savanna. In particular, there has been insufficient area excavation of settlement layouts and house plans. Nevertheless, the apparent density of sedentary settlement in the Inland Niger Delta, the Middle Senegal Valley, or the plains south of Lake Chad suggests the emergence of social complexity before a thousand years ago. So does the increasing size of some of these settlements: Jenné-jeno, for example, grew from 12 hectares early in the first millennium AD to 33 hectares towards the end of that millennium. With a population perhaps as large as 13,000 enclosed by a 2-kilometre city wall, beyond which perhaps as many people again lived within a distance of 1 kilometre, there must surely have been developments in order to maintain law and order and regulate trade. However, the McIntoshs question this assumption because of the lack of evidence for elites (McIntosh 1995: 396) and the few indications of social or economic differences (McIntosh and McIntosh 1993a: 632). Roderick McIntosh has argued that a heterarchy rather than a hierarchy existed, with authority arranged horizontally rather than vertically (McIntosh 2005). This is an idea that might explain other acephalous societies that nevertheless achieved social complexity, such as the Igbo of eastern Nigeria (p. 206). However, until more extensive excavation is done at Jenné-jeno and other early urban sites in the West

African savanna, it seems premature to assume that social stratification and despotic authority were absent, particularly as they had developed by the time the state of Ghana first appears in the documentary record in the eighth to ninth century AD. The gold earring found in the Jenné-jeno excavations appears to be of a similar date and suggests that there, also, resources were unequally distributed. Nevertheless, it is possible that social systems could undergo major changes over time, for example, from clan-based village societies to elite hierarchies and subsequently to egalitarianism. An attempt to identify archaeological evidence for such social transformations, in a Burkina Faso settlement at Kirikongo during the first and early second millennium AD, has been made by Dueppen (2012).

The burial evidence is less problematic: the size and sophisticated construction of some of the larger tumuli, and the wealth of grave goods sometimes present, are strongly suggestive of a social hierarchy. The owner of the Rao gold disc, for instance, was no ordinary person. In addition, the presence of human sacrifices with some other burials is indicative of the special status of the deceased. It is surely significant that the archaeological evidence, from some of the tumuli, compares so closely with al-Bakri's eleventh-century account of the burial of the kings of Ghana quoted above (p. 169). The Senegambian megaliths also suggest social differentiation: like the tumuli, they are evidence of the expenditure of considerable effort and resources for the benefit of a select group of people. Nevertheless, the usual burial rite in the Inland Niger Delta during the first millennium AD seems to have been inhumation in large pottery urns, presumably evidence of a large nonelite population that received more modest treatment in death. However, it seems that trade in gold and iron, and the presence of an agricultural surplus in more fortunate areas, were already stimulating social and political changes giving rise to the state of Ghana before the earliest Arab contact. In short, state formation was already in progress before the growth of trans-Saharan trade with Arabic North Africa, and it seems likely that during the earlier first millennium AD ranked chiefdoms, such as might have existed at Dhar Tichitt as early as the second millennium BC, were becoming stratified societies. Also in the first millennium AD, the development of urban centres was in progress, as the evidence from Jenné-jeno indicates. The culmination of such development can be seen at Tegdaoust or Koumbi Saleh, with their stone-built houses, and in the great walled city of Kano, which in 1851 had a population estimated by Heinrich Barth at between 30,000 and 60,000 (Barth 1857–8: vol. 2, 124). Indeed, during the second millennium AD, Kano and other Hausa cities became some of Africa's most developed city-states, supported by productive agriculture, varied technology, extensive trading connections, complex bureaucracies, defensive and offensive military organizations, and Islamic legitimization (Griffeth 2000).

As well as social stratification, the archaeological evidence suggests the development of functional specialization prior to Arab contact. Many craftsmen were already present in some West African savanna societies by the first millennium AD. There were also farmers, pastoralists, and fishermen; merchants and transporters; religious functionaries; and community leaders. Thus the social system in some parts of the West African savanna could have been particularly receptive of Arab and Islamic influences over the last millennium or so. The outcome was a complex mixture of the old and the new, of the indigenous and the alien.

Population pressures

The West African savanna is characterized by a dynamic interplay of opportunity and constraint, varying through time with fluctuations of rainfall. Not only have human populations had to come to terms with the specific constraints of each area, but the more productive areas have been bounded by less fortunate areas. Areas of greater productivity have also varied in both size and conditions in response to environmental variations, triggered by either climatic change or activities such as iron smelting or the grazing of domesticated animals. Such a situation would have been likely to produce population pressures, not only on the occupants of the advantaged areas by their poorer neighbours, but also within the more productive areas themselves if a period of environmentally good conditions was followed by environmental deterioration. From the McIntoshs' work, it seems that this is what probably happened in the Inland Niger Delta, where the unusual hydrological conditions allowed the intensification of agriculture by means of the recessional cultivation of rice. This could have encouraged a concentration of population within this area. The work done by the McIntoshs revealed a remarkable density of settlement by the middle of the first millennium AD. In addition, the area of the Inland Niger Delta is confined, and, as the McIntoshs have shown, its variety of landforms is highly susceptible to environmental fluctuations, so that by the early second millennium AD many of its settlements had been abandoned. Such an area, richly endowed with resources and yet subject to periodic stress, could well have been the location of social changes. It is thought that the Middle Niger supported a population with a relatively high density, and it has been estimated that during the first millennium AD the population of the Sahel states (Mauritania, Mali, Niger, and Chad) doubled from 1 million to 2 million – by 1975 it was about 15 million (McEvedy and Jones 1978: 238–40). Given recurrent droughts and environmental degradation, social and economic instability must have been a constant threat in this region. Intergroup violence was probably one consequence, of which the burning of the Oursi hu-beero house complex and the death of three of its occupants in the eleventh century AD provides some archaeological evidence (Petit et al. 2011: 210–14). Population pressure was surely one of the circumstances that stimulated social changes leading to urbanization and state formation.

Ideology

Historical sources indicate that Islam had an important influence on the course of West African urbanization and state formation. The Islamic world of the early second millennium AD was a world of independent states, in which substantial numbers of people lived in towns and cities that were often the centre of mercantile activities. It was also a proselytizing world, seeking, with fluctuating enthusiasm, to convert the infidel not only to its religious beliefs but also to its way of life. Archaeology has revealed the remains of early mosques in a number of places, at Koumbi Saleh, Tegdaoust, and elsewhere (Mauny 1961: 472–6; Robert 1970), and indeed some mosques still in use, such as that at Jenné, are reputed to be of great age. However, archaeology has also confirmed historical evidence that the inhabitants of the earliest cities and states of the West African savanna were not Muslims. The tumuli, in particular, indicate non-Islamic practices, as also do the urn burials of the Inland Niger Delta and the making of clay figurines in that and other regions. Some of this evidence might represent a survival of traditional practices after Islam had been introduced to the West African savanna, and historical sources indicate that this did happen. Nevertheless, urban development at Jenné-jeno by early in the first millennium shows that the origins of urbanization and state formation in the West African savanna were indeed pre-Islamic. The people involved with these developments must have been animists, and the variety of non-Islamic burial practices in the archaeological record of the West African savanna would suggest that there was considerable diversity of belief among different human groups. It is not known what these beliefs were, but the evidence of the tumuli, the megaliths, and human sacrifice suggests that funerary cults were significant. In such cults, ancestors could have had an important role in which the clay figurines were relevant, so that the monumental character of some of the associated structures might indicate that ideology provided reinforcement for elite authority.

External trade

Using historical sources, both Bovill (1968: 236) and Levtzion (1973: 10) saw long-distance trade as a vital stimulus to developments in the West African savanna. Certainly, archaeological evidence of the trans-Saharan trade of Bovill and Levtzion has been found often enough. For example, Koumbi Saleh produced stone plaques with Arabic inscriptions and Islamic decorations, not to mention stone houses said to show Maghrebian influence (Thomassey and Mauny 1951; 1956). Thus, also, Tegdaoust yielded imported pottery, oil lamps, glass vessels, glass weights, and ingots of both copper and gold (Robert 1970). Perhaps the most impressive of the archaeological evidence for the trans-Saharan trade, however, is amongst the group of twelfth- and thirteenth-century gravestones found at Sané, near Gao on the Niger in Mali. Some of these are marble gravestones with inscriptions in Kufic, an early angular form of the Arabic alphabet. These inscribed stones have been closely dated to AD 1100–1110 and are thought to have been made in Spain and carried by camel across the Sahara (Flight 1975: 82). There is even archaeological evidence of the difficulties that could assail such trans-Saharan camel transport, in the form of the abandoned loads of a caravan buried in a sand dune in the lonely Majâbat Al-Koubrâ, halfway across the desert. Dated to the twelfth century AD, these loads consisted of large numbers of brass rods and of cowrie shells of the species *Monetaria moneta* (Monod 1969). The presence of such shells, more than 9,000 kilometres from their source in the Maldive Islands, south-west of India, is eloquent testimony to the very extensive trading networks of which the trans-Saharan trade formed a part (Hogendorn and Johnson 1986: 18).

There is, indeed, a considerable amount of archaeological evidence for the trans-Saharan trade. For instance, countless sites in the West African savanna contain beads of glass or semi-precious stones; many of the earlier of these must have originated from that trade. The source and date of manufacture of such beads can be difficult to determine, but some might indicate that the trans-Saharan trade is older than has usually been thought. It is becoming apparent that relay trading networks in the Sahara, rather than trade crossing the whole desert, had already developed by Roman times (Wilson 2012). Of six Jenné-jeno glass beads selected for chemical analysis, from contexts dating from the last two centuries BC to AD 1400, the earliest is likely to have been made in India or East or South-East Asia, while one of the later ones might have come from India and another have been of Roman origin, from Egypt or Italy. Only two of the beads appear to be from an Islamic source (McIntosh 1995: 252–6). Glass beads of Asian origin from burials at Kissi, in Burkina Faso, also indicate the existence of a trans-Saharan trade during the first millennium AD before the arrival of Arab merchants (Magnavita 2003). Furthermore, analysis of copper-alloy objects from the same site has shown that most consisted of metal from North Africa and beyond (Fenn et al. 2009). Other evidence for the Saharan trade consists of the location of some of the West African cities and towns. Pushed well forward of the most viable agricultural lands of the savanna or even into the desert proper, such places as Timbuktu, Tegdaoust, or Essouk-Tadmakka were clearly located at strategic points on the trade routes, rather than in hinterlands that could support them. Also, many of the savanna urban centres appear to have grown up at environmental interfaces, between transportation systems. Thus at Timbuktu goods were transferred from camel to canoe, and at Kano from camel to donkey. A comparable situation will be seen in Chapter 7: trading centres growing up at the junction of the savanna and forest, where the tsetse fly made it necessary to transfer goods from donkey to human head.

However, archaeological evidence does not give the detailed picture of Saharan trade reconstructed by historians (Fig. 6.9). Where in the archaeological evidence is any indication of the millions of tons of salt that must have travelled south from the desert to the savanna (Lovejoy 1986)? Similarly, where is the evidence of the cloth that was carried south from North Africa, or of the thousands of slaves who were taken north (Meillassoux 1991: 44–64), or of the ivory, ostrich feathers, fine leather, and pepper? For that matter, who would realize, from the archaeological evidence, just how important the gold trade was? Clearly, some of the durable commodities, which were traded to the south, had a greater chance of surviving in archaeological contexts than the generally organic consumables, which dominated the trade to the north. Thus there will be a tendency for the West African archaeological evidence to be biased in favour of imports. This makes the discovery at Gao of a tenth- to eleventh-century AD hoard of at least fifty-three hippopotamus tusks, apparently a hidden consignment of export ivory, particularly important (Insoll 1995; 1996a: 38, 40, 98). Also the discovery at Essouk-Tadmakka of coin moulds with traces of gold, dated to the ninth to tenth century AD, has provided evidence of the early development of the gold trade (Nixon et al. 2011). Furthermore, artistic representations of black Africans in the ancient Mediterranean world is an indication that the Saharan slave trade was already active in the first millennium BC (Fentress 2011). Similarly, a review of the archaeological evidence south of the Sahara by MacDonald (2011) has traced the origins of the Saharan trade to the first millennium BC and earlier.

Of course, questions about the traded commodities lead to others. If West African agriculture is at least 3,000 years old, as the evidence appears to indicate, then why should we believe that the salt trade developed only towards the end of the first millennium AD with the advent of the Arabs and their camel caravans? According to Nenquin (1961), an adult on a mixed diet needs 12 to 15 grams of salt per day. In the West African savanna, salt could be brought from the coast where it has long been extracted from seawater, transported from the Sahara where it is quarried from rock-salt deposits, or obtained by filtering plant ashes, which is possible only in certain areas and is not very efficient (Alexander 1993b). In practice, this leaves extensive areas where the local supply is deficient but where diet and climate make salt a necessity.

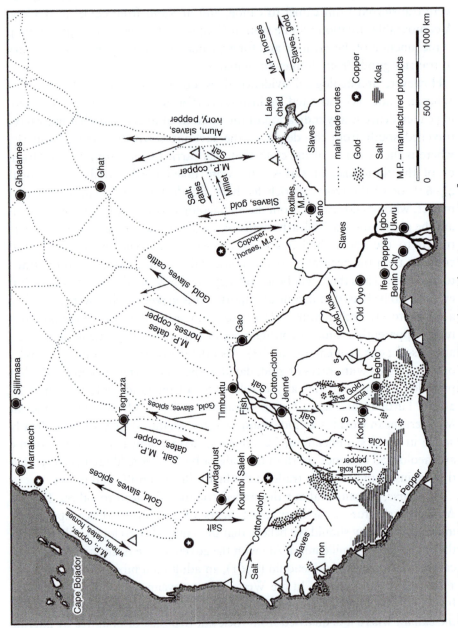

Fig. 6.9 Precolonial trade routes and commodities in West Africa. After Mauny 1961: fig. 55.

Consequently, it is probable that trade networks within West Africa are likely to be at least as old as the beginnings of food production in the region and that trading contacts with the desert are therefore nearer to 3,000 than to 1,000 years old. In addition, no one has suggested that gold mining in West Africa commenced because of stimulus from across the desert. On the contrary, historical sources tell us that West Africans were so secretive about the location of the mines that outsiders had little idea where the gold came from. Furthermore, there is evidence of gold at Jenné-jeno by AD 800. Thus there seem to be several reasons for supporting the idea that a regional network of trade routes grew up in West Africa before the advent of the Arab trans-Saharan trade. The McIntoshs (1980: vol. 2, 444–6) pointed out that because Jenné-jeno was using iron from the time of its earliest occupation, and because there was no iron ore in the vicinity, then supplies of raw materials or of finished iron must have been brought from more than 50 kilometres away. Also, situated at the interface of the dry savanna and the Sahel, on a fertile alluvial plain, and at the highest point on the River Niger for reliable seasonal river transport, Jenné-jeno was well placed to play an important role in a developing trade network.

Paintings and engravings on rocks in the Sahara of horse-drawn chariots and ox-drawn carts suggest that such a network could have had early connections with the desert (Mauny 1978; Law 1980b). These are distributed along two main axes, both of which stretch from North Africa to the Niger, axes which have been called 'chariot tracks'. It has been assumed that these rock drawings date from the first millennium BC, more likely from its second half. Most scholars now doubt that these are representations of vehicles used in commerce, however, and Camps (1982) rejected the idea of 'routes', pointing out that the distribution of this rock art merely reflects the distribution of rock outcrops in the Sahara. Nevertheless, this art is important in indicating that horse and ox traction and wheeled vehicles were known in the desert before the advent of the camel during the first few centuries AD (p. 151). Indeed, Blench has argued that the small West African ponies mentioned in historical sources 'were produced by the dwarfing of horses brought across the Sahara in the last three thousand years' (Blench 1993: 103). Even Bovill could admit, with characteristic wisdom: 'There is certainly no reason to suppose that caravan traffic in the Sahara only became possible with the arrival of the camel' (Bovill 1968: 17). Timothy Garrard has indicated that such traffic could have been at least pre-Arab in origin. He has suggested the existence of a Berber gold trade in the early first millennium AD, between the savanna and the Roman world, because the Carthage mint began issuing gold coins at the end of the third century, although it had no local gold source (Garrard 1982). In addition, the McIntoshs (1980: vol. 2, 445) have commented on the presence of copper at Jenné-jeno from the middle of the first millennium AD; the three closest known sources are all in the Sahara. The McIntoshs could well have been correct when they argued that 'the rapid establishment and expansion of Arab trade in the Western Sudan was possible because it keyed into an already-extant system of indigenous sub-Saharan trade networks' (McIntosh and McIntosh 1980: vol. 2, 450).

Conclusion

The emergence of urbanism and political centralization in the West African savanna was formerly attributed to contact with the Mediterranean world, resulting from long-distance trade. Suspiciously, the origins of that trade were usually dated to the period of the earliest historical sources that touched on the subject. Archaeology tended to play a confirmatory role in the stock historical interpretation. It was a case of so much historical information being available that archaeologists failed to ask the sort of questions that they might have asked otherwise. As a result, the quality of the archaeological data available to shed light on the origins of cities and states in the West African savanna was poor. This situation has now changed, and work at Jenné-jeno and related sites in the Inland Niger Delta, as well as in other parts of the West African savanna, has produced a very different picture. A review of the evidence makes the long-accepted external-stimulus explanation untenable. It would appear that the West African savanna by the beginning of the first millennium AD already had a sound agricultural base, with the potential for intensification of production in some more fortunate areas, and already had a varied iron-based technology. Developing social complexity is already evident at Dhar Tichitt as early as the second millennium BC, and it seems quite probable that during the first millennium AD, and prior to Arab contact, stratified societies were emerging in the West African savanna, based on resource control stimulated in part by localized population pressures. At the same time those pressures, coupled with increasing functional specialization and expanding local trade, encouraged a growth in size both of individual settlements and of aggregations of settlements, leading to some of West Africa's earliest examples of urbanism. Such developments seem to have taken place before the advent of Islam but, nevertheless, with the ideological support of a variety of animistic religions. Finally, it seems most likely that an extensive trading network existed within West Africa before the Arab trade across the Sahara began and that this network had already developed contacts across the desert. The cities and towns of the savanna were indeed to become 'ports' at the edge of the 'sea of sand', as Levtzion (1973: 10) said (p. 155), but they were ports with a vast trading hinterland that already existed. After all, what ship would ever visit a port unless there was a chance of delivering or collecting a cargo?

Chapter 7

Achieving power: the West African forest and its fringes

In the second half of the fifteenth-century AD European sailors first set eyes on the southerly coast of West Africa. What they saw was hardly encouraging: from a distance, a vague grey line pencilled in between an immensity of sea and sky; from close-in, either a dangerous, surf-pounded, sandy beach or an uninviting network of mangrove swamp, creek, and river mouth. Whatever the character of the shoreline, however, behind it there was nearly always an impenetrable tangle of trees and other vegetation. Experience soon taught such visitors that this was a coast to be reckoned with: ships' crews died of fever, and shipworms (*Teredo* spp.) ate the bottoms out of their ships. Yet it was neither altruism nor curiosity that tempted most Europeans to such a region; it was profit. The very names they gave to different parts of this coast indicate their motives: 'The Grain [pepper] Coast', 'The Ivory Coast', 'The Gold Coast', 'The Slave Coast' (Bosman 1967: frontispiece map). Europeans quickly discovered that behind the coast lay a forested and savanna hinterland rich in resources, where the inhabitants were willing to trade on a considerable scale. Not only that, but those inhabitants lived in highly organized communities, some of which took on a size and density which left the visitors in no doubt about what they were dealing with. Within some parts of the West African forest and its fringes there were, indeed, hierarchical states, towns, and cities. Because of their conspicuousness, it was these large settlements that particularly attracted European attention. Thus, writing in AD 1507–8, the Portuguese Duarte Pacheco Pereira described Ijebu-Ode (now in Nigeria) as 'a very large city' (Bascom 1959: 38). In a similar vein, the Englishman Towerson, writing in 1557, could claim, perhaps with some exaggeration, that a town in what is now Ghana was 'by the estimation of our men, as big in circuit as London' (Blake 1942: vol. 2, 406).

These quotations are selected from early in the history of European West African contact, because state development and urbanization in the West African forest and its margins have sometimes been written about as if they were developments resulting from that contact rather than pre-dating it. Although there is no doubt that European seaborne trade did play an important part in the later development of these states and their towns and cities, historical sources suggest that some were in existence before that trade started. Oral traditions give a similar impression, and, since the middle of the twentieth century, archaeological evidence has pointed in the same direction. It seems likely that there was increasing social complexity in some parts of the West African forest and its fringes from late in the first millennium AD onwards. The question is why should such developments take place in and around the West African rainforest, environments that to many outsiders have seemed to constrain rather than to encourage human endeavour?

Geographical location and environmental factors

Compared with the West African savanna (Chapter 6), the tropical rainforest of West Africa occupies a relatively small area. An extension of the equatorial rainforest, it stretches from Cameroon to Sierra Leone but is broken between the western frontier of Nigeria and eastern Ghana by a gap where forest–savanna mosaic and relatively moist woodlands and savanna reach the ocean. This is known as 'The Dahomey Gap' and its alternating absence and presence in the past indicates the role of climatic change in determining the extent of the rainforest (Salzmann and Hoelzmann 2005). At present, the belt of rainforest is never wider than 400 kilometres, and in many places it is narrower. To the south it is bounded by coastal mangrove swamp or by the Atlantic Ocean. To the north it merges into forest–savanna mosaic, often called 'derived savanna' because it has been thought to result from agricultural exploitation, over many centuries, of what was originally tropical rainforest. This would suggest high population densities, although (as with the Dahomey Gap) climatic change is also likely to have been an important factor. Whatever the cause, these northern fringes of the forest form an ecotone that has been particularly important in the history of the human race in West Africa. It is therefore impractical to consider the West African rainforest without giving attention to the adjacent savanna into which it merges.

As recently as the middle of the twentieth century the West African forest, where undisturbed, consisted of dense tropical rainforest. A few large trees grew to a height of about 42 metres and many others to a height of about 27 metres, but they protruded above the main leaf canopy that was formed at about 10 metres by most of the trees. Smaller trees and bushes densely occupied the zone below. It is possible that in its natural state the forest often lacked this dense tangle of lower growth, and the forest floor may have been relatively easy to traverse (Richards 1952: fig. 6, pp. 29–31). However, much of the forest has now been taken over by secondary growth, often of no great height but virtually impenetrable unless one chops a path through with a machete. To some extent, this results from modern timber exploitation, but even at the beginning of the twentieth century Thompson (1910–11: 131) recorded that most of the forest consisted of secondary growth. It seems probable that this situation resulted from the long practice of rotational bush-fallow agriculture. In the area around Benin City, for instance, it was shown during the 1960s that most of the apparently 'well-grown forest of considerable age' had probably 'been farmed at one time or another during the past few hundred years' (Allison 1962: 243, 244). The secondary growth that has resulted is so dense that Boisragon and Locke, fleeing for their lives after the so-called Benin Massacre in 1897, found it very difficult to travel through the forest, which was 'so thick that neither man nor beast can press through it' (Boisragon 1897: 94). An 1817 account of part of the Asante forest, in what is now Ghana, by Bowdich (1966: 20–1), indicated the problems of travel even when fear was not forcing a cross-country route. Descriptions such as these make it difficult to understand how the West African rainforest could have been the setting for the cultural developments that undoubtedly took place there.

In reality, the forest is much more complex and varied than descriptions by culture-shocked Europeans, writing to impress other Europeans, have often made it appear. In the area around Benin City, for example, it seems that vegetation on the upper interfluves might originally have been less dense than that of the lower valley slopes, and it has been shown that farming has tended to concentrate on those more easily cleared areas. Darling suggested that the forest environment around Benin varied in part because of the ever-changing mosaic of plant succession following agricultural clearance and fallowing, but also in part because of differences in soil characteristics. In addition, if we consider local perceptions of the environment, we find not the European notion of continuous forest broken only by clearings for settlements but a three-part division of the 'forest' itself into farmlands, fallow areas, and 'wild' forest. It is also possible that forest density has varied through time. Both climatic change and human activity could have resulted in more open conditions in the past. This is suggested by some historical accounts and by the extensive earthworks in the Benin City region, discussed later in this chapter. These ditches and banks are virtually invisible in dense rainforest or regrowth and must have been constructed when there was far less vegetation cover than in recent times; otherwise, they would have been of little use as boundaries (von Hellermann 2010).

In one respect the forest has an advantage over the savanna to its north: it has more water. Rainfall is higher, the wet season longer, humidity greater, and evapotranspiration lower. As a result, the forest has numerous rivers and streams, many of which flow all the year round. Also as a result, the rate and ease of vegetal growth is phenomenal; even fences take root and grow into thriving hedges or rows of trees. It is apparent that many forest soils are moderately fertile, if this is measured in terms of productivity. This is providing that farming practices minimize erosion and alternate brief cropping periods with long periods of fallow, during which the 'bush' is allowed to invade the fields.

Many resources would probably have been available in the West African forest and its fringes 2,000 to 3,000 years ago. The most significant would have been plant foods, including several species of yam, the oil palm, kola, coffee, okra, fluted gourd, and *akee* (a tree cultivated for its fruit). At the western end of the forest belt there might also have been African rice and Melegueta pepper, the so-called Grains of Paradise (Harris 1976: 329–33). Introduced plants of South-East Asian and tropical American origin (such as certain yams, plantain, banana, sugarcane, citrus fruits, cassava, sweet potato, maize, papaw, and chilli pepper) have become so important now in this region that it is easy to forget that the West African forest and its edges were already well endowed with plant foods before these others arrived. Particularly important amongst the indigenous plants would have been the various West African yams and the oil palm, the former providing carbohydrates and the latter supplementing these with both fat and vitamin A (Harris 1976: 351). It should be noticed, however, that both yams and oil palms seem originally to have belonged in the forest–savanna ecotone and must have been introduced to the forest proper by people planting them on cleared land. Thus Coursey's West African 'yam zone' (Fig. 6.1) includes extensive areas of the southern savanna as well as the more northerly parts of the forest (Coursey 1980: Fig. 1). In contrast to plant foods, the forest was not so well provided with animal foods as was the savanna. Tsetse flies precluded the keeping of domesticated livestock in the forest, with the exception of small numbers of trypanosomiasis-resistant dwarf goats and cattle (Blench 1993). Furthermore, the forest had fewer wild animals that could be hunted than did the savanna, although a wide selection of those that were present have probably been eaten in the past, including elephants, baboons, monkeys, bats, large rats, the giant land snail (*Achatina* spp.), and anything else that could be caught. In addition, fish from the sea, coastal lagoons, and rivers have almost certainly been an important source of animal protein for a long time. The forest also possessed numerous other resources, of which perhaps the most important were a great many types of wood, suitable for everything from house building to canoe making to carving to firewood. Various sorts of wood could also be burnt to produce charcoal, potash, salt, and other things. In addition, the forest could supply numerous medicinal substances, beeswax, gum, bark, rope, and other commodities. There was also ivory; inorganic raw materials included gold, iron ore, copper, lead, rocks suitable for making grindstones, good building earths, and potting clays. Last, a population density that in places was probably higher than in the more northerly savanna could be exploited as a source of slaves.

The West African forest zone and its edges suffered from constraints as well as benefiting from substantial resources. The most serious constraints were diseases that included trypanosomiasis that afflicted domestic animals and, as sleeping sickness, humans as well. The latter was only part of a heavy burden of human diseases; malaria, in particular, has been so serious a problem for so long a time that some populations in the region have developed a greater than normal incidence of the sickle-cell gene, a blood anomaly that provides a measure of protection (Livingstone 1967). Other serious diseases included yellow fever, dengue fever, filariasis, yaws, and a wide selection of parasitic infections, particularly of the intestinal tract. Disease levels in these areas might have been higher than those of the more northerly, drier savanna. Another constraint within the forest and forest–savanna mosaic was the availability of water during the dry season. In spite of a greater rainfall than most of the savanna, a long dry season together with generally permeable soils and high temperatures on cleared surfaces meant that women and children frequently had to carry water long distances from rivers and streams. Various strategies were used to alleviate this problem, including wells, underground cisterns, and even artificial ponds. The extent to which dry-season water supply could be a problem, however, particularly for large groups of people on the move, is illustrated by the experience of the British expedition against Benin City in 1897, for which water was a major worry (Home 1982). That same expedition also showed how difficult communication within the forest could be, with movement restricted to narrow paths and head loading the only means of shifting burdens. Communication problems have, indeed, been another traditional constraint, particularly during the wet season when paths are frequently reduced to rivers of mud. Nevertheless, the people who lived in and around the forest adapted well to such difficulties. Thus canoe transport on rivers and coastal lagoons was extremely important, and the very impenetrability of parts of the forest could be used as a defence by leaving a ring of uncleared land around settlements, as was recorded in the nineteenth century for the 'war-towns' of Sierra Leone (Siddle 1968).

To people not accustomed to living in the West African forest and forest fringes, the constraints might seem sufficient discouragement from developing the undoubted resources. However, states, cities, and other aspects of cultural complexity did develop in some parts of those zones, and these developments probably commenced without external stimulus, because both distance and environment attenuated influences from the northern savanna and Sahel. Nevertheless, by the end of the first millennium AD the forest and forest–savanna ecotone were probably linked with the regions to their north in a regional trading network (Insoll 1996b: 668; Casey 2010). Only the appearance of European traders on the coast of West Africa reversed this economic orientation and turned what had been a relatively remote hinterland into a major contact zone of long-distance trade.

Sources of information

Historical evidence

Most of what is known about precolonial urbanization and state formation in the West African forest and its fringes comes from historical sources. Numerous contemporary accounts by European visitors from the late fifteenth to the late nineteenth century represent the outsider's view. These visitors were of different national backgrounds: in particular, Portuguese, English, Dutch, French, Danish, and German; and of a variety of professions, including sailors, traders, explorers, and missionaries. To their number must be added others who merely stayed at home and compiled books and maps from information supplied by those who had actually visited the Guinea Coast. Some of the principal accounts by outsiders are those by Adams, Barbot, de Barros, Bosman, Bowdich, Burton, Dapper, de Marees, Landolphe, and Pacheco Pereira. Such sources throw light on some of the societies of the West African forest and its fringes during the 400 years prior to colonial takeover. A.F.C. Ryder, for instance, was able to use them as the main basis for a study of European relationships with the state of Benin (Ryder 1969). They are limited, however, not only by their sometimes imperfect understanding of what was observed but also by their short time range. Whereas external sources for the West African savanna reach back for a little over a thousand years, those for the forest zone and related areas cover only half that time. Fortunately, however, they are complemented by the insider's view, represented by the oral traditions of West African societies themselves. European scholars collected many of these in recent times, but the people to whom they refer also recorded some of them. Perhaps the most notable of these are Samuel Johnson's *History of the Yorubas*, originally published in 1921 (Johnson 1921), and Jacob Egharevba's *Short History of Benin*, first published in 1934 (Egharevba 1968). Such sources do throw a little light on the centuries before Europeans appeared on the Guinea Coast; they take us back perhaps to the beginning of the second millennium AD. Unfortunately, however, their information on the earlier periods is limited and of doubtful reliability. Their chronologies are particularly uncertain, as Bradbury demonstrated in the case of Benin City (Bradbury 1959). Overall, therefore, the written and oral historical sources have comparatively little to tell us about the origins of cities and states in the forest and adjacent savanna, except that such developments either took place during or had already taken place by the first half of the second millennium AD. From such sources, it has sometimes been implied that these developments were later than those of the savanna because it took longer for long-distance trade and postulated migrations to reach so far into the hinterland. In other words, as in the savanna, external stimulus has been advanced as an explanation, an explanation now thought to be unacceptable.

Archaeological evidence

Archaeological research, concerning recent millennia, commenced later in the West African rainforest and its margins than further north. Nevertheless, there has been a similar tendency to pursue research programmes aimed at providing more information on historically known sites. Archaeological field prospection and survey is so difficult in the forest itself that sites are not easily found; it is easier to excavate sites that are known from documentary sources or oral traditions. Patrick Darling's work on the linear earthworks of Benin and Ishan (Darling 1984; 1988; 1998) is one of the few cases where systematic search has revealed previously unknown sites. Also, the artwork associated with some of the historically known sites of southern Nigeria has often concentrated archaeological attention on those sites, such as at Ife (Willett 1967). As a result, archaeological field research and excavation has been limited to relatively few sites, particularly in Ghana and Nigeria, although there has also been activity in Sierra Leone and the Republic of Benin. More recently, increasing attention has been given to urban and state developments during the second half of the second millennium AD. The archaeological evidence is more visible than that for earlier periods, and associated documentary and oral sources enhance its interpretation, suggesting the ways in which earlier developments might have taken place.

Some of the archaeological evidence relevant to the origins of urbanization and state formation in the forest and its fringes comes from investigations into the Akan states, in what is now Ghana. These have been described as city-states, which collectively comprised a city-state culture (Kea 2000). James Anquandah (1982: 85–112) described the Akan as 'a golden civilization'; these states seem to have controlled part of the gold trade from the forest north to the Inland Niger Delta. The Akan states already existed by the beginning of the eighteenth century AD when they were mentioned by European visitors, and a considerable amount is known about the last major Akan state, that of Asante, in the eighteenth and nineteenth centuries (McLeod 1981). The earlier of these states were situated on the fringes of the forest, and archaeological investigations at the site of Begho, in this region, have revealed the remains of a large market town made up of four different 'quarters', which were 1 to 2 kilometres from one another (Posnansky 1987; 2010). These constituted a dispersed pattern of residence, probably subject to episodic mobility (Fletcher 1998). Each of these quarters consists of a group of mounds, about 1.5 metres high and 30 metres across, which are often L-shaped and which are in most cases the remains of mud-walled houses. Some 1,500 of these mounds have been counted, enabling Anquandah (1993: 648) to estimate that the population of Begho peaked at 10,000 in the seventeenth century AD, when the densest area of settlement covered about 3 square kilometres. At first, oral tradition and radiocarbon dates indicated that the town was occupied between about 1400 and 1725, being most prosperous towards the beginning of the seventeenth century, but radiocarbon dates from subsequent excavations indicated that settlement probably began as early as the eleventh or twelfth century (Posnansky and McIntosh 1976: 166, 189). Excavation of some of the house mounds has yielded evidence of a population engaged in metallurgical, textile, and ceramic industries, supported by an agricultural subsistence economy that included domestic cattle, sheep, goats, and pigs and by a substantial long-distance trade (Anquandah 1993: 649).

At Bono Manso (Fig. 7.1), another town site in the same region, occupation appears to have commenced about the thirteenth century and to have continued until about the middle of the eighteenth century (Effah-Gyamfi 1985). This seems to have been a more nucleated settlement than Begho and perhaps more homogeneous in its ethnic composition, for there was a separate settlement of aliens (probably Muslim merchants) about 4 kilometres away at Kramokrom. Like Begho, numerous small mounds, most representing the remains of houses from which population estimates could be made, characterized Bono Manso. Archaeological investigations, including excavation, showed that Phase I of the settlement had occupied a more extensive area than Phases II and III but that its population, estimated at about 4,000, had actually been lower than the approximately 10,000 and 8,000 estimated, respectively, for the two later phases. A dispersed pattern of residence had apparently changed to a more compact one, perhaps reflecting sociopolitical changes (Effah-Gyamfi 1985). This contraction to a more densely occupied form of settlement is of considerable theoretical interest because, according to Fletcher's 'interaction-communication model', 'Bono Manso contracted to precisely the maximum areal extent at which it could have been nonliterate and permanently sedentary' (Fletcher 1998: 125).

Thus Begho and Bono Manso do throw some light on the origins of urbanization, and perhaps of state formation, on the fringes of the Ghanaian forest during the early second millennium AD. Furthermore, excavations at Adansemanso and Asantemanso (Fig. 7.2) provided evidence of settlement growth within the forest itself from the late first millennium AD onwards, suggesting even earlier developments (Vivian 1996; Shinnie 2005). Also, the second phase of a site some 150 kilometres further north at New Buipe represents an

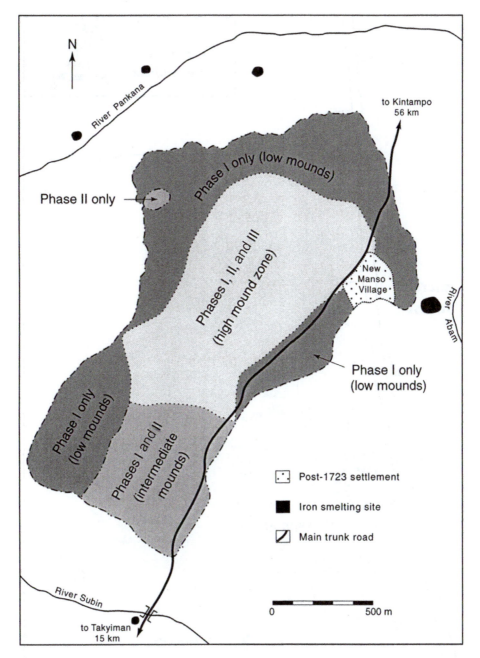

Fig. 7.1 Plan of the site of Bono Manso, in Ghana, indicating a change from a dispersed pattern of residence to a more compact one. After Effah-Gyamfi 1979: fig. 2.

iron-using community late in the first millennium AD. Consisting of three mounds with a total diameter of less than 200 metres, they seem to have been part of a larger complex (York 1973). It might also be significant that the area

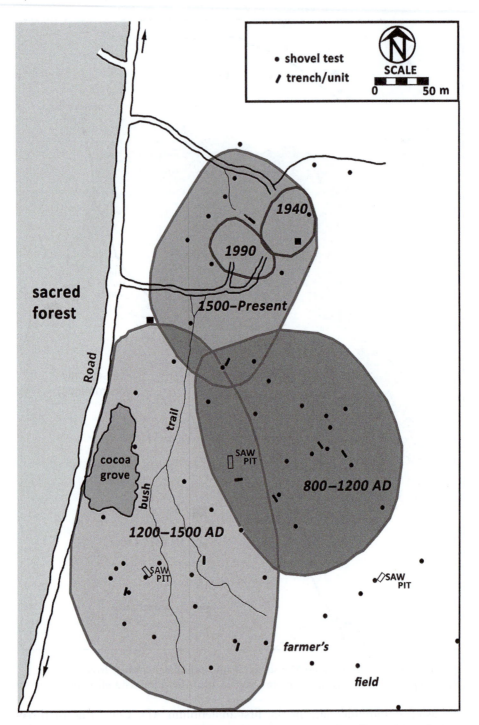

Fig. 7.2 Plan of the site of Asantemanso, in Ghana, showing areas of occupation during different periods. After Shinnie 2005: fig. 1. (Redrawn by Andrew Stawowczyk Long.)

of the early Akan states on the forest fringes (the centre of Akan power shifted into the forest proper only after European contact) is the same area that provided most of the evidence for the early food-producing Kintampo Tradition of the late third to late second millennium BC (Watson 2010). In addition, it is an area rich in iron ore and has produced a second-century AD radiocarbon date for iron smelting at Hani, near Begho (Posnansky and McIntosh 1976) and a fourth-century radiocarbon date for an iron-smelting site adjacent to Bono Manso (Effah-Gyamfi 1985: 204). The problem is linking such earlier evidence to the growth of urban communities in the second millennium AD. This is in spite of excavations by Shinnie and Kense (1989) at the town site of Daboya, on the White Volta River further north in the savanna. Occupied during the last 4,000 years or so, its earliest evidence for iron was in about the middle of the first millennium BC. A source of salt, Daboya probably became a link in an extensive trading network. However, much later evidence from the Republic of Benin, dating from the seventeenth to nineteenth centuries AD, shows how urban and state development could occur in this region. Albeit spurred by the European-sponsored Atlantic trade, the growth of urban centres, particularly at Abomey (Fig. 7.3) and Cana, and the emergence of the states of Dahomey, Allada, and Hueda provide a model for sociopolitical changes that might also have occurred earlier than archaeological evidence presently indicates (Monroe 2012; 2014).

Other important archaeological evidence relevant to urbanization and the growth of the state in the West African forest and forest fringes relates to the Yoruba people of south-western Nigeria, many of whose larger settlements were individual city-states that collectively constituted a city-state culture (Peel 2000). As Bascom wrote: 'They are undoubtedly the most urban of all African peoples' (Bascom 1955: 446). Studies of this phenomenon, however, have concentrated on historical sources, most of which are of nineteenth-century date. There has been less concern about origins, probably because many people assume that the impressive urban developments in most cases do not predate 1800. Indeed, the early-nineteenth-century Fulani attacks on northern Yorubaland, and the Yoruba civil wars that followed, do seem to have played a substantial part in the development of the urban pattern that now exists. Nevertheless, some large urban centres, such as Ijebu-Ode, clearly did exist amongst the Yoruba at an earlier date (Fletcher 1998: 128), and archaeological investigations are beginning to show this. Excavation and oral tradition have also indicated that Early Osogbo, a small town on the Upper Osun River, originated in the late sixteenth century (Ogundiran 2014). Particularly important, however, were the excavations and survey during the 1970s by Robert Soper at the site of Old Oyo, in the southern savanna, which as the capital of a large Yoruba state was at the

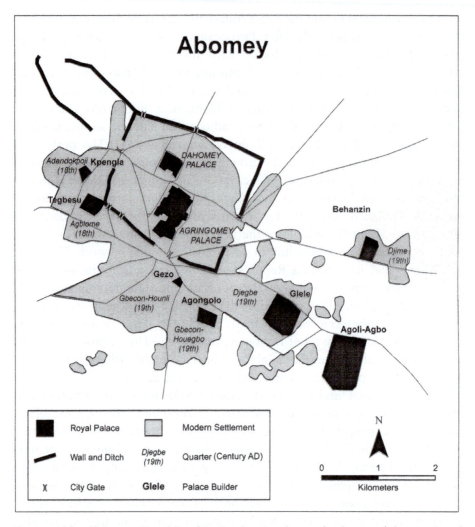

Fig. 7.3 Plan of Abomey, Republic of Benin, showing the royal palaces and the remains of the bank and ditch system. After Monroe 2014: fig. 5.5.

height of its power in the seventeenth and eighteenth centuries AD. In common with many Yoruba towns and cities (Usman 2004), Old Oyo was surrounded by a complex of earthen banks and ditches, from a study of which Soper and Darling (1980) were able to gain some idea of the shape of the former settlement and to suggest a tentative relative chronology for its development (Fig. 7.4). Soper (1993) also surveyed the site of the ruler's palace within Old Oyo and showed how closely its plan compared with that of the pre-1979 parts of the palace in the present city of Oyo, which lies about 130 kilometres to the south. Radiocarbon dates from the excavations

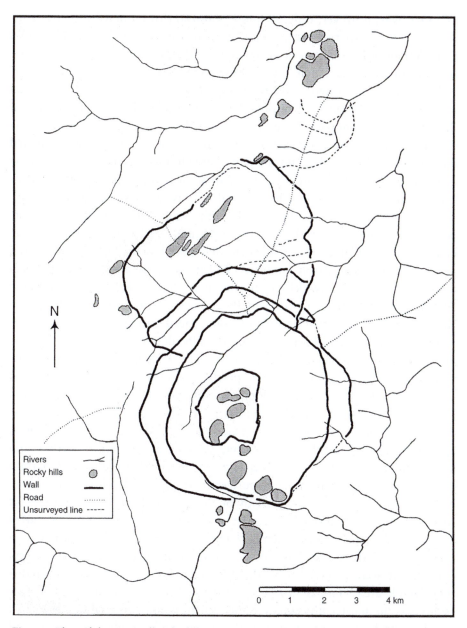

Fig. 7.4 Plan of the city walls of Old Oyo, Nigeria. After Soper and Darling 1980: fig. 1.

at Old Oyo indicate the existence of a substantial settlement of more than
1 square kilometre as early as the twelfth century AD (and perhaps as early as
the eighth century), which apparently pre-dated the earthwork complex
(Calvocoressi and David 1979: 19–20, 27; Agbaje-Williams 1990: 369).

Old Oyo was, however, only the most important of numerous towns aban-
doned in the southern savanna as a result of the Fulani attacks. Near Old
Oyo, Agbaje-Williams (1990) drew attention to the sites of Koso and Ipapo
Ile, both of which have defensive earthworks.

Even now Yoruba towns and cities tend to be concentrated in the transitional
zone between grassland and forest. Archaeologically, the most important of
those in the northern part of the forest itself is Ife, where according to Yoruba
traditions the world was created. Ife has remained of spiritual and ceremonial
importance to the Yoruba, and the remarkable terracottas, copper-based alloy
castings, and stone sculptures discovered there since the beginning of the twentieth century have focused archaeological activity on this site (Willett 1967).
The art itself suggests emerging social stratification, for some of it represents
personages of importance (Fig. 7.5); in addition, art on such a scale implies
patronage, particularly because the items of copper-based alloys are made from
materials that were probably imported (Willett and Sayre 2006). Excavations in
the present city of Ife (which covers the area of the ancient city), by Frank
Willett, Ekpo Eyo (Eyo 1974), and Peter Garlake, produced a radiocarbon
chronology suggesting that occupation commenced during the late first millennium AD. Archaeological deposits at Ife are difficult to excavate, and rarely has
mud walling been isolated in the generally shallow deposits. Nevertheless, the
excavation of pavements of edge-laid potsherds and small stones has provided
some indication of the layout of domestic buildings (Willett 1967: figs. 16 and
17, plate 66; Garlake 1974: figs. 3 and 4; 1977: figs. 4 and 8). The main period
during which such pavements were made has been dated by radiocarbon to
approximately the twelfth to the fifteenth century, and both radiocarbon and
thermoluminescence dates have been used to suggest that the most important
period of Ife art was in the late fourteenth to early fifteenth century. Little,
however, can be said of the growth of the city itself, although a series of
concentric city walls (Fig. 7.6) suggests several phases in which the city grew
up around the palace of the ruler (Ozanne 1969). These walls have not been
adequately dated, and at least some of them belonged to only the last few
centuries. It seems, nevertheless, that the ancient city must have covered a
considerable area. Garlake (1977: 92) suggested that it was probably at least
as large as the nineteenth-century walled town, because two of the excavated
sites lie outside the western wall of that town while another lies beside and
just beyond the eastern wall. He also claimed: 'There are strong indications
that buildings were sufficiently compact and close together for the settlement
to be ranked as urban.' In addition, this was an urban development with a
thriving technological base, not only in metal casting but also in other activities,
probably including the manufacture of glass from its primary materials
(Freestone 2006; Lankton et al. 2006; Babalola 2011).

Fig. 7.5 'Bronze' casting of an Oni of Ife. Height 467 millimetres. The Frank Willett Collection. Image courtesy of The Hunterian, University of Glasgow 2014.

More archaeological evidence relevant to the present discussion comes from Benin City, also in southern Nigeria. Benin (not to be confused with the Republic of Benin) is archaeologically fascinating not only because it is deep

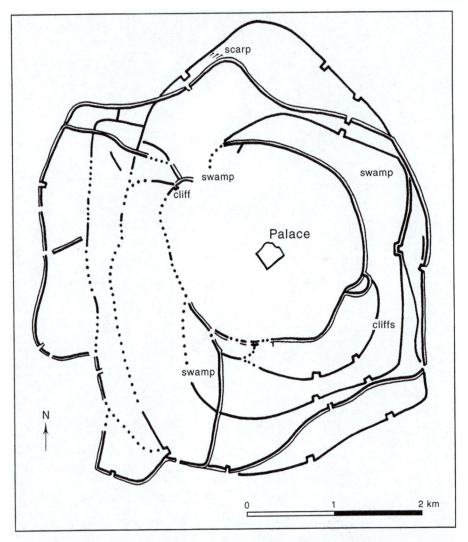

Fig. 7.6 Plan of Ife city walls, Nigeria. Single lines represent earlier walls, double lines later walls. After Ozanne 1969.

within the rainforest but also because its origins are still unclear. Excavations during the 1950s by Goodwin (1957) and by myself during the 1960s (Connah 1975) revealed substantial post-European-contact deposits (i.e. dating from after the late fifteenth century AD) on the site of the old palace. However, my own work also demonstrated occupation of the city by about the thirteenth century. The principal evidence for this consisted of radiocarbon dates for a mass burial of at least forty-one young women, who lay at a depth of more than 12.5 metres in a narrow, well-like cistern (Fig. 7.7). Wearing clothing, bracelets, finger rings, and beads, they appeared to have been dropped down the deep

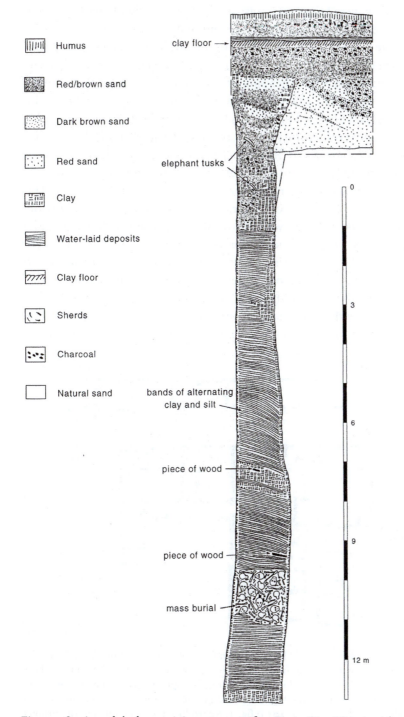

Humus

Red/brown sand

Dark brown sand

Red sand

Clay

Water-laid deposits

Clay floor

Sherds

Charcoal

Natural sand

clay floor →

elephant tusks

bands of alternating clay and silt

piece of wood

piece of wood

mass burial

0

3

6

9

12 m

Fig. 7.7 Section of shaft containing mass sacrifice, Benin City, Nigeria. After Connah 1975: fig. 18.

shaft in which they were found and must surely represent ritual sacrifice indicative of centralized authority, particularly as the shaft lay within the area of the old palace. There is documentary evidence for throwing the bodies of sacrificial victims into such pits as late as 1897 (Roth 1903). Deep beneath the modern city of Benin there must surely be other similar pits, and it is possible that some of them could be older than the one excavated. The 1960s excavations also showed that edge-laid potsherd pavements had been made in Benin City during or prior to the fourteenth century AD, a practice that appears to have ended before European contact. As at Ife, such pavements suggest the existence of formal architecture. Indeed, there is ethnohistoric, ethnographic, and archaeological evidence for postcontact architecture in coursed mud in Benin City. This was distinguished by tall, steep-roofed entrances (Fagg 1963: plate 35); horizontally grooved, polished red mud walls (Connah 1975: plates 8 and 17); and a plan in which rooms were arranged around a series of rectangular courtyards open to the sky, called impluvia (Roth 1903: figs. 180 and 185; Connah 1975: plate 1). An important example of a chief's house, which survived a fire that destroyed much of the city at the time of its British conquest in 1897, is Ogiamien's House, with its formal plan of rooms built in coursed mud that combined domestic and symbolic-sacred functions (Fig. 7.8). Its 'location and

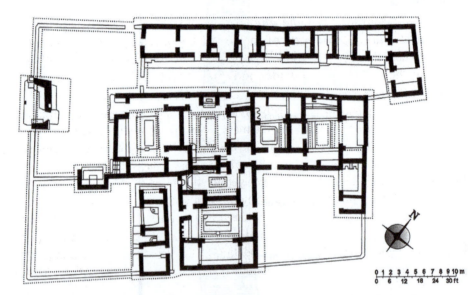

Fig. 7.8 Ground plan of Ogiamien's House, Benin City, Nigeria. Solid black indicates coursed mud walls of the main structure, open lines are compound walls, dotted lines show roof edges, and some other lines within rooms represent impluvia. The main entrance is to the left, and the row of rooms at the top are wives' quarters, with a menstruation room at the extreme right. Nevadomsky et al. 2014: fig. 1. Reproduced with permission of Springer Science+Business Media, New York, and Copyright Clearance Center's RightsLink.

design' have been claimed as 'roughly a thousand years old' (Nevadomsky et al. 2014: 67), but there is no archaeological evidence for such antiquity. Attempts to improve the dating of this house are overdue and might include dendrochronology of its major timber components or thermoluminescence of samples from its mud-wall cores.

Also important are the so-called Benin City walls, the innermost of which has been demonstrated by radiocarbon dating, historical documentation, and oral tradition to have been constructed before European contact, possibly around the middle of the fifteenth century (Connah 1975). Consisting of a massive earthen bank and ditch, with a total vertical height, from the excavated bottom of the ditch to the top of the surviving bank, of as much as 17.4 metres and a circumference of 11.6 kilometres, this earthwork represents an enormous investment of human effort that must have been directed by a powerful centralized authority. Calculations have suggested that its construction would have absorbed 5,000 people occupied for ten hours a day, if it had been completed in one dry season, or 1,000 people if spread over five dry seasons. The direction of labour on such a massive project must have implications of the greatest significance for our enquiry into state formation. That is not the whole story, however, because surveys by myself during the 1960s in the tangled vegetation around Benin City revealed a vast network of further interlocking enclosures, consisting of more than 145 kilometres of earthworks. These appeared to hint at a process of synoecism ('the union of several towns or villages into or under one capital city' (*Oxford English Dictionary* 1933)) by which a group of villages had developed into a city, at a date prior to the construction of the innermost and most massive of the 'walls'.

Subsequent work by Darling (1984; 1988; 1998) and by others (Maliphant et al. 1976; Roese 1981) showed that even this outer network mapped by me (Connah 1975) was only a small peripheral part of more extensive rural earthwork enclosures. These cover an area of about 6,500 square kilometres, with an estimated total length in excess of 16,000 kilometres (Fig. 7.9). At least 150,000,000 person-hours of work over several centuries are implied. As Darling showed, these earthworks probably have more to tell us about the process of state formation (reflecting power struggles for agricultural land) than about the urban origins of Benin City itself. Indeed, on the basis of the distribution and character of the earthworks and of a statistical analysis of surface-collected potsherds, he proposed a settlement model for both the Benin area and that of Ishan to its north from the late first millennium AD onwards. He argued that there was 'a strong southward colonization by savannah/savannah–forest ecotone Edo speakers [Edo is the language of Benin] into the rainforest'. The area over which this movement is thought to have taken place has a dense network of enclosures, 'whereas there is an almost total

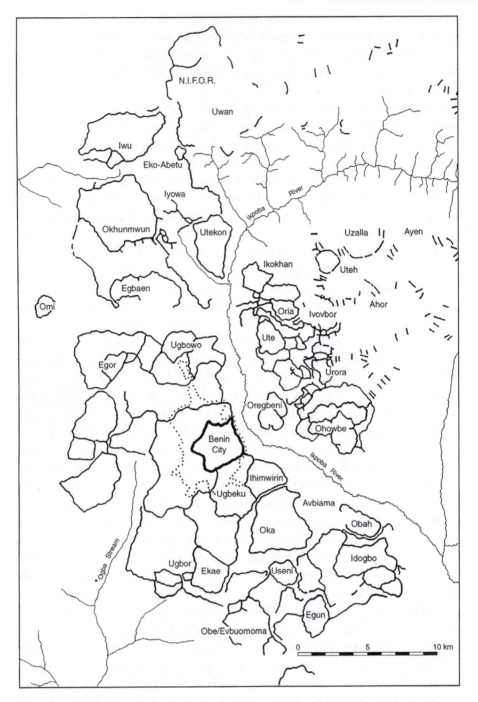

Fig. 7.9 Earthwork enclosures in the Benin City area. Dotted line indicates limits of modern city in the 1960s to 1970s. After Darling 1982.

absence of them amongst the Urhobo speakers' just to the south (Darling 1988: 122–3). Darling could well be right, but as he admitted, his archaeological survey remains 'largely undated' (Darling 1988: 133). It is regrettable that a satisfactory series of radiocarbon dates for the land surfaces beneath these earthworks has still not been obtained. Six radiocarbon determinations are available, but two of them give 'modern' dates, one gives a nineteenth-century date, and three give dates in the thirteenth to fifteenth centuries (Sutton 1982: 309, 312). Furthermore, the other radiocarbon dates for Benin City, obtained by myself in the 1960s, need to be replaced by modern assessments now that techniques have improved so greatly.

Chronological problems also remain regarding the artistic use of copper-base alloys in Benin. My excavations of the 1960s showed that these materials were used artistically as early as the thirteenth century AD, but those excavations recovered no evidence of casting these metals prior to European contact. In spite of the numerous artistic studies that have been made of the famous Benin castings (e.g., Forman et al. 1960; Dark 1973), we still have little evidence about their detailed chronology. In view of the implications of these castings, indicating both an hierarchical power structure and considerable artistic patronage, it is unfortunate that so few have been recovered from controlled stratigraphic excavations. Although a small number of Benin castings have been dated on the basis of the thermoluminescence of fired clay core remaining within them, they were all found to date from about the fifteenth century AD or later (Willett and Fleming 1976). Nevertheless, stable lead isotope analysis indicated that the source of the metal used in both Ife and during an early period in Benin was faraway France (Willet and Sayre 2006: 77), an indication of the extent of the trading networks in which these cities participated.

A question concerning Benin City and the state of which it formed the capital is whether they were always within the rainforest. As von Hellermann (2010) suggested, it is possible that forest density has varied through time; both climatic change and human activity could have created more open conditions in the past (p. 187). Talbot and Delibrias (1977) found evidence of drier conditions between 700 and 200 years ago in their investigations of Lake Bosumtwi, in Ghana, and some historical accounts support their interpretation. In addition, the extensive earthworks in the Benin City region discussed above are useless as boundaries in the heavily overgrown conditions in which many are now situated. The ditches and banks are virtually invisible in dense rainforest or regrowth. They must have been constructed when there was far less vegetation cover than at present. Rees (in Connah 1975: 237–42) raised the possibility of a formerly different environment in an area of forest near Benin City that was cleared for planting oil palms; he found pits and mounds as well as earthworks, indicating denser settlement in the past. Technology now exists in the form of aerial LiDAR (light detection and ranging) that can see through the vegetation in order to investigate this possibility (Eve 2014).

Archaeological evidence seemingly irrelevant to state formation and urbanization comes from Igbo-Ukwu, east of the River Niger in Nigeria. This is in an area occupied by the Igbo people, who have long interested anthropologists precisely because they developed neither cities nor states until recent times, in spite of a high population density. As late as the 1930s the Igbo could still boast that 'there is no one who owns us' (that is to say: we have no rulers), and their society remained characterized by 'a dispersal rather than a concentration of authority' (Green 1947: 145, 73). What, then, is one to make of Igbo-Ukwu, where the burial of a clearly important individual (Fig. 7.10), a repository of sophisticated regalia, and a ritual pit produced, amongst other things, 685 copper and bronze objects and some 165,000 stone and glass beads? Thurstan Shaw, the excavator of this site, suggested that this indicates the former existence of a local 'priest king' who was the holder of a politico-ritual title in the democratized title-taking system of this area (Shaw 1970; 1977). Some ethnohistorical evidence supports this interpretation, although it is uncertain whether this should be applied to archaeological data a thousand years old. This date, at the end of the first millennium AD, is based on radiocarbon dates that were formerly the subject of argument, but subsequently there was a greater readiness to accept them (Posnansky 1980). The approximately tenth-century date for the Igbo-Ukwu evidence is of importance not only because of the sophisticated metallurgy and unique art forms but also because it implies early trading connections between the West African rainforest and the Mediterranean or even India. Analyses have shown that some of the copper and copper alloy probably came from the lead, zinc, and copper deposits of the Benue Rift, only 100 kilometres to the east of the site (Chikwendu et al. 1989), where there is evidence of mining dating to the end of the first millennium AD (Craddock et al. 1997). Nevertheless, stable lead isotope analysis indicated that some of the metal came from Tunisia or Morocco (Willet and Sayre 2006: 77), and the glass and carnelian beads must have resulted from trade either across the Sahara or east-west through the Sahel. Indeed, Insoll (1996a: 80) suggested that elephant ivory was being shipped north up the River Niger to Gao, from where it was transported across the desert by camel caravan. If that was the case, then Gao could have been the immediate source of many of the beads found at Igbo-Ukwu, having been sent south in exchange for the ivory but originating from more distant locations (Insoll and Shaw 1997).

Clearly there was participation in both local and long-distance trade by people living in the Igbo-Ukwu area, and some of the products of this trade

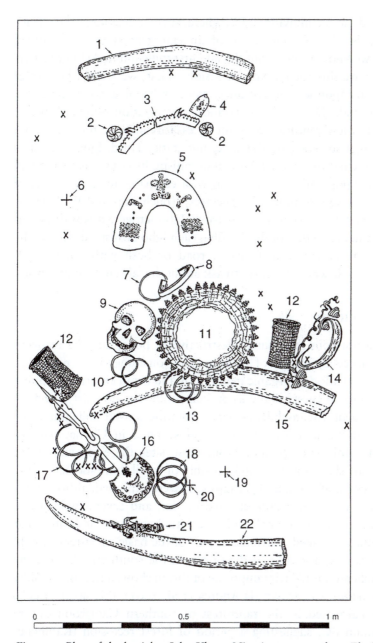

Fig. 7.10 Plan of the burial at Igbo-Ukwu, Nigeria. 1, 15, and 22, Elephant tusks; 2, decorated copper roundels; 3, crown; 4, decorated copper plate; 5, pectoral plate; 6 and 19, position of point of bracket; 7, 10, 13, 17, and 18, copper anklets; 8, copper strap; 9, skull; 11, spiral copper bosses set in wood: remains of stool; 12, beaded armlets; 14, copper handle for calabash; 16, copper fan holder; 20, position of point of rod supporting bronze leopard's skull; 21, bronze horseman hilt; X, iron nails and staples. After Shaw 1970: fig. 14.

were concentrated on one individual. Elsewhere, such archaeological evidence would probably be thought indicative of an emergent state or a ranked chiefdom. Until we know more about the late first millennium AD in this part of Nigeria, there are three tentative conclusions. First, we should be careful when deducing sociopolitical organization from archaeological evidence for 'rich burials'. Second, the social and political organization observed in any area during the last few centuries does not necessarily indicate the situation a thousand years ago; societies are dynamic, not static. Third, Igboland raises questions about the nature of West African urbanism. In 1955 this region had one of the densest populations in Nigeria, with estimates for some areas of 'well over 1000 per square mile [259 hectares]' (Buchanan and Pugh 1955: 60). Perhaps for mainly socioeconomic reasons, Igbo settlement was dispersed rather than nucleated, like that of the Yoruba, each Igbo farmstead lying in the middle of its own cultivated area near a road or bush path. Given such population densities, it seems pointless to ask about the 'absence' of urbanism.

Subsistence economy

Unfortunately, forest soils are usually destructive of bone, and the recovery of botanical evidence by means of flotation has sometimes been neglected. However, the preservation of organic materials in the Benin cistern containing the sacrificed women suggests that exceptional conditions do exist if archaeologists can find them. Meanwhile, evidence from the second millennium BC Kintampo sites, at the junction of forest and savanna in Ghana, remains of value even for this later period. From these sites there is evidence of domesticated dwarf sheep or goats and possibly of small domesticated cattle. In addition, cowpeas, oil palm, and perhaps yam were exploited, although it is unknown whether these were domesticated or not, and several wild plants were also eaten. Similarly, faunal and artefactual evidence indicates that hunting and fishing remained a significant part of the basic subsistence (Stahl 2005a; Watson 2005a; 2005b). To the north, in the southern savanna, the second to first millennium BC Kintampo site of Birimi showed that pearl millet (*Pennisetum glaucum*) was grown (D'Andrea et al. 2001); this savanna crop was also being cultivated in the rainforest of southern Cameroon during the first millennium BC, suggesting a period of forest recession (Kahlheber et al. 2009).

From sites of the late first millennium AD or early second millennium AD, there is less evidence for subsistence. At Daboya the faunal remains indicated the presence of domesticated cattle, sheep, or goats and chicken or guinea fowl over the last 2,000 years or so, and wild animals remained an important resource. However, the site provided no evidence for domesticated plants

(Shinnie and Kense 1989: 223–7). At Bono Manso the faunal material indicated the keeping of goats and chickens, as well as the exploitation of wild species, but little bone was recovered and most was undiagnostic. Furthermore, most of the bones came from the later phases, and, again, there was no evidence for cultivated plants (Effah-Gyamfi 1985: 98–9). In the case of Ife there is slight evidence of sheep or goat associated with potsherd pavements (Garlake 1977: 91), and terracottas of a bull and of a ram's head were found at Lafogido (in Ife) in a twelfth-century context (Eyo 1974). As for Benin City, there is no evidence of value (Connah 1975: 218), and although the ritual disposal pit at Igbo-Ukwu yielded a moderate number of bones, they were all of wild though edible fauna, a circumstance perhaps explained by the presumed ritual character of the pit (Shaw 1970: vol. 1, 247–8).

With so little direct archaeological evidence, it is necessary to fall back on indirect evidence and on evidence from nonarchaeological sources. As already discussed (p. 188), there were substantial plant-food resources in the rain-forest, and all the sites that have been mentioned are situated within the West African 'yam zone' (Figs. 6.1 and 6.2). Furthermore, those sites tend to be in the more northern parts of the forest or in the southern savanna, where yams and oil palm originally grew more readily, and it is those plants that are likely to have become the major components in forest subsistence (D'Andrea et al. 2006). The main deficiency would probably have been animal protein, as in recent times, but small numbers of dwarf goats and cattle, large quantities of fish, and extensive hunting in the forest (Gautier and Van Neer 2005) could have rendered this less of a problem than it is for the present, exploding population. Overall, this food-production system was almost certainly indigenous in its development and of substantial antiquity. Pottery, ground stone axes, and possible sickle components appear at the Nigerian rock shelter of Iwo Eleru during the last 5,000 years BC (Shaw and Daniels 1984: 55), and during the last few millennia BC many of the stone-using peoples of the forest made pick-like and hoe-like implements, which some archaeologists have interpreted as digging tools for the collection and eventual cultivation of yams. Sowunmi (1993: 15) detected a 'sharp rise' in the occurrence of oil palm at about 800 BC in a Niger delta deposit, along with the appearance of weeds of cultivation. Furthermore, those trypanosomiasis-resistant goats and cattle must have taken a considerable time to acquire the resistance that enables them to survive in the forest.

Apparently, by the end of the first millennium AD, and perhaps 1,000 or 2,000 years earlier, a sound agricultural system had grown up on the interfluves of the more northerly parts of the forest. This system was based on the rotational bush-fallow cultivation of extensive areas of forest land, which were cleared by slashing and burning and then abandoned to regeneration when soil exhaustion reduced productivity. The possibility that this human impact, combined with climatic change, led to a more open landscape in some parts of the forest must also be considered (von Hellermann 2010). One of the main crops was probably yams, and yams are a food that can be stored and transported. Therefore, it seems likely that by the early second millennium AD the subsistence economy of the rainforest was able to produce a surplus and to provide adequate support for the growing social complexity of which the archaeological record provides evidence. Then, during the later second millennium AD, the subsistence of the area was subject to major changes brought on by the participation of West Africa in the Atlantic trade (Stahl 2001; Ogundiran and Falola 2007; Monroe and Ogundiran 2012). Maize, cassava, various beans, tobacco, and other plants from the Americas were added to the economy. In addition, the acquisition of European trade goods from the coast had important socioeconomic consequences that stimulated the substantial urban and state developments in the West African forest and its margins that were observed by early European travellers but had originated earlier.

Technology

Killick (2004) and Alpern (2005) have reviewed the evidence for early iron smelting in Africa, and it seems that at least some of the occupants of the West African forest were working iron from early in the first millennium AD and probably earlier. Smelting was already present at Hani in Ghana, just north of the forest, by about the second century AD, and evidence from Nsukka, in eastern Nigeria, and Obobogo, in Cameroon, indicates that in the southern savanna smelting probably commenced in the second half of the first millennium BC (Okafor 1993; Woodhouse 1998). Also, iron objects from probable graves at Akonétye, in southern Cameroon, date from the first half of the first millennium AD (Meister and Eggert 2008). At the earliest Nsukka sites, the smelters were already using furnaces that were 'extremely efficient' (McIntosh 1994: 174). Certainly the iron-working skills of West African forest peoples became in time highly sophisticated; there is evidence of this by the end of the first millennium AD at Igbo-Ukwu (Shaw 1970: vol. 1, 97–103). Also, the description by Bellamy (1904), recording the operation of an impressive induced-draught furnace near Oyo in Yorubaland, indicates a long-established tradition. The adoption of iron by people living in and on the fringes of the forest must have made the agricultural exploitation of those zones more practicable than previously, enabling cultivation on a scale that could support communities of increasing size.

In addition to the working of iron, copper and copper-base alloys were being handled with great skill by the close of the first millennium AD. The evidence from Igbo-Ukwu shows that both lost-wax casting and smithing and chasing had been mastered. Indeed, by the second quarter of the second millennium AD, metalsmiths in Ife were also producing copper-base alloy castings of a technical excellence and an artistic refinement that is very impressive. A little later, craftsmen in Benin City were excelling in a similar fashion. and the Akan were producing copper-alloy weights for weighing gold dust, as well as casting an impressive range of jewellery in gold. Modern experts have described the Igbo-Ukwu material as 'extremely ambitious in design and executed by highly skilled and experienced craftsmen' (Craddock and Picton 1986: 4).

Perhaps the most impressive aspect of the forest-dwellers' technology, however, was its diversity. Thus the artists of ancient Ife excelled in the making of terracotta representations as well as ones of copper-base alloy. Furthermore, they also carved hard stone such as granite-gneiss and quartz, to produce accomplished sculptures. Some of these were decorated in a distinctive way, by driving iron nails into holes drilled into the stone (Willett 1967: 79–84, plates 72–4, 77–9). Also at Ife, the complex pavements of potsherds and stones hint at considerable architectural sophistication, a sophistication that was still apparent in the much later mud palaces of some Yoruba rulers. Indeed, some of the coursed-mud architecture of the West African forest was quite remarkable. That of the Asante, for instance, with its polished red and white walls decorated with low reliefs (e.g., McLeod 1981: 56), remained an impressive demonstration of what was possible in this building material, as also did that of Benin, with its polished, fluted red walls. Indeed, Benin City has provided a time capsule of traditional technology in the form of the varied collection of objects looted from the city at the time of its capture by the British in 1897 (e.g., Pitt Rivers 1900). The Bini were proficient not only in iron working, 'brass working', and building but also in carpentry, wood and ivory carving, mud and terracotta sculpture, pottery, leather working, weaving, and beadwork (Dark 1973). In addition, the earthworks in the Benin and Ishan areas suggest an understanding of surveying and civil engineering, as well as a capacity to move monumental amounts of earth.

The full range of technological skills amongst some forest communities, during the last 500 to 1,000 years, is too great to discuss in detail, but two other activities deserve a mention. First, a number of sites at Ife have yielded evidence of glass melting, in the form of fragments of crucibles coated with waste glass (e.g., Garlake 1977: 89–90). This might mean only that imported glass was being melted to turn into beads or other small objects (Willett 1977: 22), or it could mean that glass was being made from its primary materials, as now seems likely (Freestone 2006; Lankton et al. 2006; Babalola 2011). Radiocarbon dates for a site described as a glass-bead-making factory indicate a date between the late eleventh and the fourteenth centuries (Sutton 1982: 309, 312). Second, although there has been little archaeological investigation of gold mining in southern Ghana, there are ethnohistorical accounts of mining in the Akan forest to a depth of as much as 46 metres. Clearly, the miners must have known a considerable amount about their craft. Traces of mining have also been reported in the Nigerian lead, zinc, and copper deposits east of Igbo-Ukwu, where open cuts and tunnelling reached depths of about 10 metres (Chikwendu et al. 1989: 31). A radiocarbon date in the tenth century AD, for charcoal associated with mining debris, suggests that these mines were in use at the time that the Igbo-Ukwu copper and copper-alloy objects were being made (McIntosh 1994: 176; Craddock et al. 1997). Awaiting further investigation are the tunnels and spoil heaps of iron-ore mining in the Republic of Benin, thought to date to the first half of the second millennium AD (Randsborg 2010: 81).

Thus by early in the second millennium AD, if not before, there was a varied and sophisticated level of technology in at least some of the West African forest communities. There must have been a growth in functional specialization amongst the societies concerned.

Social system

Ethnohistorical and oral sources have more to tell us about social organization in the West African rainforest during the last half millennium than does archaeological evidence. Nevertheless, the latter can augment the other sources, and it is our major source of information for the crucial earlier formative periods. Archaeological data indicate that by late in the first millennium AD, or early in the second millennium, there was growing social stratification in some locations based on the control of trade resources and agricultural surplus. This took place particularly in the northerly parts of the forest and in the forest–savanna ecotone. It led in some places to increasing centralization of authority, particularly in the form of divine kingship. The copper-base alloy castings of Ife and Benin are evidence of that institution and, in the case of Benin, of the social and political hierarchy that supported it. In particular, it seems likely that the famous 'bronze' heads of Ife were made for attachment to wooden bodies which, provided with clothing, crowns, and other regalia, were carried in funeral processions of rulers, members of their families, and perhaps some of their more important chiefs. Such figures could have represented not only the deceased but also the authority of the office that he or she had held, much as was the case in Medieval and Early Modern Europe where similar practices were recorded (Willett 1966). Furthermore, some idea of the power that such authority could wield is given by the thirteenth-century sacrificial victims at Benin and by the scale of the earth-works of that city and its surrounding settlements.

Similarly, whatever the sociopolitical significance of the Igbo-Ukwu evidence, it clearly indicates a concentration of 'wealth' on one individual, an individual who held institutionalized power of some sort. The burial is especially persuasive in this respect. As shown in Caroline Sassoon's reconstruction painting (Shaw 1970: vol. 1, frontispiece; McIntosh 1999: fig. 1.2), the deceased sat on an ornamented stool, clothed, crowned, and with regalia and jewellery. It is likely that stools were already symbols of authority, as was later the case with the Asante of Ghana (McLeod 1981: 112–18). Indeed, some stools of exceptional workmanship from Benin, made of wood or of copper alloy (e.g., Pitt Rivers 1900: plate 41; Roth 1903: figs. 111 and 112; Dark 1973: plate 40), and from Ife, carved out of stone (e.g., Willett 1967: plate 77), must have had a similar role. Regrettably, we still lack structural evidence such as the layout of palace buildings, other than much later examples at Old Oyo, Benin City, or Abomey. Nevertheless, the material record does provide signs of emergent city-states in the West African forest by early in the second millennium AD.

There are also signs of urbanization by this time; at the very least Begho, Bono Manso, Ife, and Benin were already of increasing size with tendencies to nucleation. Archaeological evidence for the beginnings of urbanization in the West African forest is poor, but technological developments suggest a growth of specialist crafts, and with this a growth in functional specialization within society that Mabogunje thought fundamental to the development of urbanization. Furthermore, it seems that by the early second millennium AD, Mabogunje's 'limiting conditions' (p. 5) for urbanization were also being met in some parts of the West African forest. There was almost certainly a surplus of food; there were in some areas small groups of people able to exercise power; and very likely there was a class of traders and merchants. In some places, however, whether or not these conditions were met, urbanization did not take place. There is the example of the Igbo people of eastern Nigeria who, in spite of what might have been a large population, developed a form of sociopolitical organization that was dispersed rather than nucleated. The origins of Igbo society would merit careful archaeological examination, for if we understood why there were no Igbo cities, then we might understand more about the overall process of urbanization in the West African rainforest. Roderick McIntosh (2005) might well have the answer, as discussed in Chapter 6, with his idea of heterarchy, authority arranged horizontally, rather than hierarchy, authority arranged vertically. It is apparent that large numbers of people living in a small area might choose different ways of organizing their society.

Population pressures

The West African rainforest would appear to be an unlikely place for population pressures; there seems to be almost limitless unused land, and water stress is not as acute as in the savanna. Indeed, it is possible that the iron-using farmers of the first and early second millennium AD did enjoy for some centuries a virtual 'frontier' situation, in which there was always sufficient fresh land to meet increases in population. This might even be the reason why urbanization and state development were apparently later phenomena in the forest than in the savanna.

However, Darling's work around Benin City showed that forest soils and environments varied in their attractiveness to farmers. It seems probable that the best farmlands were situated on the upper interfluves, where the vegetation might have been easier to clear and the soils were better drained. Also there seems to have been a preference for ecotonal environments on the fringes of the forest. Given a rotational bush-fallow agricultural system of the sort practised in the forest during recent centuries, each piece of farmland would have to be fallowed for ten to fifteen years, after only three or four years of cultivation. During those brief periods of cultivation each piece of land would be relatively productive and capable of producing a food surplus. This might stimulate population growth, but a time would come when the best land would become harder to find, unless farmers reduced the fallowing period, thereby reducing productivity and food supplies. This is supposition, but for the area around Benin City, Allison (1962: 244) produced evidence that most of the forest had been farmed at one time or another. Indeed, the vast pattern of earthworks mapped by Darling (1984) is surely indicative of an expanding farming population competing for land. Communities do not indulge in such monumental labour unless there is good reason. Whether such competition existed also in other areas of the West African forest remains to be seen. The area occupied by the Igbo, for instance, has been said to have 'among the poorest of Nigerian soils – highly leached, extremely acid, suited only to a limited range of crops and eroding rapidly under conditions of overcropping' (Buchanan and Pugh 1955: 60). It might be that population dispersal was the most appropriate strategy for dealing with such generally poor soils, whereas nucleation on areas of better soils tended to take place where there was a greater variation in soil quality. There is also the possibility that climatic change and human impact altered the environment in the past, with a drier, more open landscape between 700 and 200 years ago, followed by a moister, more forested one in recent centuries (p. 205). This could have resulted in a high population density that led to political turmoil and warfare as conditions changed and to the decline in which British observers found the Benin state at the end of the nineteenth century (von Hellermann 2010).

Ideology

Prior to European contact, the religions of West African forest peoples seem to have consisted of a varied collection of beliefs. From ethnohistorical sources and oral tradition, it appears that pantheons of deities as well as ancestors played a part in these beliefs and that the ruler of a community often fulfilled the function of its chief priest. Thus in Benin City the Oba appears to have been the principal officiant in major religious ceremonies (Bradbury 1957: 52–60), and at least some of these involved human sacrifices in which the victim or victims were asked to carry a message to the gods (Roth 1903: 71–2). Likewise, the Oni of Ife was a spiritual leader; the Akan chiefs seem to have had spiritual as well as temporal powers (McLeod 1981); and rulers of Dahomey reinforced their control with rituals that included human sacrifices (Monroe 2012). Therefore, ideology might have played a crucial role in the emergence of West African forest states, particularly as a means of legitimizing and reinforcing centralized authority. In view of the importance of a food surplus in the development of both states and cities, it is interesting that in many parts of the forest and its fringes some of the most significant ceremonies of the religious year were concerned with the yam harvest.

There is some archaeological evidence that suggests that the role of religion might have been similar in the early centuries of the second millennium AD. In Ife, for instance, Garlake excavated fourteenth-century altars built into the edge of potsherd pavements and comparable to those dedicated to past Obas that were still to be seen in the royal palace of Benin late in the twentieth century (Garlake 1977: 69). At Benin itself there is evidence of human sacrifice in the thirteenth century. In addition, many of the Benin copper-base alloy castings of sixteenth- to nineteenth-century date, particularly those in the form of human heads, apparently represented former Obas and were important liturgical furnishings of the altars (Gore 2007). The 'bronze' and terracotta heads from Ife of fourteenth- to fifteenth-century date were perhaps intended for similar use or, in some cases, for funeral ceremonies. Herbert (1984: 302) suggested that such items were 'actual containers of power', not merely 'passive signifiers' of it. For earlier periods, however, the interpretation of religious symbolism can be difficult, such as with the thousand-year-old Igbo-Ukwu evidence for the existence of a 'priest king' (Shaw 1977). Nevertheless, whatever its significance might be, that site does suggest that the combining of spiritual and temporal authority is indeed an ancient practice in the West African forest. An amalgam of deeply embedded beliefs, rituals, and state-sponsored violence underpinned a number of the forest hierarchies and their rulers.

External trade

In Chapter 6 (p. 151) it was argued that the range of environments in West Africa would have provided both the necessity and the occasion for the exchange of raw materials and products across environmental boundaries. Thus one might expect an early development of regional trading both within and between the various ecozones and ecotones of West Africa. The forest and forest fringes must have played a part in such development, just as the drier savanna and Sahel to their north did. Furthermore, the wooded savanna in between these contrasting environments, sometimes referred to as the 'Middle Belt', would have provided a vital trading link between the two, although one that needs more attention from archaeologists (Casey 2010). Forest products that were probably exchanged in local markets and traded to greater distances could have included yams, other vegetables, vegetable oils, palm wine, dried fish, salt, Melegueta pepper, kola nuts, dyewoods, various gums, cloth, pots, canoes, charcoal, ivory, gold, and slaves. A number of these stimulated long-distance trade, particularly gold, ivory, slaves, pepper, and kola nuts. By the end of the first millennium AD some of these were being carried across the Sahara, and by the middle of the second millennium AD seaborne European traders were seeking them on the coast and, in addition, developing what was to become an almost insatiable demand for vegetable oils. Because of its gold production, it has been claimed that 'West Africa was for centuries a center of the world economy' (Kea 2012: 347).

In return for their exports, the forest and forest fringes received an assortment of goods, of which luxury items that gave status to the recipients formed a substantial part. This is not to deny that meat-on-the-hoof from the savanna was important in the forest probably from an early date or that salt from the Sahara must have reached as far south. Nevertheless, it appears that amongst the most important of the commodities reaching the forest from the Saharan trade were copper-base alloys, either as ingots or manufactures. These were much sought after by peoples of the forest, and from the time of their arrival on the West African coast European traders were quick to take advantage of this demand. Clearly, copper and its alloys were luxury materials of considerable sociopolitical and economic importance. There is evidence that France was one source of the metal used in Ife and of that used at an early date in Benin City (Willett and Sayre 2006: 77), a remarkable indication of the extent of the trading networks in which these cities participated, involving European, Mediterranean, Saharan, Sahelian, savanna, and forest transportation systems. In addition, cowrie shells were an important commodity traded into the forest, originally across the Sahara but eventually to the coast on European ships (Johnson 1970a; 1970b; Hogendorn and Johnson 1986). It has been estimated that about 16 billion cowries were brought into West Africa during the seventeenth and eighteenth centuries (Ogundiran 2007: 94). Used both decoratively and as currency, their possession was again an important indicator of status. The same could be said of many of the other imports to the West African forest. As indicated by European records of ships' cargoes, there was a demand for a variety of manufactured goods, particularly glass beads, coral beads, fine cloths, metalware of all sorts (especially iron knives), iron bars, alcohol, tobacco, gunpowder, guns, and mirrors (Ryder 1969). One of the most remarkable status symbols, however, was the horse. Used in the forest fringes, horses were also known as deep in the forest as Benin City; they were brought there from the savanna and, in later times, occasionally from European traders on the coast (Law 1980a). With trypanosomiasis in the forest, it is unlikely that horses could have lived long in such an environment. It would seem that their use in Benin represented a remarkable example of conspicuous consumption.

Much of the above is based on ethnohistory and oral tradition, mainly from post-European-contact times. The advent of European traders on the West African coast, from the sixteenth century onwards, reversed the orientation of trade from north to south; incoming commodities increasingly came via the coast, outgoing ones went the same way (Monroe and Ogundiran 2012). The trans-Saharan trade gradually faded away, so that by the twentieth century little of it survived. Consequently, to find evidence of external trade in the forest, from before about 500 years ago, we must turn to archaeology. The most important of such evidence is Igbo-Ukwu. Although it seems that some of the metal used in the items of copper-base alloy at that site came from no great distance (Chikwendu et al. 1989), it appears that the rest came from North Africa (Willett and Sayre 2006: 77), and the large number of glass and carnelian beads must imply similar or other trading links. So must the mounted horse or donkey on one of the Igbo-Ukwu castings (Shaw 1970: vol. 2, plates 365 and 366). Even if based on another work of art rather than on direct observation, this indicates a connection with the savanna. Sutton (1991) suggested trading contacts with Egypt and Nubia, and although an Indian origin has often been assumed for the carnelian because of an apparent lack of African sources, it 'occurs abundantly' in Egypt (Lucas and Harris 1962: 391).

However, irrespective of where the beads came from, the problem is to know what the people of Igbo-Ukwu were giving in exchange. Shaw (1970: vol. 1, 284–5) suggested ivory, in the form of elephant tusks, and added that probably slaves and perhaps kola nuts had also been exported. His suggestions seem reasonable, but the location of Igbo-Ukwu in the northern margin of the forest, near to the Niger River and not far from the Niger Delta, makes one wonder whether salt, dried fish, and perhaps other delta products might also have been amongst the goods traded to the north. As already mentioned (p. 206), Insoll (1996a: 80) suggested that some of the ivory was carried up the River Niger to Gao, from where it was fed into the Saharan trade, and that Gao might therefore have been the immediate source of many of the beads found at Igbo-Ukwu, whatever their remoter origin. Indeed, beads excavated from Gao are similar to those from Igbo-Ukwu (Insoll and Shaw 1997). However, Sutton (1991: 154) pointed out that both elephants (for ivory) and people (as slaves) were common south of the Sahara a thousand years ago, and he argued that to produce so much wealth as far south as Igbo-Ukwu there must have been 'some other valued commodity specific to that place'. It is an important point because, whatever else they represent, the objects found at Igbo-Ukwu do indicate a considerable concentration of wealth, which (on present knowledge) was unique in that region at that time. Sutton has suggested that the special commodity might have been silver, which apparently occurs in small quantities in copper ore in south-eastern Nigeria, and of which traces have been found in the copper-alloy objects from Igbo-Ukwu. It is an attractive idea, for here indeed was a rare commodity of considerable international value at the relevant time, particularly sought after for use in the currencies of both the Islamic and Christian worlds. However, Craddock et al. (1997: 424) have described Sutton's suggestion that silver was being smelted in the Igbo-Ukwu area as 'very unlikely'.

Further to the west, the location of Begho and other sites thought to relate to the early Akan states is surely indicative of an early trade in gold and other forest commodities. To the south of Begho lay many of West Africa's gold mines and substantial resources of kola. To the north lay more gold mines, and the Akan states seem to have developed astride a major trade route from the coast to the region of Jenné in the Inland Niger Delta. Copper-base alloy basins and bowls that have survived in eight or more localities in the Akan area provide some confirmation of this trade. These appear to have had a North African origin; indeed, three items from Nsawkaw have Arabic inscriptions, and one of those three is thought to be possibly of fourteenth-century date. Also remarkable is the fourteenth-century English bronze jug that was amongst the loot taken by the British from Kumasi in 1896. However, there was probably a wider range of imports into the Akan area than such items would suggest. Similarly, the commodities exported could have consisted of things other than just gold and kola, such as ivory, dried fish, slaves, and salt. It was on this part of the coast of West Africa that an eighteenth-century European visitor recorded salt production (by seawater evaporation) on such a scale that a number of storehouses were seen which each contained about 50 tonnes of salt (Nenquin 1961: 115–16).

At both Ife and Benin City the only firm archaeological evidence for external trade prior to European contact consists of items of copper-base alloys.

Craddock and Picton (1986: 9) found 'significant analytical differences' between such metal used at these places from the thirteenth to the fifteenth century AD and that which had been used at Igbo-Ukwu, 'showing that new sources of metal, probably imported, were now used'. Indeed, Willett and Sayre (2006: 77) have since suggested that France was its most likely origin. To some extent this reflects the growth of a trans-Saharan trade in brass, which European maritime trade later took over. As an indication of the range of pre-European trade within the forest itself, by the fourteenth century objects of copper-base alloys were even reaching the Niger Delta, implying canoe-borne trading. In the case of Ife, it has been suggested that a trade route ran north from Yorubaland to a crossing of the Niger below Bussa, where copper-base-alloy castings known as the 'Tsoede Bronzes' were found. Significantly, some of these contain a small percentage of zinc, which suggests the use of imported brass from the Saharan trade (Craddock and Picton 1986: 8–9). This could have been an important trade route from the forest zone, and the commodities probably traded out of Yorubaland would have been kola nuts (important in the savanna because kola is the only stimulant permitted by Islam), ivory, salt, dried fish, and slaves. Similar goods would probably have been exported from Benin City, although Melegueta pepper was probably more important than kola. Also trade in vegetable oils is likely to have long pre-dated European contact. The location of Benin City seems never to have been adequately explained in terms of trade routes, although it was well placed to maintain contact with both the Niger Delta to its south and the Niger River to its east.

Although direct archaeological evidence is limited, there seems no doubt that external trade was important for the peoples of the West African forest and its margins long before European traders arrived on the coast. Such trade had probably commenced at least by the first millennium AD, and its origins might be much earlier. Although long-distance contacts with trans-Saharan trade must have stimulated the movement and procurement of certain commodities, there seems no reason why the inauguration of such contacts should be claimed as the beginning of forest-zone trade. It appears that a regional network of trade routes existed in West Africa before the advent of the Arab trans-Saharan trade. Such a network must have included the forest and its margins, as well as the wooded savanna to their north.

Conclusion

Why did cities and states develop in the West African rainforest and its fringes? Why should dense settlements and hierarchical social systems appear in this region? Many explanations have drawn on external trade to explain such developments, and indeed they took place at approximately the same time as the appearance of Arab trade across the Sahara. Such an external stimulus hypothesis remains untested, however, until we know more about the archaeology of the first millennium AD within the forest and adjacent environments. Until then, it seems almost certain that the origins of these cities and states lay within the forest and its margins. The forest possessed abundant resources and the potential to produce a food surplus. By early in the first millennium AD there existed an iron-based technology sufficiently sophisticated to exploit the forest environment more successfully than before. The diversity of this technology gave rise to functional specialization, and this, probably combined with localized population pressures reflecting variations in land productivity and short-term climatic change, helped to stimulate the growth of larger, more heterogeneous communities. It was possibly population pressures also that in certain areas led to an increasing stratification of society, in which control of resources fell into fewer and fewer hands. In some places this culminated in centralization of authority on one individual, whose power was frequently reinforced by the assumption of spiritual as well as temporal attributes, with social control expressed as state-sponsored violence. This situation seems to have developed by the early second millennium AD, if not before.

However, one cannot ignore the part that trade, both local and external, did play in the development of urbanization and state formation in this zone. It was an important factor in the growth and location of cities. Such cities tended to be located in the northern part of the forest or even in the southern savanna, so that they were situated at the interface between donkey transport and human portage. There was also a tendency for them to be located on important trade routes. In addition, the growth of states within this zone was undoubtedly stimulated by control of trading resources or of the trade routes. As Law (1978) showed, for instance, West African rulers in later times drew their incomes both directly and indirectly from trade. Furthermore, imported commodities provided both status symbols to enhance the position of local rulers and a source of moveable wealth that could be used to reward supporters. It is little wonder that rulers in the West African forest often insisted that it was their right to control the trade that was carried on in their territories, particularly after Europeans drew West Africa into the Atlantic world during the second half of the second millennium AD. Trade, however, was only one factor in the appearance of cities and states in the West African forest, and, like other factors, its origins were probably within that zone rather than external to it.

Chapter 8

Indian Ocean networks: the East African coast and islands

'Kilwa is one of the most beautiful and well-constructed towns in the world.' This is how the much-travelled ibn Battuta described, first-hand, 'the principal town on the [East African] coast' in 1331. Kilwa (properly called Kilwa Kisiwani), situated in what is now Tanzania, was no isolated phenomenon. On the same coast, in what is now Somalia, was Mogadishu, of which he wrote that it was 'a very large town' (Freeman-Grenville 1975: 27–31). Ibn Battuta represented the scholarly opinion of the fourteenth-century Islamic world. By the end of the following century there were less-scholarly visitors from the Christian world of Western Europe, but they also were impressed with settlements on the East African coast. Thus in 1498, the unknown author of the *Journal of the First Voyage of Vasco da Gama, 1497–1499* compared 'the town of Malindi' (now in Kenya) to Alcouchette, a town near Lisbon in his native Portugal (Freeman-Grenville 1975: 55–6). Indeed, the account of Vasco da Gama's second voyage (1502) by Gaspar Correa (written about 1561) describes Kilwa as follows:

> The city is large and is of good buildings of stone and mortar with terraces, and the houses have much wood works. The city comes down to the shore, and is entirely surrounded by a wall and towers, within which there may be 12,000 inhabitants. The country all round is very luxuriant with many trees and gardens of all sorts of vegetables, citrons, lemons, and the best sweet oranges that were ever seen, sugar-canes, figs, pomegranates, and a great abundance of flocks, especially sheep, which have fat in the tail, which is almost the size of the body, and very savoury. (Freeman-Grenville 1975: 66)

The East African settlements would be expected to make a favourable impression on sailors several months outward bound from Portugal, who had just endured the eastern Atlantic on a dull if not inadequate diet. Nevertheless, historical sources such as these demonstrate that settlements of considerable size had already developed on the East African coast before the middle of the second millennium AD. Archaeological and oral traditional evidence supports this conclusion. The problem has been to explain how such a development took place, a development that was limited to a narrow strip comprising 3,500 kilometres of coastline, from southern Somalia to southern Mozambique and including various offshore islands, as well as the Comoro Archipelago and parts of Madagascar.

The distinctive culture that developed along this coastal strip was at least partly urban, mercantile, literate, and Islamic. Modern scholars often refer to it as the 'Swahili Culture', because many of the inhabitants are now speakers of one or another form of ki-Swahili, a north-eastern Bantu language rich in loan words from Arabic and a number of other languages, although it is uncertain if the term 'Swahili' should be used in contexts earlier than the last few centuries (Horton and Middleton 2000: 16). Nonetheless, whatever one calls the developments along this coast prior to the arrival of the Portuguese, they were clearly impressive. Consequently, it is not surprising that external stimulus was formerly advanced as the most likely explanation for such developments. Thus we were told that: 'We should picture this civilization as a remote outpost of Islam' (Chittick 1971: 137). Subsequently, however, this 'colonial-origins interpretation' has been rejected (Allen 1993), and archaeological as well as other evidence has increasingly suggested that the development of the coastal culture owed more to its African origins than to external influences, contributory though these obviously were (Horton 1987a; 1996). So, was the East African coast merely the edge of the Islamic world, or was it the centre of an indigenous African development of substantial significance? Viewed simply, the latter now seems the case, but culture change on this coast was highly complex, as might be expected in such an interaction zone, and Swahili culture did incorporate both local and foreign elements.

Geographical location and environmental factors

The area with which this chapter is concerned consists of a long narrow coastal strip and adjacent islands. Extending from about 2° north to about 16° south and perhaps to as much as 24° south, this comprises a large part of the eastern coast of Africa (Fig. 8.1). Relevant cultural developments seem to have been mainly restricted to that coast, although there are indications that the hinterland played a bigger role than is sometimes stated (Pawlowicz 2012; Kusimba et al. 2013). Nevertheless, the development of social complexity clearly had a maritime orientation. This situation contrasts with that of West Africa, discussed in Chapters 6 and 7. In that case, cities and states developed far from the coast in the northern savanna, before they did so in the forested coastal region. When such developments did take place in the forest, they were always inland and often in or near the forest–savanna ecotone. Until the advent of European sailors in the fifteenth century AD, the coast itself remained relatively remote and was not the scene of any major cultural developments. The explanation of this contrast can be found in the different locations and marine environments of these two coasts. On the West African coast, the Atlantic Ocean was a barrier rather than a highway, until knowledge

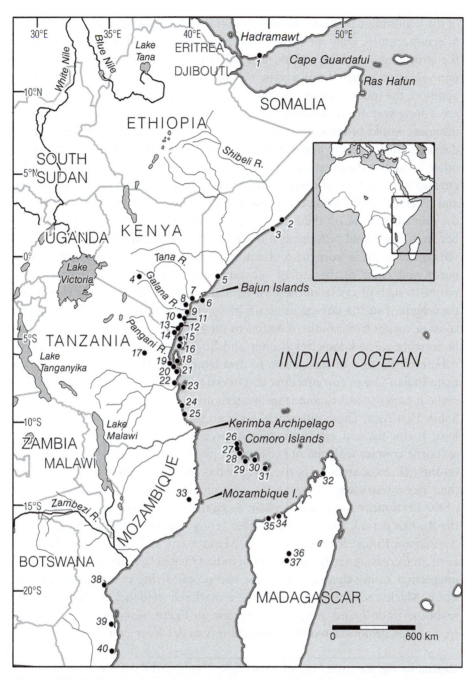

Fig. 8.1 Principal archaeological sites and places on the East African coast and islands mentioned in the text. 1, Aden; 2, Warsheikh; 3, Mogadishu; 4, Lake Naivasha; 5, Bur Gao; 6, Lamu Archipelago; 7, Ungwana; 8, Ras Kipini; 9, Malindi; 10, Mgombani; 11, Gedi; 12, Kilepwa; 13, Mombasa; 14, Vumba Kuu; 15, Mtambwe Mkuu, on Pemba Island; 16, Pujini, on Pemba Island; 17, Dakawa; 18, Unguja Ukuu, on Zanzibar Island;

of the winds improved and changes in sailing technology took place during the fifteenth century. Only then could European ships both avoid and sail against the prevailing northerly winds and currents that had previously made it impossible to return from a visit to this coast (Crosby 1986: 112–14). In addition, the more environmentally attractive parts of the West African coast are a long way from Western Europe; a voyage from Lisbon to Ghana, for instance, would be roughly 5,500 kilometres as indicated by modern marine distance tables (Caney and Reynolds 1976). The East African coast, on the other hand, has the great advantage of ease of navigation from coastal southern and western Asia. The winds and currents of the Indian Ocean are seasonal and reverse their direction every few months. Thus, from December to March the prevailing wind on the East African coast is the north-easterly monsoon, but from April until November it is the south-westerly monsoon. This enables voyages to be made from the southern Arabian coast, the Persian Gulf, and the north-west coast of the Indian subcontinent. Furthermore, it is possible to return to such places from the East African coast within the same year. Also, the length of such a voyage need not be so great as those to the West African coast; a voyage from southern Arabia to the Kenyan coast, for example, would be roughly 2,800 kilometres (Caney and Reynolds 1976). Currents also contribute to the ease of navigation to and from East Africa. In particular, the main Indian Ocean currents flow east–west, reversing each half-year, and thus make it easier to sail to and from western and southern India, Indonesia, and South-East Asia. These differences between the west and east coasts of Africa have had a marked effect on their respective histories. On the west coast, seaborne contact with the outside world has existed for only 500 years, but on the east coast such seaborne contact has certainly been a reality for more than 1,000 years (e.g., Ricks 1970), and, judging by the first-century *Periplus of the Erythraean Sea* (Casson 1989: 6–7), there was also such contact during the Roman period. Indeed, since Miller (1969: 145–8) wrote about a Roman 'Cinnamon Route' from Indonesia to Madagascar and East Africa, there has been an increasing acceptance that the Indian Ocean has long been a means of interaction rather than a barrier for the people living on its rim (Beaujard 2007; Mack 2007). In particular, the remarkable evidence for long-distance seaborne trade found at Quseir al-Qadim in Egypt, discussed in Chapter 2 (p. 39), has demonstrated this interaction (van der Veen 2011).

Caption for Fig. 8.1 (*cont.*) 19, Mkadini; 20, Ras Nunge and Kaole; 21, Mkukutu and Kivinja; 22, Dar es Salaam; 23, Ukunju Cave, on Juani Island close to Mafia Island; 24, Kilwa and Sanjé ya Kati; 25, Songo Mnara, on Songo Mnara Island; 26, Nsudjini; 27, Itsandra; 28, M'Bachile; 29, Sima; 30, Domoni; 31, Dembeni and Acoua-Agnala M'kiri; 32, Mahilaka; 33, Murrapania; 34, Antsoheribory; 35, Kingany; 36, Ankadivory; 37, Antananarivo; 38, Sofala; 39, Chibuene; 40, Inhambane. Drawn by Joe LeMonnier.

The environment varies along the East African coastal strip, although most of it belongs to the same vegetational subregion (Sinclair 1991: 181). To its north, the coast of Somalia from Cape Guardafui to round about Mogadishu is open, has few harbours, and an arid hinterland. From Mogadishu to near the present border of Somalia and Kenya, harbours are more numerous, but the coast is still exposed, hazardous, and somewhat barren. South of the border of Somalia and Kenya, however, there is a fair rainfall and numerous natural harbours. Along the northern part of this coast there is also a string of coral islands, close offshore, known as the Bajun Islands. Between them and the mainland is a sheltered channel; at their southern end are the islands of the Lamu Archipelago: Pate, Manda, and Lamu (Fig. 8.2). Only a narrow, mangrove-fringed channel separates these islands from the mainland, and from here southwards there is an almost continuous offshore coral reef, providing protected inshore waters along which there are many small creeks and harbours. Much of the mainland coast is fringed with mangrove swamps, but there are also stretches of sandy beach, the foreshores of which shelve so gradually that at low tide the sea retreats for long distances. The more protected of these beaches provide ideal landing places. The lightly built sewn boats that were used along this coast in the past could be anchored on the high tide and unloaded at low tide while they were high and dry. On the islands along the coast, fresh water could usually be obtained by digging wells, and consequently they provided locations for human settlements. To the south, the large ocean islands of Pemba, Zanzibar, and Mafia, less than a day's voyage from the mainland, are particularly important, but south of them are the inshore islands of Kilwa and Songo Mnara and further south again the Kerimba Archipelago and Mozambique Island, the last islands of the coral reef. South of the Zambezi estuary the sea is too cold for coral growth; beyond Inhambane the coast is not relevant (Chittick 1971: 108–9; Garlake 1978a: 95–6). Both the Comoro Islands and parts of Madagascar are, however, and their inclusion adds further to the range of environments. The former are volcanic, tropical, and, with the exception of Ngazidja, well watered, whilst Madagascar is characterized by environmental diversity resulting from altitudinal differences and oceanic location.

The environment of the coastal strip and adjacent islands would have been attractive to human settlement. Much of the area has a rainfall of about 1,000 millimetres per year, and its maritime, tropical climate has encouraged agriculture in areas where there are suitable soils. The character of the coast and adjacent islands would have stimulated the development of coastal shipping, and because of the winds and currents of the Indian Ocean, the people of the East African coast and islands were bound to come into contact with other maritime peoples. During the first and early second millennium AD many

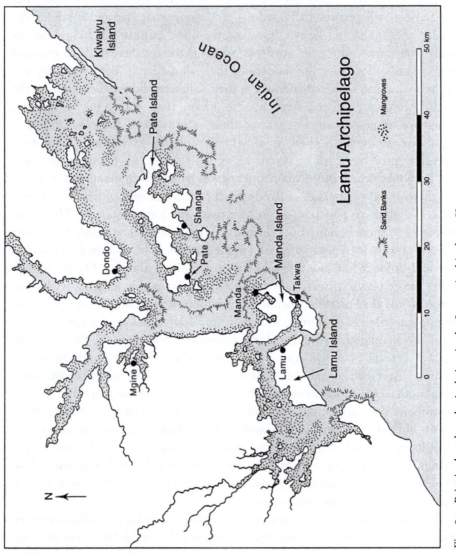

Fig. 8.2 Principal archaeological sites in the Lamu Archipelago, Kenya.

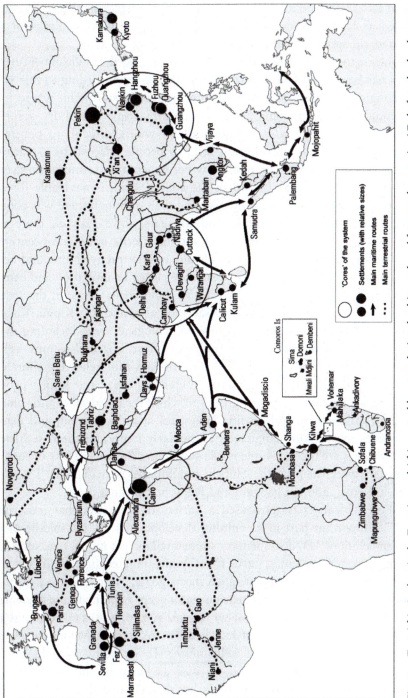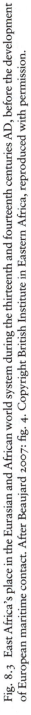

Fig. 8.3 East Africa's place in the Eurasian and African world system during the thirteenth and fourteenth centuries AD, before the development of European maritime contact. After Beaujard 2007: fig. 4. Copyright British Institute in Eastern Africa, reproduced with permission.

ports in East Africa became part of a vast trading network (Fig. 8.3), which extended as far as South-East Asia and has been called the Eurasian and African world system (Beaujard 2007).

In contrast to this narrow coastal strip and islands, the environment of the interior has been described as relatively unattractive. According to this view, behind the generally narrow, sandy, often fertile coastal plain, where fresh water could be found in many places, lies a gently rising belt of dry, scrubby, savanna bushland, 100 to 200 kilometres in width, difficult to penetrate, harbouring tsetse flies, and offering little to people adapted to a maritime environment. Furthermore, there are few permanent rivers, and of these only the Zambezi, at the southern end of the coastal strip, is navigable for any distance. Consequently, it has been assumed that, although there was contact between the coast around Sofala and the Zimbabwe Plateau, there was little between the Kenya–Tanzania coast and the interior until recent centuries. However, the idea of an attractive coast and an unattractive hinterland needs to be questioned (Kusimba et al. 2013). A closer examination indicates a greater variety of environments, at least in some areas. Thus, in the stretch of coast and hinterland between Bur Gao (Somalia) and Ras Kipini (Kenya), Horton (1987a: 292) identified a range of ecological areas including driest woodland, riverine woodland, lowland wet forest, coastal swamps, island savanna, and reefs and littorals. Consequently, within relatively short distances are pastoralists, agriculturalists, hunter-gatherers, and fishing people, comprising a wide range of ethnic groups of which the pastoralists and some of the hunter-gatherers speak Cushitic languages and the farming and fishing communities speak Bantu languages. Particularly important for East African coastal societies are the cultivable fertile soils along the lower parts of some of the coastal rivers, such as the Shibeli and Juba in Somalia, the Tana and Galana in Kenya, and the Pangani and Rufiji in Tanzania.

The East African coast possessed a variety of resources that must have played an important part in its cultural developments. By the middle of the second millennium AD, documentary sources tell us that millet, rice, sorghum, cocoyam, coconuts, bananas, citrus fruits, pomegranates, figs, sugarcane, and vegetables were being grown. Fat-tailed sheep, goats, cattle, and chickens were raised; fish and probably other marine foods were exploited; and bees were kept in hives (Chittick 1971: 136; 1974: vol. 1, 236, 248–51). Amongst the food plants were a number that had been introduced to Madagascar from South-East Asia during the first millennium AD, including rice, the greater yam, coconut, and Indian saffron, as well as bananas and taro that had reached the East African coast at an earlier date (Beaujard 2011). The most important indigenous African plant foods were probably millet, sorghum, and a number of vegetables; there is archaeological evidence from the hinterland of the Kenyan coast for the cultivation of *Sorghum bicolor* (sorghum), *Pennisetum glaucum* (pearl millet), and *Eleusine coracana* (finger millet) during the first millennium AD (Helm et al. 2012). Food resources were substantial and varied, and the environmental diversity of the coast and adjacent areas must have encouraged an early development of local exchange systems handling these and other resources (Kusimba et al. 2005; Wright 2005). Indeed, by the nineteenth century the East African coast was exporting grain, including sorghum, maize, and sesame (Spear 1978: 81–2). The last two were introduced to Africa, maize from the Americas in the sixteenth century AD and sesame from India by the second millennium BC (Bedigian 2003). By the nineteenth century AD the volume of this trade was probably much greater than in previous centuries, but it is likely that grain export to the dry lands of southern Asia had a long history. Records in Aden show that rice was imported there from Kilwa prior to Portuguese contact, and it is thought that much of the rice actually came from Madagascar.

It was with other East African resources, however, that the export trade of this coast was principally developed. Most important seems to have been ivory, already mentioned in the *Periplus of the Erythraean Sea* in the first century AD (Casson 1989: 16, 42) and still important in the nineteenth century (Spear 1978: 81–2). It appears to have been obtainable from the coast, but some tusks came from deep in the interior (Ylvisaker 1982: 221). The *Periplus* also mentions rhinoceros horn and tortoiseshell (actually from sea turtles) and pearly shell (on the latter, see Chittick 1981: 186). At a later date there were, in addition, numerous other resources that became important trade commodities during the first half of the second millennium AD. From Sofala, in the south, came gold and copper, both of which must have been from the interior. From the Horn of Africa, to the north, came frankincense and myrrh, aromatic gum resins much sought after in some parts of the world. From more central parts of the East African coast, mangrove poles, ebony, and perhaps other timbers were exported, as was iron, ambergris, and sandalwood. Slaves were probably exported from the more northerly parts of the coast, in the later second millennium AD mainly to markets in Arabia and the Persian Gulf (Vernet 2003). However, it is likely that the slave trade from this coast had a long history, judging from the revolt of apparently East African slaves that took place in southern Iraq in the late ninth century AD (Trimingham 1975: 116–18). Nineteenth-century exports also included other commodities that are an additional indication of the range of East African resources. Excluding obviously late introductions, these comprised copal (a tree resin used in the manufacture of varnish), hides, wax, hippopotamus teeth, coconuts, orchilla (a vegetable dye), beans, shells, and livestock (Spear 1978: 82).

Some of these nonfood resources, such as iron, copper, and perhaps ivory, would have been important for local use as well as for export. Timber would also have mattered, particularly for building construction and shipbuilding. In addition, there were other resources that were of local significance only or formed the basis of production for trade with the interior. Thus the coral reefs and the coral on dry land provided important building materials: both stone and lime for mortar and plaster. A considerable amount of cotton was grown on the coast and manufactured locally into cloth. Even silk was produced. Furthermore, the coast probably produced salt and also made use of some marine molluscs, either as raw material for beads or, in the case of cowries, perhaps for decoration, although in this area not as currency (Hogendorn and Johnson 1986: 102). Various coastal palms provided many things, including coconuts, wine, rope, matting, and caulking for ships. Finally, the coast had fresh water, often a problem in the dry hinterland and so crucial both for human settlements and for ships' crews anxious to replenish their supplies.

With such resources, it is difficult to understand why so many settlement sites of the first half of the second millennium AD were abandoned, in some cases prior to the arrival of the Portuguese. The main cause was probably unreliable water supply. In the Lamu Archipelago, for example, the best fresh water is found in wells closest to the sea, where it floats on the heavier, salt water. If the wells are overdrawn or the well shafts made too deep, the supply becomes salty and unusable. In fact, the wells at the abandoned settlements on these islands are today salty. As there is little or no surface water on this coast, the only alternative to such fragile well supply would have been rainwater cisterns. Another constraint on this coast would have been soil fertility, which in some places seems to have been poor and could have been damaged by agricultural exploitation. A range of tropical diseases could have provided further problems, and perhaps the maritime contacts of this coast complicated this situation by introducing and reintroducing such diseases as smallpox, cholera, and plague. There were also other constraints. Problems of overland communication, particularly with the interior of East Africa, have probably been exaggerated, but nevertheless it would have been so much easier to move by boat along the coast that communications would have concentrated around a coastal axis. The coast-clinging locations of the larger settlements, however, would have rendered them vulnerable to attack, both by those inland peoples over whom they had no control and from the sea that brought them so much of their livelihood. That vulnerability was clearly demonstrated during the fifteenth and sixteenth centuries AD by the Galla and the Zimba from inland and by the Portuguese from the sea.

Sources of information

Historical evidence

Compared with West Africa, historical documentation is extensive, commencing with the first-century *Periplus of the Erythraean Sea*, thought to have been written by an Egyptian Greek merchant from personal experience and including an account of the East African coast (Casson 1989: 7–10). Another early source is Claudius Ptolemy's *Geographia*, originally written in about AD 150 but in its final form probably an edited compilation of about AD 400 (Freeman-Grenville 1975: 3). Both of these sources contain information about the East African coast, but it is difficult to use them and there is no further information until the ninth and tenth centuries. From then on there is a series of documentary sources, mostly from Arabic authors (Trimingham 1975) but some from Chinese writers (Wheatley 1975), until the arrival of the Portuguese at the end of the fifteenth century. Perhaps the most informative of these sources are al-Masudi in the tenth century, al-Idrisi in the twelfth century, and ibn Battuta in the fourteenth century. None of these provides the wealth of ethnohistorical evidence in the sixteenth-century accounts of Portuguese writers, such as the anonymous authors of the *Journal of the First Voyage of Vasco da Gama, 1497–1499* and *The Voyage of Pedro Alvares Cabral to Brazil and India*. Other useful early Portuguese sources include Gaspar Correa's *Lendas da India*, João de Barros's *Da Asia* and an account written by Duarte Barbosa (Freeman-Grenville 1975). In addition, there are many other European sources concerning the last few centuries before colonial rule, although most date only from the nineteenth century.

All this historical documentation consists of the writings of outsiders, visitors to East Africa and some who had never even been there and merely repeated information that was at best second hand. It is fortunate, therefore, that we also have the oral traditions of the people who lived in some of the East African coastal settlements. Best known is the 'Kilwa Chronicle', available both as a sixteenth-century Portuguese version and as an Arabic version that was copied in Zanzibar in 1862. These record the traditions about Kilwa that were current in the earlier sixteenth century and give some account of its origins (Chittick 1974: vol. 1, 13–14). There are also a number of other traditional accounts, but they seem to have been written down only in the nineteenth or early twentieth century. Perhaps the best known of these is the 'History of Pate', written about 1910 but covering the period back to 1204 (Freeman-Grenville 1975: preface, 241). Although some of these traditional histories include useful information, much of their content consists of myth and genealogy, difficult to use historically. For example, a substantial literature has grown up on the interpretation of the Kilwa Chronicle story of a 'Shirazi' immigration to the East

African coast from the Persian Gulf (e.g., Chittick 1965; Allen 1982; Horton 1996: 3; Sutton 1998: 118). Nevertheless, Thomas Spear, on the traditions of the Mijikenda peoples, and J. de V. Allen, on those about Shungwaya, demonstrated how some of the inland traditions indicate a greater indigenous contribution to the coastal culture than the better-known oral histories suggest (Spear 1978; Allen 1983; 1993). However, neither oral nor documentary historical sources are able to explain the origins and early development of the coastal cities and states.

Archaeological evidence

Archaeological investigations on the East African coast commenced shortly after the Second World War. Substantial research programmes, including excavation, have been organized by the British Institute in Eastern Africa, based in Nairobi, by Uppsala University, in Sweden, and by the University of Dar es Salaam, in Tanzania. Nevertheless, until late in the twentieth century, work concentrated on sites with stone ruins, rather than looking at these sites in their overall archaeological context. This resulted from the assumption that the remarkable stone buildings derived from the cultural influence of Muslim immigrants from the Persian Gulf and parts of the Arabian coast, an assumption that the stone buildings helped to perpetuate. It was admitted that such Arab immigrants had been integrated with the local people, but it was insisted of the resulting culture that there was little contributed by Africans. This interpretation of the culture of the East African coast influenced much of the archaeological research. While the coastal cities were thought of as semi-alien trading centres clinging to the edge of the African continent and relevant only as the periphery of an international trading system, there seemed little point in investigating their relationship with the 'indigenous' settlements of the coast or the interior, nor in bothering about their local antecedents. As a result, much of the archaeological survey and excavation concentrated on the highly visible stone ruins of mosques, tombs, and houses (e.g., Kirkman 1954; 1963; 1964; 1966; Garlake 1966; Chittick 1974; Wilson 1978; 1980). There was relatively little investigation of those parts of settlements built in mud, wood, and thatch or of those settlements built only of such materials. In addition, the presence of complex architectural features, of inscriptions, of coins, and of imported glazed earthenware, porcelain, glassware, and beads tended to focus research on artefact studies and particularly on the chronology that they provided. By the 1970s and 1980s, however, the emphasis was changing, as some archaeologists realized the basically indigenous character of the coastal culture and began to see the cities as part of a process of African social and economic change, rather than the result of alien colonization (e.g., Horton 1987a; 1996; Wilson 1982).

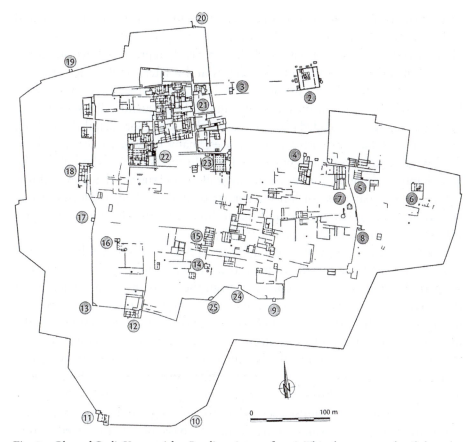

Fig. 8.4 Plan of Gedi, Kenya. After Pradines (2010: fig. 4). This shows more detail than the plans in Kirkman (1964: fig. 7) or Pradines (2004: fig. 72). Included are two phases of city walls and their gates. 1, north gate well (70 metres north of 20); 2, Great mosque, 11th to 14th centuries; 3, dated tomb, 14th century; 4, houses of the dhow and of the double court; 5, North-east Quarter; 6, mosque between the walls; 7, mosque of three bays; 8, eastern gate; 9, south defensive work; 10, south necropolis; 11, mosque against the south wall; 12, house against the south wall; 13, south-west barred corner; 14, small mosque; 15, large house with arches; 16, mosque of the sarcophagus; 17, western gate; 18, house against the west wall; 19, north-west gate; 20, north gate; 21, North-west Quarter; 22, palace and large pillar tomb; 23, Great mosque, 15th to 16th centuries; 24, south gate; 25, south barred corner. Reproduced by permission of Stéphane Pradines.

There are 173 settlement sites with stone ruins between Warsheikh (north of Mogadishu) and the Tanzania–Mozambique frontier. In addition, there are relevant sites in Mozambique, the Comoro Archipelago, and northern Madagascar (Duarte 1993; Wright 1993; Chami 1994), and many sites that lack stone ruins have not received much attention. While there must be a large number of sites spread over a great length of coast and its adjacent islands, most of the archaeological investigations have been on the Kenyan or Tanzanian coasts.

One of the first sites to be excavated was the city of Gedi, on the mainland of Kenya, where Kirkman revealed a skeletal city plan (Kirkman 1954: 185). He showed the layout of its city walls, which clearly represented two structural phases: an earlier city of about 18 hectares and a later, smaller city of about 7 hectares (Kirkman 1975: 239). Within the latter were a so-called palace, several houses, and a number of mosques and tombs. Subsequently, Pradines (2004: fig. 72; 2010: fig. 4) provided plans of the city that were more detailed (Fig. 8.4), but even these have extensive empty spaces, many of which must have been filled with buildings of mud, wood, and thatch: the houses of the bulk of the inhabitants. The angular outline of the city walls would suggest that they enclosed tightly an irregular mass of houses, similar to that at Shanga (Horton 1996: figs. 5, 9, and 10), where mud and thatch houses partly surrounded a central core of stone structures (cf. Figs. 8.4 and 8.5).

Kirkman's chronology of Gedi (1975: 237–9) was revised by Pradines (2004: 205), who identified five periods in the city's history (later revised to six periods, Pradines 2010: 199, 211), from the eleventh to the beginning of the seventeenth century. The city attained its greatest size in the late fourteenth to early fifteenth century, its outer city wall dating from the middle of the fifteenth to the middle of the sixteenth century and its inner city wall from the middle of the sixteenth to the beginning of the seventeenth century. Most of the excavated buildings were of fifteenth-century date, and house plans (Garlake 1966: 194) throw light on pre-Portuguese social organization. The coral ragstone houses comprised several narrow oblong rooms, averaging about 2.4 metres wide, the maximum rafter span. The basic plan both at Gedi and in other coastal settlements consisted of two of these long narrow rooms, one behind the other in parallel, with the first one fronting an enclosed courtyard and the rear one opening into two or three smaller rooms behind. None of these rooms had windows, but sometimes there was another courtyard behind the smaller rooms. Probably each house was intended for a separate family, with the rooms providing a graded privacy: most public in the front courtyard, most private in the back rooms. The stone houses in archaeological sites such as Gedi are in the same tradition as the mostly eighteenth-century, stone-built mansions of Lamu, some of which are still occupied (Ghaidan 1976; Donley 1987). This would suggest that by the fifteenth century there already existed a class of cultured, wealthy, mercantile urbanites (similar to those later known as the *wa-ungwana*). They reinforced their position by reserving to themselves the right to build their houses in stone, thus making use of what Linda Donley called 'house power' (Donley 1982; Donley-Reid 1990). The Gedi house plans suggest that a number of such families sometimes built their houses in interlocking groups, each group representing a distinct lineage or kin. Such people seem to have lived at a level of material comfort higher than that of most of their

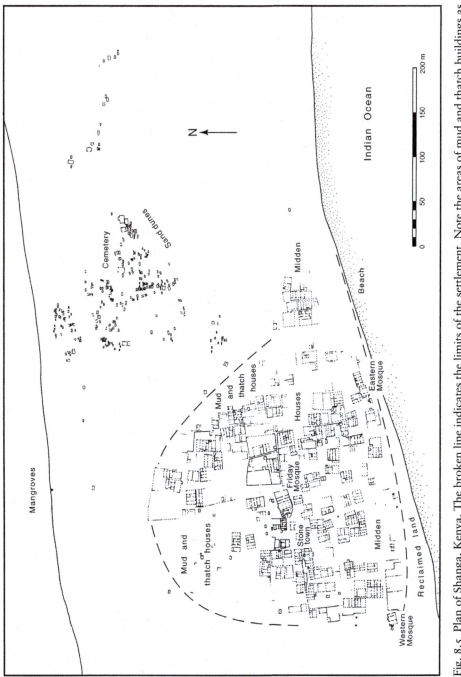

Fig. 8.5 Plan of Shanga, Kenya. The broken line indicates the limits of the settlement. Note the areas of mud and thatch buildings as well as those of stone. After Horton 1996: fig. 5. Copyright British Institute in Eastern Africa, reproduced with permission.

contemporaries. Houses had plastered walls, indoor latrines, washplaces with bidets, underfloor soakaways, and rainwater drains. Indeed, at Gedi one group of houses was identified by Kirkman as a palace. With its monumental arched entrance and its generous provision of courtyard space, this might well represent the houses of a particular lineage which, having become the hereditary ruling family, had adapted its dwellings to suit its new status.

Kirkman also excavated at other sites in Kenya and Tanzania. One was Ungwana, a walled city of about 18 hectares on the northern Kenyan coast near the estuary of the River Tana (Kirkman 1966). Kirkman concentrated on the mosques and tombs, although the ruins of stone houses were present. According to his plan, however, extensive areas of this city were empty space (Kirkman 1966: 71); as with Gedi, it seems likely that much of this space must have been filled with buildings of mud, wood, and thatch. Apparently, Kirkman's excavation strategy was not designed for this possibility. Thus at Kilepwa, a small thirteenth- to sixteenth-century settlement near Gedi, the remains consisted of a small mosque, two pillar tombs, and a group of houses. According to Kirkman, this was just a family unit, yet we are told that 'sherds of *sgraffiato* [imported glazed earthenware of eleventh- and twelfth-century date] were found all over the site, so it may have had a large population in the pre-building period' (Kirkman 1975: 239–40). To this excavator, it seems, a building that was not made of stone was not a building.

Buildings of mud, wood, and thatch must have constituted a large part of some settlements on the East African coast and islands, as some archaeologists have recognized (Fleisher and LaViolette 1999). If this was the case, the indigenous African contribution to the growth of these settlements is likely to have been important. For example, the town of Songo Mnara, on the island of that name off the Tanzanian coast, must have consisted of more structures than just a collection of stone houses, a so-called palace, and several mosques, within a large walled area. These, after all, appear to have been recorded without excavation (Garlake 1966: fig. 74). Similarly, at Kilwa (Sutton 1998), in the same area, where there have been extensive excavations, the city site covers about 1 square kilometre but the stone ruins consist of only a scatter of structures. As its excavator admitted: 'Many, and perhaps most, of the buildings at Kilwa, even at the height of its prosperity, were built of mud-and-wattle, evidently in a similar style to that which can be seen on the coast today' (Chittick 1974: vol. 1, 24). However, it appears that the ratio of buildings of stone to buildings of less permanent materials varied from site to site. For instance, the final phases of Shanga, abandoned in the fifteenth century and comprising a town of 8.68 hectares on the shore of Pate Island (Kenya), probably consisted mainly of stone structures, which took up 6.57 hectares of the occupied area (Fig. 8.5). The three mosques, approximately 400 tombs

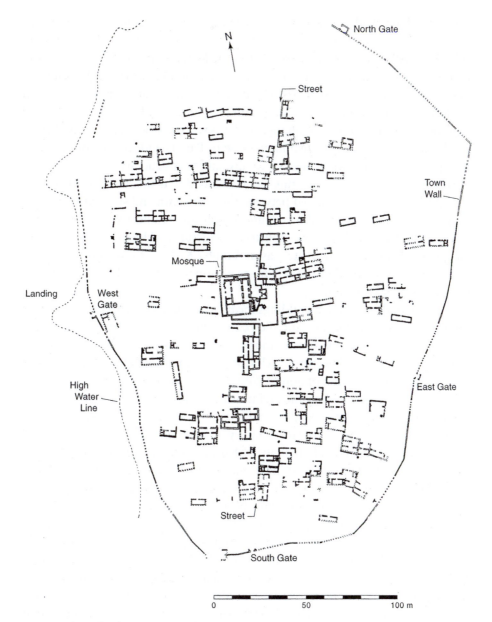

Fig. 8.6 Plan of Takwa, Kenya. After Wilson 1982: fig. 2, revised on his advice.

outside the town, other tombs within the town, and about 220 houses were all built of stone, leaving some but not much space for buildings of other materials (Horton 1996: 33, 38, 63). Another case is Takwa, a town probably occupied from the tenth to the seventeenth century (Abungu and Mutoro 1993: 695). Situated near the shore of the Kenyan island of Manda, the final phases of

237

this stone-built walled town of a little over 4 hectares contained a mosque, a well, and 137 other structures, most of which were probably houses (Fig. 8.6). Allowing for open spaces for gardens and markets, or cemeteries and public performances, as has been suggested for Songo Mnara (Fleisher and Wynne-Jones 2012; Fleisher 2013), there were still some empty areas that could have contained mud, wood, and thatch buildings, but they were limited (Wilson 1982). In contrast to Shanga and Takwa, the stone remains at Dondo, on the coast of the Kenyan mainland close to Pate Island, consist of only two mosques, two wells, two groups of tombs, and two structures suspected to be Portuguese. The excavator of this site concluded that this unwalled town, of about 5 hectares, was occupied between the fourteenth and sixteenth centuries by people of sufficient wealth to build lavish tombs and two mosques who were, nevertheless, living in nonstone structures (Horton 1996: 23–4). Geophysical survey of such sites, as at Vumba Kuu, in Kenya (Wynne-Jones 2012), has the potential to provide more information about them, particularly if followed by excavation.

If mud, wood, and thatch buildings meant indigenous contribution, does this imply that stone buildings meant alien contribution? At one time many writers thought so; now the question is more difficult to answer. Garlake, seeking the origins of the architectural styles of the stone buildings, found various parallels in different parts of South-West Asia but came to the conclusion that before the eighteenth century the architectural style of the coast was, 'to a large extent, indigenous to the coast' (Garlake 1966: 116). Clearly, alien influences might be seen in the fourteenth-century palace and commercial centre of Husuni Kubwa, just outside the city of Kilwa, with its audience court, open-sided pavilion, bathing pool, domed and vaulted roofs, and Arabic inscriptions. The same might be said of the nearby site of Husuni Ndogo, a large rectangular enclosure that could have been a mosque, a market, a barracoon (an enclosure for slaves), or possibly (Sutton 1998: 157) a caravanserai for visiting merchants and their servants. These sites, however, are exceptional, and the stone buildings of the coast and islands have a far wider range of quality. Thus, Takwa consisted mainly of small stone houses not much better than those of mud and thatch. Indeed, as already argued, stone buildings were only one aspect of these coastal settlements. Thomas Wilson showed that coastal sites in southern Somalia and Kenya could be subdivided into five classes, based on their size, ranging from more than 15 hectares to less than 2.5 hectares. Significantly, the smaller sites tended to have fewer buildings built of stone and tended to lack stone-built houses (Wilson 1982). So stone buildings were an integral part of an overall settlement pattern, rather than the major features of coast-clinging cities of alien merchants. Moreover, when that settlement pattern is analysed for location and date, it appears that this supposedly coast-clinging culture has 30 percent of the southern Somalian, Kenyan, and Tanzanian sites located in places that have poor or no harbours (including six that are actually inland), and it seems that although Swahili society became overwhelmingly sea oriented, it might have been less so in earlier centuries.

The significance of building in stone is bound up with the question of the origin of these coastal settlements. Ceramics excavated at Ras Hafun, near Cape Guardafui in the far north of Somalia, indicate trading contacts with the Red Sea, the Persian Gulf, and perhaps South Asia as early as the first century BC, and with the Persian Gulf and South Asia in the second to fifth centuries AD (Smith and Wright 1988). Nevertheless, the earliest substantial indications of trading settlements further south on the East African coast belong to the last quarter of the first millennium AD. In spite of the mention in the *Periplus of the Erythraean Sea* of an East African port called Rhapta, it has not been possible to identify this early-first-millennium site (Datoo 1970), which was most likely in the Rufiji Delta region (Chami 1999a: 210). However, potsherds from Ukunju Cave, on Juani Island close to Mafia Island, near the Rufiji Delta, have suggested contact with India, South-East Asia, and the Red Sea during the first millennium BC and the first millennium AD. In addition, four glass beads of Roman origin have been recovered from an approximately fourth-century AD deposit at Mkukutu in the Rufiji Delta (Chami 1999b), and two sherds of Roman pottery were found in a fifth-century AD context at Unguja Ukuu on the island of Zanzibar (Juma 1996). Nevertheless, none of the supposed discoveries of early-first-millennium coins on this coast is thought to be reliable.

Kilwa was an early trading settlement; its excavator Neville Chittick thought that its occupation commenced about AD 800. Dating the various excavated 'periods' was partly from imported ceramics, indicating that the settlement had overseas trading contacts from its beginning. In Period Ia (ninth century to about 1000) buildings were at first lacking and were then in mud and thatch with a little coral stone used with mud mortar. Similar buildings were found in Period Ib (about 1000 to late twelfth century). It was only in Period II (late twelfth to late thirteenth century) that the first substantial building in lime-mortared stone occurred, but Sutton (1998: 166) thought this began 150 or 200 years earlier. This period was when the first coins appeared. It was not until Periods IIIa and IIIb (late thirteenth century to about 1400, and about 1400 to about 1500, respectively) that the floruit of stone building occurred. Chittick thought that the earliest settlement was a pre-Islamic fishing village, with Islam beginning to arrive in Period Ib and becoming firmly established by Period II, by which time 'Kilwa had become a substantial and prosperous town' (Chittick 1974: vol. 1, 18–19, 28–9, 235–41). Thus the early evidence at Kilwa suggests the gradual development of both building techniques and settlement complexity, rather than any sudden arrival of these cultural characteristics from outside.

Another early settlement is Manda, on the island of the same name in the Lamu Archipelago. This was also excavated by Chittick and showed the existence of a town as early as the ninth century, occupied until perhaps the nineteenth century. Again, there was evidence of overseas trade from the beginning of the settlement, but in this case buildings of both mud, wood, and thatch and of stone were constructed from the start, the stonework of the latter sometimes being set in lime mortar, sometimes in red earth. There were also 'sea walls', some of which were of massive masonry that was set without mortar. In addition, unique on the East African coast, there were structures made of burnt bricks set in mud mortar, and it was suggested that these could have been imported from the Persian Gulf, perhaps as ships' ballast. Chittick concluded that immigrants from the Persian Gulf founded the town and that at least some of the inhabitants were Muslim from the settlement's beginning (Chittick 1971; 1984). This made Manda an exception, compared with similar sites on the East African coast, and Horton (1986) convincingly challenged Chittick's conclusions. The earliest stone buildings were shown to be later than the excavator had thought and to be influenced from the Red Sea rather than the Persian Gulf. However, later excavations at the town site of Sanjé ya Kati, near Kilwa, dating from AD 950 to 1250, did produce evidence for the arrival of people from the Persian Gulf who, it was argued, contributed to urban development on the East African coast (Pradines 2009).

Only 15 kilometres from Manda is the town site of Shanga, on Pate Island. Excavations over nine years made Shanga (Fig. 8.5) of major importance for the origins of urbanism on the East African coast. Its excavator, Mark Horton, established a building sequence from mud, wood, and thatch to stone, with imported ceramics throughout. This sequence extends from the late eighth century to the beginning of the fifteenth; mud mortar and stone buildings first appeared in the tenth century and lime-mortared stone buildings not until the twelfth century, becoming more important by the fourteenth century. It seems that the primary occupation at Shanga was non-Islamic, but there are remains of mosques from the end of the eighth century onwards. The sequence at this site suggests the indigenous origins of coastal culture, and the ten stages identified during the excavation of its central area show the evolution of the settlement over a period in excess of 600 years (Horton 1996).

Other coastal sites appear to have had an early origin. Mogadishu was occupied by the eleventh century AD (Broberg 1995; Dualeh 1996), Mombasa by about 1000 (Sassoon 1980), and Pate by about 800 (Wilson 1982: 214–15; Wilson and Lali Omar 1997: 63); in the Lamu Archipelago there are eleven

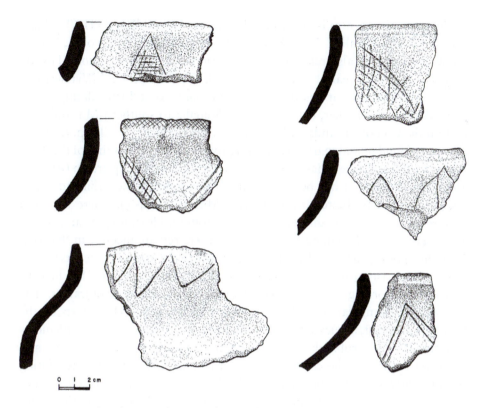

Fig. 8.7 Examples of Triangular Incised Ware sherds from the Tanzanian coast and hinterland. After Chami 1994: fig. 9.

sites with probable occupation in the ninth century (Horton 1986: 204). In addition, an archaeological study of the cultural landscape concentrating on the Tanzanian sites of Kilwa and Kaole produced evidence as early as the sixth century AD (Pollard 2008). Even more remarkable, because it is so far south on the Mozambique coast, is Chibuene, an occupation site belonging to the last quarter of the first millennium AD that contained imported Islamic glazed wares as well as glass beads and bottle fragments (Sinclair 1982; 1987: 86–91, 168; 1991: 190, 216; Sinclair et al. 2012: 734). Thus, early sites are so widely distributed that one would have to postulate a huge migration from southern Asia to attribute their simultaneous development to external stimulus. Such stimulus doubtless existed, but its relative unimportance is indicated by the very small percentage of imported wares in excavated sites (0.2 percent in Period Ia at Kilwa (Chittick 1974: vol. 2, 302)). Most of the recovered sherds are of indigenous wares, and in the earliest periods there is general uniformity amongst pottery from widely separated areas, although some regional diversity is present (Fleisher and Wynne-Jones 2011).

This pottery (Fig. 8.7) is known as 'Triangular Incised Ware' (TIW) (Chami 1994), previously called 'Early Kitchen Ware' (Chittick 1974: vol. 2, 320–2; 1984: 109–18) and also referred to as pottery of 'the Tana tradition' (Horton 1987a: 315–17) or 'early Tana Tradition' (ETT) (Fleisher and Wynne-Jones 2011: 246, footnote). It has been found on many coastal sites dating to the tenth century and earlier, extending from Somalia to southern Mozambique, and on the Comoro Islands and in northern Madagascar. Similar pottery has also been found inland, particularly along river valleys such as that of the Tana River in Kenya, where it has been recorded 250 kilometres upstream (Abungu 1995). In addition, it has been excavated from some of the Mijikenda *kaya* sites of the coastal hinterland in Kenya (Mutoro 1994–5). There has been disagreement about the antecedents of this pottery. Horton (1987a: 315–17; 1996: 410–11) and Abungu (1995: 253–5) preferred an ancestry in 'Pastoral Neolithic' pottery made by Cushitic pastoralists of the interior, whereas Chami (1994: 94–8; 1995) has seen its origins in 'Early Iron Age', or what he calls 'Early Iron-Working' (EIW) wares produced by Bantu agriculturalists. The presence of Triangular Incised Ware, in first-millennium AD contexts on the East African coast, argues strongly for an indigenous origin for the settlements concerned. This probability is strengthened by the work of Chami and Msemwa (1997) on the central coast of Tanzania, investigating sites dating from the first to the seventh century AD. They found evidence of Early Iron-Working farmers both on the coast and islands and in the interior, with Triangular Incised Ware clearly overlying Early Iron-Working pottery at the important site of Kivinja that dates to the fifth and sixth centuries. Also at that site were imported ceramics from the Middle East and glass from the Graeco-Roman world, showing that both local and transoceanic trade had already developed by the middle of the first millennium. Confirmation of this is provided by other sites, such as Unguja Ukuu, on Zanzibar Island, where again both forms of indigenous pottery have been found, in conjunction with imports dating from the fifth to seventh centuries from India, the Middle East, and even Roman sources. Indeed, both Triangular Incised Ware and Early Iron-Working pottery were also found at an eighth-century site near Dakawa, some 200 kilometres inland from Dar es Salaam on the Tanzanian coast, along with indications of substantial iron production (Haaland 1994–5). Increasingly, therefore, archaeological evidence is providing verification of the pre-Islamic origins of the East African trading network.

That network also included the Comoro Archipelago and Madagascar. The commencement of settlement was most likely in about the eighth century in the Comoro Islands (Sinclair 1995: 101–2; Allibert and Vérin 1996), but the earliest known settlement in Madagascar was in the early or middle first millennium AD, although there are traces by the third century BC (Mitchell 2004).

Linguistic evidence indicates that Malagasy, the most commonly spoken language in Madagascar, has its closest relatives in Indonesia (Adelaar 1996; Blench 2007), but archaeology has been unable to confirm the arrival of people from there (Dewar and Wright 1993; Wright 1993: 659), and it seems likely that settlers from the East African coast were also important (Dewar 1996; Beaujard 2011). By the late first millennium AD, iron-using villagers on the Comoro Islands, whose basic subsistence depended on fishing and domesticated animals and plants, were also trading with the Persian Gulf, East Asia, and the coast of East Africa, as shown by ceramics, glass beads, and glass vessels recovered from their sites (Wright 1984). Best known is Dembeni, a large village of mud, wood, and thatch buildings on the island of Maore (also known as Mayotte), its earliest occupation dating from about AD 850 to 880, and a later one from about the tenth to eleventh centuries (Allibert et al. 1990). Subsequent excavation has shown that from the ninth to the twelfth centuries this settlement received a variety of imported ceramics from Persian, Chinese, and Islamic sources, apparently mainly in exchange for rock crystal, a valuable commodity traded from Madagascar from where vessels of chlorite-schist (sometimes described as soapstone) were also obtained. Rock crystal was important in international trade because of its beauty and religious and mystical properties. Widely exchanged, it reached many distant places, including Europe (Pradines 2013). The occupants of settlements such as Dembeni were probably also supplying tortoiseshell, marine shell, and other commodities for the Indian Ocean trade. The presence of Triangular Incised Ware indicates contact with the East African coast, just as the rock crystal and chlorite-schist show connections with Madagascar. Furthermore, the bones of house mice in several Dembeni Phase sites suggest that some of the ships visiting the Comoros were large, long-distance vessels (Wright 1992: 84–5). As Sinclair (1995: 101) claimed, the Comoro Islands 'were significant hubs of the western Indian Ocean trading systems'. In origin, these developments were pre-Islamic, but Islam gradually became established as the settlements increased in size; the towns of Sima and Domoni, on the island of Nzwani, grew to about 8 hectares during the eleventh to thirteenth centuries (Wright 1992: 124). Excavations at Acoua-Agnala M'Kiri, on the northwest coast of Maore (Mayotte) Island, have revealed a walled settlement that participated in the western Indian Ocean trade between the twelfth and fifteenth centuries, providing a port of call for ships sailing from Madagascar to the Swahili coast (Pauly 2013). By the eighteenth century the Comoros seem to have been characterized by fortified towns, such as Itsandra and Ntsudjini on Ngazidja Island, which controlled adjacent territories (Dahalani 1992).

Archaeological research has also traced the process of urbanization and state formation in some parts of Madagascar. By the 1850s both developments were

Fig. 8.8 Antananarivo, Madagascar, in the 1850s, showing a royal procession passing along its eastern side. From Ellis 1859: 365.

advanced, as recorded by the Reverend William Ellis (1859) during his visits (Fig. 8.8). Amongst early archaeological evidence is that from Kingany on the north-west coast of Madagascar, a town site with stone ruins that seems to have been occupied from the ninth or tenth century AD to about the sixteenth century, and some of whose inhabitants participated in the Indian Ocean trade (Vérin 1986: 161–7). Subsequently, a town on the island of Antsoheribory, in the same area, was occupied from the late sixteenth to the early eighteenth century and has evidence of trading contacts with the Near East, the Far East, and Europe (Wright et al. 1996: 55–66). Another early town site is Mahilaka, further north along the same coast. Occupied from the tenth to the fifteenth century, this site had a walled area of more than 60 hectares, within which were a few stone structures but many others of less permanent materials (Wright 1993: 668; Radimilahy 1998). Mahilaka had wide trading connections, possibly exporting rock crystal, chlorite-schist and gold, as well as mangrove wood, copal, tortoiseshell, and slaves. Rat bones from the site suggest plague, brought to the island by visiting ships, as one possible cause of the town's abandonment (Radimilahy 1998: 110, 202–6, 208–11). However, it was in the central highlands that most sociopolitical developments took place, leading to the emergence of the Merina state by the eighteenth century (Crossland 2001). Ankadivory, near present-day Antananarivo, is one of many ditched settlements in this area and has been dated to about the thirteenth century. It has also produced evidence that by that time even inland Madagascar was in contact with the Indian Ocean trade (Wright and Rakotoarisoa 1990: 28–9; Sinclair 1991: 196–8), in which slaves from the Comoro Islands and Madagascar became particularly important from the sixteenth century onwards (Vernet 2003).

As research has progressed, attention has been given to the overall layout of Swahili towns, rather than concentrating on stone buildings. Prospecting techniques such as geophysical survey as at Kilwa (Fleisher et al. 2012), or a combination of geophysical survey, geochemical testing, and geoarchaeology as at Songo Mnara (Fleisher 2013: 271), are revealing more information about the towns and their contexts.

Subsistence economy

Archaeologists have sometimes neglected the subject of subsistence in this part of Africa, and John Mack (2007: 8) pointed out that in a maritime context such as this 'trade was itself subsistence'. Nevertheless, archaeological evidence for people's food resources is essential if we are to understand their socio-economic situation. For example, the cultivation of sorghum in the eleventh and twelfth centuries is attested by the recovery of carbonized sorghum from a layer attributed to Period Ib at Kilwa (Chittick 1974: vol. 1, 52–3). Also the early deposits at Kilwa produced evidence for the eating of fish and shellfish, while a well dated to the late thirteenth to fourteenth centuries contained the mandible of an immature camel (Chittick 1974: vol. 1, 28, 43, 98).

There is evidence from Chibuene for sheep, cattle, fish, and shellfish in the lower occupation level, dating from about AD 600 to 1000, although there are no indications of plant husbandry (Sinclair 1982: 152, 162; 1987: 88; 1991: 190, 216; Sinclair et al. 2012). Also Badenhorst et al. (2011) reported livestock, chickens, and wild animals, with fish, turtle, and shark most common. At Shanga botanical evidence is lacking but the faunal record is substantial; seafood seems to have been important and included fish of reef, inshore, and (rarely) deep-sea type; dugong; turtles; and shellfish. In addition, there were cattle, sheep, goats, camels, and chickens; cats and dogs were also kept. The hunting of wild animals contributed a small part of the diet. Significantly, the black rat was present, suggesting relatively dense human occupation and, as a vector of bubonic plague, perhaps one of the causes for the eventual abandonment of the site. Probably a mixed economy was practised at Shanga, although the absence of plant food evidence is a problem (Horton and Mudida 1993; Horton 1996: 378–93). Excavations at Manda suggested a similar subsistence economy, with evidence of sheep or goat, cattle, domestic fowl, and domesticated cat. In addition, dugong, turtles, and fish were exploited. Camel was present and a little game was hunted. Again, this site lacks evidence for plant food (Chittick 1984: 215). Fortunately, there is evidence from Mgombani, some 16 kilometres from the Kenyan coast, for the cultivation of *Sorghum bicolor* (sorghum), *Pennisetum glaucum* (pearl millet), *and Eleusine coracana* (finger millet) during the first millennium AD (Helm et al. 2012). The authors described this as 'the first significant evidence for early agriculture on the Kenyan coast'.

Excavations at Dembeni, Old Sima, and M'Bachile in the Comoro Islands provided more information on diet. There was substantial use of fish, particularly from the coral reefs; turtles and some wild animals and birds were hunted; and domesticated sheep or goats were kept, most probably goats. There was also botanical evidence for the cultivation of rice (*Oryza sativa*), millet (possibly *Setaria*), coconut (*Cocos nucifera*) and sesame (*Sesamum cf. indicum*) (Wright 1984: 48–54; Allibert et al. 1990: 153). The site of Mahilaka, in Madagascar, provided evidence of rice cultivation and the use of coconut; the keeping of cattle, sheep, goats, pigs, chickens, guinea fowl, and ducks; and the hunting of wild animals and birds; as well as fishing, turtle catching, and shellfish gathering (Radimilahy 1998: 195–9). The approximately thirteenth-century site of Ankadivory produced evidence for the keeping of cattle in the central highlands of Madagascar (Sinclair 1991: 196).

It seems that by late in the first millennium AD, when the earliest identifiable coastal cities and towns were settled (earlier sites could have been lost to coastline changes), there already existed a mixed economy exploiting the resources of both sea and land. Fishing and livestock husbandry could have provided ample animal protein, and plant food must have made a significant contribution to the diet. In particular, it is likely that plants originating in South-East Asia, introduced during the first millennium, played an important role. Asian rice, the greater yam, coconut, and Indian saffron were probably brought to Madagascar by settlers from Indonesia at that time; bananas, taro, and other yams had probably reached the East African coast from a similar source at an earlier date (Beaujard 2011). Shepherd (1982) argued that the southern end of the East African coast, particularly the Comoro Islands, played an important early role in the development of the coastal culture. If this was so, then perhaps the enhancement of the coastal subsistence economy by the South-East Asian food plants was a factor in the growth of the coastal settlements. Rather than being peripheral to the African coast, Madagascar and the Comoro Islands might have been a gateway for new ideas. Whether or not this was so, it is clear that by the second half of the first millennium AD, the subsistence economy of the East African coast must have been producing a surplus adequate to support increasing social complexity.

Technology

Archaeological evidence from East African coastal and island sites indicates considerable technological sophistication, although it is uncertain how much of it was of foreign origin rather than indigenous. Particularly important was metalworking. Iron was both smelted and forged, and evidence of one or both processes occurred, often at an early date, at Kilwa, Manda, Shanga, and Chibuene, as well as at Dembeni and Old Sima in the Comoro Islands, and at Mahilaka in Madagascar. Kusimba (1999: 101–7) emphasized the role of iron working on the Swahili coast, and indeed the twelfth-century writer al-Idrisi mentioned iron as an important export commodity (Horton 1996: 416). Probably smelting was usually in the hinterland, where more wood was available for fuel; the inland site of Dakawa had evidence of iron smelting as early as the seventh to ninth century AD (Haaland 1994–5). In addition, some of the coastal sites produced evidence of working in copper or copper-base alloy, in the form of slag or of crucibles with metal traces, and there are also indications that gold, silver, and lead were sometimes worked (Chittick 1974; 1984; Wright 1984; Sinclair 1987; Horton 1996; Radimilahy 1998). Metal artefacts seem to have been manufactured on the coast and islands, but it was the minting of coins that was most notable. These have been recovered from many coastal sites, being produced at Kilwa, Mafia, Zanzibar, Mogadishu, and perhaps other places. Usually they were of copper or copper-base alloy, like the more than 300 coins from a deposit excavated at Songo Mnara that is attributed to the end of the fourteenth or very early fifteenth century (Perkins et al. 2014). However, more than half of the coins found at Shanga are of silver (Brown 1996), and most of the more than 2,000 coins in the eleventh-century hoard found at Mtambwe Mkuu on Pemba Island are of silver (Horton et al. 1986). Also from East African coastal sites are less common coins from other parts of the Islamic world and even from China, with most of the gold coins coming from the former.

The most remarkable aspect of East African coastal technology, however, was building. As well as working in timber, mud, and thatch, considerable skills were developed in the construction of stone buildings. Coral was quarried, either from offshore reefs or on land; Horton (1996: 26–7) distinguished between well-coursed walls of dressed pieces of *Porites solida*, from the first source, and rougher walls of coral rag from the second. Traces of quarrying for both materials have been found near Shanga, and those for *Porites* coral are underwater, implying knowledge of underwater quarrying (Horton 1986: 206). Intertidal quarrying was also carried out, as at Ras Nunge, near the site of Kaole in Tanzania, although for 'cemented shelly sandstone', not coral (Pollard (2008: 180, figs 7.6 and 7.36). Both types of coral walling could be bonded with mud or lime mortar, the latter obtained

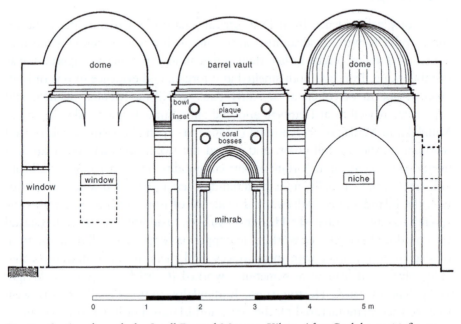

Fig. 8.9 Section through the Small Domed Mosque, Kilwa. After Garlake 1966: fig. 14.

by burning coral and mixing sand with the lime produced. Several approximately thirteenth-century lime kilns were found at Kilwa (Chittick 1974: vol. 1, 39–43). The use of lime mortar seems to have become more common with time; plaster for internal wall surfaces and rendering for external surfaces also had a lime base. Some stone structures were high, and scaffolding, presumably with lashed mangrove poles, seems to have been used. Roofs consisted usually of mangrove rafters, stone, and lime mortar but could also be supported with columns and beams or consist of vaults or domes (Fig. 8.9). Doors and windows usually had fitted woodwork; most houses possessed internal latrines and washing places; and drainage was provided both inside and outside some buildings (Garlake 1966). Wells were dug to provide convenient water supplies. This implies functional specialization: there must have been quarrymen, lime burners, stone masons, plasterers, and carpenters, as well as others. In addition, some knowledge of architecture was obviously present. Whatever the contributions to this overall expertise from alien sources, the bulk of the actual work was surely done by local craftsmen, and it is significant that the so-called pillar tomb, that is common on the East African coast, has no known parallels elsewhere.

An important part of coastal technology must have been boat building, although there is as yet no archaeological evidence for this. Nevertheless, the *Periplus of the Erythraean Sea* recorded sewn boats on this coast nearly 2,000 years ago (Casson 1989: 9), and the Portuguese remarked on them at the end of the fifteenth century (Ravenstein 1898: 26). All the materials needed to construct these boats were available on the East African coast, and it is likely that the *dau la mtepe* and the *mtepe*, with their sewn hulls and matting sails, were often built there. Although we have few details of how they were built (Prins 1982), graffiti of such boats, scratched into the wall plaster of houses and mosques along the coast, show how important they must have been (Chittick 1974: vol. 2, 266–7). Boats constructed in this manner stand up well to the frequent strandings necessary on much of the eastern coast. It is apparent that some of them were of considerable size: in 1866 David Livingstone had one loaded with 'six camels, three buffaloes, and a calf, two mules, and four donkeys' (Waller 1874: vol. 1, 9). Furthermore, it seems that the people of the East African coast had not only developed the skills to build these boats but also knew how to use them. Evidence of contact between Madagascar, the Comoro Islands, and the East African coast, as well as with South and South-East Asia, implies a substantial knowledge of seamanship.

Of the other crafts practised on the coast, probably the most important was spinning and weaving cotton cloth, suggested by the number of spindle whorls which occur in contexts dated to the first half of the second millennium (e.g., Horton 1996: 337–41). Seawater was evaporated to produce salt, an activity for which there is some evidence at Mkadini on the Tanzanian coast. In addition, ivory and bone were carved and shell beads made, as well as beads of rock crystal and carnelian (e.g., Horton 1996: 323, 332–3, 346–7, 349–50). A range of pottery included some with complex painted patterns and included lamps (Chittick 1974). Of particular interest is evidence from Mahilaka that indicates glass-bead manufacture, probably by melting broken glass from imported items (Radimilahy 1998: 184, plate 7.1d, h, j, k), and the possibility exists of similar activity at Shanga (Horton 1996: 332).

Social system

Archaeological evidence for social organization includes many settlements, some of them walled, ranging from villages to cities. The use of stone for some buildings has left clear indications of the character of urbanization prior to Portuguese contact. This was a society where many people lived in towns or cities but where many remained in the rural areas in villages, and there has been discussion of the relationship of urban and rural settlements (LaViolette and Fleisher 2005: 339–43). The level of functional specialization was probably higher in larger settlements, with most of the inhabitants of smaller settlements engaged in primary production. In addition, the degree of social stratification seems to have been greater in the larger settlements. This is suggested by the range in quality and size of the houses, both within the settlements and between different settlements. At the bottom end of the scale were mud, wood, and thatch buildings, about which less is known, although the excavations at Shanga have shed some light on them (Horton 1996: 235–42). Above these were small stone houses of one to three rooms, like those at Takwa (Wilson 1982: fig. 2), but with the larger houses provided with latrines. Higher again were multi-roomed houses with an enclosed courtyard, like some of those at Songo Mnara (Garlake 1966: fig. 74). At the top of the scale were large multiroomed houses with multiple courtyards and monumental features, such as imposing entrances, like the so-called palace at Gedi (Kirkman 1963: fig. 2).

This is an example of social and economic stratification apparent in arch-aeological evidence. A society is suggested that ranged from ruling merchant princes at the top to wealthy merchants to successful artisans to slaves or lowly menials. There are also signs that social differentiation became more marked with time. For example, building in mud, wood, and thatch was at first usual, but building in stone gradually became more common. Furthermore, the so-called palaces of Gedi and Songo Mnara probably originated as interlocking houses belonging to one extended family. These could have been subsequently transformed into a 'palace' by the addition of monumental features, when the head of that family became the hereditary ruler of the settlement (p. 236). An indication of the status to which some of these rulers eventually aspired is given by the coins bearing their names, particularly during the twelfth to fourteenth centuries. Indeed, at least one ruler seems to have been outstandingly ambitious, if the luxury of the 'palace' of Husuni Kubwa at Kilwa is considered. It appears, both from the number of medium to large stone houses and from the wide use of imported ceramics, that there emerged a socially superior merchant class comparable to the *wa-ungwana* of recent Swahili towns and cities (Donley 1982; Donley-Reid 1990). Indeed, the many stone tombs that were constructed along the East African coast also suggest the existence of such a class.

It is difficult to decide the extent to which these social developments led to state formation, because the archaeological evidence offers little relevant information. There are also geographical differences in that information. Towns on the northern Swahili coast had relatively more stone buildings and fewer mud, wood, and thatch buildings, and it has been suggested that they had 'a more horizontally differentiated power base, with numerous leaders (merchant, religious, political)'. In contrast, towns on the southern Swahili coast contained fewer stone buildings and more mud, wood, and thatch buildings, and it has been proposed that they had 'a small-scale, ranked hierarchy, whose leader ruled through custom and consent' (LaViolette and Fleisher 2005: 340). However, the existence of a few much larger settlements, and their geographical relationships to neighbouring settlements of medium or small size, suggests that some cities, for example, Mogadishu, Pate, Malindi, Mombasa, and Kilwa, controlled the territory around them, a possibility reinforced by the issue of coinage in some places. Indeed, the prosperity apparent in the early fourteenth century at Kilwa suggests an extension of control over the gold trade from Sofala, far to the south in what is now Mozambique. A coin minted in Kilwa even got as far as Great Zimbabwe. It seems likely that some of the east coast cities did function as small city-states from early in the second millennium AD and that, sometimes, certain city-states came to dominate others. In addition, collectively, the Swahili cities were part of a city-state culture, as discussed by Sinclair and Håkansson (2000: 479). In spite of local variations, they shared the same religion, same language, same architectural tradition and material culture, and a kinship-based political organization, often with both elected kings and a degree of consensus.

Population pressures

The distribution, number, and size of settlement sites along the East African coast and on its islands suggest that, prior to Portuguese contact, the region supported a substantial population. It is thought that Swahili towns with stone buildings each had in excess of 5,000 inhabitants, and places such as Kilwa and Mombasa had more than 15,000 (LaViolette and Fleisher 2005: 340). In addition, villages of mud, wood, and thatch buildings proliferated in many coastal areas, as on the island of Pemba (LaViolette and Fleisher 2009). With both land and sea resources, with food supplies augmented by South-East Asian domesticated plants, and with fresh water available in many places, the coast and its islands must have contrasted with the dry lands of the interior. Thus the coast could have stimulated population growth, but there was nowhere for excess population to go, other than north or south along the coast or onto its islands. This is because coastal peoples would have been unlikely to adapt to the dry interior. The result was the long, narrow distribution of the East African coastal culture. However, the optimum coastal conditions gradually petered out to both north and south. In addition, even within the best areas, soil character and water availability varied, making some localities more attractive for settlement than others. Thus, population pressures could have been one of the factors that contributed to urbanization and state development.

Two things suggest that such pressures existed. First, a significant number of settlements, on the coast itself and also in the Comoro Islands and Madagascar, were protected by walls, suggesting that population levels had reached a point where competition for resources was causing intergroup conflict or threat of conflict. A remarkable example is the fifteenth- to seventeenth-century fortified site of Pujini, on Pemba Island, Tanzania, which 'appears to have been a manifestation of, and contributor to, island tensions – political, economic, social' (LaViolette 1996: 81). Second, although relevant archaeological evidence is difficult to identify, the export of slaves from this coast seems to have had a long history (Trimingham 1975: 116–18; Horton 1996: 415–16), implying the existence of excess population that provided a source. However, some of the slaves might have come from inland.

Not all the hinterland is dry, unattractive country. As already pointed out (p. 228), cultivable fertile soils along the lower parts of some of the rivers must have made important contributions to the coastal economy, so that Mogadishu, for instance, although situated on a dry coast mostly unsuitable for cultivation, was largely maintained by the productivity of the Shibeli River inland to its west (Dualeh 1996). That such interaction of coast and inland riverine plains was important in the past is indicated by the coastal and interior distribution of first-millennium AD Triangular Incised Ware in both Kenya and Tanzania (Abungu 1995; Chami 1995). It was this relationship of coastal and interior peoples that must have formed the basis of the trading networks that provided the commodities sought by the Indian Ocean trade (Mutoro 1998). Like the coast, however, the more productive inland areas were limited in extent and are likely to have experienced population pressures, particularly during periods of environmental stress.

It has also been suggested that there were dry conditions in Ethiopia and Equatorial Africa between about AD 500 and 800 (Hassan 1997: 219–20). In addition, the sediments of Lake Naivasha, in Kenya, provide a climatic record for equatorial East Africa over the last 1,100 years, suggesting that it was generally drier than today from AD 1000 to 1270, but fairly wet from 1270 to 1850, although interrupted around 1380 to 1420, 1560 to 1620, and 1760 to 1840 by episodes of aridity more severe than any drought of the twentieth century (Verschuren et al. 2000). Such climatic oscillations would have allowed population growth during moister periods but caused population pressure during drier periods, periods that might be correlated with socio-economic growth or contraction on the Swahili coast and islands.

Ideology

As in the West African savanna (Chapter 6), Islam was the major ideology on the East African coast and islands (Insoll 2003). Wright (1993: 671–2) argued that Islam, along with trade, was the crucial factor in Swahili urban development. It bound together the people in the towns and bound the towns to surrounding villages, thus contributing also to state formation. Islam was not just a religion, it was a way of life. Islamic belief brought with it distinct patterns of symbolic and material culture, including social behaviour, art, music, literacy, scientific knowledge, scholarship, education, coinage, and even the layout of settlements (Insoll 1999). At many Swahili archaeological sites there is at least one stone-built mosque; significantly, the main congregational mosque usually occupies a central position within each settlement. In addition, the care and expense that was often lavished on the building of mosques show how important the role of Islam was in coastal life. Islam was the faith of urban, mercantile, literate South-West Asia, and its adoption brought East Africa into a huge common market; it ensured commercial and cultural intercourse with Arab lands to the north. In Swahili the word for 'civilization' is *ustaarabu*, often understood to mean 'becoming like an Arab' (Chittick 1971: 112; Jahadhmy 1981: 10). On the East African coast, to become like an Arab meant to follow Islam, to live in a stone house in a city, and to be involved in trade.

However, Islam was not the primary cause of urbanization and state development on the East African coast, whatever its later influence on those developments. As in the West African savanna, Islam seems to have arrived after the initial changes had taken place. Thus, in the fourteenth century when ibn Battuta visited Kilwa, Islam had already been accepted there, but in the tenth century when al-Masudi visited the East African coast some at least of its occupants were animists: 'Every man worships what he pleases, be it a plant, an animal or a mineral' (Freeman-Grenville 1975: 31–2, 16–17). The available archaeological evidence confirms that Islam was usually adopted only after initial settlement. For example, the primary occupation at Shanga, dated from about AD 760 to 780, contained no evidence for Islam, although from the late eighth century onwards there was a succession of buildings which have been interpreted as mosques (Horton 1996: 394–406). At Gedi there might have been a much longer pre-Islamic period, because houses probably occupied the site of the congregational mosque until as late as the middle of the fifteenth century (Kirkman 1954: 8–9, 14). At Kilwa its excavator thought that Islam began to arrive in the eleventh to twelfth centuries. We can conclude that although Islam played a big part in the developments on the East African coast, it did not necessarily inaugurate them. So far as ideological input was concerned, unknown animistic beliefs probably contributed substantially. The strength of those beliefs may be judged from the fact that East African Islam has remained syncretic until recent times.

External trade

So considerable is the archaeological evidence for long-distance external trade in East African coastal and island sites that it has often dominated discussion of those sites and influenced interpretations. The cities and city-states have been seen as a direct response to the growth of that trade: trading bases for overseas mercantile interests, clinging to the coast of a hostile continent, in which they had no interest other than the acquisition of primary products for export. These colonial settlements, it was thought, had little impact on the African interior and were gradually Africanized by intermarriage, as some aspects of the alien culture were adopted and the distinctive Swahili culture evolved.

This interpretation is no longer accepted, and the coastal and island settlements are now seen as part of an enormous interaction zone that included the Indian Ocean, Arabia, South and East Asia, East Africa, and the African interior. Of crucial importance for contacts within this zone were ships able to make long trading voyages and crews with the necessary knowledge of the winds and currents as well as navigational skills. In the Indian Ocean zone the ship provided the vital link, just as the camel did in the Sahara (Insoll 2003: 143). In the same way that the trans-Saharan trade penetrated deep into the lands south of the desert, so Swahili trade reached far into East and Central Africa. Historically documented inland trade routes of the eighteenth and nineteenth centuries very likely followed routes that were of great antiquity

(Wynne-Jones and Croucher 2007). The idea that there was little interaction between the coastal settlements and the African interior has become increasingly untenable (Kusimba et al. 2005).

The evidence for long-distance, overseas trade is remarkable. Much of this consists of imported ceramics, material that is quite distinct from African pottery traditions and can usually be assigned both to an area of origin and to an approximate date. At Kilwa, for example, the earliest deposits of the ninth and tenth centuries contained Islamic glazed wares that probably originated in the Persian Gulf or were trans-shipped there. Although the wares changed with time, and the places from which they came also changed to some degree, such Islamic glazed wares continued to be imported until well after Portuguese contact. In addition, from about the thirteenth century, Chinese ceramics began to arrive in Kilwa; indeed, from about the fourteenth century onwards they equalled or exceeded the quantity of Islamic glazed wares. It is these Chinese products, at both Kilwa and other East African coastal sites, which have convinced archaeologists of the extent of the long-distance trade of this coast. No doubt the Chinese material was usually trans-shipped several times, but the distances involved are still most impressive. In addition, imports other than ceramics have also been found in East African coastal sites. At Kilwa, for instance, glass vessels and beads of glass, carnelian, and other semi-precious stones were found, widely distributed through time. The carnelian and perhaps the glass beads might have come from western India; the other items probably from various parts of the Islamic world (Chittick 1974; Insoll et al. 2004). Furthermore, these trade goods consist only of those that happen to have survived in the archaeological record. As was the case with the trans-Saharan trade discussed in Chapter 6 (p. 181), one wonders about the imports that have left no trace. For instance, it is thought that cloth would have been one of the principal imports, particularly high-quality cloth and coloured cloth. Such a commodity could have come from a very wide area indeed. So extensive and substantial was East Africa's international trade that Islamic, Indian, Sri Lankan, and Chinese coinage reached the Swahili coast, and, to facilitate commercial transactions, local rulers struck their own coins. Remarkably, many bronze coins were exported from China, for use as a metal source in regions around the Indian Ocean, including East Africa. For example, a bronze lion figurine excavated from Shanga was either cast in India or more probably cast in East Africa by Indian craftsmen, possibly using Chinese coins (Horton and Blurton 1988; Horton 1996: 358).

In return for the things supplied to the East African coast and islands, overseas traders were tapping the natural resources of the coast and interior. These primary products included ivory, rhinoceros horn, tortoiseshell, ambergris, gold, copper, iron, rock crystal, frankincense, myrrh, mangrove poles, ebony and other timbers, sandalwood, and slaves, not to mention spices, about which there is less certainty. Without access to these commodities, the socio-economic development of the Swahili coast would not have occurred, because its settlements could not have attracted interest from the Indian Ocean traders. Many of the exports would have come from deep in the African interior, but the imported goods have rarely been found in the interior. A notable exception is a very small quantity of the Chinese pottery known as 'celadon', which reached the site of Great Zimbabwe in the fourteenth century. In addition, glass beads reached sites in the Limpopo Valley, such as Indian and Persian examples found in a ninth-century context at Schroda (p. 270) (Pwiti 2005: 382). Glass beads also occurred in the Upemba Depression in south-east Democratic Congo, in the thirteenth to fifteenth centuries, along with cowrie shells, which had already appeared there by the tenth to twelfth centuries (p. 311). This is 1,500 kilometres from the East African coast, from which the cowries must have come and presumably the glass beads as well (Insoll 2003: 378). Furthermore, at a date around the fourteenth century, a few glass beads, along with a single cowrie shell (probably *Monetaria annulus*), found their way to Kibiro on the eastern shore of Lake Albert (Connah 1996).

Nevertheless, evidence for coastal-interior contacts remains limited; so what sort of a trade could have gathered so many African resources but apparently given so little in exchange? The answer lies partly in the differential preservation of the archaeological evidence, for not only would imported cloth not have survived, but, without historical sources, we would know little even about the exports. However, this does not explain why imports that survive in the coastal sites are not in general found in the interior; after all, Chinese ceramics are tough material. The most likely explanation is that trade was more complex than a simple exchange of overseas goods for African commodities. Chittick distinguished not two categories of goods that were traded, that is to say imports and exports, but four categories. These consisted of (1) African goods sought for export, (2) goods imported for trade with the interior, (3) goods imported for use in the coastal towns, and (4) goods produced in those towns for trade with the interior. Thus, the East African coastal settlements were acting as entrepôts, that is to say, as commercial centres of import, export, collection, and distribution. Two sorts of imports arrived from overseas: cloth that could be traded into the interior and luxury goods that were sought by the more successful occupants of the coastal cities and towns for prestige purposes. These exotic manufactures, of which ceramics and some other items are all that have survived, were probably restricted by economic and social factors to the coastal elite. To trade with the peoples of the interior, the merchants of the coastal settlements used much of the cloth that had been imported from overseas, but they also transported into the interior cotton

cloth manufactured in the coastal settlements. In addition, before the thirteenth century, beads of marine shell were manufactured on the coast, and
large numbers of cowrie shells were collected. Both of these were probably
used for the inland trade, although imported glass beads seem to have taken
the place of shell beads in later times.

It is also likely that coastal communities traded some agricultural surplus into
the interior, just as inland riverine cultivators must have traded surplus both to
the coast and to more immediate neighbours (Kusimba et al. 2005: 260).
Nomadic pastoralists, hunter-gatherers, and even the farmers of the drier areas
would probably have welcomed additions to their diet. They would also have
welcomed salt, which was probably produced on the coast. In return for these
and other commodities, recipients in the inland gave the primary products
that the coastal merchants sought and which they exported overseas. The
antiquity of such contacts between coast and inland is indicated by the seated
burial excavated at the site of Murrapania IV, near Nampula, in the interior of
Mozambique. Dated to the beginning of the first millennium AD, the burial was
associated with an elephant tusk and pottery decorated with marine-shell
impressions (Sinclair 1991: 188).

A key factor in this complex trade was local input, of primary products and
manufactures from the coast itself. Environmental diversity and the consequent unevenness of resource distribution must have necessitated the early,
pre-Islamic development of local exchange systems on the East African coast
and between it and its hinterland. In particular, coastal trading in small vessels
would have developed early on a coast that was generally suited to inshore
navigation. Some indication of this trade network was found at Kilwa, where
stone vessels made of chlorite-schist appeared from about the eleventh to
twelfth centuries onward. These are thought to have originated in Madagascar
(Chittick 1974: vol. 1, 237). In addition, it was no doubt because of such a
coastal trading network that Kilwa was able to profit from the export of gold,
from the Zimbabwe Plateau, by southern Mozambique coastal settlements.
Indeed, it seems that the more successful of the coastal cities, such as Kilwa,
were successful not only because of their location on trade routes connecting
the interior to overseas markets but also because of their location on coastal
trade routes which enabled them to act as collecting points for local products
and as distribution points for imports. Horton (1987b) wrote of what he called
'The Swahili Corridor', stressing movement of goods along the coast, but
Sinclair (1995: 107) preferred the idea of a 'Swahili trading wheel', with its
hub located in different places at different times, such as the Comoro Islands,
Kilwa, or Zanzibar. Insoll (2003: fig. 4.4) provided a map of how the pre-
Islamic trade networks might have looked. Such a circular trading network, or
a series of such networks, might have linked the long East African coastal strip

to the offshore islands and to Madagascar, as well as to parts of the African interior such as the Zimbabwe Plateau, and then linked the whole system into the Indian Ocean trade.

Thus the East African towns and cities did not result simply from the development of external trade with overseas markets. Such trade had a substantial influence on their subsequent history but was only part of a complex network involving local exchange systems, which almost certainly pre-dated the overseas connections and definitely pre-dated the arrival of Islam.

Conclusion

Urbanization and state formation on the East African coast and adjacent islands have sometimes been treated as though they resulted from external stimulus. In particular, the larger settlements of this coast have been regarded as Islamic trading cities, founded by colonists who originated from the Persian Gulf at the end of the first millennium AD. Such a view has held that this coast was significant only as the edge of the Indian Ocean trading network, to which it supplied the products of the African interior and from which it received some of the products of the most sophisticated cultures of its time. Unfortunately, this interpretation has been arrived at by looking at the results rather than at the causes of the remarkable East African coastal developments.

Eventually, external trade was extremely important to the settlements of this coast; no doubt there were some mercantile colonists from outside. However, it is necessary to ask what already existed on this coast to attract such attention. This question cannot be answered by excavating the stone-built settlements of the thirteenth to fifteenth centuries, on which much of the archaeological field research has been concentrated. It is doubtful if it can even be answered by excavating the important settlement deposits of the ninth and tenth centuries, which have also commanded attention. The answer must lie in the investigation of the coastal settlement archaeology of the last millennium BC and the earlier part of the first millennium AD, a task to which archaeologists are now giving attention. In addition, the large coastal settlements of the first half of the second millennium AD will undoubtedly be better understood if they can be viewed in the context of the whole settlement pattern of which they formed a part: in short, archaeologists are having to look for and investigate the smaller settlements that were contemporary with such places as Kilwa, Gedi, or Shanga. As these things are done, it is becoming clear that the indigenous contribution to cultural development on the East African coast was much more substantial than previously thought and that the origins of the East African coastal culture were African, not Asiatic.

We have seen that there existed a strong subsistence base, capable of producing a surplus, encouraging complex local exchange networks. It is also probable that the introduction of South-East Asian food plants, some 2,000 years ago, had a catalytic effect on coastal cultural evolution. To these things should be added the existence of a sophisticated technology that encouraged functional specialization, and there should also be added the possibility of complex population pressures within increasingly hierarchical societies, whose socioeconomic order could be legitimized first by indigenous animism and later by Islam. It is significant that, during the later first millennium AD, similar locally made pottery was in use both at widely separated coastal settlements and in parts of the interior. It is also significant that some early coastal sites show a gradual change from construction in mud, wood, and thatch to stone and that some of the later coastal sites remained substantially settlements of mud, wood, and thatch buildings, some of the less important ones almost entirely so. In addition, so widespread were these coastal and island settlements that a massive immigration would have to be invoked if they are to be explained as alien foundations. One must conclude that the large settlements of the East African coast and islands were not merely the edge of an Indian Ocean trading network but the focus of complex African networks, which subsequently incorporated substantial elements from the Indian Ocean world.

Chapter 9

Cattle, ivory, and gold: social complexity in Zambezia

Zambezia is the region between the Zambezi and Limpopo Rivers and between the Kalahari Desert and the Indian Ocean. The name was already in use by 1890 (Maund 1890) and has remained relevant (Pikirayi 2001b). This region comprises modern Zimbabwe, southern Mozambique, north-eastern Botswana, and the extreme north of South Africa. From the archaeological perspective, it is characterized by widespread evidence for the development of social complexity, commencing in the first millennium AD and continuing until the nineteenth century. Most famous of this evidence is the site of Great Zimbabwe, perhaps one of the most ill-used of Africa's archaeological sites. Its fame is such that it has given its name to the country in which it is situated, the country formerly known as Rhodesia and before that as Southern Rhodesia. Its ill usage has been both intellectual and physical, starting when it first became known to Europeans. The first such visitor was a German geologist, Carl Mauch, in 1871. After giving an account of the impressive stone ruins, Mauch felt it necessary to explain their presence deep in the African interior and did so by associating them with King Solomon and the Queen of Sheba. Perhaps it is understandable that a nineteenth-century European should grasp at such an unlikely biblical explanation, but unfortunately the myth of alien origin for the Great Zimbabwe structures was to survive for a long time, even surfacing as a political issue in the 1960s and 1970s (Garlake 1973: 209–10). This was probably because such a belief became psychologically essential for some European colonial settlers in this part of Africa. Perhaps the most damaging aspect of the African colonial experience was the attempted denial to African peoples of their own cultural heritage, of which the attribution of Great Zimbabwe to outside influence must be the classic example.

For those who understood the archaeological evidence, there was never any doubt about the African origins of Great Zimbabwe (e.g., Garlake 1973; 1978a). Nevertheless, the resulting controversy has influenced much of the research that has been conducted at this famous site. Intellectually, it has dictated the questions that have been asked by researchers; physically, it has sometimes occasioned excavations and restoration work that damaged or destroyed archaeological evidence. Excavations by Theodore Bent in 1891, Richard Hall in 1902–4, David Randall-MacIver in 1905, and Gertrude Caton-Thompson in 1929 were all directed principally at the problem of who built the ruins and when (Bent 1896; Hall 1905; Caton-Thompson 1971;

Randall-MacIver 1971). The first two excavators were determined to prove that alien builders were responsible and ignored indications to the contrary; the second two treated the evidence objectively and were able to demonstrate its indigenous identity. Dating, however, remained a problem, and later excavation and survey in 1958 was still principally concerned with the chronological sequence of occupation within the stone ruins (Robinson et al. 1961). It was only as radiocarbon dates became increasingly available that archaeologists were able to turn their attention to other questions.

In the latter part of the twentieth century, for instance, archaeologists began to ask themselves what the stone ruins of Great Zimbabwe and similar sites represented in social, economic, and political terms. In particular, it was realized that the stone-walled enclosures of at least some of these sites were merely the central and most important features of quite large former settlements. At Great Zimbabwe, the recognition of extensive areas of densely packed huts caused the revision of Peter Garlake's 1973 population estimate, of 1,000 to 2,500 adults (Garlake 1973: 195), to one of about 18,000 (Huffman 1986: 323; 1996: 125). It is unfortunate, therefore, that archaeologists have been so obsessed by the stone structures at Great Zimbabwe and related sites that for a long time they virtually ignored other parts of these sites. Sinclair calculated that of the estimated 600 square metres excavated and published from all zimbabwe sites (here called 'zimbabwe-tradition sites') after the time of Randall-MacIver, all except about 20 square metres had been excavated inside and immediately outside stone-walled enclosures (Sinclair 1984). This meant that 'at least at Great Zimbabwe over 90 percent of archaeological effort has been focused upon 2 percent of the population' (Morais and Sinclair 1980: 351). Attention concentrated on the elite; commoners were ignored. However, changes in research orientation have occurred, and Huffman's excavations of the early 1970s (p. 290) provided information about an extensive area of commoner housing (Huffman 2007: 398).

Great Zimbabwe has indeed been ill used. The only 'mystery' or 'riddle' connected with this site is why it took archaeologists so long to recognize its urban character. By the 1970s Huffman was calling it southern Africa's first town, and others saw it as the capital of the earliest state in its area. We have little documentary or oral traditional evidence to support these claims, but it seems likely that these sites, on and around the Zimbabwe Plateau, do indicate the presence of both urbanization and state formation during the first half of the second millennium AD. The real 'problem' of zimbabwe-tradition sites has been to explain why and how these developments took place. In particular, what economic factors led to a growth in the size of some settlements and to increased centralization of authority? Furthermore, how did those factors change so that by the late nineteenth century there were merely ruins scattered through a rural landscape? Indeed, answering such economic questions is only part of the task of explaining the Great Zimbabwe phenomenon. Both this and the related sites can be understood only by seeing them in their full context: chronological, geographical, economic, and sociocultural; only then might it be possible to explain their rise and fall.

Geographical location and environmental factors

Most of the well-known sites of zimbabwe tradition are located on the Zimbabwe Plateau, an area of high land much of which is more than 1,000 metres above sea level. However, there are also comparable sites on the lowveld to the south of the plateau (Manyanga 2007), in areas to its west (van Waarden 1998; 2012), and in one known case to its east (Garlake 1976a). The plateau is situated between about 16° south and about 22° south, bounded on the north by the valley of the Zambezi River, on the south by the valley of the Limpopo River, and on the east by an escarpment that runs down to the wide coastal plain of the Indian Ocean. To the west the plateau merges gradually with the Kalahari Desert (Fig. 9.1). It might seem that Zambezia would have been isolated in the past, but this was not the case. There was apparently contact with areas now in Zambia, southern Democratic Congo, the Transvaal (now Limpopo Province of South Africa), and north-eastern Botswana, as well as with the Indian Ocean coast. Via the latter there were even connections with more distant parts of the world: in earlier times with the Persian Gulf and China, in later times with Western Europe. Travel outside the plateau itself was made easier by the river valleys which dissect its sides, particularly those of the tributaries of the Save and Mazoe Rivers.

The Zimbabwe Plateau has a wet season from November to March and a dry season from April to October. Temperatures are highest late in the dry season, are slightly lower during the wet season, and can fall below freezing point. Rainfall tends to be heavier in the north and east of the plateau than in the south and west. Geologically, the plateau consists mainly of igneous and metamorphic rocks, particularly of granites and schists, amongst some of which there has been extensive mineralization (Collins 1965: 40–1). Much of the landscape comprises gently rolling plains broken by granite inselbergs and by bare, rounded hills of granite. Parts of the plateau are deeply dissected by river valleys, however, leaving rugged ranges of hills between them. In addition, there are the mountains of the Eastern Highlands, which contrast with much of the rest of the plateau. Variations in the geology of the plateau have resulted in a variety of soil conditions: some soils are remarkably fertile, while others are very poor. Natural vegetation varies with both altitude and soil but generally consists of savanna–woodland, with trees scattered among

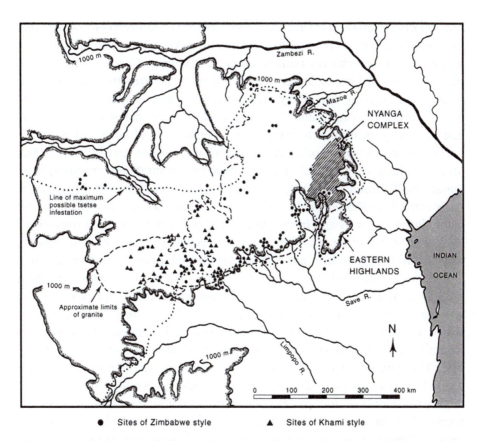

Fig. 9.1 Distribution of zimbabwe-tradition sites of Great Zimbabwe and Khami style. After Garlake 1973: figs. 25 and 26.

wide grassy spaces. The trees tend to be more numerous in lower areas, but some of the highest parts of the plateau consist of almost treeless grassy plains. The Eastern Highlands, on the other hand, have a variety of trees as well as grassland, while the lowlands off the edge of the plateau are usually thickly wooded, mostly by *mopane* trees (Phimister 1976; Beach 1980).

Much of the Zimbabwe Plateau would have been attractive to early human settlement. Its relatively cool, well-watered plains provided a generally healthy environment. The plateau and surrounding areas also possessed a variety of resources, of which agricultural and pastoral potential was probably the most important. Extensive pasturage made parts of the plateau, and of areas to its west, good country for sheep, goats, and particularly cattle. The considerable range in altitude between the plateau and the coastal plain offered the possibility of transhumant pastoralism for overcoming seasonal variations in pasture and other conditions. Suitable climate and soils also made cultivation important in some areas, however, and provided the staple foods of sorghum, millet, beans, and squashes (Garlake 1978a: 73). The significance of food production amongst the region's resources was clearly indicated by a Portuguese, Antonio Bocarro, writing in the seventeenth century about the Mwene Mutapa state, one of the successors of Great Zimbabwe. According to Bocarro the land 'abounds with ... millet, some rice, many vegetables, large and small cattle, and many hens ... and the greater number of ... [people] ... are inclined to agricultural and pastoral pursuits, in which their riches consist' (Theal 1964: vol. 3, 355).

There were, however, other resources on the plateau and in surrounding areas, of which ivory and gold were the most important (Summers 1969; Swan 1994: van Waarden 1998: 144, see table 6.3 for later statistics). Much of the ivory came from the Shashe-Limpopo Basin, and gold could be obtained both from alluvial deposits and from quartz reefs, particularly on the plateau itself (Miller et al. 2000: fig. 2). Together, they became the basis of long-distance trade from the first millennium AD into the first half of the second millennium. Other metals included iron, copper, and tin. Silver might also have been present (Pikirayi 2001b: 226, 263). In addition, there appears to have been salt available (Pikirayi 2001b: 146). A further resource was granite, of which much of the plateau consisted. This continually exfoliated in thin layers from the many rock surfaces exposed to the marked daily changes of temperature. The thin, parallel-sided slabs produced in this way collected as a scree around granite domes and inselbergs and could be readily broken up into rectangular blocks of uniform size. These provided abundant building material, needing little or no preparation. Indeed, supplies were virtually inexhaustible, because lighting fires on the rock surfaces and quenching them with water produced exfoliation artificially (Garlake 1973). It was the ready availability of building stone in such a uniform size and shape that gave many of the walls of Great Zimbabwe, and of some other sites, their unusually regular appearance. For although drystone building was widely practised in precolonial Africa, the neat, horizontal coursework of some of the zimbabwe-tradition ruins is unusual. The resources of the plateau also included other building material: wood and grass for house construction and clays derived from decomposed granite, which formed the main ingredient of the 'mud' used in building. Known in this part of Africa as *daga*, this was sometimes of such high quality that it was used for free-standing structures that could survive considerable exposure. Some of the earlier excavators at Great Zimbabwe erroneously called this material 'cement' (Garlake 1973: 19). Also amongst the plateau's resources were clays suitable for potting and soapstone for carving. Finally, there was abundant wild fauna, which not only provided important sources of ivory but could also supplement human food supplies.

Counterbalancing these resources were a number of environmental constraints that would have influenced the character of precolonial settlement on and around the Zimbabwe Plateau. Probably most important was the tsetse fly, particularly *Glossina morsitans*, whose presence discouraged human settlement both because of the danger to human health and because it killed the livestock on which so many human groups were dependent. Much of the plateau is free of tsetse, as Garlake showed (1978b: fig. 1); however, Summers (1967) suggested that tsetse distribution could have expanded at times during the last two millennia, given slightly warmer and wetter conditions. Although Garlake doubted the evidence for such climatic changes, he showed how the location of zimbabwe-tradition sites might have been influenced by transhumant pastoralism on the seasonally fluctuating boundaries of tsetse fly infestation (Garlake 1978b). At lower elevations than the plateau, particularly in the Shashe-Limpopo Basin, tsetse could have been more of a problem, although it has been suggested that the danger of disease for livestock and humans in that area has been exaggerated (Manyanga 2007: 59). In such places, malarial mosquitoes could also have been an inhibiting factor for settlement.

Another constraint of importance was climatic variability, which often led to what the Shona (the principal inhabitants of the Zimbabwe Plateau) called *shangwa* (Beach 1980: 28–9). This was drought or some other natural disaster. Thus the rains might arrive too late or fail completely or even be so abundant as to destroy the crops. Records exist of droughts and extreme weather from 1790 to 2003, with comparable conditions back to the fifteenth century (Manyanga 2007: 56). There is also evidence for longer climatic fluctuations, from cool and dry to warm and wet, from AD 100–200 to 1810 (van Waarden 1998: 116). Alternatively, locusts or other pests, whose appearance was climatically linked, might be destructive. The result, according to Beach, was that although four years out of five might have normal rainfall, it was probable that the fifth would see some such disaster. The keeping of livestock (goats were the most numerous) was a strategy for surviving years of that sort, for not only could the animals be eaten during a famine but they could be exchanged for grain with neighbours who had not suffered so badly.

Variable soil fertility was also a constraining factor for settlement on the plateau and in surrounding areas. There were undoubtedly some areas of fertile red clay soil and some areas of fertile alluvial soil, but large expanses of the plateau were covered by poor sandy soils developed on the granite (Sinclair 1987: 38–40). Off the plateau the best soils were along river margins or on the edges of seasonally flooded areas, both important in an otherwise dry environment. Thus it is probable that good land was limited, and control of such land might have been one of the means by which rulers exerted economic control over their people (Sinclair 1984). Soil conditions affected not only cultivated crops but also the nutritional value of the pastures available for livestock. In addition, some parts of the land were agriculturally useless because they consisted of bare rock surfaces or because they were too steep to exploit. In the latter case, terracing was a solution; this was extensively employed in the Nyanga (formerly Inyanga) area of the Eastern Highlands from the sixteenth to the early nineteenth century AD. In that area, not only were cultivation terraces constructed on hillsides but also stone-lined pits to house livestock within the stone-built homesteads (Soper 2002).

The interplay of environmental assets and constraints that characterized the Zimbabwe Plateau and surrounding areas seems to have concentrated precolonial population around the watershed between the middle Zambezi to the west and the lower Zambezi and Save-Limpopo rivers to the east. Ethnohistorical and archaeological evidence shows that there was a huge curved area of denser settlement, particularly to the east of this watershed, which David Beach called 'The Great Crescent of population' (Beach 1994: 19–23). It was in this area that the sociopolitical developments associated with the best-known of the zimbabwe-tradition sites took place, although the plateau must also be seen in the context of developments in adjacent environments.

Sources of information

Historical evidence

Our knowledge of Great Zimbabwe and comparable sites is heavily dependent on archaeological evidence. However, there are also historical documentation and oral tradition that are relevant. Stone buildings on the Zimbabwe Plateau were known to the Portuguese, who in the sixteenth and seventeenth centuries AD had trading posts along the Zambezi River and on adjacent parts of the plateau (Pikirayi 1993: 71–4). They wanted to control the gold trade, by exerting influence on the Mwene Mutapa, a ruler of part of an area of similar culture from the Zambezi to the Limpopo and from the Kalahari to the Indian Ocean. Unfortunately, the Portuguese had little direct knowledge beyond the area of the Mwene Mutapa's own Karanga kingdom, on the northern end of the Zimbabwe Plateau. Nevertheless, it is thought that this kingdom was one of the successor states to that of Great Zimbabwe, on the southern part of the plateau. If this was so, then the Portuguese descriptions of what they observed in the territories of the Mwene Mutapa must have some relevance for Great Zimbabwe itself. They seem to have been told about Great Zimbabwe, although they never visited it. One of them, João de Barros, published a secondhand account in 1552 (Theal 1964: vol. 6, 267–8), and Garlake thought that the place described was Great Zimbabwe, which had been virtually abandoned by that time. Although subsequent archaeological research has shown that it was still inhabited, it was no longer as important as it had been (Garlake 1973: 53; Huffman and Vogel 1991: 69).

The de Barros description is the nearest that historical documentation comes to providing details about Great Zimbabwe, but it was based on information obtained after its heyday. To understand the economic, social, and political organization of this place, it is necessary to draw on later Portuguese accounts. Also it is necessary to consider oral traditions, but again there are problems. Great Zimbabwe was most prosperous about 600 years ago, which is a long time for oral traditions to have real value. In addition, it is probable that the Ngoni invasions of the 1830s, and other ethnic movements during the nineteenth century, caused a break in those traditions. When Carl Mauch reached the site in 1871 he found people living there who seemed to know little about its history and significance. Nevertheless, sufficient oral traditions exist to show that Great Zimbabwe was built by the ancestors of the present Shona people, for whom it apparently formed an important political and religious centre. From these traditions it has been possible to reconstruct something of its religious significance (Garlake 1973), social organization (Huffman 1981), and position in Shona history (Beach 1980). Indeed, it has been claimed that oral and ethnohistorical evidence concerning the Venda, a people to the south of the Shona but said to be related to them, can be used to reconstruct life in Great Zimbabwe (Huffman 1996). This has been done by applying the Venda evidence to the layout of the seventeenth- to nineteenth-century site of Danangombe (formerly called Dhlo Dhlo), and then back to the fifteenth- to seventeenth-century site of Khami, and even further back to the thirteenth- to fifteenth-century site of Great Zimbabwe and its thirteenth-century predecessor at Mapungubwe. The result is a stimulating picture of life at Great Zimbabwe and in similar sites but one that is imposed on the physical evidence rather than generated from it, occasioning much discussion, some of it critical (Beach et al. 1997; Beach 1998). Subsequently, Chirikure and Pikirayi challenged Huffman's interpretation and used the archaeological evidence to argue that the various parts of Great Zimbabwe represent not contemporary activities by different occupants but 'the work of successive rulers, each founding a new residence and power centre in accord with Shona practice' (Chirikure and Pikirayi 2008: 976). Inevitably, Huffman (2010a) objected to their approach, which they then defended (Pikirayi and Chirikure 2011). Publication concerning Great Zimbabwe has become almost an industry in itself.

Archaeological evidence

It is archaeological evidence that has the greatest potential for informing us about Great Zimbabwe and similar sites (Fig. 9.2). Great Zimbabwe is the largest of an extensive group of stone ruins situated on the high granite

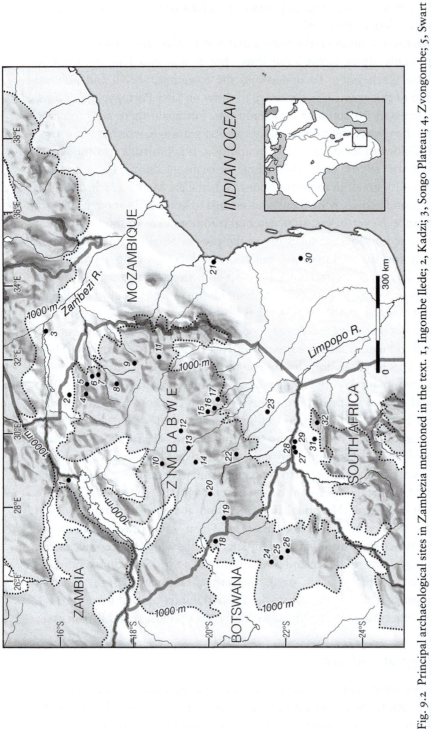

Fig. 9.2 Principal archaeological sites in Zambezia mentioned in the text. 1, Ingombe Ilede; 2, Kadzi; 3, Songo Plateau; 4, Zvongombe; 5, Swart Village; 6, Baranda; 7, Ruanga; 8, Nhunguza; 9, Lekkerwater (Tsindi); 10, Mtelegwa; 11, Chipadze's Ruin (Harleigh Farm); 12, Tebekwe Mine; 13, Naletale; 14, Danangombe (Dhlo Dhlo); 15, Chivowa Hill; 16, Montevideo Ranch; 17, Great Zimbabwe; 18, Domboshaba; 19, Leopard's Kopje; 20, Khami; 21, Sofala; 22, Chummungwa; 23, Malumba; 24, Bosutswe; 25, Taukome; 26, Toutswe; 27, Mapungubwe; 28, Bambandyanalo; 29, Schroda; 30, Manyikeni (Manekweni); 31, Machemma; 32, Dzata. Note that the site of Bambandyanalo is also known as 'K2'. Drawn by Joe LeMonnier.

268

country of the Zimbabwe Plateau. It has been estimated that about 150 ruins built in the Great Zimbabwe style, or in the later Khami style, survive in this area (Fig. 9.1) and that perhaps another fifty have been destroyed since the 1890s (Garlake 1973: 162). Outside the area, similar sites have been located in north-eastern Botswana, northern Transvaal (now Limpopo Province of South Africa), and Mozambique, and both these and the sites in Zimbabwe are part of a widespread practice of drystone construction in southern Africa (e.g., Walton 1956). The characteristic feature of the Great Zimbabwe-style sites is the presence of single or multiple enclosures of drystone walls, which are usually free standing and broad based relative to their height. These walls are constructed of either regularly coursed, dressed masonry or poorly coursed masonry; both types of walling are often found on the same site. Occasionally the walls are decorated with courses of stonework set in a chevron, herringbone, or other pattern or with courses of darker stone. Other typical architectural features include rounded 'bastions', stepped platforms, and upright monoliths. The walls are usually built of granite blocks, but on sites where granite was not available they are constructed of whatever stone was to hand. These stone-walled enclosures were evidently intended as 'containers', for apparently they usually sheltered small groups of circular huts with solid *daga* walls and thatched roofs. Alternatively, on occasion they might have sheltered granaries (Huffman 1981: 6) or even groups of religious emblems (e.g., the Eastern Enclosure of the Hill Ruin at Great Zimbabwe).

Sites of this tradition are called 'zimbabwe' (*madzimbabwe* is the more correct plural form) because this is what the Shona called them. This has been said to be a contraction of *dzimba dza mabwe*, meaning 'houses of stone', and has also been claimed to be derived from *dzimba woye*, meaning 'venerated houses', a phrase used to describe chiefs' houses or graves (Garlake 1973: 11; 1978b: 479). Shona linguists, however, point out that *dzimbahwe* itself means court, home, or grave of a chief. Most of these sites are situated on the Zimbabwe Plateau and within the modern state of Zimbabwe. To avoid confusion, it has become customary amongst archaeologists to refer to the largest and most researched site as 'Great Zimbabwe'. However, sites of the same tradition do occur in more distant locations, and there might be more than are yet known. One example is Manyikeni (formerly known as Manekweni) on the coastal plain of Mozambique, only 50 kilometres from the Indian Ocean and some 270 kilometres from the nearest other known zimbabwe-tradition site. This small site is dated principally to the thirteenth to fifteenth centuries and consists of a single stone enclosure of poorly coursed limestone blocks. The enclosure is subdivided by internal walls and contains traces of occupation in the form of an eroding hut floor of *daga* and two middens. Outside the stone ruin there is extensive evidence of habitation consisting of low mounds, most of which are middens, and house-floor remains. In addition, an overall scatter of broken pottery defines the site limits at approximately 368 by 264 metres; the population has been estimated at 150 to 200 (Garlake 1976a; Sinclair 1987: 91–9). Another outlying site of zimbabwe tradition, although probably of a later date, is on the Songo Plateau, near the Cabora-Bassa Dam in central Mozambique (Ramos 1980; Macamo and Duarte 1996). Also a number of stone ruins of either the Zimbabwe or Khami style exist in north-eastern Botswana, of which Domboshaba has been dated to the fifteenth to sixteenth centuries (Denbow 1986: 25–6). Furthermore, some of the numerous precolonial stone structures in the former Transvaal show similarities with zimbabwe-tradition sites, notable examples being Dzata and Machemma in the Zoutpansberg (Walton 1956: 123, 125; Huffman and Hanisch 1987; Huffman 1996: 40, 75).

For many years Great Zimbabwe was studied in isolation, but it has become increasingly apparent that it needs to be seen in its chronological and geographical context. It represents the apogee of socioeconomic developments that first become evident in the archaeological record of Zambezia during the first millennium AD. Agropastoral people on and around the Zimbabwe Plateau were keeping herds of cattle that are thought to have been indicators of wealth and power, as well as a source of food. To the south, in the Shashe-Limpopo Basin, the settlement sites of Schroda, Bambandyanalo (K2), and Mapungubwe provide a dated sequence from AD 900 to 1300; increasing settlement size indicates growing social complexity at the same time that there is increasing evidence of trade with the East African coast (Leslie and Maggs 2000; Calabrese 2007). Occupants of these sites were receiving glass beads (p. 294) manufactured in places from the Persian Gulf to China (Wood 2000: fig. 1). Cloth and other manufactures were probably also being obtained. In exchange were a variety of African commodities, of which ivory was important, as mentioned in the first-century *Periplus of the Erythraean Sea* (Horton 1996: 414). Furthermore, 'the Mapungubwe area is capable of supporting large herds of elephants' (Huffman 2009: 37). It has been shown that these could have met the trade demand for ivory but that the area was also attractive for cultivation and domestic livestock, as well as large wild mammalian herbivores (Forssman et al. 2014: 75). By the thirteenth century ivory and other resources had made Mapungubwe the urban capital of southern Africa's first state (Fouché 1937; Gardner 1963), with structures of dry-stone walling and elite burials accompanied by gold grave goods (Duffey 2012). It was succeeded in this role by Great Zimbabwe, Mapungubwe's abandonment probably being caused by climatic deterioration in the Limpopo Valley, exotic diseases introduced by the Indian Ocean trade, and a shift north in the trade routes to the coast. These routes were particularly important for the trade in gold, because the gold mines were more accessible from Great Zimbabwe, and by the thirteenth century the trade in gold had become more important than that in ivory (van Waarden 1998: 123). Similar to the developments in the Shashe-Limpopo Basin, a three-tiered social structure emerged in the Toutswe Complex of north-east Botswana, also based on cattle herding. Most common were small settlements of 2,000 to 5,000 square metres. Above these were fewer sites, always on hilltops, of about 10,000 square metres, such as Taukome and Thatswane. At the top of the socioeconomic pyramid were three much larger hilltop sites, each of more than 40,000 square metres: Toutswemogala, Bosutswe, and Sung (Denbow 1999; Reid and Segobye 2000). Glass beads reached some of these sites but far fewer than were received in the Limpopo Valley. In exchange, Toutswe sites were probably supplying ivory for trade with the East Coast.

Such is the background for the emergence of Great Zimbabwe. It consists of two main areas of stone ruins: a group of enclosures clustered around boulders at the top of a precipitous granite hill and another group of enclosures on the far slope of an adjacent valley. Much of the 'Hill Ruin', as it has been called, consists of small enclosures separated by narrow twisting passages, but at one end is the large 'Western Enclosure', which is bounded by walls more than 9 metres high, capped by turrets and monoliths. This enclosure contained deposits over 4 metres in depth, the remains of a succession of *daga* structures, and had room for about fourteen dwelling huts. At the other end of the Hill Ruin is the 'Eastern Enclosure', much smaller than the Western Enclosure and bounded on one side by a high wall originally capped by two courses of decorative stonework. The ground inside this enclosure slopes steeply upwards; it was originally terraced and supported groups of stone platforms in which were set some of the large number of monoliths found in this enclosure. Some were of soapstone and were surmounted by carved birds (Matenga 1998). The most remarkable of the ruins in the valley is a large stone enclosure with a maximum diameter of 89 metres, which has been variously called the 'Temple', the 'Circular Ruin', the 'Great Enclosure', and the 'Elliptical Building'. Garlake, who preferred the last of these names, described its outer wall as 'by far the largest single prehistoric structure in sub-Saharan Africa' (Garlake 1973: 27). This wall is 244 metres long and, at its greatest, 5 metres thick and 10 metres high. It has been estimated to contain 5,151 cubic metres of stonework. Parts of the wall consist of exceptionally sophisticated drystone masonry, comprising the most regular coursing at Great Zimbabwe and with the top of the wall capped by monoliths and a decorative frieze. Other walls, many of which appear to belong to an earlier period than the outer wall, subdivide the space within this enclosure. There is also a conical tower, about 5.5 metres in diameter and more than 9 metres high, built of solid drystone masonry, in itself one of Africa's most remarkable precolonial structures. Spreads of *daga* within the enclosure suggest that parts of its interior were originally occupied by *daga* structures, most of them probably huts. The remainder of the ruins in the valley at Great Zimbabwe consist of small enclosures, a number of which were formerly named after early European visitors. Thus there was the 'Mauch Ruin', the 'Renders Ruin', the 'Posselt Ruin', the 'Philips Ruin', and the 'Maund Ruin'. Others had names such as the 'East Ruin', the 'No. 1 Ruin', the 'Ridge Ruins', the 'Camp Ruin', and the 'Outspan Ruin' (Garlake 1973: 25–30). Although these appear to have been renamed, the Posselt, Philips, and Maund Ruins, for instance, becoming, respectively, the Western, Central, and Eastern Valley Enclosures (Collett et al. 1992), their former names are common in the older literature.

Investigations at Great Zimbabwe and other zimbabwe sites have been architectural and archaeological. Architecturally, it was shown that there was an indigenous evolution of masonry techniques at Great Zimbabwe, from poorly coursed (P) to regularly coursed (Q) stonework, which finally devolved into uncoursed, loosely piled (R) walling (Robinson et al. 1961). Radiocarbon dating subsequently confirmed the sequence from P to Q masonry but showed that R stonework was contemporary with them rather than belonging to a separate late phase (Huffman and Vogel 1991: 69). Architectural studies at Great Zimbabwe have also identified a number of distinctive features in the Great Zimbabwe style of building. Thus the poorly coursed, early walls were frequently built among and over boulders, which were incorporated into their fabric (Fig. 9.3). Regularly coursed, later walls, on the other hand, were usually built on level ground free from boulders. Doorways in these later walls are distinctive, having rounded sides and high thresholds that frequently have curved steps, each successive step curving more sharply into the doorway and merging into the walls at the sides. Pairs of semi-circular projections, often called 'bastions', are inside most doorways and passages in later walls and have the effect of making entrances narrower and longer. Slots in the sides of many of these bastions and in other locations might originally have held upright stone slabs (but see Huffman 1996). Similar slabs were also set upright as monoliths, in the ground, grouped on low *daga* platforms, or along the tops of some of the walls. Other features associated with the regularly coursed later walling are stepped, curved platforms, perhaps intended as seats or as display stands for ceremonial objects, and small stone turrets, either on the ground within enclosures or on the tops of walls (Garlake 1973: 21–5).

Archaeological investigations of Great Zimbabwe and at related sites have concentrated on the date of the stone structures and the identity of their

Fig. 9.3 Stonework in the Hill Ruin at Great Zimbabwe. Note the skill with which the masonry has been built around the natural outcrops of granite. Photograph by the author, 1994.

builders. Considerable attention has also been given to the question of why these structures were built. It appears that building in stone at Great Zimbabwe dates mainly from AD 1275 to 1450, with a late period from 1450 to 1550 (Huffman and Vogel 1991: 68). The builders might have been descendants of earlier occupants of the site during the first millennium AD, a people whose culture was related to that of cattle-oriented groups in south-eastern Zimbabwe (Huffman 1982). As already discussed, Great Zimbabwe seems to have inherited the role of Mapungubwe, a hilltop settlement on the south side of the Limpopo Valley, which has been described as 'the first Zimbabwe Culture capital' (Huffman 1982: 146) and seems to have been at its most important in the thirteenth century AD. Thus the site of Great Zimbabwe was already occupied before the earliest stone walls were constructed. According to Huffman and Vogel (1991: 69), continuity in the pottery at Great Zimbabwe from the twelfth century onwards 'definitely establishes a Shona identity' for the builders, but why were the walls constructed? Archaeologists seem agreed that all zimbabwe-tradition stone structures were intended to be indicators of status for the dwelling places of the elite. In short, their first appearance may be regarded as a sign of social and political change. That being the case, it is unfortunate that so much archaeological attention has been given to the stone ruins at zimbabwe-tradition sites and so little to the rest of the settlement of which each ruin must have formed a part. As a result, not only has most attention been concentrated on a very small part of the population of these settlements, as Morais and Sinclair claimed (p. 261), but the impressive character of the stone ruins at Great Zimbabwe has led to a concentration of work on that site, while inadequate attention has been given to other zimbabwe-tradition sites. Indeed, so single-minded were the earliest excavators that they virtually destroyed the archaeological deposits within the main stone-walled enclosures at Great Zimbabwe. Fortunately, both Randall-MacIver (1971) and Caton-Thompson (1971) recognized the necessity to excavate at other sites also, if they were to understand Great Zimbabwe itself. In addition, both of them realized that the stone structures at Great Zimbabwe and similar sites were only part of the story. Thus Randall-MacIver wrote in 1906: 'It is, properly speaking, the huts which constitute the really essential part of the ruin in every case; the stone wall which the visitor so much admires is only the skin, the huts are the flesh and bone' (Randall-MacIver 1971: 84). Caton-Thompson went further by demonstrating, with her Great Zimbabwe excavations in 1929 at the Maund Ruin, now the Eastern Valley Enclosure (Fig. 9.4), how a jumble of stone walls made sense when one included in the plan the *daga* huts, of which they were the courtyard walls (Caton-Thompson 1971: plate 57; Garlake 1973: fig. 3). Collett et al. (1992: figs. 2 and 3) show the same for the Western and Central Valley Enclosures but from surface evidence. However, it was not till the 1970s that attention again turned to area excavation and that interest at last focused on the whole settlement, of which the enclosures and their inhabitants formed only a part.

Work by Thomas Huffman, in the 1970s, showed that the stone enclosures at Great Zimbabwe were the principal structures within an extensive settlement of *daga* huts (Fig. 9.5), and a plan (Fig. 9.6) was provided of the entire site (Huffman 1981: fig. 1). Huffman's work led to a revision of the population estimate for Great Zimbabwe made by Garlake in 1973. Instead of a population of 1,000 to 2,500 adults (Garlake 1973: 195), it was suggested that the population might have numbered 5,000 adults (Sinclair 1984) and also that the total population was 10,000 (Morais and Sinclair 1980: 351) and might have been as high as 11,000 or even 18,000 (Huffman 1986: 323; 1996: 125). The conclusion was inescapable: Great Zimbabwe had a density of population sufficient for it to be called a town or city. Beach provided a description of what it might have been like, commenting: 'The effect of having so many people on a single site may easily be imagined: this was urban living' (Beach 1980: 46). His analogy with London or Paris at a similar date was a salutary reminder of the environment that could have existed at Great Zimbabwe. Manyanga et al. (2010: 584)

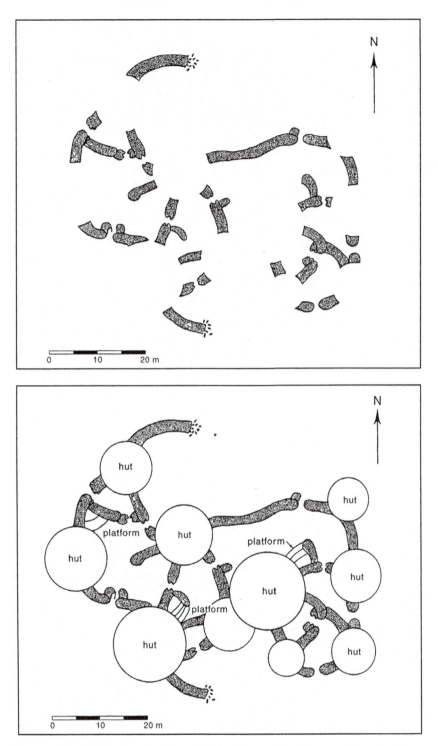

Fig. 9.4 Great Zimbabwe: the Maund Ruin. Above, plan of stone walls only. Below, plan of stone walls and daga huts as revealed by excavation. After Garlake 1973: fig. 3.

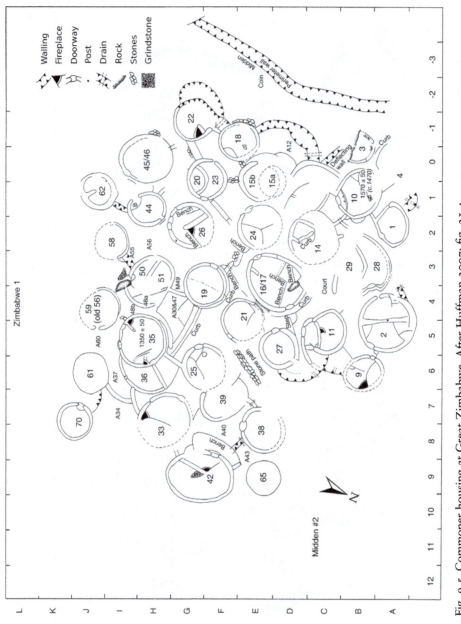

Fig. 9.5 Commoner housing at Great Zimbabwe. After Huffman 2007: fig. 21.4.

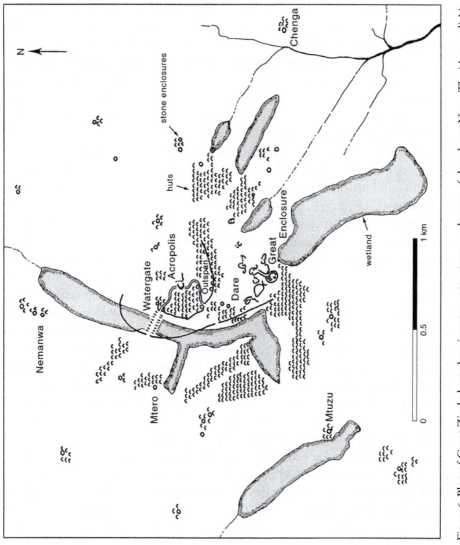

Fig. 9.6 Plan of Great Zimbabwe showing stone structures and areas of *daga* huts. Note: The 'Acropolis' is more usually referred to as the 'Hill Ruin'. After Huffman 1981: fig. 1.

were more specific and wondered 'how waste disposal [including sewage] was handled at such crowded places' in southern Africa.

The problem for archaeologists has always been that the sheer size of an urban site makes it difficult to get an overall picture. This is what makes the investigations of Sinclair so important. Soil samples were collected at random from more than 600 hectares, allowing geophysical analysis, measurement of soil colour, and geochemical analysis of phosphate concentrations to be carried out over the whole of the Great Zimbabwe site. In addition, more than 200 cores each of 50 millimetres in diameter were drilled across the centre of the site, covering an area of about 20 hectares. To all of this data were added observations from field walking, local informants, and the records of previous archaeological investigations, resulting in a series of maps that showed the developmental history of Great Zimbabwe, covering both its growth and its subsequent decline, from the fourth century AD to the nineteenth century. This work provided a picture that would have taken many years of excavation to obtain, and provided it with minimal impact on the archaeological deposits (Sinclair et al. 1993: 710, 712–13).

Yet if Great Zimbabwe was the scene of an urban development on the scale now suggested, then the question arises of how it related to the other, smaller zimbabwe-tradition sites. Insufficient attention was formerly given to these sites by archaeologists, but fieldwork and excavation have thrown some light on them. Chipadze's Ruin at Harleigh Farm near Rusape, for instance, seems to have been the earlier of two ruins at this place and excavation showed that it comprised a small settlement with cultural affinities to Great Zimbabwe. Occupied from about AD 1300 to after 1500, and with an apparent emphasis on cattle keeping, this settlement consisted of stone screening walls enclosing areas within which were massive *daga* huts (Robins and Whitty 1966). It seems that what the excavators investigated were the dwellings of a small political or religious elite and that somewhere nearby must have been the rest of the settlement in which lived the ordinary people.

A similar impression is gained from other zimbabwe-tradition sites that have been excavated. Thus both Nhunguza Ruin and Ruanga Ruin are small sites, dated to about the fifteenth century AD, where stone screening walls enclosed only a small number of *daga* huts. Garlake was of the opinion that the adult population of such enclosures could never have been more than thirty and was probably more often nearer ten (Garlake 1973: 164). Several pieces of evidence at the Nhunguza and Ruanga sites reinforce the impression that the occupants of the stone-walled enclosures were merely an elite section of a larger settlement. First, at Nhunguza the largest hut seems to have been for a person of authority to sit in audience, backed by symbols of that authority that were housed in an adjacent, secluded room. Second, at both Nhunguza and Ruanga the pottery consisted of a limited range of vessels and excluded cooking vessels and bowls for eating and serving. This has also been observed at other zimbabwe-tradition sites, indicating that food was prepared outside the stone enclosures, then brought into them and the vessels later removed. Third, at both these sites there is a suggestion that there were other habitations outside the stone enclosures. At Ruanga it is possible that people of a lesser status were living on the Lower Platform, while at Nhunguza the remains of at least six small huts were found outside the enclosure but were not investigated (Garlake 1972). It is from the zimbabwe-tradition site of Manyikeni (Manekweni), however, that has come some of the best evidence for social differentiation. There is extensive surface evidence for occupation outside the stone enclosure (Garlake 1976a: 29), and excavation has confirmed the presence of huts in this peripheral area (Morais and Sinclair 1980: 352; Sinclair 1987: 91–9). In addition, analysis of the faunal remains indicated that whereas cattle dominated the meat diet of the people living in the central enclosure and immediately around it, sheep or goat and game dominated that of the people living on the periphery of the site (Barker 1978).

The elite status of those who lived within zimbabwe-tradition structures, or the special function of those structures, is also suggested by excavations at the sites of Lekkerwater (Tsindi) and Zvongombe. At Lekkerwater a small number of *daga* huts nestled within stone enclosures on the top of a bare granite hill, one of them with an internal dividing wall like that in the largest hut at Nhunguza and two of them with finely moulded *daga* features, some with complex relief decoration. Material culture, economy, and occupation from the tenth to the nineteenth century associate the site with the overall zimbabwe-tradition complex (Garlake 1973: plates 17 and 99; Rudd 1984; Turner 1984). Like Nhunguza and Ruanga, the two zimbabwe-tradition sites at Zvongombe show that this complex extended also to the northern Zimbabwe Plateau, where it seems to have been imposed on the unrelated Musengezi and Harare traditions, suggesting an expansion from a core area in the south (Pwiti 1996: fig. 42, table 20b). It is uncertain whether these two sites, known as Zvongombe North and Zvongombe South (Fig. 9.7), were contemporary, although both appear to have belonged to the fifteenth century AD. Several *daga* huts were located within the stone enclosures, and internal dividing walls and moulded *daga* features were present (Soper and Pwiti 1992). As with other similar sites, the number of occupants of the Zvongombe enclosures seems to have been small.

Just as the stone structures at Great Zimbabwe can be understood only in the context of the substantial number of people who lived outside them, so also the associated smaller zimbabwe-tradition sites scattered over the landscape need to be examined in the context of the overall settlement pattern of which

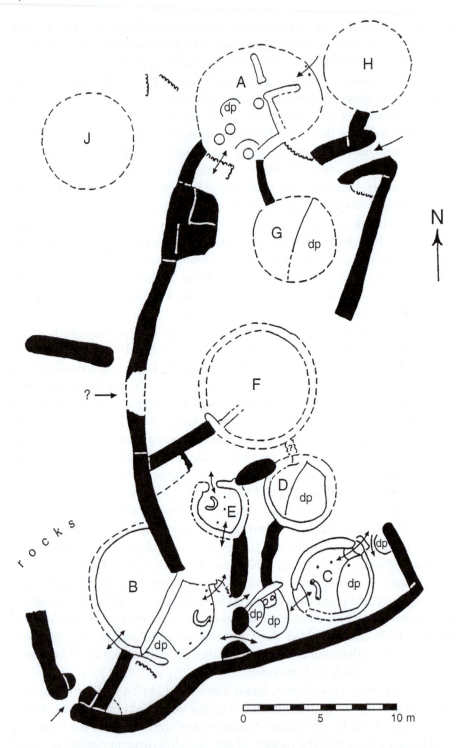

Fig. 9.7 Zvongombe South, Zimbabwe, reconstructed layout. Stone walls are shown solid, *daga* huts in outline. dp, daga platform; small circles in A represent pots, small black dots are postholes, and arrows indicate entrances. After Soper and Pwiti 1992: figs. 3 and 4.

they formed a part. On the Zimbabwe Plateau there are some sites that are culturally and chronologically related to zimbabwe-tradition sites but have few or no stone structures. Two relevant sites that have been excavated are Chivowa Hill (which has very little stone walling) and Montevideo Ranch (which has no walling), both quite near to Great Zimbabwe itself. These sites yielded evidence of communities engaged in both pastoralism and (probably) sorghum and millet cultivation, for whom cattle seem to have been particularly important. They would appear to have been rural peasant communities that were contemporary with the various zimbabwe-tradition sites (Sinclair 1984; 1987: 99–109). A similar situation was also revealed on part of the northern Zimbabwe Plateau, when a random stratified sampling strategy was applied to an area of approximately 12 by 10 kilometres around Zvongombe. The 'Centenary Survey', as this fieldwork project was called, showed that whereas the zimbabwe-tradition stone structures of the area tended to cluster, there were 'unwalled sites ceramically related to the zimbabwes' that were more widely scattered (Soper 1990: 73). It was concluded that the evidence suggested 'a group of more important GZ [Great Zimbabwe] communities, perhaps a "political elite" ... supported by a network of small subordinate settlements' (Soper 1990: 74). Subsequently, Soper (1992) discussed the sociopolitical status of the zimbabwe-tradition sites on the northern Zimbabwe Plateau, where they appear to represent a cultural intrusion from the south, but found that the evidence was inadequate for any confident inferences to be made. However, the overall evidence from the various sites that are thought to be culturally related to Great Zimbabwe suggests that there existed a graded series of settlements, from capital city to regional centre to rural village. If this was the case, then it seems likely that a formally organized state did exist on the Zimbabwe Plateau during the second quarter of the second millennium. However, the manner of its emergence remains one of the most significant issues in the archaeology of southern Africa (Kim and Kusimba 2008; Huffman 2010b).

Radiocarbon dating and imports from the East African coast, of which ceramics are the most significant, have enabled archaeologists to piece together a reasonably consistent chronology for the zimbabwe-tradition sites of Great Zimbabwe style. This indicates that they had ceased to be important by the end of the fifteenth century and indeed that Great Zimbabwe had declined sharply, at least as an urban centre, by the middle of that century. It used to be thought that the site was virtually abandoned at that time, but it seems more likely that it continued to be inhabited until the nineteenth century, although it had lost both its economic and political importance and most of its population (Huffman and Vogel 1991: 69; Collett et al. 1992: 157–8; Sinclair et al. 1993: fig. 43.2). However, more attention needs to be given to the archaeology of Great Zimbabwe concerning the period after about 1450 (Pikirayi 2013a).

Documentary and oral sources indicate that the kingdom of the Mwene Mutapa, on the northern end of the Zimbabwe Plateau, was the immediate successor of the state that had been centred on Great Zimbabwe, and archaeological research has provided some support for this. In the Mount Fura area, Innocent Pikirayi investigated sites which he identified with the Mutapa state. During the sixteenth and seventeenth centuries the Portuguese had trading posts in this area, attracted, it would appear, by its gold resources. Excavations at the large settlement site of Baranda produced imports of those and later dates, including glazed ceramics from the Near East, the Far East, and Europe, as well as large quantities of Indian glass beads and other imported glass. However, indigenous burnished graphite pottery was far more abundant than imported wares and is similar to pottery from zimbabwe-tradition sites at the time of their maximum development. Smaller sites in the same locality told a similar story, although less imported material was present. Although there was no indication of building in stone at any of these sites, others of possibly later date and different cultural tradition, located on hills in the vicinity, do have stone-built enclosures that contain evidence of occupation and in some cases have loopholes, perhaps for firearms, but these are quite different from the stone structures of zimbabwe-tradition sites. Thus, some sites in this area seem to have inherited parts of the zimbabwe cultural tradition, but sophisticated building in stone was not one of them (Pikirayi 1992; 1993; Sinclair et al. 1993: 725–31).

It was in the south-western part of the plateau, not its north, that the zimbabwe tradition of building in stone was to survive and develop. The sites of Khami, Danangombe (Dhlo Dhlo), and Naletale are remarkable examples of this phenomenon. These and a number of similar sites belong to the period from the fifteenth to the nineteenth century AD. The stone structures typical of this later period consist mainly of revetment walls for building platforms, on which *daga* huts were erected. Belonging to the Khami style of the zimbabwe tradition, these walls made considerable use of decorative features (Garlake 1973: 166–8, plates 16 and 103). The most extensively investigated site is the fifteenth- to seventeenth-century Khami, where Keith Robinson excavated parts of a group of elite buildings, some of which were approached by underground passages and many of which were provided with drains (Robinson 1959: 105). Khami is thought to have been the capital of the Butua State, associated with the Torwa dynasty (Huffman 1996: 51), where many people might have moved after the decline of Great Zimbabwe. For this reason, Huffman (1981: 15–16) used the settlement pattern at Khami to throw light on the earlier one at Great Zimbabwe and so provided a plan of the Khami site (Fig. 9.8). This demonstrates that Khami, like Great Zimbabwe, consisted mainly of peasant housing, with the buildings of the elite occupying only a small part of the total area of the settlement. Subsequently, Huffman (1996)

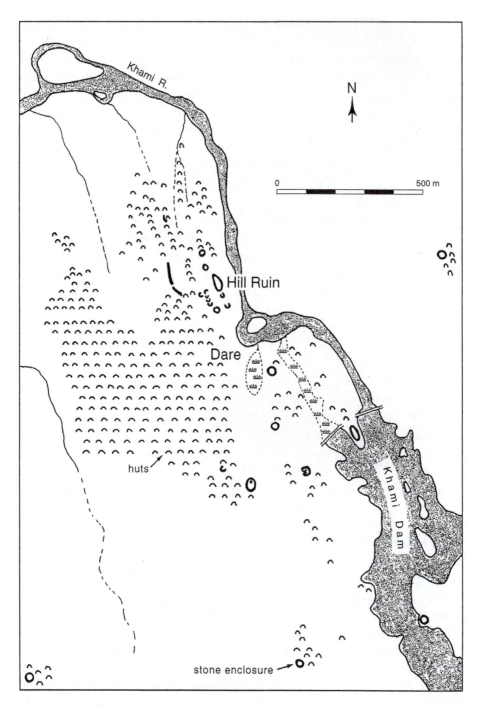

Fig. 9.8 Plan of Khami, showing stone structures and areas of *daga* huts. After Huffman 1981: fig. 13.

also used both Khami and the seventeenth- to nineteenth-century site of Danangombe, which became the capital of the Changamire dynasty (Beach 1994: 120), to help explain the symbolic use of space within Great Zimbabwe itself and even in the earlier Mapungubwe. However, whatever the actual level of cultural continuity over this long period, it appears that state formation and urban living had a long history in this area. Indeed, van Waarden has studied what she identifies as the Butua State, which occupied much of western Zimbabwe and eastern Botswana from 1425 to 1830 and which 'for four centuries ... was the largest and most powerful state in southern Africa'. It collapsed only in the nineteenth century due to repeated Ndebele invasions (van Waarden 2012).

Building in stone also continued in the Nyanga area of the Eastern Highlands, where numerous structures have been thought to date from the sixteenth to the early nineteenth century AD, although the so-called ruin complexes have been dated to the fourteenth and fifteenth centuries (Soper 1996). Nyanga stone building (p. 266) differs from that of the zimbabwe-tradition sites, however, and it has been claimed that it has little relevance for understanding the latter (Garlake 1973: 172). Nevertheless, it does form part of the wider context within which Great Zimbabwe, Khami, and their related sites should be considered.

The economic basis of the relatively large populations, indicated by the settlements with stone walling, was a combination of cereal agriculture and cattle and small stock husbandry. These were societies in which cattle became wealth and their possession gave power; cattle even determined the layout of settlements and the symbolic use of space within them (Kuper 1980; 1982; Evers 1984). The 'Bantu Cattle Pattern', as it has been called, can be discerned in many sites, including the Toutswe settlements of north-east Botswana, which date from about AD 600 to about 1300 and show evidence of a graded settlement hierarchy based on the possession of large herds of cattle (Denbow 1984; 1986). Similar developments also took place in the Limpopo Valley from the ninth century onwards, eventually giving rise to the important centre of Mapungubwe, which by the thirteenth century had grown powerful and wealthy from its participation in long-distance trade with the Indian Ocean coast. At the peak of its power, 3,000 to 5,000 people are thought to have lived at Mapungubwe, making it 'the largest urban settlement in Southern Africa in its time' (Huffman 1996: 184). In conjunction with a number of associated sites, it also seems that Mapungubwe became one of the earliest identifiable states in the area (Hall 1987: 74–90). However, although it has been thought that the zimbabwe-tradition sites were its successors, a reexamination of the chronology of Great Zimbabwe has suggested that the latter actually over-lapped with that of Mapungubwe (Chirikure et al. 2013a; 2013b).

There is archaeological evidence for precolonial mining, particularly for gold, on the Zimbabwe Plateau. These 'ancient workings', as they have been called, have been associated with the zimbabwe-tradition sites and it was formerly suggested that the distribution of workings and ruins was similar (Summers 1969: 137–41). Summers (1969: 105) listed 1,267 ancient workings, most of which resulted from gold mining. Both alluvial and quartz reef gold was mined, with stopes, shafts, and sometimes adits used to exploit the latter. The miners rarely penetrated deeper than about 25 metres, because of the harder rocks met at depth, as well as ventilation or drainage problems (Phimister 1976). Nevertheless, it has been claimed that of the 3,041 kilometres of gold reef pegged by European miners by 1894, some 611 kilometres were covered by 'ancient workings'. The mining of placer deposits, both alluvial and eluvial, seems to have been important, and they were comparatively easy to exploit. Indeed, it has been suggested that placer deposits in the vicinity influenced the location of Great Zimbabwe. However, the problem with archaeological evidence for precolonial mining on the Zimbabwe Plateau, which included mining for copper and iron as well as gold, is that so many of the old workings were destroyed by mining early in the twentieth century.

Because of this, the work of Lorraine Swan, looking at changes in the proximity of settlements to gold mines (excluding alluvial workings), has been particularly useful (Swan 1994). Although gold production seems to have peaked from the twelfth to the early fifteenth centuries (Phimister 1976: 16), she found 'a close relationship' between mines and first-millennium settlements in the north-east of the Zimbabwe Plateau and indications of a movement of the latter towards the mines in the south-west between the seventh and ninth centuries (Swan 1994: 125). She also showed that mining was the work of a lower-status population living near the mines, while smelting was carried out at the elite zimbabwe-tradition sites, from which have come most of the gold artefacts that have been found. Furthermore, Swan was able to excavate a rare surviving portion of backfill in a stope at the Tebekwe Mine, in central Zimbabwe (Swan 1994: 103–16). This provided information on hard-rock mining techniques and was dated by radiocarbon to the mid-fifteenth to mid-seventeenth centuries. Huffman argued that gold mining did not develop on the plateau until the eleventh century AD at the earliest and that the rise of the Great Zimbabwe state was a direct consequence of that mining and of the gold trade with the East African coast. Swan's work, and the presence of marine shells and beads in early to mid first-millennium contexts on the Zimbabwe Plateau (Swan 1994: 72–3), suggests that gold mining actually began during the first millennium AD. Nevertheless, the greater part of the production of 7 to 9 million ounces that Phimister (1976: 16–17) estimated for the period from the late tenth century to the nineteenth seems to have been produced during the time of greatest building activity at Great Zimbabwe, and the significance of gold mining for the zimbabwe phenomenon seems incontrovertible.

Subsistence economy

In the economy that supported urbanization and state developments in Zambezia, livestock husbandry was particularly important, dominated by cattle. Consider, for example, the analysis of a large quantity of animal bones excavated from a midden on the lower slopes of the hill at Great Zimbabwe, on the top of which is the so-called Hill Ruin. It was estimated that this collection consisted of about 140,000 pieces of bone. Of these, 15,298 were selected as easily recognizable; on examination it was found that all except 218 pieces came from cattle. The more recognizable material was also analysed for skeletal part, bone treatment and fragmentation, and minimum number of individuals. It was concluded that cattle dominated the food remains from the Hill Ruin and that more than 75 percent of the 1,330 animals represented were immature when killed. It also appeared that the cattle had been butchered on the hilltop rather than elsewhere (Brain 1974).

A similar emphasis on cattle has been found at other sites. At Ruanga Ruin the animal bones excavated by Garlake indicated that mature domestic cattle were the main source of meat, although smaller animals – domestic sheep, goats, or small buck – were also eaten (Garlake 1972: 134). Cattle were the most common animal at Harleigh Farm (Robins and Whitty 1966); Sinclair found the same thing at Chivowa Hill and Montevideo Ranch (Sinclair 1984; 1987: 102, 108); and Turner the same thing at Lekkerwater (Tsindi) (Turner 1984). At these sites sheep or goat and wild animals were also present but of considerably less importance. The cattle seem to have been of the Sanga type, which are still kept by the Shona people of the area today. Garlake suggested that transhumant pastoralism for the intensive production of beef was a major factor in the location of zimbabwe-tradition settlements, many of which were situated on the edge of the tsetse-free highlands so as to exploit lowland grazing when it was relatively tsetse-free during the dry seasons. Indeed, Garlake argued that such specialist pastoralism is as likely to have formed part of the basis for the rise of Great Zimbabwe and its associated sites as gold mining and long-distance trade, to which the development has so often been attributed (Garlake 1978b). Although his transhumance model has since been questioned (Thorp 1995: 73), there seems little doubt about the important role of cattle in the economy.

Perhaps those immature cattle bones at the base of the hill at Great Zimbabwe should make us pause. If the Hill Ruin was occupied by an elite group or if the ethnohistorical evidence for cattle sacrifice collected by Carl Mauch in 1871 is relevant for 400 to 600 years earlier (Brain 1974: 308–9), then the bones from the hill midden might not constitute reliable evidence for the role of cattle in the overall subsistence economy. Indeed, there is a general danger that faunal evidence from within or near stone structures at zimbabwe-tradition sites will throw light only on the diet or rituals of the elite. A comparison by Carolyn Thorp of the age of cattle from the hill midden at Great Zimbabwe with the age of cattle from an area of commoners' houses in the valley showed that the former indicated the killing of a significantly larger number of young animals (Thorp 1995: 73). Furthermore, it was found at Manyikeni (p. 279) that whilst those people within and near the stone enclosure mainly ate beef, those living on the edge of the site ate mainly sheep or goat and game (Barker 1978). In addition, a sample of faunal material from Khami contained not only a preponderance of cattle but also a wide variety of other species.

The location and apparently continuous occupation of the zimbabwe-tradition sites suggest that pastoralism was only a part of the subsistence economy. Ethnohistorical evidence indicates that it was grain cultivation, particularly of sorghum and millet, which provided the basic staple foods. In addition, there was probably a wide range of vegetables cultivated. Carbonized seeds from Great Zimbabwe and from related sites of the Leopard's Kopje tradition (Robinson et al. 1961: 170) confirm that sorghum was grown, as well as finger millet (*Eleusine coracana*), pearl millet (*Pennisetum americanum*), and a variety of beans (*Voandzeia subterranea*) and peas (*Vigna* spp.). Furthermore, two grains of finger millet were recovered from deposits dated to the second half of the first millennium at the site of Kadzi, in the middle Zambezi Valley (Pwiti 1996: 132). Also the eleventh- to fourteenth-century site of Malumba, in southern Zimbabwe, yielded large quantities of sorghum. The role of livestock in such mixed farming economies was largely to cushion the effect of crop failure in bad years and, particularly in the case of cattle, to provide a means of amassing wealth in a negotiable form, wealth that could form the basis of power. Apparently, Bocarro (p. 264) was not exaggerating in the seventeenth century when he claimed that most of the people in this area were 'inclined to agricultural and pastoral pursuits, in which their riches consist'.

Technology

Archaeological evidence from zimbabwe-tradition sites indicates considerable technological expertise. Most obvious is building in stone; the construction of free-standing, drystone walls, especially on the scale and of the quality of some of those at Great Zimbabwe, requires skill. Admittedly the tabular nature of the exfoliated granite provided a supply of superb building material, but the builders knew how best to use it within their own technological limitations. Although they never seem to have grasped fully the importance of bonding, either between courses or between separate walls, their building technique, at its best, exhibited remarkable sophistication. Walls were broad based to spread their load and tapered to their tops. They were rubble filled, to economise on labour and resources, but the faces of the walls, so vital to the success of such a technique, were constructed with great care. Sharp corners and rectangular layouts were avoided, and plans consisted of random curved forms. This emphasis on curves is also evident in the distinctive architectural features that were constructed. Over-all, the stone structures of the zimbabwe-tradition sites, and of Great Zimbabwe particularly, imply remarkable technological skill. These structures indicate the development, from an indigenous tradition, of what Garlake called 'an architecture that is unparalleled elsewhere in Africa or beyond' (Garlake 1973: 50).

However, the stone walls of the zimbabwe-tradition sites were merely one component of the building technology. Fragmentary evidence from a number of sites suggests that building in *daga* (or 'mud') was just as important as building in stone. Indeed, it seems that originally much of the impressive stonework at Great Zimbabwe would have been plastered with *daga* up to a height of some 2 metres above the ground (Garlake 1973: 20). This material was used for a variety of constructional purposes, including floors and other internal fittings, and was skilfully moulded into decorative patterns, as well as being beautifully finished to a hard, smooth, almost polished surface. Other building skills of which we have no direct evidence must have included wood working and thatching.

An important aspect of the technology of Zambezia during the first half of the second millennium AD comprised mining and metallurgy. Archaeological evidence (p. 285) indicates that mining was a widespread activity conducted on a considerable scale, although in the case of gold mining it was limited in depth, and recovery methods were inefficient (Phimister 1976: 15). The metals that were produced probably consisted of iron, copper, gold, and tin, and Great Zimbabwe has yielded evidence of metal working in all of these. Iron working seems to have been particularly well developed, producing a range of hoes, axes, spearheads, arrowheads, knives, and other things. Excavations at two sites in northern Zimbabwe, Swart Village, dated from 800 to 1200 AD, and Baranda, dated from 1500 to 1700, have thrown light on smelting and smithing practices, indicating both continuities and differences through time (Chirikure and Rehren 2006). Copper, bronze, and gold were used mainly for decorative purposes, often in the form of wire made with the assistance of iron tongs and drawplates but also as sheet or cast metal (Garlake 1973: 113–16). The gold-covered rhinoceros figurine and other objects found in twelfth-century burials at Mapungubwe are a sad reminder of the objects that must have been lost to looters, particularly during the period 1895 to 1900 when more than 2,000 ounces (62,200 grams) of gold were estimated to have been taken from ruin sites (Swan 1994: 70).

Other crafts indicated by the archaeological evidence from zimbabwe-tradition sites include the manufacture of pottery, much of which had polished and graphited exteriors. In addition, spinning, presumably of cotton, is suggested by the large numbers of perforated discs of potsherd that have been found, although they might have had other uses (Garlake 1973: 116–17). If they were spindle whorls, then the presence of spinning would suggest that weaving was taking place and that textile manufacture was of some significance (Davison and Harries 1980). The carving of soapstone is also worth noting, with most of the evidence coming from Great Zimbabwe itself. Ritual bird figures, monoliths, flat-bottomed dishes, figurines, and open moulds for casting cross-shaped ingots of copper were all carved from this easily worked and locally available stone. The manner in which the soapstone was carved suggests a familiarity with wood carving and is another reminder of the many crafts in perishable materials that must also have existed at the zimbabwe-tradition settlements (Garlake 1973: 119–23, 130–1). There are, however, examples of ivory carving and bone working from the site of Bambandyanalo (K2) and from nearby Mapungubwe, dating from the end of the first millennium and the beginning of the second millennium AD (Hall 1987: 80–1). More durable are the many pottery figurines of humans and animals, recovered from more than 200 sites and dating from about the third century AD to the end of the nineteenth century (Matenga 1993).

The technology associated with zimbabwe-tradition settlements indicates that by the second quarter of the second millennium AD, there had developed a degree of functional specialization within the society to which these settlements belonged.

Social system

Zimbabwe-tradition sites provide many indications of social and economic stratification. The stone structures that characterize most of these sites are symbols of privilege and power, in the opinion of Pikirayi (2013b) creating elite power as well as reflecting it. They have no other obvious role, such as defence. Rather, they seem to have been intended as containers, behind whose high walls could be hidden both the living and the ceremonial areas of a ruling elite. Indeed, the walls themselves demonstrate the power of the ruling group, able to spend its surplus wealth on such conspicuous consumption and able to exert the necessary control over substantial bodies of skilled and unskilled labour. Although the work actually extended over some three centuries, a British drystone building contractor has estimated that the structures at Great Zimbabwe would take eighty-four men, working six days a week, two years to complete (Reader 1997: 338). Furthermore, some of the items recovered from within these stone-walled compounds confirm the elevated status of their

289

occupants. Thus there are objects of gold, copper, bronze, or soapstone; there are also exotic objects such as glass beads and, at Great Zimbabwe itself, glass vessels and Islamic and Chinese ceramics, products of long-distance trade via the East African coast. Moreover, there are significant absences from the artefacts found in the stone enclosures. Garlake remarked on the 'extraordinarily limited range' of pottery, comprising drinking and brewing/storage vessels but lacking open bowls for cooking, serving, and eating and lacking pots for fetching water. Garlake thought that this suggested a limited range of domestic activities within the enclosures and pointed out that there is also an almost complete absence of grindstones (Garlake 1973: 112–13). Add to this the fact that many of the enclosures contained huts with finely finished *daga* walls, at least one of which (at Nhunguza) seems to have been an 'audience hut', and the elite character of the occupants is almost certainly established. The small populations of the enclosures provide further evidence of this; Garlake estimated the total population of those at Great Zimbabwe as between 100 and 200 adults and the population of enclosures at all the other known zimbabwe-tradition sites at any one time as about 750 adults (Garlake 1973: 195–6).

By the 1970s archaeologists began to ask questions about the rest of the population of these settlements. Evidence became available that the stone enclosures were merely central structures within more extensive settlements, which in the case of Great Zimbabwe might have had a total population of 18,000 people. With some justification, Huffman referred to Great Zimbabwe as southern Africa's first town. The ordinary townspeople lived in cramped conditions (Fig. 9.5), at a density of about three times that of the elite. Further, judging from the evidence at Manyikeni (p. 279), they did not eat so well. However, there was probably already social differentiation amongst the townspeople themselves, with functional specialization giving a different status to craftsmen such as blacksmiths and builders.

At Great Zimbabwe, at least, urbanization was already in progress. Furthermore, if this site is examined in the context of all the other zimbabwe-tradition sites that are culturally and chronologically related, then it is possible to discern a graded series of settlements that suggests the existence of a formally organized state (p. 281). At one end of the scale was the capital at Great Zimbabwe, with its large population controlled by a powerful elite; at the other end were rural villages with their peasant communities. In between were regional centres: smaller towns, each of which was controlled by its own elite group that probably owed allegiance to that of the capital. It also seems probable that the occupants of these settlements shared a similar worldview, originating from Kuper's 'Bantu Cattle Pattern' (p. 284) but developing into something quite distinctive. The attempt by Huffman (1996) to reconstruct the

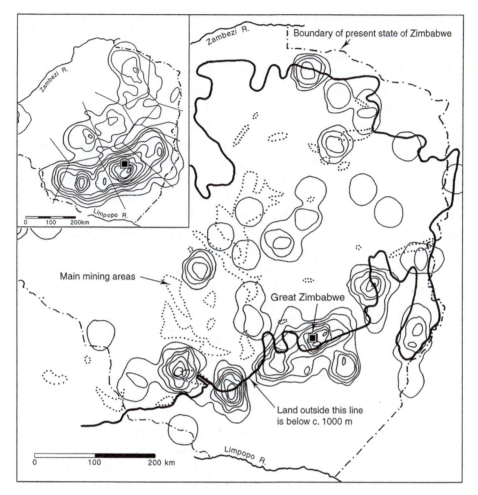

Fig. 9.9 Spatial analysis maps of Zimbabwe sites. Large map shows 50 km clustering level; inset map shows 155 km clustering level and Garlake's (1978b) Thiessen polygon study. After Sinclair and Lundmark 1984: fig. 5.

symbolism that shaped the material record at Great Zimbabwe and related sites provides a stimulating picture of how society might have been organized, although it remains difficult to verify.

Population pressures

Spatial analysis (Fig. 9.9) of the distribution of zimbabwe-tradition sites on the Zimbabwe Plateau (possibly the distribution of research rather than of sites) has demonstrated a settlement pattern in which the population showed a marked tendency to cluster. A similar analysis of Khami sites again shows obvious clustering but in a different place (Sinclair and Lundmark 1984; Sinclair 1987: 123–4). The locations of these clusters, which are thought to indicate the areas, respectively, of the Great Zimbabwe and the Butua State, were presumably influenced by environmental factors. Tsetse fly, climatic variability, and differences in soil fertility must all have played a part in making some areas more attractive to human settlement than others. For example, zimbabwe-tradition sites tended to be on the southern edge of the plateau, which was high enough to be tsetse-free, was within reach of lowland grazing only exploitable during its relatively tsetse-free dry season, had local areas with a higher rainfall, and possessed some areas of high soil fertility. As Pikirayi (2001a: 148) concluded: 'Land was always an important issue in the past. It was necessary to control it for its resources'. In addition, Tsheboeng (2001: 128) thought that 'two variables appear to have been important in settlement location decision, namely soils and water needs'. Although this picture was complicated by settlement clusters of lesser importance in the mining areas of the central plateau, it appears that the places most attractive to human settlement were relatively limited. Many seem to have lain within what Beach (1994: 19–23) called 'The Great Crescent of population'. This could well have caused local population pressures sufficient to give rise to the social changes inherent in the processes of urbanization and state formation. As Sinclair concluded, 'pressure on land and the accompanying possibility to control access to productive areas should be included in the analysis of relations between élite and others and even of differentiation within the élite itself' (Sinclair 1987: 144).

Some confirmation of the existence of local population pressures might, indeed, be provided by the eventual abandonment of Great Zimbabwe itself. Both Garlake and Huffman were of the opinion that abandonment resulted from environmental deterioration brought on by the large population, and Sinclair (1987: 114, 116) thought that there was a 200-year periodicity in the sociopolitical history of the area resulting from this factor, so that Bambandyanalo–Mapungubwe, Great Zimbabwe, and Khami each lasted for about that time. Certainly the large number of people that are now thought to have lived in Great Zimbabwe must have placed a tremendous demand on the natural resources of the surrounding area. Firewood would soon have become locally unavailable, necessitating its laborious transport by head from ever-increasing distances; wildlife to serve as a supplement to human diet would have become scarce (Brain 1974: 309); and the relatively limited areas of better soils must have been gradually exhausted by overcultivation and overgrazing. As might have been the case with Aksum, it is possible that it was overexploitation of the strong resource base of Great Zimbabwe that brought about its destruction. Without fundamental changes in technology and agricultural system, it was fated to destroy itself.

Ideology

Religion seems to have permeated many aspects of Shona life, as suggested by the numerous pottery figurines from Zimbabwe, widespread in space and time, which have been discussed by Matenga (1993). Therefore, it is probable that it was a contributory factor in the rise of Great Zimbabwe and of the state that it seems to have controlled. Indeed, one of the two main schools of thought concerning the origins of these developments sees religion as the major factor in their initiation. However, our knowledge of Shona religion is drawn from oral tradition and ethnography, and from such sources it is difficult to estimate its role in changes that took place some seven centuries ago, although Huffman (1996) made a bold attempt to do so. According to Garlake (1973: 184), 'Great Zimbabwe was very probably always a major religious centre', where Mwari, the Shona supreme god, was particularly revered and where cults of the *mhondoro*, spirits associated with the ruling dynasties, also flourished (Garlake 1973: 174). Certainly there are archaeological features and artefacts at Great Zimbabwe that suggest religious and ancestral associations – particularly the monoliths, some surmounted by carved birds, most of which originally stood in the Eastern Enclosure of the Hill Ruin. Furthermore, Herbert (1996: 645) emphasized 'the ideological dimensions of technology and the negotiations over power' represented by 'the insignia of office such as spears, axes and double gongs'. However, there is no archaeological evidence to support Garlake's assumption that religion was 'probably the most important single factor in bringing about the first steps towards the cohesion, organization and stratification of the society', and Garlake himself recognized this (1973: 184). Indeed, although Shona religious ideology might have been important as a means of reinforcing the authority of a ruling elite, the hypothesis that the rise of Great Zimbabwe and its associated sites was due to a religious minority, of either migrant or local origin, is unconvincing. The alternative is the trade hypothesis, which maintains that Zimbabwe was a result of surplus wealth from the East African gold trade. This, at least, is an hypothesis that is susceptible to archaeological evaluation.

External trade

Both Arabic and early Portuguese documentary sources mention the existence of trade between the Sofala area (p. 251), on the southern coast of Mozambique, and the interior. That area seems to have been a clearing house, where trade goods from the Islamic world and from India and China were imported for onward transmission to the interior, which exported primary products via the same area. Most sought-after of those products was gold, although at the time of the first Portuguese contact ivory was another important export, and it is probable that other commodities, including copper, were also handled. The imports, according to the Portuguese, were principally cloth, beads, and glazed ceramics. The source of the gold that passed through the Sofala area was said by ibn Battuta, early in the fourteenth century, to be Yufi in the land of the Limiin, one month's march from the coast (Freeman-Grenville 1975: 31), and it has been suggested that the land of the Limiin was the Zimbabwe Plateau and that Yufi was Great Zimbabwe itself. A number of questions arise from this. First: does the archaeological evidence at zimbabwe-tradition sites throw any light on this trade? Second: to what extent was this trade unusual and to what extent was it merely part of a complex network of trade that involved both long-distance and interregional exchange? Third and most important: what role, if any, did this trade play in the rise of Great Zimbabwe and its associated sites? Is it really possible that the Zimbabwe Culture was simply an indigenous reaction to external stimulus in the form of the East Coast gold trade?

Archaeological evidence for trade between Zambezia and the East African coast is abundant for the sixteenth and seventeenth centuries AD, when the Portuguese had trading posts in the Zambezi Valley and on the northern part of the plateau (Pikirayi 1993). For the earlier periods there is less evidence, but some of the earliest comes from the site of Schroda, near the confluence of the Shashe and Limpopo Rivers, occupied between the eighth and tenth centuries and containing imported glass beads as well as indications that ivory was being worked and traded. In the same area the eleventh-century site of Bambandyanalo (K2) has produced similar evidence, and by the thirteenth century, glass beads and gold-covered objects from Mapungubwe suggest trade in gold and ivory with the East Coast (Hall 1987: 75–85; Huffman 1996: 175–80). Perhaps the most important evidence for trade, however, comes from the 'Renders Ruin' at Great Zimbabwe itself, where a hoard included a glazed Persian bowl of thirteenth- or fourteenth-century date. With it were a number of Chinese celadon dishes, some sherds of a Chinese stoneware vessel, another glazed Persian bowl, and fragments of engraved and painted Near Eastern glass, all of about the same date. In addition there were a piece of coral, an iron spoon, an iron lamp holder with a copper suspension chain, a copper box, two copper finger rings, and two small bronze bells. There were also several tens of thousands of glass beads, some brass wire, and a quantity of cowrie shells. Hall excavated this hoard in 1903, but in 1941 Goodall found some 30,000 beads in another part of the same ruin (Garlake 1973: 131–3). These exotic objects demonstrate that in about the fourteenth century Great Zimbabwe was in contact with the trading cities of the East African coast. The hoard has been interpreted as part of the stock of a visiting Arab trader, but the diverse nature of the goods and their location within what might have been the royal wives' living area make it more likely that they were part of a royal repository (Huffman 1981: 6). The unique character of this collection suggests that it must have had considerable prestige value for its owner. Indeed, as late as the beginning of the sixteenth century imported Chinese porcelain was still reaching Great Zimbabwe (Collett et al. 1992: 139, 157–8).

Another piece of archaeological evidence for trading contacts between the Zimbabwe Plateau and the coast consists of a coin minted in Kilwa probably in the early fourteenth century. This coin was excavated at Great Zimbabwe and appears to be the only one ever recovered from a scientific context at that site. Of more use as evidence for trade with the coast, because they are more common, are the large numbers of glass beads recovered both from Great Zimbabwe and from many other zimbabwe-tradition sites. The ultimate origin of these beads is unknown, but they are similar to beads found in the East Coast cities and, like them, they came from the Indian Ocean trade (p. 256). Indeed, beads from the earlier sites of Bambandyanalo and Mapungubwe have been shown by rare earth element analysis to have been made at al-Fustat in Egypt (Saitowitz et al. 1996). However, changes in the glass chemistry of beads from southern African sites between the eighth and fifteenth centuries suggest different sources around the Indian Ocean at different times (Wood 2011). Cowries are also very occasionally found at other zimbabwe-tradition sites, as well as at Great Zimbabwe. Otherwise, evidence of imports from the coast is limited, although the appearance at zimbabwe-tradition sites of spindle whorls, which are absent from earlier sites, has been interpreted as indicating that the craft of spinning spread from the coast as a result of trading contacts (Garlake 1973: 117). It should be no surprise that a trade in which textiles and gold were the most important commodities has left relatively little archaeological evidence. Nevertheless, there is strong circumstantial evidence for the importance of trading between the Zimbabwe Plateau and the coast. There was a sudden and considerable increase in building activity at Great Zimbabwe during the fourteenth century, at the same time that equally sudden and considerable expansion was taking place in the cities of the East African coast, particularly at Kilwa. Equally, the fortunes of both Great Zimbabwe and the coastal cities declined at about the same time during the fifteenth century. The most likely explanation for such a coincidence of prosperity must be that there was a 'close economic connection' (Garlake 1976b: 224). Sutton (1997) has suggested that depression in the coastal economy actually began in the second half of the fourteenth century, following a fall in the international price of gold, possibly resulting from the Black Death of 1346 to 1349. Thus one of the factors in the decline of Great Zimbabwe might have been a reduced demand for gold on the 'world' market.

The second question that was asked concerned the extent to which this overseas trade was part of a more general network of long-distance and interregional exchange. In addition to items that must have derived from the East Coast trade, the Renders Ruin hoard contained a large quantity of material that suggests the existence of a substantial internal African trade. Thus there were about 30 kilograms of iron wire and about 100 kilograms of iron hoes, axes, and chisels. With them were 'cakes of copper', ivory, two unusual spearheads, three iron gongs, and three iron rods that were probably strikers for the gongs. There were also a soapstone dish, twenty small pieces of perforated gold sheathing, some gold wire, and a handful of gold beads (Garlake 1973: 133). The gongs are bell shaped and were made of two sheets of iron welded together round the flanges, although welding seems not to have been practised in Zambezia. Seven similar gongs have been found at Great Zimbabwe and single examples have been found at Chumnungwa Ruins and Danangombe (Dhlo Dhlo) Ruins. Such gongs are characteristic of parts of Zambia, the Congo Basin, and West Africa, and it has been suggested that their distribution indicates contact between different African states (Vansina 1969). Indeed, gongs of this type accompanied two of the burials at the Zambezi Valley site of Ingombe Ilede, in Zambia (Fagan et al. 1969: 92–4), and their presence at Great Zimbabwe presumably indicates trading connections with the Ingombe Ilede area. This probability is reinforced by the discovery of single examples of cross-shaped copper ingots, of a characteristic Ingombe Ilede form, at the zimbabwe-tradition site of Chumnungwa and at another ruin site in the Great Zimbabwe area. Three similar ingots have also been found in the Mtelegwa Ruin. It seems that during the fourteenth and fifteenth centuries the Ingombe Ilede people were mining copper on some scale, and as there are salt deposits in their area, it is likely that they traded salt as well as copper to the Zimbabwe Plateau. In exchange they probably took gold beads and ornaments, and iron tools and weapons. The comparatively few glass beads at Ingombe Ilede sites suggest that the trade was with other internal African communities, rather than with the East Coast (Garlake 1976b: 224). Furthermore, this Ingombe Ilede–Zimbabwe Plateau trade was probably just a small part of a complex internal trading network, of which the rest has left little archaeological evidence. Documentary and oral traditional sources indicate a network of trade routes stretching deep into the interior (van Waarden 2012: fig. 7.2). Brian Fagan demonstrated for the region north of the Zimbabwe Plateau that the demand for raw materials, particularly iron, copper, and salt, ensured the growth of such networks (Fagan 1969). As in other parts of Africa, it is likely that internal trading of this sort substantially pre-dated long-distance external trade. If this was the case, then the East Coast gold trade probably took advantage of an existing trading network.

The third and final question concerned the role of the East Coast trade in the rise of Great Zimbabwe and other zimbabwe-tradition sites. The quick answer is that it was probably very important but that its role in the social and economic changes that led to urbanization and state formation was to facilitate rather than to originate. The cause of these developments was deeper and more complex than a mere trade in luxuries, but without doubt that trade provided the elite with prestige goods and with a form of wealth that could be used to enhance their authority.

Conclusion

Great Zimbabwe and its related sites comprise the archaeological evidence for social and political developments that took place in Zambezia during the first half of the second millennium AD. The stone structures that have dominated archaeological research housed a small ruling elite, who governed settlements varying in size from the capital city of Great Zimbabwe itself, with a population of perhaps 18,000, to smaller regional towns. The authority of this elite probably extended also to rural villages that were too small to justify elite residences. The size of Great Zimbabwe would suggest that urbanization was already in process, at least at this place. The presence of comparable elite structures in so many of the other settlements would suggest that some progress had also been made towards the formation of a state. Why and how had this happened?

The basic reason was almost certainly the successful subsistence agriculture of this area. As a generally healthy environment that was tsetse-free and with access to other areas that were seasonally tsetse-free, it supported a mixed farming economy in which grain, vegetables, and livestock – particularly cattle – all played a part. This combination of cultivation and livestock would have helped to even out the effects of bad years and must inevitably have led to an increase in the population. However, good soils were limited and it is probable that the tsetse boundaries fluctuated. Thus some areas must have been more productive than others, and those who controlled such areas must in time have come to control the less fortunate members of an expanding population.

However, there were alternatives to agriculture: mining, trade, and crafts of various sorts. The development of these activities provided some escape from the problem of limited productive land. They also provided the emerging elite with further sources of wealth that could be controlled and that were more negotiable than land or cattle. In particular, it is likely that a far-reaching and complex network of interregional trade in raw materials had developed within south central Africa, before Indian Ocean merchants were able to benefit from it. How could the latter have known that there was gold to be had from the relatively remote Zimbabwe Plateau, unless that gold was already reaching the coast? Nevertheless, the gold trade with the East Coast must in time have become extremely important in creating surplus wealth that further enhanced the power of the Zimbabwe Plateau elite. Even the most conservative estimate suggests that between 7 and 9 million ounces of gold were made available for trade and internal consumption before the end of the nineteenth century (Phimister 1976: 16–17). It is not difficult to imagine the impact on Plateau society of the volume of goods (particularly cloth and beads) that must have been received in exchange prior to the middle of the second millennium AD. It seems unlikely that the gold trade 'caused' the rise of Great Zimbabwe, but nevertheless it must have had a great effect on it.

The apparent reasons for the decline and abandonment of Great Zimbabwe and its associated sites consist of a reversal of the factors that gave rise to their growth. The gold trade declined, probably because of falling world prices and the depletion of the more easily worked deposits on the Zimbabwe Plateau. More important, however, the environment around Great Zimbabwe collapsed: overcropped, overgrazed, overhunted, overexploited in every essential aspect of subsistence agriculture, it ceased to be able to carry the concentration of people to whom it had given rise. To begin to understand this episode of growth and decay, it is essential to see it in the broadest possible context, in spatial, temporal, and social, economic, and political circumstances. Great Zimbabwe was only ever a mystery when viewed in isolation.

Chapter 10

Central Africa: the Upemba Depression, Interlacustrine Region, and Far West

This book presents case studies of archaeological evidence for urbanization and state formation in precolonial Africa. The choice of areas has been dictated by the character of the archaeological evidence and by the extent of archaeological research, resulting in an incomplete picture. Not only might the individual case studies be unrepresentative of developments in the selected areas, but also there were precolonial cities and states in Africa, known from the evidence of ethnohistory or oral tradition, that are excluded. This omission is because the relevant archaeological evidence is either absent or severely limited.

The basic problem is archaeological visibility (Connah 2008). Some manifestations of early urbanization and state formation in Africa are of such a character that their archaeological investigation is peculiarly difficult. For instance, the capital city of Buganda (Gutkind 1963), a state near Lake Victoria, was described in 1889 as 'one of the great capitals of Africa' (Ashe 1889: 52), but it was constructed totally of grass, wood, and other organic materials and it moved frequently, particularly on the death of the Kabaka, the ruler of Buganda (Gutkind 1960: 29). The sites of these large settlements are, therefore, unlikely to have much depth of deposit or structural remains, and no archaeological investigation of them has been attempted (the last two are covered by modern Kampala). Thus there is no archaeological information about a settlement that John Hanning Speke, its first European visitor, described as 'a magnificent sight. A whole hill was covered with gigantic huts such as I had never seen in Africa before' (Speke 1863: 283).

There is, however, no reason why archaeologists should not be able to investigate such short-lived settlements of ephemeral materials, as was done, for example, at the South African site of Mgungundlovu (Parkington and Cronin 1979). Provided that subsequent activity or erosion has not destroyed the inevitably shallow evidence, survey and excavation techniques do exist that enable information to be obtained from sites of this type. Nevertheless, they have been seldom applied in Africa, and a lack of sophistication in research design has led to the excavation of many larger African settlement sites with structures of stone, fired brick, or mud, while sites with less substantial structural remains have been ignored. Although this situation is now changing, there are large areas of Africa where political and economic problems make it difficult, and sometimes impossible, to conduct archaeological field research, so that the excavation of sites of supposed low archaeological visibility still lacks the necessary attention.

This could apply to many parts of Africa but is particularly relevant to a huge area of the continent extending across the modern states of the Congo Republic, Democratic Congo, Angola, Zambia, Rwanda, Burundi, Uganda, and western Tanzania. This area straddles the equator, although situated mostly to its south. Ethnohistorical and oral traditional evidence indicate that it was the location of a succession of cities and states from at least the sixteenth century AD onwards. Some of these, such as the Kingdom of Kongo in the sixteenth century or the state of Buganda in the nineteenth century, clearly impressed European visitors. The latter were often particularly interested in the cities that they came across, such as Loango in what is now the Congo Republic (Dapper 1686: 320–1). Nevertheless, archaeology has contributed relatively little to our knowledge of precolonial cities and states in this part of Africa. At its southern margin, for instance, the Lozi Kingdom is known from oral history, not archaeology. For all periods in the enormous area covered by equatorial rainforest there has been only 'a meager scattering of excavated archaeological sites' (Vansina 1990: 8), although the situation is improving.

For the Kingdom of Kongo, there is the site of its capital city, Mbanza Kongo (São Salvador), in northern Angola (Fig. 10.1), but it has never been excavated (de Maret 1982: 80). Indeed, excavated evidence relevant to the Kongo state was for long limited to a cemetery at Mbanza Mbata, where elite graves produced indications of European trading contacts during the seventeenth and eighteenth centuries (de Maret 1982: 82). However, there has now been other fieldwork that indicates the potential of archaeology to throw light on this region during the last 400 to 500 years (Clist et al. 2013a; 2013b). Nevertheless, archaeological evidence for Kongo, a state described in detail in both contemporary accounts (e.g., Pigafetta 1591) and historical studies (e.g., Randles 1968), remains limited. Further to the north, for example, the city of Concobela (Ngombela) has been identified with the site of Kingabwa, near Kinshasa, but it has since been destroyed by clay digging and covered by a garbage dump (de Maret 1982: 83). Similarly, the mounds of Mashita Bansa, the site of a city in south-central Democratic Congo, can tell us little, although test excavations were carried out there in 1984. Even the excavation of some of the royal tombs of Rwanda was of limited value, as the three graves investigated contained burials of the late nineteenth and early twentieth centuries. One of these was of Cyirima Rujugira, a king who had been dead since the seventeenth or eighteenth century but was buried only in 1930 or 1931. This burial was accompanied by numerous grave goods that had also remained unburied until the twentieth century; these are of interest because they included items symbolic of royalty (Van Noten 1972). A similar problem

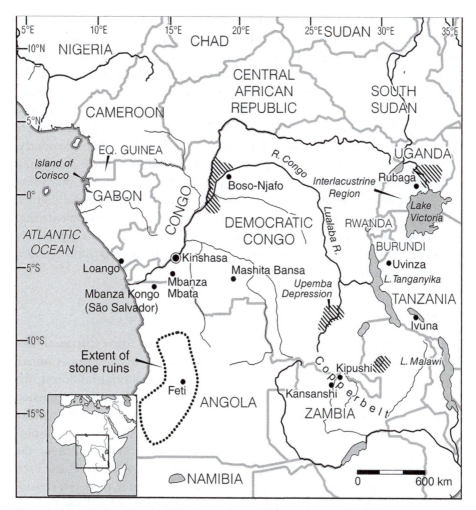

Fig. 10.1 Principal archaeological sites in Central Africa mentioned in the text. Note the locations of the Upemba Depression and the Interlacustrine Region, for which see Figs. 10.2 and 10.4. Hatched areas are subject to inundation. Drawn by Joe LeMonnier.

of limited time depth exists for the site of Ryamurari, the old capital of the Ndorwa Kingdom in Rwanda. Remains of circular mud walls indicate the king's enclosure, and there are also cattle kraals built of cattle dung and garbage, but excavation has produced radiocarbon dates of the eighteenth and twentieth centuries (Van Noten 1982: 75).

Fortunately there are two areas in Central Africa where archaeological research has contributed significantly to our knowledge of socioeconomic and political developments over the last millennium or so. One of these is the Upemba Depression, in south-east Democratic Congo, and the other is the Interlacustrine Region, particularly the part in Uganda (Fig. 10.1). The first has shed light on the origins of the Luba state, which is known to have existed by the eighteenth and nineteenth centuries (Reefe 1981: 60–1); the second has provided information on the antecedents and early phases of several states which oral tradition suggests might have developed by about the middle of the second millennium AD (Sutton 1993). A third area, where archaeological research has been more limited, consists of a vast area of Central Africa to the west of the first two areas (Vansina 2004). For convenience, it is called here the 'Far West', and more is now known of its archaeology than previously. Situated in the heart of Africa, the relative isolation of these three areas from influences outside the continent makes it particularly likely that increasing social complexity was the result of indigenous rather than external factors. For this reason, it is especially important to examine the developments that took place, recollecting in doing so that the three selected areas are merely representative of a huge region for much of which there is little relevant archaeological evidence.

Geographical location and environmental factors

Situated roughly 1,000 kilometres apart, the main two areas discussed here have similarities but some differences (Winterbotham et al. 1944; Connah 1996). Both lie within the savanna that fringes the equatorial rainforest, the Interlacustrine Region actually straddling the equator, the Upemba Depression more than 8° south of it. This gives both areas an annual rainfall in many places of about 1,000 millimetres, which tends to fall in two wet seasons. However, climatic conditions are modified by altitude, with much of the Interlacustrine Region being more than 1,000 metres above sea level and even the Upemba Depression lying above 500 metres. In addition, there is a considerable altitudinal range within each area: the northern one is bordered by both the Western Rift Valley and the Ruwenzori Mountains, and the southern by the Hakansson Mountains to its north-west and the Mitumba Mountains to its south-east. The resulting environmental diversity of both areas is made even more complex by the presence of major bodies of water: the Victoria Nile and Lakes Victoria, Kyoga, Albert, George, Edward, and Kivu in the one case, and the River Lualaba (the Upper Congo) and Lakes Upemba and Kisale in the other. The Interlacustrine Region, however, is much larger than the Upemba Depression, with a greater variety of environments, although only small parts of the area have been investigated archaeologically. In addition, the Upemba Depression is dominated by a vast floodplain through which runs the Lualaba and to which archaeological research has so far been confined. Contrasting with the relatively dispersed natural resources of the Interlacustrine Region, those of the Upemba Depression are markedly concentrated.

Less detail is known about the environment in the Far West, the third area on which attention is focussed here and the archaeology of which is limited. Its environment consists of a mix of rainforest, savanna, and grassland, through which in this case flow the Congo River and its tributaries (Vansina 2004: map 6). There is marked variation in relief, soil fertility, and rainfall (Vansina 2004: maps 2, 3, and 5). Food production in about AD 1000 probably consisted of agriculture, agropastoralism, cattle pastoralism, and foraging, in appropriate environments (Vansina 2004: map 10). Population densities between AD 1000 and 1500 were probably varied (Vansina 2004: map 16). Like the Upemba Depression and the Interlacustrine Region, the Far West offered both opportunities and constraints for human settlement, facilitating an increase in sociopolitical complexity in some places but not in others.

Compared with much of the African savanna, the first two areas provided environments rich in resources and attractive to human settlement. In the Upemba Depression fish were particularly important, being the main export of the area when Europeans first visited it (de Maret 1982: 90). However, fertile, well-watered, alluvial soils and access to mountain grasslands permitted a mixed agricultural economy, to which hunting of the prolific local game also made a contribution. Maize, cassava, groundnuts, and sweet potatoes seem to have been the main crops in recent times, but these were introductions from the Americas since the sixteenth century; African millets and sorghum were also important. In addition, bananas, originally from South-East Asia, were grown, as were indigenous beans and cowpeas. Domesticated animals consisted mainly of chickens and goats. In the Upemba Depression, farmers controlled water levels with dams, and canoe channels were maintained to give fishermen access to open water (Reefe 1983: 163). So successful was the human exploitation of the area that for centuries a 'high population density supported by the richness of the ecosystem, appears to have strongly contrasted with neighboring less-populated areas' (de Maret 1997: 499). The Upemba Depression seems to have become the heartland of the Luba people. Occupants of the Interlacustrine Region, however, might have been even more fortunate. Generally good rainfall, equatorial temperatures moderated by altitude, and relatively fertile soils enabled the growing of a range of crops that now include, amongst other things, finger millet, cassava, sweet potatoes, beans, and above all bananas. Many varieties of the latter have been grown in the area for a long time, particularly the vegetable banana known as *matooke*, which in its cooked form has become a staple food for large numbers of people. Given adequate rainfall, moderate heat all year round, and suitable soil, bananas need only modest inputs of land and labour, will yield within ten to eighteen months of planting, and can produce for thirty years or more (Wrigley 1989). Furthermore, in the drier parts of the Interlacustrine Region

303

were some of Africa's best grasslands, often free of tsetse, which supported extensive pastoralism, particularly of cattle. In addition, the lakes and rivers of the area yielded important supplies of fish, and until recent times there were also substantial resources of wild game. Overall, this range of subsistence choices, especially those based on bananas or cattle (Schoenbrun 1993), not only supported local concentrations of population but also provided the wealth and power that brought about sociopolitical changes leading to the emergence of the Interlacustrine kingdoms.

As well as an exceptional subsistence base, however, both of these areas possessed other resources of importance. In the case of the Upemba Depression, to its south-east lies one of the richest and largest copper deposits in the world, which extends some 400 kilometres from the extreme south-east of Democratic Congo into northern Zambia (Winterbotham et al. 1944: 401–2). There are also sources of iron ore and salt in the area (Reefe 1983: 162), and, like the Interlacustrine Region, there would formerly have been substantial supplies of ivory. For this latter region, however, it was iron and salt that were the most important commodities, iron having been smelted in Rwanda, Burundi, and north-west Tanzania for more than 2,000 years (Woodhouse 1998: 181) and salt having been produced at Katwe on Lake Edward and Kibiro on Lake Albert probably for much of the second millennium AD (Connah 1996). Given such resources and the transport potential of the rivers and lakes as well as the relatively easy conditions of overland routes, both areas are likely to have played an important part in the development of trading networks within Central Africa, which must have further stimulated sociopolitical changes.

Nevertheless, there were constraints, as even Winston Churchill realized in 1908 when eulogizing Uganda as 'from end to end one beautiful garden' (Churchill 1962: 60). Over the relatively short period for which written records have been kept, both human and animal diseases have had major demographic impacts, and it seems possible that the same was the case in the remoter past. As in much of Africa where there are substantial bodies of water, malaria, schistosomiasis, filariasis, and other scourges must have long been a problem. In addition, as population densities increased in some parts of the areas, so did the likelihood of disease transmission, particularly of gastrointestinal infections and intestinal parasites (Patterson 1993: 448). It was sleeping sickness, however, that most impressed Churchill in the early years of the twentieth century, which by the end of 1905 killed 'considerably more than two hundred thousand persons' in parts of Uganda, out of a population estimated at not more than 300,000 (Churchill 1962: 67). In the area between Lakes George and Edward, an especially nightmarish situation developed. In 1891 rinderpest swept through this country, and most of the cattle and much of the game died. The amount of thicket increased with the reduction of grazing, creating suitable environments for tsetse flies, which in turn spread trypanosomiasis that killed more cattle, and sleeping sickness that killed large numbers of people. By 1912 the area was so badly affected that the British colonial authorities removed much of the remaining population, as was also done at about the same time in other areas along the eastern side of Lake Albert and along the lower Victoria Nile. Large parts of these areas became game reserves and national parks with very few inhabitants (Good 1972: 571–7; Uganda National Parks n.d.). Admittedly, colonial movements of livestock and people triggered these epidemics; previously an ecological balance could have existed between disease vectors, animals, and humans. However, even the threat of these diseases must have constituted a constraint on the distribution and density of population in these areas.

A final constraint in these areas might have resulted from the very population densities to which the exceptional subsistence base, and other resources, gave rise. At times the two areas might have supported some of the densest populations in tropical Africa, particularly in Rwanda, Burundi, and parts of Uganda. Increasing pressure on resources, especially competition for productive land, could have produced intergroup violence in the absence of major epidemics, substantial emigration, or fundamental technological change. Although compounded by the sociopolitical dislocation of the colonial and postcolonial experience, the explosion of violence in Rwanda in 1994 is a reminder of the potential for self-destruction within dense human populations. An estimated 500,000 to 850,000 people were killed over a period of about three months – more than 10 percent of the population – and another 30 percent were forced into exile (Reader 1997: 717–19). Political scientists, anthropologists, and others might agonize about the reasons for this appalling series of events, but one thing is clear: human beings can become a major constraint to other human beings.

Sources of information

Historical evidence

The Kingdom of Kongo, in the Far West, was first described by Portuguese visitors in the late fifteenth century AD (de Maret 1998), but for both the Upemba Depression and the Interlacustrine Region historical documentation is of limited time depth. The former became known to the outside world only towards the end of the nineteenth century, and accounts of the latter area began in the 1860s with the visits of Speke, Grant, and Baker (Winterbotham et al. 1944: fig. 36; Connah 1996: 1). It was indeed these writers who first brought some of the Interlacustrine states to international attention, providing accounts of Karagwe, Buganda, and Bunyoro before the impact of European colonial ambitions. Late-nineteenth-century and early-twentieth-century European visitors, officials, soldiers, traders, missionaries, and scientists, not only left writings that have become a source of ethnohistorical data for the Upemba and Interlacustrine areas but also made some of the earliest records of their oral traditions, a source of information for precontact periods. However, for the Luba area, 'individual tales yield only an occasional, tantalising glimpse of what happened before about AD 1700' (Reefe 1983: 165), and for the Interlacustrine states, attempts to interpret the traditions about the supposed former state of Kitara and the Bacwezi dynasty have generated an extensive but inconclusive literature (Sutton 1993). It seems probable that these latter sources refer to about the middle of the second millennium AD and concern the antecedents of the states first visited by Europeans in the 1860s, but interpretations have ranged from seeing the Bacwezi as the rulers of an early pastoral state (Oliver 1953) to arguing that they were merely mythical figures (Wrigley 1958), and from suggesting that their origins lay in the first millennium AD (Berger 1980) to concluding that they belonged to the fourteenth and fifteenth centuries (Steinhart 1981: 118). Collectively, the documentary and oral records seem unlikely to throw much light on sociopolitical developments in these areas of Central Africa before, at best, the last four or five centuries. A source of information with greater potential is the study of historical linguistics, particularly concerning cultivated plants and domesticated animals. Schoenbrun (1993), by setting his linguistic evidence in a broad interdisciplinary context, has been able to suggest that banana farming and pastoralism were already established in the Interlacustrine Region by the beginning of the second millennium. He has also examined the possible social dimensions of those agricultural developments. This has provided a useful set of hypotheses, but the chronological validity of the evidence remains uncertain. Much the same might be said for another potentially important source of information, the genetic history of the plants and animals themselves. For example, it is largely on the basis of such evidence, as well as linguistics, that De Langhe et al. (1995) proposed that plantains reached the Interlacustrine Region, from the other side of the Indian Ocean, by 2,500 years ago. In such matters we need physical evidence, particularly evidence that can be subjected to absolute dating.

Archaeological evidence

For the Upemba Depression (Fig. 10.2), archaeological evidence provides a cultural sequence from the fifth century AD to the beginning of the nineteenth century and indicates the emergence of an hierarchical society by the end of the

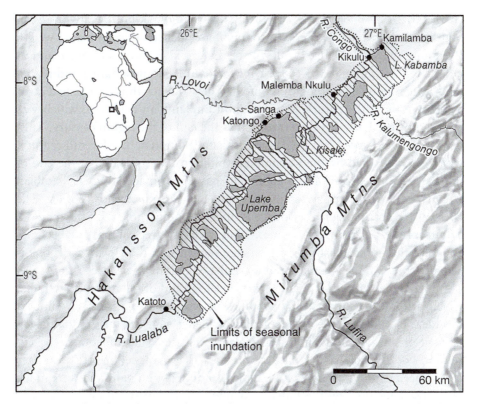

Fig. 10.2 Archaeological sites in the Upemba Depression, Democratic Congo. After de Maret 1992: fig. 48. Drawn by Joe LeMonnier.

first millennium (de Maret 1979). The sequence is supported by more than fifty radiocarbon dates (de Maret 1997: 499) and constitutes a most successful piece of archaeological research. Unfortunately, however, the evidence consists entirely of burials, clustered in cemeteries in the Upemba Depression, particularly on the banks of Lake Kisale on the upper Lualaba River. Settlement sites are known but appear to have only shallow deposits that have been extensively disturbed by continuous occupation or cultivation. As a result, they have not been excavated, but a total of more than 265 graves have been. These were situated at the sites of Sanga, Katongo, Kamilamba, Kikulu, and Malemba Nkulu (de Maret 1982: 89).

The Upemba Depression sequence can, therefore, tell us little about early urbanization in this area, but it is informative about social evolution and early state emergence. This first became apparent after the excavations of Jacques Nenquin at Sanga in 1957 and of Jean Hiernaux in 1958, which produced evidence of a remarkably sophisticated material culture from the seventh to ninth century AD. Called by Nenquin the 'Kisalian', this culture was characterized by finely made and distinctive pottery, skilful metalworking in both iron and copper, and graves containing evidence of accumulated wealth (Nenquin 1963; Hiernaux et al. 1971). Later excavations at Sanga and at other sites (de Maret 1979; 1982; 1992) revised Nenquin's dating and placed the Kisalian in its chronological context. The sequence thus established commenced in the fifth century AD with the Kamilambian tradition, which was replaced by the Early Kisalian tradition at the end of the eighth century. This, in turn, was succeeded by the Classic Kisalian tradition in the eleventh century, which was followed by the Kabambian tradition that appeared at the end of the fourteenth century. The Kabambian has been divided into Kabambian A and B, the latter ending at the beginning of the nineteenth century. The latest of the archaeological evidence is, indeed, comparable with the material culture of the Luba in recent times. Thus, as de Maret claimed, 'It becomes apparent that in establishing an Iron Age sequence in the Upemba rift one is actually studying the emergence of the Luba Kingdom' (de Maret 1979: 234).

Anthropometric studies of the Sanga skeletons and of the present-day Luba, which are said to show strong affinities between the two, seem to support this idea. In addition, the archaeological evidence suggests the gradual development of social stratification, political organization, and functional specialization. For example, as far back as the Early Kisalian, ceremonial iron axes were placed in graves. These had handles decorated with nails and were much like those later used by the Luba as symbols of authority. In one such Early Kisalian grave, the deceased had also been buried with an iron anvil, another symbol of power among Bantu-speaking peoples (Fig. 10.3). At Katoto, a cemetery in the southern part of the Upemba Rift belonging to a tradition approximately contemporaneous with the Kisalian, the richest graves included not only ceremonial axes and anvils but also evidence of child sacrifices. Social stratification was further indicated in the Classic Kisalian by the unequal distribution of grave goods between the various burials. It was observed that the few graves that contained an unusually large number of pots also contained uncommon things like cowries and ivory pendants. Furthermore, such wealth appeared to be partly hereditary, because some children's graves were among the wealthiest (de Maret 1979; 1982).

Following Bisson (1975), the development of political organization in the Luba area might be inferred from the archaeological evidence for the use of copper. This metal was particularly valued in much of Africa during precolonial times, being variously used as a medium of exchange, for personal adornment, for status symbols, and for cult objects (Herbert 1984). In the Upemba Depression sequence (de Maret 1979) there is no evidence of copper in the Kamilambian, and its first appearance is in the Early Kisalian when there were a few copper objects, mainly in the form of hammered bangles. It is very

Fig. 10.3 Early Kisalian burial at Kamilamba, Democratic Congo. Note ceremonial iron axe at left centre and iron anvil to left of skull. Reproduced by permission of Pierre de Maret.

common, however, in the Classic Kisalian, when it was used both for personal ornaments and for some functional objects. Thus far it would appear that the role of copper was principally as an indicator of wealth, prestige, and status. With the Kabambian came a marked change; distinctive copper *croisettes* (little crosses) appeared, probably originally as ingots but later used as currency. As time went by, these crosses grew smaller and more uniform in shape (de Maret 1981), and it is thought that they might have first been used as a special-purpose currency (e.g., for buying wives) but gradually evolved into a general-purpose unit of exchange. Thus the smaller, later crosses could have been used for a variety of small purchases. The use of these crosses as a form of money is suggested by evidence at Sanga, where they were often found in or near the hands of the deceased; one grave containing 140 of the smallest crosses had them tied in groups of five (Bisson 1975: 287). The presence of such a currency would imply the existence of political sophistication.

The craftsmanship indicated by the archaeological evidence for the Kisalian suggests a degree of functional specialization by the early part of the second millennium AD. The skilful handling of iron, copper, ivory, bone, and pottery hints at the presence of professional artisans. The range of metalwork alone is one of the most impressive in tropical Africa, including (for the Kisalian) iron hoes, knives, axes, spears, arrows, harpoon heads, fish hooks, necklaces, pendants with chains, together with copper artefacts such as belts, necklaces, bangles, bracelets, small knives, spearheads, and fish hooks. There might have been specialist traders bringing copper from the Copperbelt, some 200 kilometres to the south-east (de Maret 1979).

The relative proximity of one of the richest sources of copper in Africa must, indeed, have played a part in the developments in south-east Democratic Congo. From Kansanshi and Kipushi, in northern Zambia, Bisson (1976) obtained precolonial evidence for both mining and smelting copper. Exploitation of the Kansanshi deposits commenced possibly as early as the fourth century AD, and there is evidence that copper was being smelted at a similar date in the Lubumbashi region of south-east Democratic Congo (Anciaux de Faveaux and de Maret 1984; de Maret 1985: 138). The Kansanshi evidence led Bisson to reject the hypothesis sometimes advanced that Arab or Swahili traders were responsible for both the origin of states and the start of large-scale copper mining in this part of Africa. Similarly, de Maret argued that the Kisalian evidence for an hierarchical society as early as the end of the first millennium AD ruled out long-distance trade as a possible cause of this development. Rather, he saw a combination of fishing, hunting, and agriculture as permitting a high population density that 'led to a need for political integration' (de Maret 1979: 234). Certainly, the evidence for the Classic Kisalian is suggestive of some form of early state, and this in an area where throughout the earlier archaeological sequence the only indication of contact with the outside world consists of a few glass beads and a small number of marine shells from the Indian Ocean coast (Hiernaux et al. 1971: 55; 1972: 154–5; de Maret 1992: 170). Nevertheless, the possible role of internal trading networks should not be forgotten; local exchanges of copper, iron, and salt were probably particularly important (Fagan 1969). The people of the Classic Kisalian might well have participated in such networks by trading dried fish from the lakes and rivers of the Upemba Depression, as was still occurring when Europeans first entered the area (de Maret 1982: 90).

Although important, the archaeological evidence from the Upemba Depression provides information on only a relatively small area. In the case of the Interlacustrine Region the situation is rather better: the available information is scattered but covers a larger geographical area and provides more varied data (Fig. 10.4). Uganda, in particular, has had a long record of archaeological research, unfortunately interrupted by periods of political instability during the 1970s and 1980s. One of the most important of the nineteenth-century states in this area was Buganda (from which modern Uganda takes its name), although there is no archaeological evidence to throw light on the development of Bugandan urbanization. However, the origins of urbanization elsewhere in the Interlacustrine Region can be identified (p. 324). Also, Oliver (1959b) was able to make a study of the Bugandan royal tombs and of their associated human jaw-bone shrines. Other archaeological work has been carried out on Ankole, also one of the Interlacustrine states. As with that of Buganda, the capital of Ankole moved many times, but careful use of oral tradition enabled Oliver (1959a) to identify a number of capital sites in the field, which were reexamined years later by Andrew Reid and Peter Robertshaw (1987). Bweyorere, seemingly the largest, was excavated by Merrick Posnansky (1968), demonstrating the difficulties of extracting useful information from this type of site. It consists of a series of low banks on the top of a hill, forming irregular, incomplete enclosures. The banks seem to be mainly of cattle dung, and there are also several hollows that might have been cisterns. Posnansky excavated thirty-one trenches into the site and was able to identify the remains of the palace, a circular building of organic material over 15 metres in diameter, which had been destroyed by fire. The deposit was shallow, however, and no other habitation structures were found, although pottery and bones were generally distributed. Oral tradition indicated occupation of this site at three different periods: in the seventeenth, eighteenth, and nineteenth centuries. Radiocarbon dating was in general agreement with this timespan. Animal bones from the site indicated the importance of cattle to its occupants but also suggested that hunting was common. Glass beads and fragments of pottery pipes for smoking probably belonged to the latter part of the sequence.

Fig. 10.4 Principal archaeological sites and places in the Ugandan part of the Interlacustrine Region. After Connah 1996: fig. 2.2. Drawn by Joe LeMonnier.

Posnansky concluded that Bweyorere represented 'a large pastoral settlement with evidence of a palace site' but with a population of 'probably no more than a few hundred people' and that it was 'not a town' (Posnansky 1968: 165, 173). Indeed, Reid and Robertshaw pointed out that, as the traditions say that the site was occupied on several occasions, not all of it is likely to have been occupied at the same time, so that this relatively large site 'may be simply a palimpsest of several small sites'. They concluded that further excavation of such sites was unlikely to throw new light on 'the establishment and organization of the Ankole state' (Reid and Robertshaw 1987: 87–8).

Of more value for the archaeological investigation of sociopolitical change in western Uganda is a series of large earthwork enclosures to the north of Ankole, extending from the Katonga River towards the south-eastern part of Lake Albert, of which the best known are Kibengo, Munsa, and Bigo (Lanning 1953). Most investigated of these is Bigo, one of the most famous sites in east Central Africa. It consists of some 10 kilometres of ditches and banks, enclosing an area of about 5 square kilometres (Fig. 10.5). The earthworks form two main enclosures, within the larger of which is a central group of smaller enclosures. The height and width of bank and ditch vary greatly; the greatest height from the bottom of the ditch to the top of the bank is more than 7 metres. Situated within and around the central enclosures are three large mounds. Bigo was first described in 1909, was first mapped properly in 1921, and has been the subject of considerable published discussion. Tenuous oral tradition ascribes the site to the so-called Bacwezi dynasty, whose uncertain historical status has already been mentioned (p. 306). The site is associated with two smaller earthwork enclosures – Kagogo to its north-west and Kasonko to its north-east – and with the large open settlement site at Ntusi some 15 kilometres to its south-west (p. 315). All four of these sites are situated within an area less than 20 kilometres across (Wayland 1934; Shinnie 1960; Posnansky 1969).

Bigo has been excavated on two occasions: by Shinnie in 1957 (Shinnie 1960) and by Posnansky in 1960 (Posnansky 1969). These excavations indicated that there was settlement at Bigo prior to the construction of the bank and ditch system, and radiocarbon dates suggested an overall occupation date in the fifteenth and sixteenth centuries AD. Although few traces of timber structures were found, Posnansky claimed to identify the location of a royal enclosure (Posnansky 1969: 135), and Shinnie thought that 'there was considerable human occupation at the centre of the complex' (Shinnie 1960: 27). The excavated animal bones, however, revealed an emphasis on cattle; it seems possible that the outer enclosures were intended for penning cattle rather than for defence. There is some support for this: more attention seems to have been given to digging the ditch than to constructing the bank, but the protection of agricultural fields is also likely. Furthermore, as Posnansky suggested (1969: 145), it is also possible that the immensity of the earthworks was intended to bestow prestige on those who lived there. Certainly they may be regarded as a form of monumental construction: in one place Shinnie found the rock-cut ditch to be nearly 4 metres deep (Shinnie 1960: 17), and Posnansky (1969: 144) estimated that more than 200,000 cubic metres of earth and rock had been removed in making the ditches. The size and direction of the labour force necessary to accomplish such work, together with the presence at this site of a royal enclosure, would imply the existence of some degree of political

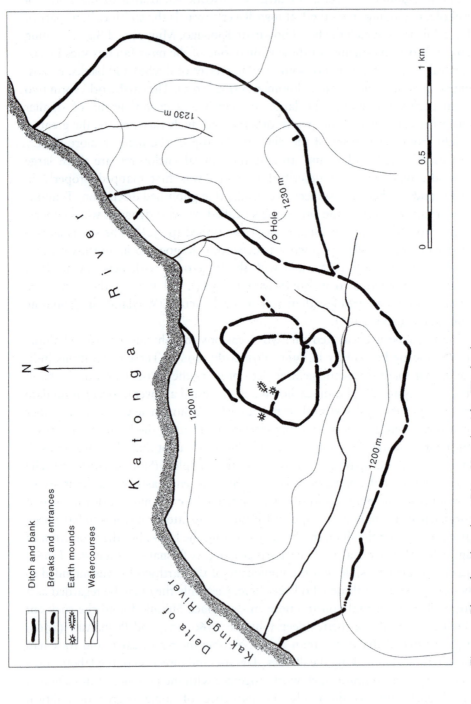

Fig. 10.5 Plan of earthworks at Bigo, Uganda. After Wayland 1934.

Ditch and bank

Breaks and entrances

Earth mounds

Watercourses

N

Katonga River

Delta of
Kakinga River

1230 m

1230 m

o Hole

1200 m

1200 m

0   0.5   1 km

centralization. It would appear that Bigo was a settlement of importance, the centre perhaps of an emerging state.

Such an assumption fails to recognize 'the ability of non-stratified societies to produce feats of construction over long periods of time' (Reid 1996: 621), but inevitably Bigo and the other earthwork sites have been interpreted as archaeological evidence of a Bacwezi-ruled Kitara state. Of the other sites, only Munsa and Kibengo have been subjected to archaeological investigation, first by E.C. Lanning (1955; 1960) and later by Peter Robertshaw (Robertshaw 1997). The earthworks at these sites were probably constructed in about the fifteenth and sixteenth centuries AD, at roughly the same time as those at Bigo, although there is evidence of occupation at Munsa as early as around the tenth century and at Kibengo from the late thirteenth to the mid-seventeenth century. Like Bigo, cattle dominated the faunal remains at Munsa, but Kibengo showed more variation and, like Bigo, lacked the evidence for smelting and iron working present at Munsa. These and other differences between the sites led Robertshaw and others to suggest that they might have acted as the centres of three polities, rather than of a single one. Excavations have also been conducted at shrine sites associated with the Bacwezi at both Mubende and Kasunga, but the former produced only the remains of a small village dating to the late thirteenth or fourteenth century, and the latter, which yielded both occupation and burial evidence, might date to as late as the seventeenth century.

It is the site of Ntusi, with neither earthworks nor a demonstrated association with the Bacwezi traditions, that has proved most informative so far as sociopolitical changes in the first half of the second millennium are concerned (Sutton 1993; Reid 1996). Lanning (1970: 39) described it as 'an ancient capital site', and, indeed, survey and excavations conducted by Andrew Reid in the late 1980s and early 1990s showed that this open settlement site has archaeological material scattered over approximately 100 hectares and was occupied between the eleventh and fifteenth centuries AD (Fig. 10.6). Excavation of two large midden mounds and of an area associated with some of the low banks that characterize the site produced large quantities of broken pottery, a faunal assemblage dominated by young cattle, numerous grindstones, curved iron knives thought to have been for cereal harvesting, burnt grain which appeared to be sorghum, storage pits probably for grain, evidence of iron working, fragments of ivory of which some were worked, ostrich eggshell beads, traces of circular houses dated to the fourteenth to fifteenth century (Fig. 10.7), and glass and cowrie shell beads indicating contact with the Indian Ocean coast by about the thirteenth century. Thus Ntusi was first occupied earlier than Bigo, whose dates have been revised to the period from the thirteenth to sixteenth century, but they apparently overlapped. Reid

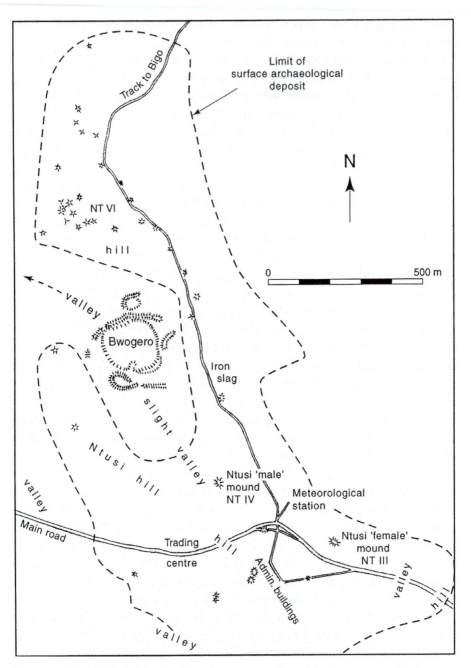

Fig. 10.6 Plan of Ntusi, Uganda. After Sutton 1993: fig. 4 based on a survey by Andrew Reid in 1987–9.

Fig. 10.7 Traces of fourteenth- to fifteenth-century circular houses at Ntusi. Reproduced by permission of Andrew Reid.

conducted a survey of 5 percent of 560 square kilometres around Ntusi and Bigo and found more than fifty other sites of second-millennium date, of which several when excavated revealed faunal remains overwhelmingly dominated by cattle. However, these sites were in general less than half a hectare in area, and the lack of sites of intermediate size suggests that, by the fourteenth and fifteenth centuries, Ntusi was a chiefdom based on cattle pastoralism and sorghum cultivation rather than a centralized state. A social hierarchy based on cattle had perhaps not yet emerged, but the fifteenth-century abandonment of Ntusi and the construction of the Bigo earthworks might indicate that this occurred subsequently. Perhaps Bigo, bordered by the Katonga River, offered a more viable centre for cattle than the dry grassland area of Ntusi. The existence near the latter site of the huge artificial depression and associated mounds and banks known as the Bwogero, sometimes called the Ntusi 'dams', suggests that this might indeed have been so (Fig. 10.6). Reid described this rather suspect feature as 'functionally ambiguous' (1996: 623), but Sutton (1985: 174) suggested that it resulted from exposing the water table for use by cattle. If he was correct, then the scale of the feature (Reid thought that almost 30,000 cubic metres of material had been removed) would suggest that this activity continued for some centuries and that demand was extreme. In such circumstances Ntusi could have been abandoned in favour of Bigo, particularly if cattle rather than a balance of pastoralism and cultivation were becoming economically dominant. However, the Bwogero remains undated and its association with the site of Ntusi has never been demonstrated.

Comparable to Reid's survey around Ntusi and Bigo were Robertshaw's investigations of the country south and west of Munsa. Some 130 archaeological sites were recorded, which all appeared to belong to the second millennium AD. By comparing the sizes and locations of these sites and grouping them on the basis of a statistical analysis of the pottery found on them, Robertshaw was able to suggest how the state of Bunyoro had developed in this area prior to the nineteenth century. Early settlements tended to be small, but it appears that a hierarchy of sizes existed from about the fourteenth century, some of the larger being protected with earthworks by the fourteenth and fifteenth centuries. A period of 'competing polities' (Robertshaw 1994: 127) between about the fourteenth and sixteenth centuries might eventually have led to collapse, which the Babito dynasty, the rulers of Bunyoro when the first Europeans arrived, were able to exploit. Thus Bunyoro might have emerged only during the seventeenth or eighteenth century but the sociopolitical changes that gave rise to it could have originated in the earlier part of the second millennium (Robertshaw 1994). Support for this model came from my excavations of the settlement site at Kibiro on the eastern shore of Lake Albert, the salt production of which was so important to the economy of nineteenth-century Bunyoro. The exploitation of this resource could also be traced back to the early second millennium (Connah 1996). Furthermore, evidence from the surface of other sites adjacent to the north-eastern part of Lake Albert and along the lower part of the Victoria Nile suggests widespread cultural homogeneity in this area over the last thousand years and gives some idea of the background of Bunyoro's development.

Control of salt production and trading was probably of importance in the rise of Bunyoro, but in the case of both this and other Interlacustrine states, such as Buganda (Reid 2001; 2003; Reid and Young 2003), the smelting and exchange of iron must also have been of significance. In the Mwenge Kingdom of western Uganda, this has been investigated archaeologically for the second millennium AD (Iles 2013b). However, in the Buhaya area, in north-west Tanzania, work by Peter Schmidt has shown that iron smelting was already practised more than 2000 years before Europeans visited that area (Schmidt and Avery 1996). Given its probable socioeconomic role, it is hardly surprising that iron also took on political and religious symbolic meaning, so that iron anvils were amongst the royal insignia of the states of Karagwe (now part of Tanzania), Ankole, Buganda, and Rwanda.

The third part of Central Africa discussed in this chapter is the Far West. Until recently there was little archaeological evidence for the emergence of social

Fig. 10.8 Axes and other iron artefacts in a burial on Corisco Island, Equatorial Guinea, first to second century AD. González-Ruibal et al. 2011, cover photograph. Reproduced by permission of Alfredo González-Ruibal and Africa Magna Verlag, Frankfurt am Main.

complexity in this area, but this is changing. Most remarkable are sites on the Island of Corisco, also known as Mandji, off the coast of Equatorial Guinea, where burials dating from the first to second century AD were accompanied by iron axes, spearheads, anklets, bracelets, spoons, knives, sickle knives, and other items, as well as complete pots (Fig. 10.8). Copper and bronze were notably absent; it seems to have been the production of iron that provided a major resource in this area (González-Ruibal et al. 2011; 2013). Little bone seems to have survived from the burials, but the iron grave goods were well preserved and possibly the graves had held both secondary and primary burials. The evidence from these sites has been associated with an 'ancient and common tradition' identified by Vansina for Equatorial Africa, from which later developments grew (Vansina 1990: 71–100; González-Ruibal et al. 2013: 141). It has been claimed that 'the new archaeological data reveal the existence of another core area for the emergence of inequalities in sub-Saharan Africa' (González-Ruibal et al. 2011: 65). In this respect it is significant that 'special-purpose currency' is present amongst the iron artefacts from Corisco (González-Ruibal et al. 2013: 129–30), suggesting that as in the Upemba Depression a sophisticated economic and sociopolitical situation was developing.

In their discussion of the Corisco evidence, González-Ruibal et al. (2011: 64) refer to the Angolan site of Feti, 'a royal tumulus' dated to between the ninth and thirteenth centuries AD, which also yielded iron hoes, knives, arrowheads, spearheads, anvils, and hammers. Vansina (2004: 170) described this site as 'one of the largest known ancient sites anywhere in West Central Africa'. Consisting of several mounds, surrounding ditches, and stone walls, it was 7.5 hectares in extent; Vansina claimed that in its later stages it was 'the capital of a very large kingdom'. In spite of incompetent excavation during the 1940s and subsequent destruction by a hydroelectric dam, the evidence from Feti suggests the development of social complexity on the *planalto* (Benguela Plateau) of Angola and in the wider Cuanza basin. Indeed, it was only one of four sites that Vansina (2004: map 17) showed on a map of 'Stone Ruins in Angola'. According to some of his other maps, these ruins were in an area with an 'ancient population cluster' and with both greater altitude and soil fertility than adjacent areas (Vansina 2004: maps 2, 3, and 16). Clearly, this part of Angola has considerable archaeological potential and needs further investigation by excavators. However, this is the case for the most of the Far West as identified here. In spite of detailed study of ceramic traditions associated with the Kingdom of Kongo, for instance, archaeology has been unable as yet to provide much information on its origins (Clist 2012). Nevertheless, ongoing archaeological research promises to shed new light on the latter subject, particularly regarding the role of copper exploitation in state development (Clist et al. 2013a; 2013b; Nikis et al. 2013).

Subsistence economy

It is uncertain to what extent the two main areas discussed are representative of Central Africa, but both have archaeological evidence for growing social complexity. It is significant that in both instances there seems to have been a subsistence economy that was stronger than in surrounding regions. Mixed farming, relying on the cultivation of cereal and other crops as well as on the herding of domestic animals, was supplemented by fishing and hunting.

In the Upemba Depression fishing was particularly important, but fertile alluvial soils that were inundated seasonally provided a productive agricultural base. Archaeological evidence limited to burials and a lack of information from settlement sites makes it difficult to assess the subsistence economy, but clearly it was a successful one that supported a substantial population. Direct evidence is sparse, but oil-palm nuts (*Elaeis guineensis*), grain that was very probably finger millet (*Eleusine* [*coracana*?]), and the bones of goats and chicken were found in various contexts, as well as fish bones, mollusc shells, and bones from wild animals (de Maret 1992: 157, 170, 239–43).

In the Interlacustrine Region there is more evidence, with probable sorghum at Ntusi in the fourteenth to fifteenth century; finger millet from an approximately fourteenth-century context at Kibiro; cattle dominating faunal evidence at Ntusi, Bigo, Munsa, and other sites; and sheep or goats as important as cattle at Kibiro (Posnansky 1969; Connah 1996; Reid 1996). In the more fertile areas with higher rainfall, cereal cultivation was apparently supplemented by banana growing, although bananas are difficult to identify in the archaeological record. Impressions of banana pseudostems in slag from iron-smelting sites in Buganda are 'possibly only a hundred or so years old' (Reid and Young 2003: 122), and claims of banana phytoliths from Munsa dated to the fourth millennium BC (Lejju et al. 2006) have been questioned (Neumann and Hildebrand 2009). Nevertheless, bananas seem to have had an important role in the emergence of the Bugandan state, because of their low-input and high-yield production (Reid 2001). Cattle herding so successfully exploited the drier grasslands that it came to be sociopolitically if not economically dominant. It would appear that both these areas had a successful subsistence base that was capable of producing a surplus that could be accumulated: in the form of grain, dried fish, cattle, or small stock. Some parts of these areas were probably able to support locally dense populations. Concerning the subsistence economy of the Far West, archaeological evidence remains sparse, although the first-millennium BC site of Boso-Njafo, further to the East, in the Inner Congo Basin, has produced grains of domesticated pearl millet (*Pennisetum glaucum*), suggesting a drier period than at present (Kahlheber et al. 2014).

Technology

Archaeological evidence from the three areas of Central Africa discussed indicates a sound technological base. Because the Upemba Depression and Far West evidence consists of grave goods, with a high incidence of intact artefacts, and the Interlacustrine Region evidence consists of material from settlement sites, where items are often fragmented, our knowledge of technology in the first two areas is substantial. Metalworking, of both iron and (not in the Far West) copper, was sophisticated. In the Upemba Depression the carving of ivory and bone and the making of high-quality pottery also indicate considerable craftsmanship, while evidence for basket making is a reminder of skills using organic materials that have not survived.

For the Interlacustrine Region we have more information on processes than products. Thus numerous sites indicate skill in iron smelting and smithing, and sites in north-west Tanzania have been claimed to show evidence of a preheated air blast and a direct steel process, although these claims might need qualification (Killick 1996; Woodhouse 1998). Furthermore, the smelters of western Uganda between the fourteenth and twentieth centuries must have been highly skilled; archaeological excavations and fieldwork in the Mwenge Kingdom suggest that metal yield was increased by the addition of manganese oxide to the ore (Iles 2013b). A fourteenth-century furnace excavated at Munsa is amongst the earliest evidence for iron smelting in this region (Iles et al. 2014). Analysis of iron furnaces and other remains from Kooki and Masindi, in western Uganda, has also shed light on iron-working technology over the last three centuries (Iles 2013a). In addition, the evidence from Kibiro demonstrates the existence, from early in the second millennium, of a salt-making technique using the sun's capillary action on waterlogged deposits, producing salt of 97.6 percent purity (Connah 1996). Salt was also made at Katwe, on Lake Edward, and at Lake Bunyampaka, near Lake George, by the more usual solar evaporation technique, although it is unknown for how long this had been done prior to its recording in the nineteenth century (Connah 1998a). In contrast, the making of pottery was well established by the first millennium AD, and during the second millennium produced an impressive range of vessel forms. Relatively late in the Kibiro sequence graphite slip was used on some high-status items, requiring the mining of graphite for which evidence was found at Kigorobya nearby (Connah 1996: 129, 180). The pottery is also technologically informative in other ways: acquiring clay and tempers needed an understanding of geology, making flexible roulettes used in decoration required a knowledge of plant fibres, and the fine carving of wooden roulettes also used in decoration suggests the existence of wood-carving skills. Finally, perhaps the most impressive aspect of the technology of the Interlacustrine Region is indicated by the existence of the earthwork sites, of which Bigo is the best known. Requiring the excavation of earth, the quarrying of rock, and the construction of substantial banks of these materials, something more than massed hoes and copious sweat was needed: civil engineering skills must have been present.

Social system

In all three of the areas reviewed there is archaeological evidence for the emergence of a social hierarchy. Some of the Upemban burials were accompanied by more grave goods than others, some even by child sacrifices, and the existence of wealthy children's graves suggested that wealth was partly hereditary. Large numbers of high-quality pots, iron and copper artefacts, items of ivory, and even glass beads and cowrie shells from the Indian Ocean coast were probably indicative of one or more elite groups. Furthermore, some graves contained probable symbols of power, such as an iron axe, anvil, or bell, suggesting that the individuals with whom they were buried were invested with political or sacred authority. Indeed, the eventual use of copper *croisettes* as a form of currency suggests that a sophisticated political structure had developed. It seems likely that several privileged groups that had attained chieftain status, one of which by the eighteenth century founded the Luba state, ruled a society of cultivators, herdsmen, and fishermen. The diverse technological skills indicated by the artefactual assemblage would suggest that some degree of functional specialization also developed. In the Far West, iron grave goods on the Island of Corisco, and at Feti where there are earthworks and stone structures, with the latter also in other places, suggest the emergence of social hierarchies during the first and second millennia AD.

In the Interlacustrine Region it is the construction of large earthworks, with all that this implies for control of resources, planning, and direction of labour, that suggests the existence of powerful elites whose wealth was accumulated in the form of cattle. In addition, at both Bigo and Bweyorere the sites of supposed elite structures were found, and it is possible that the two large midden mounds at Ntusi were associated with the dwellings of sociopolitical leaders. That some members of society were wealthier and perhaps more powerful than others is also suggested by several approximately eleventh-century burials excavated at Munsa that were accompanied by the earliest glass beads found in the area as well as by bracelets of iron and one of copper (Robertshaw 1997: 13–14). Furthermore, the roughly fourteenth-century female burial at Kibiro that had iron and copper jewellery with it, as well as beads of glass and of freshwater shell, suggests that women as well as men were among the elite (Connah 1996: 90–2). From the evidence of Robertshaw's survey south and west of Munsa (Robertshaw 1994) and from Reid's research in and around Ntusi (Reid 1996), it seems likely that the process of sociopolitical change followed much the same course as in the Upemba Depression, with separate chiefdoms gradually giving way to a number of Interlacustrine states by the eighteenth century. At the same time the archaeological evidence for iron working, salt making, and perhaps other activities suggests that some functional specialization was also occurring. Finally, although the Upemba Depression and Far West lack evidence from settlement sites that could throw light on the subject, at least in the Inter-lacustrine Region the beginnings of urbanization were apparent. For example, by the fifteenth century Ntusi was an extensive settlement, probably covering much of its approximately 100 hectares; round about the sixteenth century the massive enclosures at Bigo might at times have sheltered large numbers of people and their cattle; and in 1894 Kibiro was described as 'the only manufacturing town in [B]Unyoro' (Thruston 1900: 143). Apparently all three of the areas of Central Africa discussed had already attained a substantial level of social complexity before the advent of sustained contact with the outside world. Clearly, this was also the case for the Kingdom of Kongo, in the Far West, which so impressed Portuguese visitors in the late fifteenth century.

Population pressures

A causative factor in these changes might have been localized population pressures, which resulted in competition for an important but limited resource that had stimulated population growth. Greater resources than were available in adjacent areas characterized each of the areas discussed in this chapter. In the Upemba Depression this could have been access to prime fishing areas or to fertile alluvial soils in an environment where '[d]ense populations had to compete for the few stretches of land not inundated during the annual flood' (Reefe 1983: 163). In the Interlacustrine Region it is more likely to have been access to dryland grazing rights and to the more fertile cultivable soils in higher rainfall areas, but water for livestock and sources of salt, iron ore, and even charcoal are also possibilities. For the Far West, specialized iron production seems to have provided a major resource, and marked population clustering has been claimed for the first half of the second millennium AD (Vansina 2004: map 16). It seems that exceptional natural resources might have promoted population growth in areas that were so endowed but that such growth inevitably led to competition for control of the best of those resources. Those who succeeded in gaining that control could then accumulate a surplus in one form or another and use this as a means of establishing authority over large numbers of less fortunate people. However, these propositions have yet to be tested with relevant archaeological evidence, and Parker Shipton argued that in agrarian East Africa it was areas of low population pressure, not high population pressure, that were characterized by the development of political hierarchy (Shipton 1984).

Ideology

The archaeological evidence for the role of religious ideology in the socio-political changes that took place in the Upemba Depression, the Interlacus-trine Region, and the Far West is limited, although both oral tradition and the ethnohistorical record suggest that it must have been an important contributory factor. In these areas, the placing of valuable and sometimes numerous items as grave goods in burials indicates a concern with the spirit world, and the collection of both secular and sacred objects placed with the 1930/1 burial of the seventeenth- or eighteenth-century Rwandan king Cyirima Rujugira suggests that this was particularly the case with state rulers (Van Noten 1972: fig. 8; 1982: fig. 36). Evidence of the association of kingship and the sacred is also provided by the large number of royal tombs in both Bunyoro and Buganda, which were still maintained and venerated during the twentieth century (Uganda 1967: 71). Indeed, in these states it was customary to remove the mandible from the deceased and house it in a separate 'jaw-bone shrine', specifically because it represented part of the credentials of his successor (Oliver 1959b). It is possible that these various tombs and shrines extend back to the fifteenth century, but other shrines associated with the supposed earlier Bacwezi rulers could be developments subsequent to these possibly mythical figures. This might be the case at Mubende, Kasunga, and Masaka Hill, and certainly is the case at Bigo where such a shrine seems to have appeared only in the 1990s. Nevertheless, it is likely that those who ruled emergent states in Central Africa based their power on the spiritual world as well as on material resources. Indeed, de Maret (2012) focussed on the Far West of Central Africa and on the Upemba Depression in his examination of the role of ritual power in African kingship and in the emergence of political complexity. For the Interlacustrine Region, the importance of belief systems is indicated by the late-first- to early-second-millennium AD Luzira Head (Fig. 10.9), and associated terracottas, found near Kampala in Uganda (Ashley and Reid 2008).

External trade

It has often been assumed that until late in the second millennium, Central Africa remained so remote from the world outside the continent that external long-distance trade could not have played a part in sociopolitical changes (e.g., Connah 1996: 1, 213). Indeed, archaeological evidence indicates that such changes were already in progress at an earlier date. However, the idea of an isolated Central Africa needs modification, particularly because of its origin in the nineteenth century amongst Europeans who believed they

0   5 cm

Fig. 10.9 Ceramic head from Luzira, near Kampala, Uganda. Late first to early second millennium AD. Ashley and Reid 2008: fig. 2a. Copyright British Institute in Eastern Africa, reproduced with permission.

were ending the timeless isolation of the continent's heart. Can Central Africa have been previously so isolated, when nineteenth-century European visitors found American crops such as maize, cassava, sweet potatoes, and groundnuts already growing there? Furthermore, tobacco was also being grown and was being smoked in pottery pipes that were similar in form to pipes found in other parts of Africa and beyond (Shaw 1960). It might be countered that none of these introductions is likely to pre-date the sixteenth century, by which time the Portuguese were already present in the Kingdom of Kongo. However, there is also the problem of bananas to explain, for it has been proposed that they were introduced to Central Africa, from the other side of the Indian Ocean, 2,500 years ago (De Langhe et al. 1995). Indeed, a small amount of archaeological evidence does suggest that contacts with the outside world go back to early in the second millennium AD. Such is the approximate date of a few glass beads and a small number of marine shells (from the Indian Ocean coast) that were found at the site of Katoto in the Upemba Depression (Hiernaux et al. 1972: 154–5), while glass and cowrie shell beads were excavated from a roughly thirteenth-century context at Ntusi and glass beads from a grave of about the fourteenth century at Kibiro (Connah 1996: 90–2). In addition, glass beads were also recovered from several approximately eleventh-century burials at Munsa (Robertshaw 1997: 13–14). In short, Central Africa was not totally isolated from the rest of the world, but the evidence for long-distance trade from outside the continent before the middle of the second millennium AD is tenuous. Surface collections from no less than thirty-six sites in the Ugandan part of the Western Rift Valley, for instance, produced only seven glass beads (Connah 1996: 213).

In such circumstances, although isolation was not total, external trade is unlikely to have been an important factor in the development of social complexity. On the other hand, internal African trading networks, particularly in salt, iron, and copper, could have played a significant role in this development. Salt was produced at Uvinza, in western Tanzania, from the middle of the first millennium AD (Sutton and Roberts 1968); at Ivuna, also in western Tanzania, from early in the second millennium (Fagan and Yellen 1968); at Kibiro, in Uganda, from a similar date (Connah 1996); and at Katwe, also in Uganda, from an unknown date prior to the nineteenth century (Connah 1998a). Iron production was clearly important in the Interlacustrine Region, and one of the world's great copper deposits was already being exploited in south-east Democratic Congo and northern Zambia. In addition, it is probable that numerous other commodities were traded widely in Central Africa, such as dried fish, millet, sorghum, charcoal, bark cloth, wild animal skins, and ivory. With landscapes over which movement was relatively easy, many trade goods could have travelled long distances as head loads, but this is a land of lakes and rivers in which there is ethnohistorical evidence for substantial development of water transport. In the course of a thousand years or more a complex series of overlapping trading networks could have developed, of which we still know very little, although Vansina (2004: map 12) thought that trade routes could have already extended across the continent, from the Indian Ocean to the Atlantic, by early in the second millennium AD. It was possibly these that spread the bananas and the other new crops, as well as the occasional glass beads and marine shells, all of them picked up at the periphery of the networks from international sources. It might also have been these internal trading networks that generated concentrations of wealth in particular areas, brought disparate groups of people into contact, and stimulated competition and conflict, by these and other means contributing to the social, political, and economic transformations that took place in some parts of Central Africa.

Conclusion

The relative isolation of much of Central Africa from influences external to the continent, until the middle of the second millennium AD, makes it particularly important to understand the processes that led in some places to state emergence and/or the growth of larger, denser settlements. Explanation of such developments in this context might help us to comprehend similar sociopolitical changes in other parts of Africa, and perhaps even elsewhere in the world. Unfortunately, however, a relatively low level of archaeological visibility and a very uneven distribution of archaeological research given the huge area involved make it difficult to draw any general conclusions. Nevertheless, for the relatively small Upemba Depression, the larger but still limited Interlacustrine Region, and parts of the Far West, there is sufficient archaeological evidence to throw a little light on the matter, assuming that they can be taken as representative of Central Africa. Potentially highly productive environments, with access to other major resources, distinguished all these areas. In spite of the constraints of periodic disease and human conflict, each of them could have supported locally dense populations sustained by cereal, banana, and other cultivation; pastoralism; fishing; and hunting and with a varied metallurgy-based technology. The archaeological evidence also suggests that increasingly hierarchical social systems were developing during the first half of the second millennium, stimulated by competition for prime resources as population pressures increased in some areas. Elite individuals were able to manipulate large groups of people, legitimizing their position by assumption of ritual status but basing their power on economic control. Extensive trading networks within Central Africa are also likely to have played an important contributory part in these developments, with only attenuated input from outside the continent. Many commodities were probably involved, but the importance of salt (so keenly sought for both human and livestock use), iron (the very basis of the technology on which society depended), and copper (such a valued symbol of status and means of exchange) can hardly be exaggerated. It is apparent that all of these factors helped to shape the complex sociopolitical landscape, which impressed nineteenth-century European explorers deep in the heart of Africa.

Chapter 11

Settlement growth and emerging polities: South Africa

In this chapter, 'South Africa' describes the extremity of the continent south of a line from the Limpopo River, in the east, to Walvis Bay, in the west. It consists of the Republic of South Africa, together with southern parts of Namibia, Botswana, and Mozambique, as well as Lesotho and Swaziland, although attention will be limited to the first of these modern states. Two characteristics of the archaeology of this region are of relevance to the subject of urban and state origins in Africa. First, environments in which trees were rare or absent resulted in the use of drystone construction for parts of many settlements, rendering them highly visible archaeologically, particularly if subsequently abandoned during the turbulent history of recent centuries. This allows detailed analysis of the layout of settlements and their relationship to landscapes. Second, the sociopolitical developments that are the subject of this book took place in South Africa within the last five hundred years at most and in many cases more recently, so that both documentary records and oral traditions are copious and valuable sources of information. In addition, linguistic and genetic studies can provide information on the relationships and movements of ethnic groups, to which investigations of pottery and other aspects of material culture can contribute. Thus, in the case of South Africa, we can examine processes of change for which there is much less evidence in some other parts of the continent at earlier dates. Not only can this throw light on the development of complexity in Africa as a whole, but an investigation of the South African data also has global relevance.

Geographical location and environmental factors

Mixed farming seems to have been well established in South Africa by the middle of the second millennium AD. However, the western and south-western parts of this huge area were too dry to grow African cereal crops or had winter rainfall instead of the necessary summer rainfall. In those parts of southern Africa, livestock-herding, hunter-gathering, or a combination of the two remained the subsistence strategies until European colonization over the last three hundred years or so. In contrast, to the east and north-east both cultivation and livestock, particularly cattle, were important. This was especially the case on the Highveld between the Vaal River and the Gariep

River (formerly the Orange River) and some way north of the Vaal. In this area there are numerous deserted partly stone-built settlements belonging to the last few centuries, and some of them were the scenes of substantial social and political changes (Fig. 11.1). This is an area of temperate grassland, in South Africa referred to as the Veld, a word meaning grassland and open country. Indeed, the area is both of these, but it is also more than 1,000 metres above sea level, so that it has a relatively cool and healthy climate. Much of it is good grazing country for livestock. It comprises two of the ten biomes, or ecological zones, into which the South African environment can be divided (Mitchell 2002:15). These have been referred to as 'Grassland' and 'Mixed Woodland Savanna'. Significantly, the majority of the archaeological sites discussed in this chapter are located within these zones (Mitchell 2002: fig. 12.2).

In addition to livestock, both rainfall and soil in these zones are generally suitable for cereal cultivation, with sorghum and pearl millet formerly grown but after the seventeenth century increasingly maize, introduced from America. The latter can yield up to three times as much as the indigenous cereals and requires less labour for its cultivation. However, it needs 25 percent more rain, and in an environment prone to rainfall fluctuations and serious drought, this was to have disastrous consequences (Mitchell 2002: 372). The existence of such fluctuations is why livestock became so important; cattle-keeping, in particular, helped to protect against food shortages and provided a means of accumulating wealth and gathering supporters by loaning animals. Understandably, cattle became the centre around which life revolved, even dictating the layout of the settlements in which farmers lived, a layout known as the Central Cattle Pattern that still characterizes patrilineal Eastern Bantu-speaking people (Mitchell 2002: 179–280). Concerning this matter more is known than usual, because many of the settlements were built partly in stone; specifically they included extensive drystone enclosure walls whose ruins are often still visible. As already mentioned, this was a response to the grassland environment, for the general lack of trees meant that there was little wood available for building, it being reserved for the framework of otherwise mud-built houses; in some cases houses were even built of stone. Such was the shortage of wood that dried dung had to be used for fuel in many places (Chirikure et al. 2008: fig. 5.2), and iron tools and weapons had to be obtained by trade with other areas where there was sufficient wood for smelting and smithing. However, in spite of the rounded character of much of the landscape, there were also outcrops of rock that broke into pieces ideally suited for building. Settlements were often located on the ridges formed by such outcrops, giving ready access to building material as well as a commanding view of the surrounding plains.

UNIVERSITY OF WINCHESTER
LIBRARY

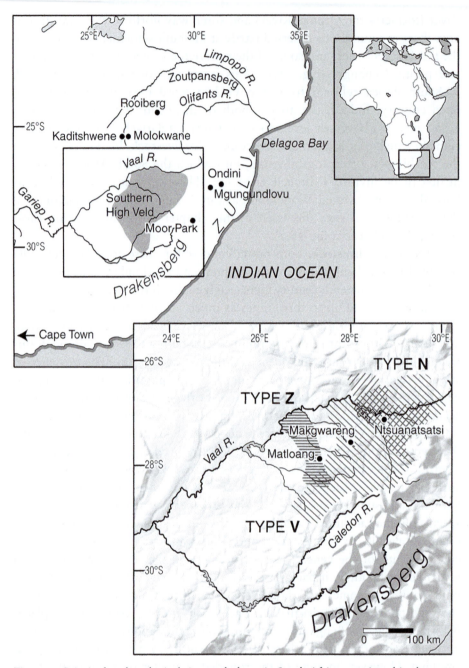

Fig. 11.1 Principal archaeological sites and places in South Africa mentioned in the text, showing the distribution of the three types of stone-walled settlement units on the South African Highveld. After Maggs 1976: fig. 15 and Whitelaw 1997: fig. 65. Drawn by Joe LeMonnier.

Sources of information

Historical evidence

The earliest European settlements in South Africa were during the sixteenth century, so that substantial historical documentation provides information on African communities since that time (Theal 1964). Explorers, missionaries, traders, and others recorded what they saw, and these ethnohistorical sources indicate that urban development was already occurring in some places by the nineteenth century. For example, in 1801 Truter and Somerville estimated the number of huts at the Thlaping settlement of Old Lithako (which lacked stone structures), in north-eastern Cape Province, to be between 2,000 and 3,000, and the population between 10,000 and 15,000 (Walton 1956: 52). Furthermore, in 1835 Gardiner reckoned the number of inhabitants at the Zulu capital of Mgungundlovu, in KwaZulu-Natal, at 5,500 (Parkington and Cronin 1979: 136), and the later Zulu capital of Ondini is thought to have housed up to 5,000 people at times during the 1870s (Watson and Watson 1990: 34). Neither of these places possessed stone structures. In the case of Mgungundlovu, some of these visitors left plans and drawings of its layout, as well as descriptions. Another important documentary source is the account by John Campbell of his visit to Kaditshwene, the early nineteenth-century capital of the Hurutshe group of the Tswana, in 1820. He estimated its population as either 16,000 or 20,000; Stephen Kay, who visited in 1821, thought that it contained 13,000 to 14,000 people. In comparison, an 1824 official census recorded 18,668 occupants for Cape Town, the biggest colonial settlement at that time (Boeyens 2000: 3).

Historical documentation also provides evidence of state emergence, in several of the more densely populated parts of South Africa, by the nineteenth century. Best known is the Zulu kingdom, because of its violent conflict with other ethnic groups and with European colonial interests. However, there were also related Nguni polities and those of the Ndebele, Swazi, and others, which appeared during and after the Mfecane, a period of wars and population movements during the early nineteenth century (Fage and Verity 1978: 42). Oral traditions are another important source of information concerning these developments, and many of these traditions have been systematically recorded. This has provided substantial information on the ethnic identities of many of the people occupying the south-eastern part of South Africa, particularly the Sotho-Tswana of the Highveld. Anthropological and ethnological investigations have further contributed to these contextual studies, so that much more is understood about the development of sociopolitical complexity in South Africa during the later second millennium AD than is the case for other parts of Africa during earlier periods. A major factor contributing to this difference was European settlement and trade, both of which expanded on an unprecedented scale in South Africa during the nineteenth century.

Archaeological evidence

Some of the earliest archaeological evidence for the emergence of social complexity in South Africa is in the Zoutpansberg Range, in what was formerly the northern Transvaal (now Limpopo Province). This seems to be dated to the fifteenth century AD. Some sites with drystone structures in this region have similarities to the zimbabwe-tradition sites of Zambezia, notable examples being Dzata and Machemma. These are situated in a region later associated with the Venda, whose culture has been used to interpret symbolism at Great Zimbabwe (Huffman 1996). The Zoutpansberg had metal ores, good soils and pasture, and formerly abundant game, particularly elephants, and it is thought to be where the Sotho-Tswana people originated (Whitelaw 1997: 451). This was during a period with a cooler, drier climate; in some parts of South Africa, severe aridity probably occurred. As a consequence, farmers apparently had little interest in the Highveld, and it was probably only the increasing importance of cattle in their economy that led to substantial settlement in this zone. This occurred from about 1300; the site of Moor Park, in KwaZulu-Natal, is dated from the fourteenth to sixteenth centuries and consisted of a stone-walled enclosed hilltop, with evidence of domesticated cattle and sorghum cultivation (Mitchell 2002: 348; Huffman 2007: 33–4). Subsequently, a warmer, wetter period with more regular summer rains, which provided favourable conditions for cereal cultivation, might also have encouraged increased settlement of this high country. Radiocarbon dates suggest that this could have happened as late as the seventeenth century (Mitchell 2002: 348–9), although formerly a date two centuries earlier was suggested (Maggs 1976: 320). It was at this time that the earliest of many stone-walled settlements were built, in the northeastern corner of the southern Highveld. Each of these consisted of a cluster of settlement units with layouts known to archaeologists as Type N (Fig. 11.2), after a site at Ntsuanatsatsi, in Free State Province. These settlement units had a central ring of circular livestock enclosures which were connected by walling to form a large secondary enclosure, outside of which were houses of reeds and mud, the whole complex being surrounded by a low outer wall. The layout allowed livestock to be penned in the centre of the unit, away from the living area around the huts. Each settlement unit seems to have housed an extended family and its livestock; settlements consisted of as many as a hundred such units, possibly containing up to 1,500 people. However, these early settlements were widely spaced compared with later ones, suggesting that the overall

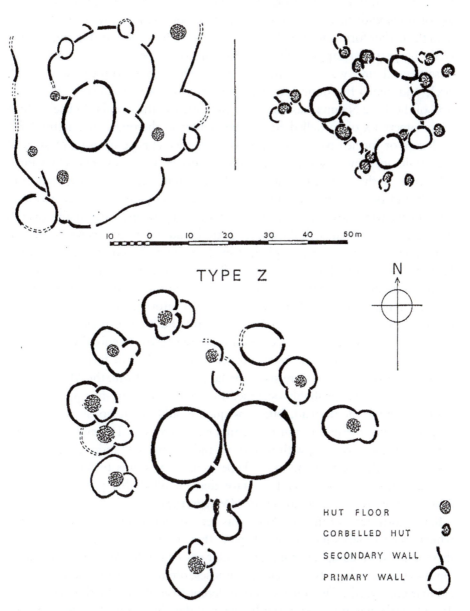

Fig. 11.2 Types of stone-walled settlement units on the South African Highveld. After Maggs 1976: fig. 16. Copyright Taylor & Francis Ltd: www.tandfonline.com.

population was still small. Excavation has produced broken pottery, clay figurines of cattle, iron and bone tools, bones of both domesticated and wild animals, stone platforms for grain bins, and indications that the houses were dome-like structures, sometimes with paved floors (Maggs 1976).

335

After some time, the layout of the individual settlement units changed to one that is referred to by archaeologists as Type V (Fig. 11.2). Settlements consisting of units with this plan were much more common and more widespread than the earlier form and were located in areas with the best arable and grazing land, in part overlapping the distribution of Type N units. Each Type V settlement unit was made up of circular enclosures arranged in a rough circle and joined by connecting walls to form one large enclosure. The outer wall of the Type N units was no longer present, and the circular houses, which were sometimes of corbelled stone, were either in the open outside the large enclosure or formed part of the enclosure. Settlements comprising clusters of such units in some cases housed many hundreds of inhabitants. Occasional differences in the sizes of individual settlement units suggest that differences in wealth and power were developing within these communities. Furthermore, settlements were now closer together, indicating an increase in the overall population compared with the earlier period, and older settlements continued to be occupied or were reoccupied, stone from Type N settlement units often being robbed to build in the new style. Type V settlement units date from the seventeenth and eighteenth centuries, and excavations at the settlement site of Makgwareng, in the Free State, have provided information on the history of one of them. In this case the earliest occupants built enclosures of reeds, not stone, and constructed houses of mud-plastered reeds. Eventually these were replaced by five large stone enclosures that were linked to form a secondary enclosure, around which were six stone houses. In this form, the Makgwareng settlement unit was probably occupied by eighteen to forty-five people, comprising a family homestead, but subsequently additional houses were built, suggesting that the number of occupants had increased. The end was apparently sudden and violent, with iron tools and weapons abandoned at the site. Like many other settlements with Type V units, it seems to have been destroyed during the widespread warfare that engulfed this part of southern Africa in the early nineteenth century (Maggs 1976).

In the north-west of the Free State was yet another design of settlement unit, which archaeologists have called Type Z (Fig. 11.2). At the centre of each of these units was a compact group of circular enclosures for livestock; surrounding these were eight to twenty circular houses, often with front and back semicircular courtyards. The houses were different from those of either Type N or Type V settlement units. Apparently they had thatched conical roofs supported mainly by a ring of poles set outside the mud wall of the building itself, thus providing it with a veranda. Again, these settlement units were grouped together into settlements, of which one particularly large example at Matloang has been surveyed and partly excavated. At that place, tightly packed houses and livestock enclosures extended for more than a kilometre along a ridge and might have had a population of more than 1,000 people. Such settlements were probably occupied during the eighteenth century, but the earliest of them might be older. When oral traditions, historical accounts, and linguistic data are compared with the archaeological evidence, it appears that all three types of settlement unit were probably built by speakers of Sotho-Tswana languages but that whereas both Type N and Type V were the work of Sotho people, the first style developing into the second, Type Z settlement units were built by Tswana people. Thus it seems that the differences in layout amongst the stone ruins of the Highveld reflect differences in its past populations (Maggs 1976).

During the 1960s and 1970s, the classification of the stone-walled structures discussed above was based on aerial photographs. More recently, technologies such as Google Earth satellite imagery and Geographic Information System software have allowed more sophisticated analysis of such sites. Remotely sensed settlement data from the Suikerbosrand Nature Reserve near Johannesburg have shown significant changes in settlement patterns from dispersed homesteads to nucleated towns during the last two or three centuries before the colonial period. These changes are similar to those in other stone-walled structures, where they have been interpreted as indicating an evolution in social, political, and economic complexity. It is thought that climatic stress and conflict might have helped bring about these changes in settlement patterns. Structures have been classified into three groups: Group I dates from the fifteenth to the seventeenth century and Groups II and III from the seventeenth to the nineteenth, although Group III might have been chronologically intermediate between Groups I and II (Sadr and Rodier 2012).

During the eighteenth century some Tswana settlements in the western Transvaal (now North-West Province) grew to a remarkable size, culminating in populations of 10,000 people or more. Kaditshwene appears to have been one of the largest, with a population in the early nineteenth century approaching 20,000, making it similar in size to contemporary Cape Town (Boeyens 2000: 3). Molokwane, also in North-West Province, dating from the beginning of the eighteenth century, is thought to have been even larger. It was a settlement 3 kilometres in length, averaging 1.5 kilometres in width and with an area of approximately 4 to 5 square kilometres. It has to be regarded as urban in character, although it was called a 'village' by its investigator, who also described it as 'the largest stone-walled archaeological site in South Africa' (Pistorius 1992: 17). Excavation of one of its smaller settlement units, covering an area of 1 hectare and loosely comparable in layout to the Type Z units, has provided a valuable picture of the life of its occupants (Fig. 11.3). Over 79 percent of the meat consumed came from domestic animals, cattle outnumbering sheep and goats, and there was evidence for the preparation of plant food, including grain. In addition, the internal arrangements of the settlement

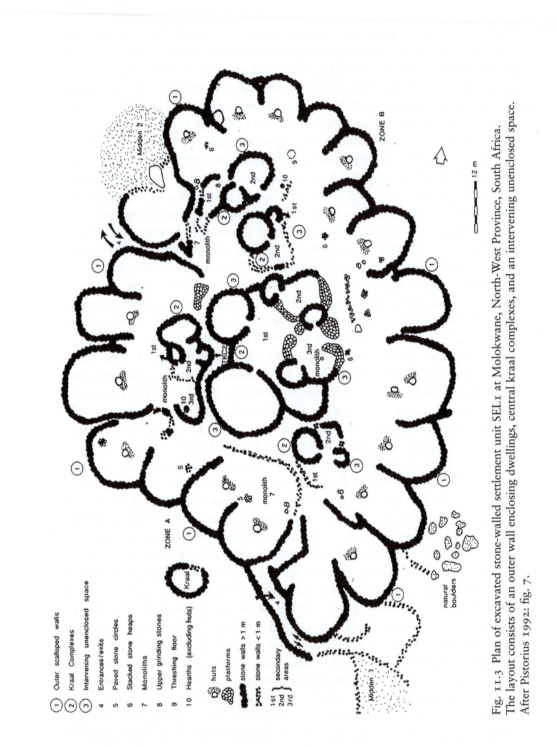

Fig. 11.3 Plan of excavated stone-walled settlement unit SEL1 at Molokwane, North-West Province, South Africa. The layout consists of an outer wall enclosing dwellings, central kraal complexes, and an intervening unenclosed space. After Pistorius 1992: fig. 7.

Legend:
1 Outer scalloped walls
2 Kraal Complexes
3 Intervening unenclosed space
4 Entrances / exits
5 Paved stone circles
6 Stacked stone heaps
7 Monoliths
8 Upper grinding stones
9 Threshing floor
10 Hearths (excluding huts)

huts
platforms

stone walls > 1 m
stone walls < 1 m

1st
2nd } secondary
3rd } areas

Kraal

12 m

ZONE A
ZONE B

Midden 2
Midden 3

natural boulders

monolith

unit shed light on the social structure of its inhabitants as well as on their daily activities. Considered as a whole, this huge settlement and others like it indicate increasing centralization of economic and political power by local rulers, at least partly in response to growing instability. Population expansion, partly fuelled by the introduction of maize, had led to greater competition between chiefdoms for arable land and grazing and to more frequent cattle raiding as a means of augmenting wealth. In addition, the onset of drought made the situation even worse, setting the stage for disaster (Antonites and Antonites 2014).

During the early nineteenth century there erupted a series of wars and population movements that originated in KwaZulu-Natal but subsequently affected much of south-eastern Africa. Known as the Mfecane by the Nguni, meaning 'the crushing', this explosion of violence seems to have been principally sparked by intense competition for the control of resources, particularly those sought by European traders at Delagoa Bay, the location of the Mozambique port formerly known as Lourenço Marques (now Maputo). Slaves appear to have been one of those resources, but ivory was the principal one, as much as 50 tonnes (representing about 500 elephants) being exported each year from 1750 to 1790. This was mainly in exchange for glass beads, cloth, and brass. Such imports increased the wealth and power of those rulers who gained access to them, and the competition for elephants grew ever more intense as they became more difficult to find. In addition, there were the effects of population growth, resulting from the cultivation of maize, as mentioned earlier. Several severe drought episodes as well as crop rust and cattle disease made the situation even worse. Out of the resulting chaos emerged the Zulu state, centred in KwaZulu-Natal, but for the settlements of the Highveld the period has been remembered as the Difaqane by the Sotho-Tswana, meaning 'the scattering of tribes'. As European settlers moved north in the so-called Great Trek of the late 1830s, they found only deserted stone ruins in many places, not the thriving communities of people and animals that had formerly existed (Mitchell 2002: 369–79).

The increasing number and size of the stone-walled sites of the Highveld can be regarded as indications of urban development. Furthermore, the emergence of powerful centralized polities, such as that of the Zulus, out of the chaos of the Mfecane is a remarkable example of state development. In the Zulu case this was centred on a permanent army of young men of a given age, based in purpose-built military homesteads. Warfare enabled control of land, cattle, food, and agricultural labour, while the king controlled iron production and imported prestige goods. The success of the Zulu state is indicated by the Battle of Isandlwana in 1879, when the Zulus inflicted one of the most devastating defeats suffered by a British Army during colonial wars in Africa. Later that year the British retaliated at the Battle of Ulundi, breaking the military power of the Zulu nation by defeating its army, destroying the capital of Zululand, Ulundi, and capturing the Zulu king, Cetshwayo. The existence of the Zulu state had been brief, but it was an impressive example of indigenous state development in Africa.

The ruins of other stone-walled settlements exist in the south-east of South Africa, although individual settlement units are often relatively small. Nevertheless, as already seen, in some instances the dense distribution of such structures and the size of some of them suggest the presence of substantial populations, with the potential for urban growth and state development. Such is the case in the Rustenburg region of North-West Province (Hall et al. 2008) and on the Mpumalanga Escarpment in Mpumalanga Province (Delius and Schoeman 2008). It was this potential that was most famously realized in the case of the Zulu; fortunately there are two sites of Zulu state capitals that have been investigated archaeologically. These are Mgungundlovu, in KwaZulu-Natal, occupied from 1829 to 1838 (Parkington and Cronin 1979), and the later capital of Ondini, dating from 1873 to 1879, in the same general area (Watson and Watson 1990). Each of these are thought to have housed about 5,000 people at times, and although they both lacked stone structures, they were clearly impressive settlements. Mgungundlovu had an area of about 22.5 hectares and a circumference of about 1.7 kilometres; Ondini covered about 35 hectares. Because they were constructed in timber, reed, and thatch and in both cases had been destroyed by fire, hut floors were fired brick-hard, enabling excavation at Mgungundlovu to uncover the plans and layout of many huts as well as some of their internal details. At Ondini, excavation concentrated instead on midden deposits, permitting a detailed study of faunal remains. On the basis of the meat weights estimated from the bones recovered, cattle overwhelmingly dominated the animal input of the diet. This was as expected from historical evidence for the major role of cattle in Zulu society at that time, providing hides for shields and clothing, as well as food, and also individual wealth for acquiring wives and for ritual and religious ceremonies. Together, the sites of Mgungundlovu and Ondini have contributed an important insight into the character of nineteenth-century capitals in South Africa, enabling both urban and state development to be better understood.

Subsistence economy

Historical documentation and oral traditions indicate that mixed farming, consisting of cereal cultivation and livestock herding, was the basis of the subsistence economy of the stone-walled and related settlements of south-east South Africa. Perhaps as a result, relatively little attention appears to have been given to archaeobotanical evidence from excavations. Nevertheless, carbonized remains of sorghum, cowpeas, tsamma melons, and (from the eighteenth century onwards) maize have been recorded, as well as granaries and grain bins for storage. In addition, different forms of grindstones, used to prepare the grains as food, indicate the change from sorghum and millet growing to maize growing (Huffman 2007: 453–4; Antonites and Antonites 2014). More attention has been given to the meat supply, which overwhelmingly depended on cattle, although goats and sheep were kept and hunting and wild plant foods continued to be significant resources (Mitchell 2002: 349). In contrast, the importance of cultivation to the economy is confirmed by the distribution of stone-walled structures relative to the best arable soils. This suggests 'a strong correlation between political courts and the best farmlands' (Sadr and Rodier 2012: 1038). Although it is apparent that population growth, drought, and both animal and plant disease did cause periodic crises, the very existence of a growing population suggests that the subsistence economy was sound.

Technology

Two aspects of the technology of the Highveld and related settlements were particularly important. One was the building skill evident in the drystone structures at many sites, as well as in the use of reeds, mud, and thatch to produce serviceable and attractive houses. By the early nineteenth century, if not before, numerous houses in Tswana settlements were even provided with the sophistication of sliding doors. European visitors recorded these, and excavators have found the grooves in which they ran, as well as the remains of wood from the doors themselves. In addition, contemporary accounts mention finely polished mud floors, verandas, courtyards, internally plastered walls and ceilings, a void in the conical roof above the ceiling (presumably for insulation), painted decorations, and the general cleanliness of the houses (Maggs 1993). Clearly the occupants of these settlements were accomplished builders with a pride in their work. The second aspect of technology that deserves attention was metalworking, from the early second millennium AD, including both iron and copper smelting and manufacturing (Fig. 11.4) and mining to obtain the necessary ores (Hall et al. 2006). Tin was also mined and alloyed with copper to produce bronze (Huffman 2007: 87–8). At Rooiberg, in the Southern Waterberg of Limpopo Province, is the only source in southern Africa of cassiterite (a tin oxide) that has provided evidence of its mining before European colonization (Bandama et al. 2013). Because of the shortage of wood in many areas, communities with access to fuel for smelting and smithing, as well as the necessary ores, specialized in metalworking. They then traded their products to populations whose lack of fuel prevented such work

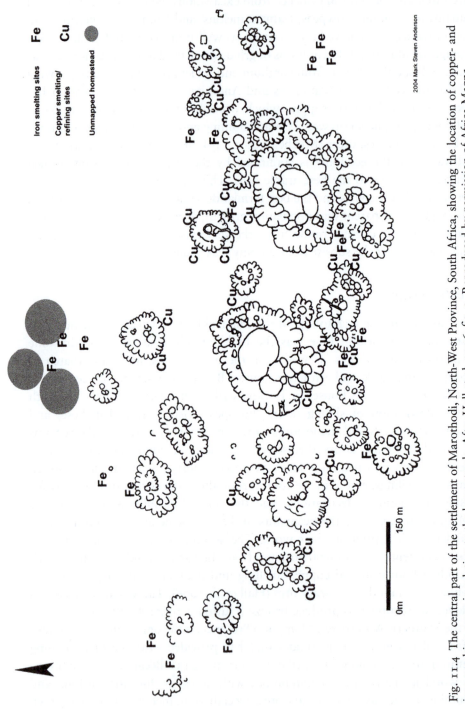

Fig. 11.4 The central part of the settlement of Marothodi, North-West Province, South Africa, showing the location of copper- and iron-working areas in relation to the homesteads. After Hall et al. 2006: fig. 2. Reproduced by permission of Africa Magna Verlag, Frankfurt am Main.

(Chirikure et al. 2008). A wide range of utilitarian iron goods was produced for both agriculture and warfare; copper (and sometimes bronze) was used for personal adornment. Other significant aspects of technology included the manufacture of salt and the mining of ochre (Huffman 2007: 90–1). There was also the production of fine pottery and the making of leather goods such as clothing and shields. In addition, the Lydenburg Head and associated artefacts from Mpumalanga Province (Huffman 2007: 67), although earlier in date than the period discussed here, indicate a tradition of technical skill in the forming and firing of terracotta sculpture. Overall, archaeological and other evidence suggests that the occupants of the stone-walled and related settlements had a sophisticated technology and that a degree of functional specialization had already developed within a context of sociopolitical change.

Social system

The archaeological evidence, like the documentary and oral evidence, indicates the existence of a hierarchical society of chiefs and kings based on populations of subsistence farmers. If the clusters of stone-walled settlement units consisted of those occupied at the same time, then the larger clusters represented larger settlements, and it is thought that the size of settlements reflected wealth and political power. Large middens also indicate greater political power, as they represent court, rather than household garbage. Sadr and Rodier (2012) used the ranked sizes of individual settlements to suggest the relative political and economic stratification of their different settlement groups. Clearly, varying degrees of urbanism were developing amongst the Sotho-Tswana, as well as state formation at different levels. For these changes to take place, social organization based on age sets and circumcision-initiation schools tended to be replaced by militaristic governance, of which Shaka's Zulu state was the best known example. Young men of similar age were formed into regiments that lived together, were not allowed to marry until they had served in action, and were under the control of commanders answerable to the king. In addition, lineage heads lost power to an elite centred on the royal lineage (Mitchell 2002: 372–3). This was a state produced by interethnic conflict and dependant on warfare; it was inevitable that it should eventually collapse when confronted by expanding European interests in southern Africa, in spite of fielding an army of 20,000 at the Battle of Ulundi. Assegais (short iron-tipped stabbing spears) and obsolete or captured firearms were no match for late-nineteenth-century European military technology. Although polities similar to that of the Zulu emerged or began to emerge amongst other people, they also were swept away in the sociopolitical maelstrom of nineteenth-century southern Africa.

Population pressures

The Mfecane appears to have been largely the consequence of population increase during agriculturally productive periods, followed by drought and food shortages leading to severe sociopolitical dislocation. The adoption of maize, more productive than sorghum or millet but more vulnerable to fluctuations in rainfall (p. 331), is thought to have contributed to this crisis. Although competition for access to overseas trade was another cause of the violence that erupted, there seems little doubt that the Mfecane was itself an indication of population pressures in southern Africa during the nineteenth century. More people meant less food, a shortage that could be relieved only by taking other people's food, by force if necessary. Archaeological evidence for population stress is present amongst Bokoni settlements of the Mpumalanga Escarpment, dated to within the last 400 years. These settlements are remarkable because 'not only are the homesteads preserved but there are also networks of linking roads and vast areas of agricultural terraces' (Maggs 2008: 173). It has been suggested that such developments represent 'islands of agricultural intensification', capable of supporting larger populations (Maggs 2008: 178–9); part of the Lydenburg valley, for example, had a maximum population of perhaps 19,000 to 57,000 (Maggs 2008: 172–3). It seems that population pressures did contribute to the development of sociopolitical complexity in this part of southern Africa.

Ideology

Little appears to have been known of Sotho-Tswana religious beliefs and practices until the nineteenth century, when Christian missionary endeavour was already transforming traditional ideas as well as misunderstanding them. Shamanism, in which altered states of consciousness enabled interaction with the spirit world, with ancestors acting as intermediaries, seems to have been central to these ideas. Herbalist healers and diviners functioned as shamans, spiritual counsellors, and protectors against evil spirits and black magic. Political leaders were often expected to preside over rituals of fertility, rain making, and warfare that strengthened the people and the land. In many African societies, kingship was essentially divine kingship, in which '"ceremonies" and the importance of the "following of people" were at the core of the notion of power' (de Maret 2012: 315). As de Maret stressed, it is necessary to recognize sacred power in the archaeological record, focussing on palaces, cities, burials, and regalia. In the case of the Sotho-Tswana occupants of the stone-walled settlements in south-eastern South Africa, aspects of such evidence do show religious ideology providing the basis of political control.

Archaeological evidence of the role of ideology in the functioning of these societies is also present in the form of rain-making sites (Huffman 2007: 71–3).

External trade

By the nineteenth century, international maritime activity along South Africa's eastern coast had stimulated a major expansion of its external trade. The Sotho-Tswana stone-walled settlements and adjacent areas, although inland, were within relatively easy reach of that coast, where Delagoa Bay (now Maputo) provided access to international markets and suppliers. The most important African export commodity was probably ivory, to satisfy a growing European demand for piano keys and a variety of other items, as well as for raw material to feed a long-standing tradition of ivory carving. Slaves were another export, along with rhinoceros horn, gold, tin, skins, and African exotica. In addition, visiting ships needed provisions, particularly meat, with European and American whalers calling at Delagoa Bay for that purpose. In exchange, glass beads, cloth, brass, ceramics, and other manufactured goods were imported, providing wealth that rulers and associated elite could use to accumulate more cattle and therefore strengthen their power base. Significantly, the Zulu state, the most successful and aggressive polity in the coastal region, was adjacent to Delagoa Bay. As already stated, competition for access to overseas trade is thought to have been a contributory factor to the violence that erupted in the Mfecane, for which the Zulus have often been blamed. Another view is that the Zulu part in this was a defensive response by Shaka to slave raiding from Delagoa Bay and aggression from Cape Colony (Cobbing 1988; Gordon 2009), but this interpretation has been questioned (Mitchell 2002: 370). Whatever the case, it seems that external trade played a part in the sociopolitical developments that occurred.

As in other parts of Africa, however, the role of external trade must be seen in the context of indigenous African trading networks. Differential distribution of resources meant that there was a complex internal network of trade in iron, copper, salt, specularite, pigments, animal skins, feathers, ostrich eggshell beads, a variety of foodstuffs, and other things (Mitchell 2002). Any consideration of the part that trade played in the development of sociopolitical complexity in parts of southern Africa must consider internal trade as well as external trade and the interaction between the two.

Conclusion

The Highveld and associated areas of South Africa have large numbers of archaeological sites that constitute the remains of farming settlements dating to only the last few centuries. Drystone construction ensures the archaeological visibility of many of these sites, and both documentary records and oral traditions are informative. Consequently, we are provided with an opportunity to see the emergence of aspects of sociopolitical complexity actually in progress. Study of evidence from this recent past reveals examples of the beginnings of urbanization and of state formation. These nineteenth-century developments were inevitably hesitant, constrained as they were by indigenous political instability and growing colonial interference, but they do enable us to see the circumstances in which the changes took place.

To begin with, relatively good soil and pasture in some areas supported mixed farming, to which cereals and cattle herding were the main contributors and which in some instances involved intensive production. This resulted in both population increase and greater local population density, so that the number of settlements and their individual sizes became greater. Furthermore, some of the occupants of these settlements had technological skills, particularly in building with stone, mud, and organic materials, and in metal mining, smelting, and manufacture, resulting in a degree of functional specialization. However, population size and density contributed to the growth of a hierarchical social system that was based on subsistence farming, varying in scale from small chiefdoms to emergent states. Unfortunately, population pressures also caused social instability, a situation made worse by the introduction of maize, a cereal with a greater yield than sorghum or millet but vulnerable to the periodic droughts of the region. Religious ideology provided the basis of political control by rulers, but this was often weakened by severe competition for resources. In addition, access to commodities from external trade and to the means of paying for these brought on serious interethnic conflict. Added to the violence and disruption that resulted was the increasing pressure of colonial settlement. In the end, the South African evidence shows not only how sociopolitical complexity can develop but also how it can fail.

Chapter 12
What are the common denominators?

The examples of African precolonial urbanization and state formation discussed in Chapters 2 to 11 come from a wide range of environments. These include river valley, such as Egypt and Nubia; mountain plateau, for example, Aksum and Zambezia; savanna plain, for instance, Kano; rainforest, such as Ife and Central Africa; maritime fringe, as with the Swahili coast; grassland, such as the South African Highveld; and desert margins, for example, North Africa. The geographical locations of these developments within the continent are equally diverse. Egypt and Nubia were so positioned that they had substantial and long-standing contacts with the eastern Mediterranean. Aksum was situated beside a major trade route between the Mediterranean world and the lands of the Indian Ocean. Zambezia also had contact with Indian Ocean trade, although more remotely. The West African savanna, on the other hand, was separated from the outside world by one of the greatest deserts on earth, the traversal of which weakened external cultural influences. This was even more the case in the West African forest, situated far to the south of the desert margins and backed by the empty Atlantic Ocean that for many centuries was a more effective barrier than the Sahara. Different again were the cities and towns of the East African coast, which looked out on the Indian Ocean that provided links with distant but technologically sophisticated cultures. More remote from such contacts was Central Africa, which had relatively little contact with the outside world until quite late, as was also the case for the South African Highveld. North Africa looked north to the heart of the ancient world but also south into the Sahara, with some remarkable adaptations to its extreme environments. Such environmental and geographical diversity would suggest that we must look elsewhere for any common factors that might explain the appearance of social complexity in some parts of the African continent and, equally, its failure to appear in other parts.

Nevertheless, each area had its own characteristic environmental and geographical opportunities. In every case there were also environmental constraints, but the ingenuity of human culture partly mitigated their impact. Nowhere is this more starkly illustrated than on the middle Nile; on the one hand, the river offered life, but on the other hand, parts of the surrounding environment were so dry as to be scarcely habitable. Yet by means of a combination of irrigation, rainfed cultivation, and pastoralism, human populations were able to exploit both the river and the adjacent savanna and

347

desert margins. So successfully were the environmental constraints overcome that this area was the scene of some of Africa's earliest states and cities and a long succession of such developments. A similar interplay of environmental opportunity, environmental constraint, and human culture can be discerned (to varying extents) in each of the cases that have been considered. This interplay was a dynamic one, and its outcome in each case was normally in favour of the human inhabitants, except when episodic imbalance threatened collapse of the often delicately balanced system. However, this does not go very far in explaining the emergence of social complexity in Africa; obviously, human beings thrive better in some places than in others, but this is no reason why they should build cities or create states.

However, it is the numbers of people who thrived that might be significant. Population sizes and densities in the relevant areas seem to have been higher than was usual in this generally thinly populated continent. As a result, localized population pressures probably developed, but all of the areas discussed had a strong subsistence base with potential for a storable, transportable surplus that could normally alleviate such pressures. Most people were agriculturalists, growing a range of food plants suited to local environments and keeping livestock, though the latter was limited by trypanosomiasis in the West African forest and in some other parts of Africa. The importance of pastoralism (Smith 1992) can hardly be overstated: herds of cattle and flocks of sheep and goats converted grass into wealth during good years and could provide relief from starvation when crops failed in bad years. The farmers and the pastoralists were often different groups of people, interacting with one another, but from this symbiosis came strength, just as weakness resulted from their periodic conflicts. In addition, in some areas there was an intensification of agricultural strategy, and this in a continent where agricultural systems have tended to be extensive rather than intensive. Thus, on the middle Nile more efficient irrigation was achieved by introducing the ox-driven waterwheel; in the Inland Niger Delta of Mali recessional cultivation of rice was developed; and in the Ethiopian Highlands slopes were terraced and water-storage dams constructed. Developments of this sort would suggest that populations in such areas were indeed increasing, creating a demand for more food and for more labour to produce it. It is surely significant that people became such an important trade commodity in some parts of Africa; slaves have a long history in the continent for both export and internal use. In Africa, as elsewhere in the world, one should remember George Orwell's remark about 'those hundreds of millions of slaves on whose backs civilization rested generation after generation' (Orwell 1966: 238).

In each of the areas considered, the exploitation of resources included not only a mixed agricultural strategy but also a varied and sometimes sophisticated metallurgically based technology. Most of the relevant societies were proficient in the working of iron; iron technology has been extremely important in Africa as an enabling and intensifying agent during the last two millennia or so. Without iron, the farmers of the West African forest could not have exploited their heavily vegetated environment as successfully as they did, nor could the occupants of Bigo in Uganda have dug such impressive rock-cut ditches. Iron provided both the tools to exploit available resources and the weapons to discourage others who coveted them. In addition to iron working and other metallurgical skills, the technology of the groups of people discussed in this book covered a range of abilities. Although engineering knowledge of the sort indicated by the Aksumite stelae seems to have been unusual, there was, nevertheless, a widespread understanding of building techniques, in stone, fired brick, mud-brick, coursed mud, wood, grass, and in other organic materials. Building technology was both diverse and accomplished. Furthermore, there appear to have been other crafts, including pottery making, wood working, textile production, and leather working. In some instances, there must also have been people with skills specific to the region, such as boat builders and sailors on the middle Nile or the East African coast, and scribes in Meroë or Aksum where indigenous alphabets were developed. When it is considered that a number of the cases studied also have evidence of religious functionaries, government officials, and specialist traders, it becomes apparent that some degree of functional specialization was probably present in the areas examined.

Inevitably, some resources were more limited than others, and as Haas (1982: 151) claimed, it is control of resources that gives rulers their power (p. 7). All of the cases examined in this book show unmistakable signs of the emergence of an elite who told other people what to do. The question is, what were the vital resources that they controlled? Most commonly this has been answered by pointing to the existence of raw materials such as gold, ivory, and other things that commanded a high price on the world market. Control of these meant control of long-distance trade, and control of such trade provided prestige and wealth. Thus appeared the African elites; thus developed the cities and the states. The problem with this explanation is not that it is incorrect but that it is wrongly timed. Looking at the archaeological evidence in North Africa, on the middle Nile, in the Ethiopian Highlands, or along the East African coast, it is clear that external long-distance trade did sometimes play a major role in African urbanization and state formation, but it seems that this was as an intensifier rather than as an originator. We now have evidence that suggests an indigenous origin for the development of social complexity on the East African coast; the earliest urbanization in the West African savanna pre-dates the growth of large-scale trans-Saharan trade; and in Central Africa

349

there are signs of increasing social complexity at a time before there was any substantial long-distance trade with the outside world. Furthermore, neither Zambezia nor the West African forest has evidence for early long-distance trade on a large scale, and even in the middle Nile and the Ethiopian Highlands the origins of sociopolitical changes seem to have pre-dated such a development.

If external long-distance trade was merely an intensifier of changes that had already commenced, then the question remains of what started them. There seem to be two possibilities. The first is that extensive *internal* trading networks preexisted external trading contacts and that African elites first gained power by controlling resources within such internal exchange systems. Copper, iron, and salt are likely to have been amongst these resources, but there could have been many more, including the gold and ivory that subsequently became so vital to the overseas trade. Indeed, the earliest commodities to be exchanged by internal trade were probably foodstuffs and other plant and animal resources. The ecological diversity of much of Africa makes this likely, and, in fact, the movement of such commodities has remained significant down to modern times. For example, shea butter has been exported from northern Nigeria to the south of that country, whilst kola nuts travelled in the opposite direction (Shaw 1984: 156); Africa has many other, similar instances of resource exchange. Although archaeology tends to be silent on perishable goods, there is some indication that early internal trading networks did exist, particularly in Central Africa, West Africa, and Ethiopia. This being the case, it seems likely that external long-distance trade merely plugged into the extant circuitry of the internal networks.

A second possible explanation is that elite power was first acquired by the control of land – not any land but land with an unusually high production potential. The role of this factor is seen as possibly complementary to that of internal trade, rather than as an alternative to it. Given the relatively poor quality of many African soils, together with their often moisture-stressed condition, and given expanding populations in some places, the greatest competition was likely to be around land which was more highly productive. In all of the case studies examined, it is possible to find indications that such land might have existed. Thus, in an environment surrounded by desert, the lower Nile had seasonal floods carrying fertile silt, which benefitted some places more than others. In the middle Nile area, fertile silts that could be reached by the available irrigation technology were limited, and the proportion of each year for which they could be watered varied with location. As a result, some areas of land must have been more productive than others. On the north-eastern Ethiopian plateau, some soils were more fertile than others and more suitable for plough cultivation of cereals, giving them a significant role during episodes of famine. The generally water-stressed environment of the West African savanna gave the limited areas available for recessional cultivation, such as parts of the Inland Niger Delta, a particular importance. In the West African forest, it seems to have been the upper interfluves and the forest–savanna ecotonal areas that provided the best farmlands, and these were limited. For the East African coast it was a matter of fertile soils and water availability, some areas being better provided for than others. On the Zimbabwe Plateau, it was again a matter of soils, where some soils were particularly fertile in an otherwise rocky area with granite-derived soils of poor fertility. For the Upemba Depression it was access to seasonally inundated fertile alluvium and to the most productive fishing grounds. In the Interlacustrine Region, in areas of good rainfall it was control of the best soils for cultivation, and in drier areas it was control of the best grazing lands for cattle. In both North and South Africa there were also areas with more rainfall or better pasture.

So it is possible that the crucial common factor underlying the emergence of African elites was access to, and control of, more highly productive land. If this was the case, then we have an indigenous explanation for the origin of social complexity in some parts of Africa. Doubtless, local trading networks also played an important role, and, clearly, external long-distance trade eventually came to act as an intensifying agent of significance. Nevertheless, this 'productive land hypothesis', as it might be called, does provide an originating agent, within each locality, of the developments that we are seeking to understand. It also provides an hypothesis that is testable, as field research progresses. Nevertheless, those who argue that control of people was more important than control of land have challenged this explanation (Edwards 1994: 9; Peel 2000: 515). After all, they claim, in the past there was no shortage of land in an essentially underpopulated Africa, but their argument fails to allow for the extensive areas of the continent where land is of limited use due to low fertility, rocky surfaces, hard topsoils of laterite (clay high in iron oxides), and other factors. In reality, a combination of land *and* people as a controllable resource has greater explanatory value; land is needed to support increasing numbers of people, but increasing numbers of people are needed to make the land productive.

With the emergence of an elite, a social hierarchy also developed. All of the archaeological examples that have been examined show signs of such social differentiation to a greater or lesser degree. There were clearly those few who were in charge and those masses who did what they were told. Less easy to recognize are the people in the middle, who acted on behalf of the elite but were neither of their ranks nor of the labouring majority. Whatever the details of the hierarchy, however, in each of the cases reviewed in this book it was

351

legitimized and reinforced by one form or another of religious ideology. In all instances, the earliest manifestations of this were indigenous, presumably animistic, religions, but in cases where there was prolonged contact with the outside world Christianity or Islam eventually replaced these. Whatever its form, however, it does seem that in each case the spiritual came to the aid of the material. That is to understate the importance of African indigenous religions, particularly during the earlier phases of the processes with which this book is concerned. Such religions were often a means of manipulating the forces believed to control fertility, in all senses of that word, and therefore gave power to those who were thought to be able to do this. In that case, the role of religion could have been much more than merely validating the authority of those who had acquired power by other means; African power holders were frequently priests themselves. As such, they could indeed have claimed control of the best land and of the people to work it, or of the internal exchange systems, or even, eventually, of their end of external long-distance trade networks, and who would have been prepared to deny them? As for the ordinary people, they needed to be assured that the sun would really rise tomorrow and the rain fall when needed, and in exchange they had no choice but to accept their condition.

This book has been more concerned with archaeological evidence than with theoretical matters, which often generate esoteric explanations incomprehensible to people in general and difficult even for some anthropologists and sociologists to understand. Its objective has been to explain how we know what we think we know. Nevertheless, any attempt to identify the main factors that gave rise to the cities and states of precolonial Africa has theoretical implications. For example, it appears that the power theory of state formation advocated by Haas (p. 7) does help us to understand the African situation and therefore does have some explanatory value. Furthermore, it seems that Lonsdale (p. 7) was correct in concluding that state formation in Africa was a very slow process, involving the coercive centralization of power and resulting from local politics, not from external ideas. This being the case, one is inclined to agree with Renfrew (p. 7) that the division into 'pristine' and 'secondary' states, which has so often been made, is a meaningless exercise. It was Renfrew's insistence that 'to understand the origins and development of any civilization' it is necessary to look at its local conditions, which suggested an analytical framework for each chapter of this book, hence the repeated subsections examining those conditions.

What of the idea of heterarchy, instead of hierarchy, as a basis for sociopolitical organization? This has been advanced as an alternative model for the development of complexity (p. 160), a model in which society is most simply described as organized horizontally rather than vertically (McIntosh 2005: 187).

It is an important idea but one that appears to depend on a lack of evidence for hierarchy rather than on the presence of positive evidence for heterarchy. Probably such evidence will become available only after there has been much more extensive excavation of relevant urban sites.

Unfortunately, all the attempted explanations for the origins of social complexity that have been discussed above are somewhat mechanistic; in terms of argument it is a case of A plus B plus C must equal D, but surely the reality is more complex than that. Inevitably there is a temptation to claim that the problem is insoluble, simply because it is so complex and involves so many interrelated factors whose associations are obscure. In the end it is perhaps Jared Diamond who has come nearest to an explanation that is both coherent and comprehensible. He argues that as the size of human groups increases, 'Considerations of conflict resolution, decision making, economics, and space thus converge in requiring large societies to be centralized' (Diamond 1998: 288). In short, increasing levels of social complexity become essential if larger and larger groups of people are to live together successfully. For sure, the other factors discussed in this book are important contributors to change – subsistence, technology, social system, population pressures, ideology, and external trade – they provide what Diamond calls 'autocatalysis' (Diamond 1998: 285), a condition where the individual factors stimulate each other and collectively trigger the developments that we seek to understand but do not individually cause them ('catalysis of a reaction by one of its products', *Concise Oxford English Dictionary* 2011: 88).

Clearly the development of cities and the formation of states in Africa were not aspects of a single process; not all cities were capitals of significant states and not all states had large, static centres of population. Nevertheless, they were both important manifestations of precolonial complex societies, and it is sometimes difficult to discuss them in isolation. Centralization of power, social stratification, functional specialization, and other related developments, together with population growth and population pressures, are phenomena that can be associated with both the appearance of cities and the emergence of states. Furthermore, their separate identification in the archaeological record can be particularly difficult. In some cases we do have physical evidence for the existence of settlements in which relatively large numbers of people were congregated; whether they are called large villages, towns, or even cities, the important point is that they were relatively dense aggregations of population, recalling Mabogunje's straightforward definition of urbanization (p. 6). More ambiguous, however, are the instances of archaeological evidence that might suggest the extension of political authority, or at least some commonality of culture, over a substantial geographical area. Indeed, even in the minds of some of the African people involved, it seems that the ideas of city and state might at times have been inextricably associated. Thus, in 1893, Lugard found it necessary to emphasize the close association of state, ruler, and city in the case of Buganda: 'The Waganda consider their country to be where the King is, and if no Kabaka of the Royal blood is installed in Mengo [the capital], the result would be a break-up of the people' (Lugard 1893: 36). It is with the opposite process of the coming together of people in tropical Africa that this book has been concerned.

In the African case this coming together occurred in a diversity of forms. Varied in their indigenous origins, states were also variously influenced by Pharaonic Egypt, by the ancient Mediterranean, by the Christian world, by Islamic North Africa, by Indian Ocean traders, and by each other. Urban centres also showed considerable variety: some were densely occupied for long periods, some only briefly occupied, some completely mobile, some with transient residence from season to season and year to year, and some with dispersed settlement covering enormous areas. Such diversity would suggest that the physical evidence for African social complexity would merit far more attention from archaeologists than it has yet had and that the African developments might have a far greater role in the formation of global social theory than has yet been the case.

References

Abungu, G.H.O. 1995. Agriculture and settlement formation along the East African coast. *Azania* 29–30, 248–56.

Abungu, G.H.O., and Mutoro, H.W. 1993. Coast–interior settlements and social relations in the Kenya coastal hinterland. In *The archaeology of Africa: food, metals and towns*, ed. T. Shaw, P. Sinclair, B. Andah, and A. Okpoko, 694–704. Routledge, London and New York.

Adams, R.McC. 1981. *Heartland of cities: surveys of ancient settlement and land use on the central floodplain of the Euphrates*. University of Chicago Press, Chicago and London.

Adams, W.Y. 1961. The Christian potteries at Faras. *Kush* 9, 30–43.

1974. Sacred and secular polities in ancient Nubia. *World Archaeology* 6(1), 39–51.

1976. Meroitic north and south: a study in cultural contrasts. *Meroitica* 2, 11–26.

1977. *Nubia: corridor to Africa*. Allen Lane, London. (Reprinted 1984.)

1981. Ecology and economy in the Empire of Kush. *Zeitschrift für Ägyptische Sprache* 108, 1–12.

1982. Qasr Ibrim: an archaeological conspectus. In *Nubian studies: proceedings of the Symposium for Nubian Studies, Selwyn College, Cambridge, 1978*, ed. J.M. Plumley, 25–33. International Society for Nubian Studies, Aris & Phillips, Warminster, UK.

1984. The first colonial empire: Egypt in Nubia, 3200–1200 BC. *Comparative Studies in Society and History* 26(1), 36–71.

1994. Castle-houses of late medieval Nubia. *Archéologie du Nil Moyen* 6, 11–46.

1996. *Qasr Ibrim: The Late Mediaeval period*. Egypt Exploration Society, Excavation Memoir 59, London.

2000. *Meinarti I: The Late Meroitic, Ballaña and transitional occupation*. Sudan Archaeological Research Society Publication Number 5. BAR International Series 895, Archaeopress, Oxford.

2001. *Meinarti II: The Early and Classic Christian phases*. Sudan Archaeological Research Society Publication Number 6, London. (Also forms BAR International Series 966.)

2002. *Meinarti III: The Late and Terminal Christian phases*. Sudan Archaeological Research Society Publication Number 9. BAR International Series 1072, Archaeopress, Oxford.

2009. *The churches of Nobadia*, 2 vols. Sudan Archaeological Research Society Publication Number 17. BAR International Series 2000, Archaeopress, Oxford.

2011. *Kulubnarti I: the architectural remains*. Sudan Archaeological Research Society Publication Number 18. BAR International Series 2241, Archaeopress, Oxford.

Adelaar, K.A. 1996. Malagasy culture-history: some linguistic evidence. In *The Indian Ocean in antiquity*, ed. J. Reade, 487–500. Kegan Paul International, London and New York.

Africanus, Leo. 1896. *The history and description of Africa*, 3 vols., ed. R. Brown. Hakluyt Society, London.

Agbaje-Williams, B. 1990. Oyo ruins in NW Yorubaland, Nigeria. *Journal of Field Archaeology* 17 (3), 367–73.

Ahmed, K.A. 1984. *Meroitic settlement in the Central Sudan*. BAR International Series 197, Oxford.

Alexander, J. 1988. The Saharan divide in the Nile Valley: the evidence from Qasr Ibrim. *African Archaeological Review* 6, 73–90.

1993a. Beyond the Nile: the influence of Egypt and Nubia in Sub-Saharan Africa. *Expedition* 35(2), 51–61.

1993b. The salt industries of West Africa: a preliminary study. In *The archaeology of Africa: food, metals and towns*, ed. T. Shaw, P. Sinclair, B. Andah, and A. Okpoko, 652–7. Routledge, London and New York.

1995. The Turks on the Middle Nile. *Archéologie du Nil Moyen* 7, 15–35.

2001. Islam, archaeology and slavery in Africa. *World Archaeology* 33(1), 44–60.

Allen, J. de V. 1982. The 'Shirazi' problem in East African coastal history. In *From Zinj to Zanzibar: studies in history, trade and society on the eastern coast of Africa* (*Paideuma* 28), ed. J. de V. Allen and T.H. Wilson, 9–27.

1983. Shungwaya, the Mijikenda, and the traditions. *International Journal of African Historical Studies* 16(3), 455–85.

1993. *Swahili origins: Swahili culture and the Shungwaya phenomenon*. James Currey, London.

Allibert, C., and Vérin, P. 1996. The early pre-Islamic history of the Comores Islands: links with Madagascar and Africa. In *The Indian Ocean in antiquity*, ed. J. Reade, 461–70. Kegan Paul International, London and New York.

Allibert, C., Argant, A., and Argant, J. 1990. Le site de Dembeni (Mayotte, Archipel des Comores) Mission 1984. *Etudes Océan Indien 11. Archéologie des Comores: I: Maore et Ngazidja*. Institut des Langues et Civilisations Orientales, Paris, 63–172.

Allison, P.A. 1962. Historical inferences to be drawn from the effect of human settlement on the vegetation of Africa. *Journal of African History* 3(2), 241–9.

Alpern, S.B. 2005. Did they or didn't they invent it? Iron in sub-Saharan Africa. *History in Africa* 32, 41–94.

al-Sa'di. 1964. *Tarikh es-Soudan*, texte Arabe édité et traduit par O. Houdas. Adrien-Maisonneuve, Paris.

Anciaux de Faveaux, E., and de Maret, P. 1984. Premières datations pour la fonte du cuivre au Shaba (Zaïre). *Bulletin de la Société Royale Belge d'Anthropologie et de Préhistoire* 95, 5–20.

Anderson, D.M., and Rathbone, R. (eds.) 2000. *Africa's urban past*. James Currey, Oxford.

Andrews, F.W. 1948. The vegetation of the Sudan. In *Agriculture in the Sudan*, ed. J.D. Tothill, 32–61. Oxford University Press, London.

Anfray, F. 1967. Matara. *Annales d'Ethiopie* 7, 33–88.

1968. Aspects de l'archéologie éthiopienne. *Journal of African History* 9(3), 345–66.

1972a. L'archéologie d'Axoum en 1972. *Paideuma* 18, 60–78.

1972b. Fouilles de Yeha. *Annales d'Ethiopie* 9, 45–64.

1973. Nouveaux sites antiques. *Journal of Ethiopian Studies* 11(2), 13–27.

1974. Deux villes Axoumites: Adoulis et Matara. *IV Congresso Internazionale di Studi Etiopici (Roma, 10–15 aprile 1972)*. Tomo I, Accademia Nazionale Dei Lincei, Roma, 745–65 et planche I–VI.

1981. The civilization of Aksum from the first to the seventh century. In *General history of Africa*, vol. 2: *Ancient civilizations of Africa*, ed. G. Mokhtar, 362–80. Heinemann, University of California, UNESCO; London, Berkeley, Paris.

1990. *Les Anciens Ethiopiens: siecles d'histoire*. Armand Colin, Paris.

Annequin, G. 1965. Château de Gouzara. *Annales d'Ethiopie* 6, 22–5.

Anquandah, J. 1982. *Rediscovering Ghana's past*. Longman, Harlow; Sedco, Accra.

1993. Urbanization and state formation in Ghana during the Iron Age. In *The archaeology of Africa: food, metals and towns*, ed. T. Shaw, P. Sinclair, B. Andah, and A. Okpoko, 642–51. Routledge, London and New York.

Antonites, A., and Antonites, A.R. 2014. The archaeology of farming communities in South Africa: a review. In *Archaeology of African plant use*, ed. C.J. Stevens, S. Nixon, M.A. Murray, and D.Q. Fuller, 225–32. Left Coast Press, Walnut Creek, CA.

Ashe, R.P. 1889. *Two Kings of Uganda*. Sampson Low, London.

Ashley, C., and Reid, A. 2008. A reconsideration of the figures from Luzira. *Azania* 43, 95–123.

Aubet, M.E. 2001. *The Phoenicians and the West: politics, colonies and trade*, 2nd ed. Translated by M. Turton. Cambridge University Press, Cambridge.

Ayele Tarekegn 1996. Aksumite burial practices, the 'Gudit Stelae Field', Aksum. In *Aspects of African archaeology: papers from the 10th Congress of the PanAfrican Association for Prehistory and Related Studies*, ed. G. Pwiti and R. Soper, 611–19. University of Zimbabwe, Harare.

Babalola, A.B. 2011. Archaeological investigation at Ile-Ife, southwest Nigeria: a preliminary report on the 2010 test excavations. *Nyame Akuma* 76, 33–46.

Badenhorst, S., Sinclair, P., Ekblom, A., and Plug, I. 2011. Faunal remains from Chibuene, an Iron Age coastal trading station in central Mozambique. *Southern African Humanities* 23, 1–15 (KwaZulu-Natal Museum).

Baines, J. 1983. Literacy and Ancient Egyptian society. *Man* 18(3), 572–99.

Baines, J., and Malek, J. 2000. *Cultural atlas of Ancient Egypt* (rev. ed.). Checkmark Books, New York.

Bandama, F., Chirikure, S., and Hall, S. 2013. Ore souces, smelters and archaeometallurgy: exploring Iron Age metal production in the Southern Waterberg, South Africa. *Journal of African Archaeology* 11(2), 243–67.

Bard, K.A. 2000. The emergence of the Egyptian state (c.3200–2686 BC). In *The Oxford history of ancient Egypt*, ed. I. Shaw, 61–88. Oxford University Press, Oxford.

Bard, K.A., and Fattovich, R. 1993. The 1993 excavations at Ona Enda Aboi Zague (Aksum, Tigray). *Nyame Akuma* 40, 14–17.

Bard, K.A., Fattovich, R., Manzo, A., and Perlingieri, C. 1997. Archaeological investigations at Bieta Giyorgis (Aksum), Ethiopia: 1993–1995 field seasons. *Journal of Field Archaeology* 24(4), 387–403.

Bard, K.A., Coltorti, M., DiBlasi, M.C., Dramis, F., and Fattovich, R. 2000. The environmental history of Tigray (Northern Ethiopia) in the Middle and Late Holocene: a preliminary outline. *African Archaeological Review* 17(2), 65–86.

Bard, K.A., Fattovich, R., Manzo, A., and Perlingieri, C. 2014. The chronology of Aksum (Tigrai, Ethiopia): a view from Bieta Giyorgis. *Azania: Archaeological Research in Africa* 49(3), 285–316.

Barker, G. 1978. Economic models for the Manekweni Zimbabwe, Mozambique. *Azania* 13, 71–100.

Barnett, R., Yamaguchi, N., Shapiro, B., and Sabin, R. 2008. Ancient DNA analysis indicates the first English lions originated from North Africa. *Contributions to Zoology* 77(1), 7–16.

Barnett, T. 1999. Quiha rock shelter, Ethiopia: implications for domestication. *Azania* 34, 10–24.

Barth, H. 1857-8. *Travels and discoveries in North and Central Africa: being a journal of an expedition undertaken under the auspices of H.B.M.'s Government in the years 1849–1855*, 5 vols. Longman, Brown, Green, Longmans, & Roberts, London.

Bascom, W. 1955. Urbanization among the Yoruba. *The American Journal of Sociology* 60(5), 446–54.

1959. Urbanism as a traditional African pattern. *Sociological Review* (NS) 7, 29–43.

Beach, D. 1980. *The Shona and Zimbabwe 900–1850*. Heinemann, London.

1994. *The Shona and their neighbours*. Blackwell, Oxford, UK, and Cambridge, MA.

1998. Cognitive archaeology and imaginary history at Great Zimbabwe. *Current Anthropology* 39(1), 47–72.

Beach, D., Bourdillon, M.F.C., Denbow, J., Hall, M., Lane, P., Pikirayi, I., Pwiti, G., and Huffman, T.N. 1997. Review feature: Snakes and crocodiles: power and symbolism in ancient Zimbabwe, by Thomas N. Huffman. *South African Archaeological Bulletin* 52, 125–43.

Beaujard, P. 2007. East Africa, the Comoros Islands and Madagascar before the sixteenth century: on a neglected part of the world system. *Azania* 42, 15–35.

2011. The first migrants to Madagascar and their introduction of plants: linguistic and ethnological evidence. *Azania: Archaeological Research in Africa* 46(2), 169–89.

Bedaux, R.M.A., Constandse-Westermann, T.S., Hacquebord, L., Lange, A.G., and van der Waals, J.D. 1978. Recherches archéologiques dans le Delta Intérieur du Niger (Mali). *Palaeohistoria* 20, 91–220.

Bedigian, D. 2003. Sesame in Africa: origin and dispersals. In *Food, fuel and fields; progress in African archaeobotany*, ed. K. Neumann, A. Butler, and S. Kahlheber, 17–36. Heinrich-Barth-Institut, Köln.

Bellamy, C.V. 1904. A West African smelting house. *Journal of the Iron and Steel Institute* 66, 99–126.

Benco, N.L. (ed.) 2004. *Anatomy of a medieval Islamic town: Al-Basra, Morocco*. BAR International Series 1234, Archaeopress, Oxford.

Bent, J.T. 1893. *The sacred city of the Ethiopians*. Longmans, Green, and Co., London.
  1896. *The ruined cities of Mashonaland*, New edition (Reissue). Longmans, London.
Berger, I. 1980. Deities, dynasties, and oral tradition: the history and legend of the Abacwezi. In *The African past speaks: essays on oral tradition and history*, ed. J.C. Miller, 60–81. Dawson, Folkestone.
Berthier, S. 1997. *Recherches archéologiques sur la capitale de l'empire de Ghana: étude d'un secteur d'habitat à Koumbi Saleh, Mauritanie. Campagnes II–III–IV–V (1975–1976) – (1980–1981)*, Cambridge Monographs in African Archaeology 41, BAR International Series 680, Oxford.
Bisson, M.S. 1975. Copper currency in central Africa: the archaeological evidence. *World Archaeology* 6(3), 276–92.
  1976. *The prehistoric coppermines of Zambia*. Ph.D. thesis, University of California, University Microfilms International, Santa Barbara.
Bivar, A.D.H., and Shinnie, P.L. 1962. Old Kanuri capitals. *Journal of African History* 3(1), 1–10.
Blake, J.W. 1942. *Europeans in West Africa, 1450–1560*, 2 vols. Hakluyt, London.
Blench, R. 1993. Ethnographic and linguistic evidence for the prehistory of African ruminant livestock, horses and ponies. In *The archaeology of Africa: food, metals and towns*, ed. T. Shaw, P. Sinclair, B. Andah, and A. Okpoko, 71–103. Routledge, London and New York.
  2000. African minor livestock species. In *The origins and development of African livestock: archaeology, genetics, linguistics and ethnography*, ed. R.M. Blench and K.C. MacDonald, 314–38. UCL Press, London.
  2006. *Archaeology, language, and the African past*. AltaMira Press, Lanham, MD.
  2007. New palaeozoogeographical evidence for the settlement of Madagascar. *Azania* 42, 69–82.
Blench, R.M., and MacDonald, K.C. (eds.) 2000. *The origins and development of African livestock: archaeology, genetics, linguistics and ethnography*. UCL Press, London.
Bloom, J.M. 2007. *Arts of the city victorious: Islamic art and architecture in Fatimid North Africa and Egypt*. Yale University Press, New Haven, CT.
Boeyens, J.C.A. 2000. In search of Kaditshwene. *South African Archaeological Bulletin* 55, 3–17.
Boisragon, A. 1897. *The Benin Massacre*. Methuen, London.
Bonnet, C. 1992. Excavations at the Nubian royal town of Kerma: 1975–91. *Antiquity* 66, 611–25.
  1997.The Kingdom of Kerma: 2500–1500 BC. In *Sudan: ancient kingdoms of the Nile*, ed. D. Wildung, 87–116. Flammarion, Paris and New York.
Bonnet, C. (ed.) 1990. *Kerma, royaume de Nubie*. Mission archéologique de l'Université de Genève au Soudan, Genève.
Bonnet, C., and Valbelle, D. 2006. *The Nubian Pharaohs: black kings on the Nile*. The American University in Cairo Press, Cairo and New York.
  2014. *La ville de Kerma, une capitale nubienne au sud de l'Egypte*. Favre, Lausanne.
Bosman, W. 1967. *A new and accurate description of the coast of Guinea*, 4th ed. Cass, London, (1st English ed. 1705).

Boullier, C., Person, A., Saliège, J.-F., and Polet, J. 2002–3. Bilan chronologique de la culture Nok et nouvelles datations sur des sculptures. *Afrique: Archéologie and Arts* 2, 9–28.

Bourriau, J. 1991. Relations between Egypt and Kerma during the Middle and New Kingdoms. In *Egypt and Africa: Nubia from prehistory to Islam*, ed. W.V. Davies, 129–44. British Museum Press, London.

Bovill, E.W. 1968. *The golden trade of the Moors*, 2nd ed. Oxford University Press, London.

Bowdich, T.E. 1966. *Mission from Cape Coast Castle to Ashantee*, 3rd ed. Cass, London (1st ed. 1819).

Bradbury R.E. 1957. *The Benin Kingdom and the Edo-speaking peoples of south-western Nigeria*. International African Institute, London.

　1959. Chronological problems in the study of Benin history. *Journal of the Historical Society of Nigeria* 1(4), 263–87.

Bradley, R.J. 1982. Varia from the city of Meroë. *Meroitica* 6, 163–70.

Brain, C.K. 1974. Human food remains from the Iron Age at Zimbabwe. *South African Journal of Science* 70, 303–9.

Breunig, P. 1996. The 8000-year-old dugout canoe from Dufuna (NE Nigeria). In *Aspects of African archaeology: papers from the 10th Congress of the PanAfrican Association for Prehistory and Related Studies*, ed. G. Pwiti and R. Soper, 461–8. University of Zimbabwe, Harare.

Breunig, P., Neumann, K., and Van Neer, W. 1996. New research on the Holocene settlement and environment of the Chad Basin in Nigeria. *African Archaeological Review* 13(2), 111–45.

Broberg, A. 1995. New aspects of the medieval towns of Benadir in southern Somalia: topography, climate and population. In *Islamic art and culture in Sub-Saharan Africa*, ed. K. Ådahl and B. Sahlström, 111–22. Acta Universitatis Upsaliensis, Figura Nova Series 27, Uppsala.

Brooks, G.E. 1998. Climate and history in West Africa. In *Transformations in Africa: essays on Africa's later past*, ed. G. Connah, 139–59. Leicester University Press, London and Washington.

Brown, H. 1996. The coins. In *Shanga: the archaeology of a Muslim trading community on the coast of East Africa*, ed. M. Horton, 368–75. Memoir 14, British Institute in Eastern Africa, London.

Brunk, K., and Gronenborn, D. 2004. Floods, droughts, and migrations: the effects of Late Holocene lake level oscillations and climate fluctuations on the settlement and political history in the Chad Basin. In *Living with the lake: perspectives on history, culture and economy of Lake Chad*, ed. M. Krings and E. Platte, 101–32. Studien zur Kulturkunde 121, Rüdiger Köppe Verlag, Köln.

Buchanan, K.M., and Pugh, J.C. 1955. *Land and people in Nigeria: the human geography of Nigeria and its environmental background*. University of London Press, London.

Bulliet, R.W. 1975. *The camel and the wheel*. Harvard University Press, Cambridge, MA.

Butzer, K.W. 1981. Rise and fall of Axum, Ethiopia: a geo-archaeological interpretation. *American Antiquity* 46(3), 471–95.

Buxton, D.R. 1970. *The Abyssinians*. Thames and Hudson, London.

1971. The rock-hewn and other medieval churches of Tigré Province, Ethiopia. *Archaeologia* 103, 33–100.

Buxton, D.R., and Matthews, D. 1974. The reconstruction of vanished Aksumite buildings. *Rassegna di Studi Etiopici* 25, 53–77 and figs. 1–31.

Calabrese, J.A. 2007. *The emergence of social and political complexity in the Shashi-Limpopo Valley of southern Africa, AD 900 to 1300: ethnicity, class, and polity.* BAR International Series 1617, Archaeopress, Oxford.

Calvocoressi, D., and David, N. 1979. A new survey of radiocarbon and thermoluminescence dates for West Africa. *Journal of African History* 20(1), 1–29.

Camps, G. 1982. Le cheval et le char dans la préhistoire Nord-Africaine et Saharienne. In *Les chars préhistoriques du Sahara*, ed. G. Camps and M. Gast, 9–22. Université de Provence, Aix-en-Provence.

Caney, R.W., and Reynolds, J.E. 1976. *Reed's marine distance tables*, 3rd ed. Reed, London.

Cappers, R.T.J. 2006. *Roman foodprints at Berenike: archaeobotanical evidence of subsistence and trade in the Eastern Desert of Egypt*. Monograph 55, Cotsen Institute of Archaeology, University of California, Los Angeles.

Carneiro, R.L. 1970. A theory of the origin of the state. *Science* 169: 733–8.

Carter, P.L., and Foley, R. 1980. A report on the fauna from the excavations at Meroë, 1967–1972. Appendix B in *The capital of Kush 1: Meroë excavations 1965–1972, (Meroitica 4)*, ed. P.L. Shinnie and R.J. Bradley, 298–312. Akademie-Verlag, Berlin.

Casey, J. 1998. The ecology of food production in West Africa. In *Transformations in Africa: essays on Africa's later past*, ed. G. Connah, 46–70. Leicester University Press, London and Washington.

2010. Between the Forest and the Sudan: the dynamics of trade in Northern Ghana. In *West African archaeology: new developments, new perspectives*, ed. P. Allsworth-Jones, 83–92. BAR International Series 2164, Archaeopress, Oxford.

Casson, L. 1989. *The Periplus Maris Erythraei: text with introduction, translation, and commentary*, Princeton University Press, Princeton.

Caton-Thompson, G. 1971. *The Zimbabwe culture: ruins and reactions*, 2nd ed. Cass, London (1st ed. 1931).

Chaix, L. 2013. The fauna from the UNO/BU excavations at Bieta Giyorgis (Aksum) in Tigray, Northern Ethiopia: campaigns 1995–2003; Pre-Aksumite, 700–400 BC to Late Aksumite, AD 800–1200. *Journal of African Archaeology* 11(2), 211–41.

Chami, F.A. 1994. *The Tanzanian coast in the first millennium AD: an archaeology of the iron-working, farming communities*, Studies in African Archaeology 7. Societas Archaeologica Upsaliensis, Uppsala.

1995. The first millennium AD on the East Coast: a new look at the cultural sequence and interactions. *Azania* 29–30, 232–7.

1999a. Graeco-Roman trade link and the Bantu migration theory. *Anthropos: Internationale Zeitschrift für Völker-und Sprachenkunde* 94(1/3), 205–15.

1999b. Roman beads from the Rufiji Delta, Tanzania: first incontrovertible archaeological link with the Periplus. *Current Anthropology* 40(2), 237–41.

Chami, F.A., and Msemwa, P.J. 1997. A new look at culture and trade on the Azanian coast. *Current Anthropology* 38(4), 673–7.

Chandler, T., and Fox, G. 1974. *3000 years of urban growth*. Academic Press, New York and London.

Chikwendu, V.E., Craddock, P.T., Farquhar, R.M., Shaw, T., and Umeji, A.C. 1989. Nigerian sources of copper, lead and tin for the Igbo-Ukwu bronzes. *Archaeometry* 31(1), 27–36.

Childe, V.G. 1950. The urban revolution. *The Town Planning Review* 21: 3–17.
    1957. Civilization, cities and towns. *Antiquity* 31 (121), 36–8.

Chirikure, S., and Pikirayi, I. 2008. Inside and outside the dry stone walls: revisiting the material culture of Great Zimbabwe. *Antiquity* 82 (318), 976–93.

Chirikure, S., and Rehren, T. 2006. Iron smelting in pre-colonial Zimbabwe: evidence for diachronic change from Swart Village and Baranda, northern Zimbabwe. *Journal of African Archaeology* 4(1), 37–54.

Chirikure, S., Hall, S., and Maggs, T. 2008. Metals beyond frontiers: exploring the production, distribution and use of metals in the Free State grasslands, South Africa. In *Five hundred years rediscovered: southern African precedents and prospects*, ed. N. Swanepoel, A. Esterhuysen, and P. Bonner, 87–101. Wits University Press, Johannesburg.

Chirikure, S., Manyanga, M., Pikirayi, I., and Pollard, M. 2013a. New pathways of sociopolitical complexity in southern Africa. *African Archaeological Review* 30(4), 339–66.

Chirikure, S., Pollard, M., Manyanga, M., and Bandama, F. 2013b. A Bayesian chronology for Great Zimbabwe: re-threading the sequence of a vandalised monument. *Antiquity* 87 (337), 854–72.

Chittick, N. 1965. The 'Shirazi' colonization of East Africa. *Journal of African History* 6(3), 275–94.
    1971. The coast of East Africa. In *The African Iron Age*, ed. P.L. Shinnie, 108–41. Clarendon Press, Oxford.
    1974. *Kilwa: an Islamic trading city on the East African coast*, 2 vols. British Institute in Eastern Africa, Memoir 5, Nairobi.
    1981. The Periplus and the spice trade. *Azania* 16, 185–90.
    1984. *Manda: excavations at an island port on the Kenya coast*, Memoir 9, British Institute in Eastern Africa, Nairobi.

Christides, V. 2000. *Byzantine Libya and the march of the Arabs towards the West of North Africa*. BAR International Series 851, John and Erica Hedges, Oxford.

Churchill, W.S. 1962 [first published 1908]. *My African journey*. Heron Books.

Cissé, M., McIntosh, S.K., Dussubieux, L., Fenn, T., Gallagher, D., and Smith, A.C. 2013. Excavations at Gao Saney: new evidence for settlement growth, trade, and interaction on the Niger Bend in the first millennium CE. *Journal of African Archaeology* 11(1), 9–37.

Claessen, H.J.M., and Oosten, J.G. (eds.) 1996. *Ideology and the formation of early states*. Brill, Leiden.

Claessen, H.J.M., and Skalník, P. (eds.) 1978. *The early state*. Mouton, The Hague.

Claessen, H.J.M., and van de Velde, P. (eds.) 1987. *Early state dynamics*. Brill, Leiden.

Clarke, S. 1912. *Christian antiquities in the Nile Valley: a contribution towards the study of the ancient churches*. Clarendon Press, Oxford.

Clist, B. 2012. Pour une archéologie du royaume Kongo: la tradition de Mbafu. *Azania: Archaeological Research in Africa* 47(2), 175–209.

Clist, B., de Maret, P., de Schryver, G. M., Kaumba, M., Matonda, I., Cranshof, E., and Bostoen, K. 2013a. The KongoKing Project: 2012 fieldwork report from the Lower Congo Province (DRC). *Nyame Akuma* 79, 60–73.

Clist, B., de Maret, P., Livingstone-Smith, A., Cranshof, E., Kaumba, M., Matonda, I., Mambu, C., Yogolelo, J., and Bostoen, K. 2013b. The KongoKing Project: 2013 fieldwork report from the Lower Congo Province (DRC). *Nyame Akuma* 80, 22–31.

Clover, F.M. 1993. *The Late Roman West and the Vandals.* Variorum, Ashgate Publishing Limited, Aldershot, UK.

Cobbing, J. 1988. The Mfecane as alibi: thoughts on Dithakong and Mbolompo. *Journal of African History* 29(3), 487–519.

Cohen, R., and Service, E.R. (eds.) 1978. *Origins of the state: the anthropology of political evolution.* Institute for the Study of Human Issues, Philadelphia.

Collett, D.P., Vines, A.E., and Hughes, E.G. 1992. The chronology of the Valley Enclosures: implications for the interpretation of Great Zimbabwe. *African Archaeological Review* 10, 139–61.

Collins, M.O. (ed.) 1965. *Rhodesia: its natural resources and economic development.* M.O. Collins, Salisbury, Rhodesia.

Concise Oxford English Dictionary, 12th edition. 2011. Oxford University Press, Oxford.

Connah, G. 1975. *The archaeology of Benin.* Oxford University Press, Oxford.

1981. *Three thousand years in Africa: Man and his environment in the Lake Chad region of Nigeria.* Cambridge University Press, Cambridge.

1985. Agricultural intensification and sedentism in the firki of N.E. Nigeria. In *Prehistoric intensive agriculture in the tropics*, ed. I.S. Farrington, 765–85. BAR International Series 232, Oxford.

1987. *African civilizations: precolonial cities and states in tropical Africa: an archaeological perspective.* Cambridge University Press, Cambridge.

1996. *Kibiro: the salt of Bunyoro, past and present.* Memoir 13, British Institute in Eastern Africa, London.

1998a. Resource exploitation and population aggregation: the case of Kibiro. In *The development of urbanism from a global perspective*, ed. P. Sinclair, Department of Archaeology and Ancient History, Uppsala University, Sweden. www.arkeologi.uu.se/Forskning/Publikationer/Digital/Development_of_Urbanism/ Accessed 4 November 2014.

1998b. Static image, dynamic reality. In *Transformations in Africa: essays on Africa's later past*, ed. G. Connah, 1–13. London and Washington, Leicester University Press.

2000a. African city walls: a neglected source? In *Africa's urban past*, ed. D.M. Anderson and R. Rathbone, 36–51. James Currey, Oxford.

2000b. Contained communities in tropical Africa. In *City walls: the urban enceinte in global perspective*, ed. J. Tracy, 19–45. Cambridge University Press, New York.

2008. Urbanism and the archaeological visibility of African complex societies. *Journal of African Archaeology* 6(2), 233–41.

Conrad, D.C. 1994. A town called Dakajalan: the Sunjata tradition and the question of ancient Mali's capital. *Journal of African History* 35(3), 355–77.

Coursey, D.G. 1980. The origins and domestication of yams in Africa. In *West African culture dynamics: archaeological and historical perspectives*, ed. B.K. Swartz and R.E. Dumett, 67–90. Mouton, The Hague.

Craddock, P.T., and Picton, J. 1986. Medieval copper alloy production and West African bronze analyses — Part II. *Archaeometry* 28(1), 3–32.

Craddock, P.T., Ambers, J., Hook, D.R., Farquhar, R.M., Chikwendu, V.E., Umeji, A.C., and Shaw, T. 1997. Metal sources and the bronzes from Igbo-Ukwu, Nigeria. *Journal of Field Archaeology* 24(4), 405–29.

Crosby, A.W. 1986. *Ecological imperialism: the biological expansion of Europe, 900–1900*, Cambridge University Press, Cambridge.

Crossland, Z. 2001. Time and the ancestors: landscape survey in the Andrantsay region of Madagascar. *Antiquity* 75 (290), 825–36.

Curtis, M.C. 2009. Relating the Ancient Ona Culture to the wider Northern Horn: discerning patterns and problems in the archaeology of the first millennium BC. *African Archaeological Review* 26(4), 327–50.

Dahalani, S.A. 1992. Itsandramdjini: espace et société. In *Urban origins in Eastern Africa: proceedings of the 1991 workshop in Zanzibar*, ed. P.J.J. Sinclair and A. Juma, 180–6. Central Board of National Antiquities, Stockholm.

Dalziel, J.M. 1937. *The useful plants of west tropical Africa*. Crown Agents for the Colonies, London.

D'Andrea, A.C., Klee, M., and Casey, J. 2001. Archaeobotanical evidence for pearl millet (*Pennisetum glaucum*) in sub-Saharan West Africa. *Antiquity* 75 (288), 341–8.

D'Andrea, A.C., Logan, A.L., and Watson, D.J. 2006. Oil palm and prehistoric subsistence in tropical West Africa. *Journal of African Archaeology* 4(2), 195–222.

D'Andrea, A.C., Manzo, A., Harrower, M.J., and Hawkins, A.L. 2008. The Pre-Aksumite and Aksumite settlement of NE Tigrai, Ethiopia. *Journal of Field Archaeology* 33(2), 151–76.

Daniel, G. 1968. *The first civilizations: the archaeology of their origins*. Thames and Hudson, London.

Dapper, O. 1686. *Description de l'Afrique ... Traduite du Flamand*, Chez Wolfgang, Waesberge, Boom & van Someren, Amsterdam.

Dark, P.J.C. 1973. *An introduction to Benin art and technology*. Clarendon Press, Oxford.

Darling, P.J. 1982. Ancient linear earthworks of Benin and Ishan, Southern Nigeria, 2 vols. Ph.D. thesis, University of Birmingham.

   1984. *Archaeology and history in southern Nigeria*, 2 vols. Cambridge Monographs in African Archaeology 11, BAR International Series 215(i) and (ii), Oxford.

   1988. Emerging towns in Benin and Ishan (Nigeria) AD 500–1500. In *State and society: the emergence and development of social hierarchy and political centralization*, ed. J. Gledhill, B. Bender, and M.T. Larsen, 121–36. Unwin Hyman, London.

   1998. A legacy in earth – ancient Benin and Ishan, southern Nigeria. In *Historical archaeology in Nigeria*, ed. K.W. Wesler, 143–97. Africa World Press, Trenton and Asmara.

Datoo, B.A. 1970. Rhapta: the location and importance of East Africa's first port. *Azania* 5, 65–75.

Davies, V., and Friedman, R. 1999. *Egypt*. British Museum Press, London.

Davison, P., and Harries, P. 1980. Cotton weaving in south-east Africa: its history and technology. *Textile History* 11, 175–92.

de Contenson, H. 1961. Les fouilles à Ouchatei Golo, près d'Axoum, en 1958. *Annales d'Éthiopie* 4, 3–14.

    1962. Les monuments d'art Sud-Arabe découverts sur le site de Haoulti (Ethiopie) en 1959. *Syria: Revue d'art oriental et d'archéologie* 39, 64–87.

    1981. Pre-Aksumite culture. In *General history of Africa*, vol. 2: *Ancient civilizations of Africa*, ed. G. Mokhtar, 341–61. Heinemann, University of California, UNESCO; London, Berkeley, Paris.

De Langhe, E., Swennen, R., and Vuylsteke, D. 1995. Plantain in the early Bantu world. *Azania* 29–30, 147–60.

Delius, P., and Schoeman, M.H. 2008. Revisiting Bokoni: populating the stone ruins of the Mpumalanga Escarpment. In *Five hundred years rediscovered: southern African precedents and prospects*, ed. N. Swanepoel, A. Esterhuysen, and P. Bonner, 135–67. Wits University Press, Johannesburg.

de Maret, P. 1979. Luba roots: the first complete Iron Age sequence in Zaïre. *Current Anthropology* 20(1), 233–5.

    1981. L'évolution monétaire du Shaba Central entre le 7e et le 18e siècle. *African Economic History* 10, 117–49.

    1982. The Iron Age in the west and south. In *The archaeology of Central Africa*, ed. F. Van Noten, 77–96. Akademische Druck – und Verlagsanstalt, Graz, Austria.

    1985. Recent archaeological research and dates from Central Africa. *Journal of African History* 26, 129–48.

    1992. *Fouilles archéologiques dans la vallée du Haut-Lualaba, Zaïre III: Kamilamba, Kikulu, et Malemba-Nkulu, 1975*. Musée Royal de l'Afrique Centrale, Tervuren, Belgium.

    1997. Savanna states. In *Encyclopedia of precolonial Africa: archaeology, history, languages, cultures, and environments*, ed. J.O. Vogel, 496–501. AltaMira Press, Walnut Creek, CA.

    1998. Urban origins in central Africa: the case of Kongo. In *The development of urbanism from a global perspective*, ed. P. Sinclair, Department of Archaeology and Ancient History, Uppsala University, Sweden. www.arkeologi.uu.se/Forskning/Publikationer/Digital/Development_of_Urbanism/ Accessed 4 November 2014.

    2012. From kinship to kingship: an African journey into complexity. *Azania: Archaeological Research in Africa* 47(3), 314–26.

Denbow, J.R. 1984. Cows and kings: a spatial and economic analysis of a hierarchical Early Iron Age settlement system in eastern Botswana. In *Frontiers: southern African archaeology today*, ed. M. Hall, G. Avery, D.M. Avery, M.L. Wilson, and A.J.B. Humphreys, 24–39. Cambridge Monographs in African Archaeology 10, BAR International Series 207, Oxford.

    1986. A new look at the later prehistory of the Kalahari. *Journal of African History* 27, 3–28.

1999. Material culture and the dialetics of identity in the Kalahari: AD 700–1700. In *Beyond chiefdoms: pathways to complexity in Africa*, ed. S.K. McIntosh, 110–123. Cambridge University Press, Cambridge.

Denham, D., Clapperton, H., and Oudney, W. 1826. *Narrative of travels and discoveries in Northern and Central Africa, in the years 1822, 1823, and 1824*. Murray, London.

Desplagnes, L. 1903. Etude sur les Tumuli du Killi, dans la région de Goundam. *L'Anthropologie* 14, 151–72.

1951. Fouilles du tumulus d'El Oualedji (Soudan); annoté par R. Mauny. *Bulletin de l'IFAN*, Dakar, 13(4), 1159–73.

de Voogt, A. 2010. Mancala players at Palmyra. *Antiquity* 84 (326), 1055–66.

Dewar, R.E. 1996. The archaeology of the early settlement of Madagascar. In *The Indian Ocean in antiquity*, ed. J. Reade, 471–86. Kegan Paul International, London and New York.

Dewar, R.E., and Wright, H.T. 1993. The culture history of Madagascar. *Journal of World Prehistory* 7(4), 417–66.

Diamond, J. 1998. *Guns, germs and steel: a short history of everybody for the last 13,000 years*. Vintage, London.

Donley, L.W. 1982. House power: Swahili space and symbolic markers. In *Symbolic and structural archaeology*, ed. I. Hodder, 63–73. Cambridge University Press, Cambridge

1987. Life in the Swahili town house reveals the symbolic meaning of spaces and artefact assemblages. *African Archaeological Review* 5, 181–92.

Donley-Reid, L.W. 1990. A structuring structure: the Swahili house. In *Domestic architecture and the use of space: an interdisciplinary cross-cultural study*, ed. S. Kent, 114–26. Cambridge University Press, Cambridge.

Dowler, A. 2011. Introduction. In *Money, trade and trade routes in Pre-Islamic North Africa*, ed. A. Dowler and E.R. Galvin, 1–10. Research Publication 176, British Museum, London.

Dualeh, A. 1996. *The origins and development of Mogadishu AD 1000 to 1850: a study in urban growth along the Benadir coast of southern Somalia*. Studies in African Archaeology 12, Uppsala.

Duarte, R.T. 1993. *Northern Mozambique in the Swahili world: an archaeological approach*. Studies in African Archaeology 4, Central Board of National Antiquities, Sweden, Eduardo Mondlane University, Mozambique, and Uppsala University, Uppsala.

Dueppen, S.A. 2011. Early evidence for chickens at Iron Age Kirikongo (c.AD 100–1450), Burkina Faso. *Antiquity* 85 (327), 142–57.

2012. *Egalitarian revolution in the savanna: the origins of a West African political system*. Equinox Publishing, Sheffield, UK.

Duffey, A. 2012. Mapungubwe: interpretation of the gold content of the *Original Gold Burial M1, A620*. *Journal of African Archaeology* 10(2), 175–87.

Dunbabin, K.M.D. 1978. *The mosaics of Roman North Africa*. Clarendon Press, Oxford.

Dunham, D. 1950. *The royal cemeteries of Kush*, vol. 1: *El Kurru*. Harvard University Press, Cambridge, MA.

1955. *The royal cemeteries of Kush,* vol. 2: *Nuri.* Museum of Fine Arts, Boston, MA.

Earle, T. 1997. *How chiefs come to power: the political economy in prehistory.* Stanford University Press, Stanford, CA.

Edwards, D.N. 1989. *Archaeology and settlement in Upper Nubia in the 1st millennium AD.* Cambridge Monographs in African Archaeology 36, BAR International Series 537, Oxford.

1994. Power and the state in the Middle Nile: Meroe in context. An example for the study of state development in Sudanic Africa. *Archaeological Review from Cambridge* 13(1), 5–19.

1996. *The archaeology of the Meroitic state: new perspectives on its social and political organisation.* Cambridge Monographs in African Archaeology 38, BAR International Series 640, Tempus Reparatum, Oxford.

2004. *The Nubian past: an archaeology of the Sudan.* Routledge, London.

2007. The archaeology of Sudan and Nubia. *Annual Review of Anthropology* 36, 211–28.

Effah-Gyamfi, K. 1979. Bono Manso archaeological research project. *West African Journal of Archaeology* 9, 173–86.

1985. *Bono Manso: an archaeological investigation into early Akan urbanism.* University of Calgary Press, Calgary.

1986. Ancient urban sites in Hausaland. *West African Journal of Archaeology* 16, 117–34.

Egharevba, J. 1968. *A short history of Benin,* 4th ed. Ibadan University Press, Ibadan.

Ehret, C. 2002. *The civilizations of Africa: a history to 1800.* James Currey, Oxford.

Eisenstadt, S.N., Abitbol, M., and Chazan, N. (eds.) 1988. *The early state in African perspective: culture, power and division of labor.* Brill, Leiden.

Ellis, W. 1859. *Three visits to Madagascar during the years 1853–1854–1856. Including a journey to the capital. With notices of the natural history of the country and of the present civilisation of the people.* John Murray, London.

Elzein, I.S. 2004. *Islamic archaeology in the Sudan.* Cambridge Monographs in African Archaeology 60, BAR International Series 1289, Archaeopress, Oxford.

Emery, W.B. 1938. *The royal tombs of Ballana and Qustul,* 2 vols. Government Press, Cairo.

1948. *Nubian treasure: an account of the discoveries at Ballana and Qustul.* Methuen, London.

1965. *Egypt in Nubia.* Hutchinson, London.

Ennahid, S. 2002. *Political economy and settlement systems of medieval northern Morocco: an archaeological-historical approach.* BAR International Series 1059, Archaeopress, Oxford.

Ethiopian Mapping Authority. 1988. *National atlas of Ethiopia.* Ethiopian Mapping Authority, Addis Abebe.

Eve, S. 2014. An undiscovered county? New field systems found on the South Downs. *Past: the newsletter of the Prehistoric Society* 78, 3–5.

Evers, T.M. 1984. Sotho-Tswana and Moloko settlement patterns and the Bantu Cattle Pattern. In *Frontiers: southern African archaeology today,* ed. M. Hall, G. Avery, D.M. Avery, M.L. Wilson, and A.J.B. Humphreys, 236–47. Cambridge Monographs in African Archaeology 10, BAR International Series 207, Oxford.

Exell, K. 2011. *Egypt in its African context: proceedings of the conference held at The Manchester Museum, University of Manchester, 2–4 October 2009*. BAR International Series 2204, Archaeopress, Oxford.

Eyo, E. 1974. Odo Ogbe Street and Lafogido: contrasting archaeological sites in Ile-Ife, Western Nigeria. *West African Journal of Archaeology* 4, 99–109.

Fabre, J.-M. 2009. La métallurgie du fer au Sahel burkinabé à la fin du 1er millénaire AD. In *Crossroads/Carrefour Sahel: cultural and technological developments in first millennium BC/AD West Africa*, ed. S. Magnavita, L. Koté, P. Breunig, and O.A. Idé, 167–78. Africa Magna Verlag, Frankfurt am Main.

Fagan, B.M. 1969. Early trade and raw materials in south central Africa. *Journal of African History* 10(1), 1–13.

Fagan, B.M., and Yellen, J.E. 1968. Ivuna: ancient salt-working in southern Tanzania. *Azania* 3, 1–43.

Fagan, B.M., Phillipson, D.W., and Daniels, S.G.H. 1969. *Iron Age cultures in Zambia (Dambwa, Ingombe Ilede and the Tonga)*, vol. 2. Chatto and Windus, London.

Fage, J.D., and Verity, M. 1978. *An atlas of African history*, 2nd ed. Edward Arnold, London.

Fagg, W. 1963. *Nigerian images*. Lund Humphries, London.

Fattovich, R. 1990. Remarks on the Pre-Aksumite Period in northern Ethiopia. *Journal of Ethiopian Studies* 23, 1–33.

1991. At the periphery of the empire: the Gash Delta (Eastern Sudan). In *Egypt and Africa: Nubia from prehistory to Islam*, ed. W.V. Davies, 40–8. British Museum Press, London.

2009. Reconsidering Yeha, c.800–400 BC. *African Archaeological Review* 26(4), 275–90.

2010. The development of ancient states in the Northern Horn of Africa, c.3000 BC–AD 1000: an archaeological outline. *Journal of World Prehistory* 23(3), 145–75.

Fauvelle-Aymar, F.X., Bruxelles, L., Mensan, R., Bosc-Tiessé, C., Derat, M.-L., and Fritsch, E. 2010. Rock-cut stratigraphy: sequencing the Lalibela churches. *Antiquity* 84 (326): 1135–50.

Feinman, G.M., and Manzanilla, L. 2000. *Cultural evolution: contemporary viewpoints*. Kluwer Academic/Plenum, New York.

Fenn, T.R., Killick, D.J., Chesley, J., Magnavita, S., and Ruiz, J. 2009. Contacts between West Africa and Roman North Africa: archaeometallurgical results from Kissi, northeastern Burkina Faso. In *Crossroads/Carrefour Sahel: cultural and technological developments in first millennium BC/AD West Africa*, ed. S. Magnavita, L. Koté, P. Breunig, and O.A. Idé, 119–46. Africa Magna Verlag, Frankfurt am Main.

Fentress, E. 2011. Slavers on chariots. In *Money, trade and trade routes in Pre-Islamic North Africa*, ed. A. Dowler and E.R. Galvin, 65–71. Research Publication 176, British Museum, London.

Filipowiak, W. 1969. L'expédition archéologique Polono-Guinéenne à Niani, en 1968. *Africana Bulletin* 11, 107–17.

Finneran, N. 2002. *The archaeology of Christianity in Africa*. Tempus, Stroud, Gloucestershire, UK.

2007. *The archaeology of Ethiopia.* Routledge, London and New York.

2009. Settlement archaeology and oral history in Lasta, Ethiopia: some preliminary observations from a landscape study of Lalibela. *Azania: Archaeological Research in Africa* 44(3), 281–91.

2012. Lalibela in its landscape: archaeological survey at Lalibela, Lasta, Ethiopia, April to May 2009. *Azania: Archaeological Research in Africa.* 47(1), 81–98.

Flannery, K.V. 1999. Process and agency in early state formation. *Cambridge Archaeological Journal* 9, 3–21.

Flannery, K.[V.], and Marcus, J. 2012. *The creation of inequality: how our prehistoric ancestors set the stage for monarchy, slavery, and empire.* Harvard University Press, Cambridge, MA.

Fleisher, J. 2013. Performance, monumentality and the 'built exterior' on the eastern African Swahili coast. *Azania: Archaeological Research in Africa* 48(2), 263–81.

Fleisher, J., and LaViolette, A. 1999. Elusive wattle-and-daub: finding the hidden majority in the archaeology of the Swahili. *Azania* 34, 87–108.

Fleisher, J., and Wynne-Jones, S. 2011. Ceramics and the early Swahili: deconstructing the early Tana Tradition. *African Archaeological Review* 28(4), 245–78.

2012. Finding meaning in ancient Swahili spatial practices. *African Archaeological Review* 29(2–3), 171–207.

Fleisher, J., Wynne-Jones, S., Steele, C., and Welham, K. 2012. Geophysical survey at Kilwa Kisiwani, Tanzania. *Journal of African Archaeology* 10(2), 207–20.

Fletcher, R. 1995. *The limits of settlement growth: a theoretical outline.* Cambridge University Press, Cambridge.

1998. African urbanism: scale, mobility and transformations. In *Transformations in Africa: essays on Africa's later past,* ed. G. Connah, 104–38. Leicester University Press, London and Washington.

Flight, C. 1975. Gao, 1972: first interim report: a preliminary investigation of the cemetery at Sané. *West African Journal of Archaeology* 5, 81–90.

Forman, W., Forman, B., and Dark, P. 1960. *Benin art.* Hamlyn, London.

Forssman, T., Page, B., and Selier, J. 2014. How important was the presence of elephants as a determinant of the Zhizo settlement of the Greater Mapungubwe Landscape? *Journal of African Archaeology* 12(1), 75–87.

Fouché, L. 1937. *Mapungubwe: ancient Bantu civilization on the Limpopo.* Cambridge University Press, Cambridge.

Freeman-Grenville, G.S.P. 1975. *The East African coast: select documents from the first to the earlier nineteenth century,* 2nd ed. Collings, London.

Freestone, I.C. 2006. An indigenous technology? A commentary on Lankton et al. 'Early primary glass production in southern Nigeria'. *Journal of African Archaeology* 4(1), 139–41.

Fried, M.H. 1967. *The evolution of political society: an essay in political anthropology.* Random House, New York.

Fulford, M.G. 1989. To east and west: the Mediterranean trade of Cyrenaica and Tripolitania in antiquity. *Libyan Studies* 20, 169–91.

Fuller, D.Q. 2003. Pharaonic or Sudanic? Models for Meroitic society and change. In *Ancient Egypt in Africa,* ed. D. O'Connor and A. Reid, 169–84. Left Coast Press, Walnut Creek, CA.

2014. Agricultural innovation and state collapse in Meroitic Nubia: the impact of the Savannah Package. In *Archaeology of African plant use*, ed. C.J. Stevens, S. Nixon, M.A. Murray, and D.Q. Fuller, 165–77. Left Coast Press, Walnut Creek, CA.

Gallay, A. 2010. Sériation chronologique de la céramique mégalithique Sénégambienne (Sénégal, Gambie), 700 cal BC–1700 cal AD. *Journal of African Archaeology* 8(1), 99–129.

Gallay, A., Pignat, G., and Curdy, P. 1982. Mbolop Tobé (Santhiou Kohel, Sénégal): contribution à la connaissance du mégalithisme sénégambien. *Archives suisses d'anthropologie générale (Genève)* 46(2), 217–59.

Gallay, A., Huysecom, E., Honegger, M., and Mayor, A. 1990. *Hamdallahi, capitale de l'Empire peul du Massina, Mali. Première fouille archéologique, études historiques et ethnoarchéologiques*. Sonderschriften des Frobenius-Instituts 9, Franz Steiner, Stuttgart.

Gardner, G.A. 1963. *Mapungubwe*, vol. 2. Van Schaik, Pretoria.

Garlake, P.S. 1966. *The early Islamic architecture of the East African coast*. Memoir 1, British Institute in Eastern Africa, Oxford University Press, London.

1972. Excavations at the Nhunguza and Ruanga Ruins in northern Mashonaland. *South African Archaeological Bulletin* 27, 107–43.

1973. *Great Zimbabwe*. Thames and Hudson, London.

1974. Excavations at Obalara's Land, Ife: an interim report. *West African Journal of Archaeology* 4, 111–48.

1976a. An investigation of Manekweni, Mozambique. *Azania* 11, 25–47.

1976b. Great Zimbabwe: a reappraisal. In *Proceedings of the Panafrican Congress of Prehistory and Quaternary Studies: 7th Session, Addis Ababa, December 1971*, ed. B. Abebe, J. Chavaillon, and J.E.G. Sutton, 221–6. Provisional Military Government of Socialist Ethiopia, Ministry of Culture, Addis Ababa.

1977. Excavations on the Woye Asiri family land in Ife, Western Nigeria. *West African Journal of Archaeology* 7, 57–96.

1978a. *The kingdoms of Africa*. Elsevier–Phaidon, Oxford.

1978b. Pastoralism and Zimbabwe. *Journal of African History* 19(4), 479–93.

2002. *Early art and architecture in Africa*. Oxford University Press, Oxford.

Garrard, T.F. 1982. Myth and metrology: the early trans-Saharan gold trade. *Journal of African History* 23(4), 443–61.

Garstang, J., Sayce, A.H., and Griffiths, F.W. 1911. *Meroë, the city of the Ethiopians*. Oxford University Press, Oxford.

Gauthier-Pilters, H., and Dagg, A.I. 1981. *The camel: its evolution, ecology, behavior, and relationship to man*. University of Chicago Press, Chicago and London.

Gautier, A., and Van Neer, W. 2005. The continuous exploitation of wild animal resources in the archaeozoological record of Ghana. *Journal of African Archaeology* 3(2), 195–212.

Gerster, G. 1970. *Churches in rock: early Christian art in Ethiopia*. Translated by R. Hosking. Phaidon, London.

Ghaidan, U. (ed.) 1976. *Lamu: a study in conservation*. East African Literature Bureau, Nairobi.

Gibbon, E. 1952. *The decline and fall of the Roman Empire*, 2 vols. Encyclopaedia Britannica, Chicago.

Godlewski, W. 1991. Old Dongola 1988–1989: House PCH 1. *Archéologie du Nil Moyen* 5, 79–101.

Godlewski, W., and Medeksza, S. 1987. The so-called mosque building in Old Dongola (Sudan): a structural analysis. *Archéologie du Nil Moyen* 2, 185–205.

González-Ruibal, A., Gelabert, L.P., and Mañé, A.V. 2011. Early Iron Age burials from Equatorial Guinea: the sites of Corisco Island. *Journal of African Archaeology* 9(1), 41–66.

González-Ruibal, A., Sánchez-Elipe, M., and Otero-Vilariño, C. 2013. An ancient and common tradition: funerary rituals and society in Equatorial Guinea (first–twelfth centuries AD). *African Archaeological Review* 30(2), 115–43.

Good, C.M. 1972. Salt, trade, and disease: aspects of development in Africa's northern Great Lakes Region. *International Journal of African Historical Studies* 5(4), 543–86.

Goodwin, A.J.H. 1957. Archaeology and Benin architecture. *Journal of the Historical Society of Nigeria* 1(2), 65–85.

Gordon, D. 2009. A revisionist view of Shaka (book review). *Journal of African History* 50(2), 315–16.

Gore, C. 2007. *Art, performance and ritual in Benin City.* Edinburgh University Press, Edinburgh.

Green, M.M. 1947. *Ibo village affairs: chiefly with reference to the village of Umueke Agbaja.* Sidgwick and Jackson, London.

Griffeth, R. 2000. The Hausa city-states from 1450 to 1804. In *A comparative study of thirty city-state cultures*, ed. M.H. Hansen, 483–506. The Royal Danish Academy of Sciences and Letters, Copenhagen.

Griffith, F. Ll. 1922. Oxford excavations in Nubia. *Annals of Archaeology and Anthropology* 9, Liverpool Institute of Archaeology, Liverpool University Press, Liverpool.

Gronenborn, D. 2001. Princedoms along the lakeshore. Historical-archaeological investigations considering the development of complex societies in the southern Chad Basin. *Berichte des Sonderforschungsbereichs 268*, Band 14, 55–69.

(ed.) 2011. *Gold, Sklaven und Elfenbein: Mittelalterliche Reiche im Norden Nigerias [Gold, slaves, and ivory: Medieval empires in northern Nigeria]*, parallel texts in German and English. Verlag des Römisch-Germanischen Zentralmuseums, Mainz.

Gronenborn, D., Adderley, P., Ameje, J., Banerjee, A., Fenn, T., Liesegang, G., Haase, C.-P., Usman, Y.A., and Patscher, S. 2012. Durbi Takusheyi: a high-status burial site in the western Central *bilad al-sudan*. *Azania: Archaeological Research in Africa*, 47(3), 256–71.

Grzymski, K. 1984. Population estimates from Meroitic architecture. *Meroitica* 7, 287–9.

Gutkind, P.C.W. 1960. Notes on the kibuga of Buganda. *Uganda Journal* 24(1), 29–43.

1963. *The royal capital of Buganda.* Mouton, The Hague.

Håland, R. 1980. Man's role in the changing habitat of Mema during the old kingdom of Ghana. *Norwegian Archaeological Review* 13, 31–46.

Haaland [Håland], R. 1994–1995. Dakawa: an early Iron Age site in the Tanzanian hinterland. *Azania* 29–30, 238–47.

Haas, J. 1982. *The evolution of the prehistoric state.* New York University Press, New York.

Haase, C.-P. 2011. The metal bowl from Tumulus 7. In *Gold, Sklaven und Elfenbein: Mittelalterliche Reiche im Norden Nigerias [Gold, slaves, and ivory: Medieval empires in northern Nigeria],* parallel texts in German and English, ed. D. Gronenborn, 103. Verlag des Römisch-Germanischen Zentralmuseums, Mainz.

Hall, M. 1987. *The changing past: farmers, kings and traders in southern Africa, 200–1860.* David Philip, Johannesburg.

Hall, R.N. 1905. *Great Zimbabwe.* Methuen, London.

Hall, S., Anderson, M., Boeyens, J., and Coetzee, F. 2008. Towards an outline of the oral geography, historical identity and political economy of the late precolonial Tswana in the Rustenburg region. In *Five hundred years rediscovered: southern African precedents and prospects,* ed. N. Swanepoel, A. Esterhuysen, and P. Bonner, 55–85. Wits University Press, Johannesburg.

Hall, S., Miller, D., Anderson, M., and Boeyens, J. 2006. An exploratory study of copper and iron production at Marothodi, an early 19th century Tswana town, Rustenburg District, South Africa. *Journal of African Archaeology* 4(1), 3–35.

Harlan, J.R., and Pasquereau, J. 1969. Décrue agriculture in Mali. *Economic Botany* 23(1), 70–4.

Harris, D.R. 1976. Traditional systems of plant food production and the origins of agriculture in West Africa. In *Origins of African plant domestication,* ed. J.R. Harlan, J.M.J. de Wet, and A.B.L. Stemler, 311–56. Mouton, The Hague.

Hassan, F.A. 1997. Holocene palaeoclimates of Africa. *African Archaeological Review* 14(4), 213–30.

　2007. The Aswan High Dam and the International Rescue Nubia Campaign. *African Archaeological Review* 24(3/4), 73–94.

　(ed.) 2002. *Droughts, food and culture: ecological change and food security in Africa's later prehistory.* Kluwer Academic/Plenum, New York.

Helm, R., Crowther, A., Shipton, C., Tengeza, A., Fuller, D., and Boivin, N. 2012. Exploring agriculture, interaction and trade on the eastern African littoral: preliminary results from Kenya. *Azania: Archaeological Research in Africa* 47(1), 39–63.

Hendrickx, S., and Vermeersch, P. 2000. Prehistory: from the Palaeolithic to the Badarian culture (c. 700,000–4000 BC). In *The Oxford history of ancient Egypt,* ed. I. Shaw, 17–43. Oxford University Press, Oxford.

Herbert, E.W. 1984. *Red gold of Africa: copper in precolonial history and culture,* University of Wisconsin Press, Madison.

　1996. Metals and power at Great Zimbabwe. In *Aspects of African archaeology: papers from the 10th Congress of the PanAfrican Association for Prehistory and Related Studies,* ed. G. Pwiti and R. Soper, 641–7. University of Zimbabwe, Harare.

Hiernaux, J., de Longrée, E., and De Buyst, J. 1971. *Fouilles archéologiques dans la vallée du Haut-Lualaba. I Sanga 1958.* Musée Royal de l'Afrique Centrale, Tervuren, Belgium.

Hiernaux, J., Maquet, E., and De Buyst, J. 1972. Le cimetière protohistorique de Katoto (Vallée du Lualaba, Congo-Kinshasa). In *Congrès panafricain de préhistoire, Dakar 1967: Actes de 6e session,* ed. H.J. Hugot, 148–58. Les Imprimeries Réunies de Chambéry, Chambéry.

Hinkel, F.W. 2000. The Royal Pyramids of Meroe. Architecture, construction and reconstruction of a sacred landscape. *Sudan and Nubia* 4, 11–26 and plates X–XV.

Hogendorn, J., and Johnson, M. 1986. *The shell money of the slave trade*. Cambridge University Press, Cambridge.

Holl, A.F.C. 1985. Background to the Ghana Empire: archaeological investigations on the transition to statehood in the Dhar Tichitt region (Mauritania). *Journal of Anthropological Archaeology* 4, 73–115.

1996. Genesis of central Chadic polities. In *Aspects of African archaeology: papers from the 10th Congress of the PanAfrican Association for Prehistory and Related Studies*, ed. G. Pwiti and R. Soper, 581–91. University of Zimbabwe, Harare.

2006. *West African early towns: archaeology of households in urban landscapes*. University of Michigan, Ann Arbor, Michigan.

2009. Iron metallurgy in West Africa: an early iron smelting site in the Mahoun Bend, Burkina Faso. In *Crossroads/Carrefour Sahel: cultural and technological developments in first millennium BC/AD West Africa*, ed. S. Magnavita, L. Koté, P. Breunig, and O.A. Idé, 59–68. Africa Magna Verlag, Frankfurt am Main.

Home, R. 1982. *City of Blood revisited: a new look at the Benin expedition of 1897*. Collings, London.

Horton, M. 1986. Asiatic colonization of the East African coast: the Manda evidence. *Journal of the Royal Asiatic Society*, Pt 2, 201–13.

1987a. Early Muslim trading settlements on the East African coast: new evidence from Shanga. *Antiquaries Journal* 67, 290–323.

1987b. The Swahili Corridor. *Scientific American* 257(3), 76–84.

1996. *Shanga: the archaeology of a Muslim trading community on the coast of East Africa*, Memoir 14, British Institute in Eastern Africa, London.

Horton, M., and Blurton, T.R. 1988. 'Indian' metalwork in East Africa: the bronze lion statuette from Shanga. *Antiquity* 62 (234), 11–23.

Horton, M., and Middleton, J. 2000. *The Swahili: the social landscape of a mercantile society*. Blackwell, Oxford.

Horton, M., and Mudida, N. 1993. Exploitation of marine resources: evidence for the origin of the Swahili communities of east Africa. In *The archaeology of Africa: food, metals and towns*, ed. T. Shaw, P. Sinclair, B. Andah, and A. Okpoko, 673–93. Routledge, London and New York.

Horton, M., Brown, H.M., and Oddy, W.A. 1986. The Mtambwe hoard. *Azania* 21, 115–23 and plate 1.

Hoyos, D. 2010. *The Carthaginians*. London and New York, Routledge.

Huffman, T.N. 1981. *Snakes and birds: expressive space at Great Zimbabwe*, Inaugural lecture, University of Witwatersrand, Johannesburg. Witwatersrand University Press, Johannesburg. (Also published in 1981 in *African Studies* 40(2), 131–50.)

1982. Archaeology and ethnohistory of the African Iron Age. *Annual Review of Anthropology* 11, 133–50.

1986. Iron Age settlement patterns and the origins of class distinction in southern Africa. *Advances in World Archaeology* 5, 291–338.

1996. *Snakes and crocodiles: power and symbolism in ancient Zimbabwe*, Witwatersrand University Press, Johannesburg.

2007. *Handbook to the Iron Age: the archaeology of pre-colonial farming societies in southern Africa*. University of KwaZulu-Natal Press, Scottsville, South Africa.

2009. Mapungubwe and Great Zimbabwe: the origin and spread of social complexity in southern Africa. *Journal of Anthropological Archaeology* 28, 37–54.

2010a. Revisiting Great Zimbabwe. *Azania: Archaeological Research in Africa* 45(3), 321–8.

2010b. State formation in southern Africa: a reply to Kim and Kusimba. *African Archaeological Review* 27(1), 1–11.

Huffman, T.N., and Hanisch, E.O.M. 1987. Settlement hierarchies in the northern Transvaal: zimbabwe ruins and Venda history. *African Studies* 46, 79–116.

Huffman, T.N., and Vogel, J.C. 1991. The chronology of Great Zimbabwe. *South African Archaeological Bulletin* 46, 61–70.

Hull, R.W. 1976. *African cities and towns before the European conquest*. New York, Norton.

Hunwick, J. 1971. Songhay, Bornu and Hausaland in the sixteenth century. In *History of West Africa*, vol. 1, ed. J.F.A. Ajayi and M. Crowder, 202–39. Longman, London.

Hurst, H. 1979. Excavations at Carthage 1977–8: fourth interim report. *Antiquaries Journal* 59(1), 19–49.

Iles, L. 2013a. Analysis of iron working remains from Kooki and Masindi, western Uganda. *Nyame Akuma* 80, 43–58.

2013b. The development of iron technology in precolonial western Uganda. *Azania: Archaeological Research in Africa* 48(1), 65–90.

Iles, L., Robertshaw, P., and Young, R. 2014. A furnace and associated ironworking remains at Munsa, Uganda. *Azania: Archaeological Research in Africa* 49(1), 45–63.

Iliffe, J. 1995. *Africans: the history of a continent*. Cambridge University Press, Cambridge.

Insoll, T. 1995. A cache of hippopotamus ivory at Gao, Mali; and a hypothesis of its use. *Antiquity* 69 (263), 327–36.

1996a. *Islam, archaeology and history: Gao region (Mali) ca. AD 900–1250*. Cambridge Monographs in African Archaeology 39, BAR International Series 647, Tempus Reparatum, Oxford.

1996b. Settlement and trade in Gao, Mali. In *Aspects of African archaeology: papers from the 10th Congress of the PanAfrican Association for Prehistory and Related Studies*, ed. G. Pwiti and R. Soper, 663–9. University of Zimbabwe, Harare.

1999. *The archaeology of Islam*. Blackwell, Oxford.

2003. *The archaeology of Islam in sub-Saharan Africa*. Cambridge University Press, Cambridge.

Insoll, T., and Shaw, T. 1997. Gao and Igbo-Ukwu: beads, interregional trade, and beyond. *African Archaeological Review* 14(1), 9–23.

Insoll, T., Polya, D.A., Bhan, K., Irving, D., and Jarvis, K. 2004. Towards an understanding of the carnelian bead trade from Western India to sub-Saharan Africa: the application of UV-LA-ICP-MS to carnelian from Gujarat, India, and West Africa. *Journal of Archaeological Science* 31, 1161–73.

Jaabiri, F., and Yahia, B. 2000. Le Mzâb Cité-état. In *A comparative study of thirty city-state cultures*, ed. M.H. Hansen, 445–62. The Royal Danish Academy of Sciences and Letters, Copenhagen.

Jahadhmy, A.A. 1981. *Learner's Swahili-English, English-Swahili Dictionary*, Evans, London.

Jakobielski, S. 1982. Polish excavations at Old Dongola in 1976 and 1978. In *Nubian studies: proceedings of the Symposium for Nubian Studies, Selwyn College, Cambridge 1978*, ed. J.M. Plumley, 116–26. International Society for Nubian Studies, Aris & Phillips, Warminster, UK.

Jansen, M. 1989. Water supply and sewage disposal at Mohenjo-Daro. *World Archaeology* 21(2), 177–92.

Jesse, F., Kröpelin, S., Lange, M., Pöllath, N., and Berke, H. 2004. On the periphery of Kerma – The Handessi Horizon in Wadi Hariq, Northwestern Sudan. *Journal of African Archaeology* 2(2), 123–64.

Johnson, M. 1970a. The cowrie currencies of West Africa, Part I. *Journal of African History* 11(1), 17–49.

1970b. The cowrie currencies of West Africa, Part II. *Journal of African History* 11(3), 331–53.

Johnson, S. 1921. *The history of the Yorubas*. Routledge, London.

Joire, J. 1955. Découvertes archéologiques dans la région de Rao (Bas-Sénégal). *Bulletin de l'IFAN*, Dakar, 17(B), 249–333.

Juma, A.M. 1996. The Swahili and the Mediterranean worlds: pottery of the late Roman period from Zanzibar. *Antiquity* 70, 148–54.

Kaegi, W.E. 2010. *Muslim expansion and Byzantine collapse in North Africa*. Cambridge University Press, Cambridge.

Kahlheber, S., Bostoen, K., and Neumann, K. 2009. Early plant cultivation in the Central African rain forest: first millennium BC pearl millet from south Cameroon. *Journal of African Archaeology* 7(2), 253–72.

Kahlheber, S., Eggert, M.K.H., Seidensticker, D., and Wotzka, H.-P. 2014. Pearl millet and other plant remains from the Early Iron Age site of Boso-Njafo (Inner Congo Basin, Democratic Republic of the Congo). *African Archaeological Review* 31(3), 479–512.

Kea, R.A. 2000. City-state culture on the Gold Coast: the Fante city–state federation in the seventeenth and eighteenth centuries. In *A comparative study of thirty city-state cultures*, ed. M.H. Hansen, 519–30. The Royal Danish Academy of Sciences and Letters, Copenhagen.

2012. The local and the global: historiographical reflections on West Africa in the Atlantic Age. In *Power and landscape in Atlantic West Africa: archaeological perspectives*, ed. J.C. Monroe and A. Ogundiran, 339–75. Cambridge University Press, Cambridge.

Keay, R.W.J. 1959. *Vegetation map of Africa south of the Tropic of Cancer*. Oxford University Press, London.

Kemp, B.J. 1991. *Ancient Egypt: anatomy of a civilization*. Routledge, London.

2013. *The city of Akhenaten and Nefertiti: Amarna and its people*. Paperback edition, Thames and Hudson, London.

Kendall, T. 1991. The Napatan palace at Gebel Barkal: a first look at B1200. In *Egypt and Africa: Nubia from prehistory to Islam*, ed. W.V. Davies, 302–13. British Museum Press, London.

1997. *Kerma and the Kingdom of Kush 2500–1500 BC: the archaeological discovery of an ancient Nubian empire*. Smithsonian Institution, Washington.

Kenrick, P. 1986. *Excavations at Sabratha 1948–1951*. The Society for the Promotion of Roman Studies, London.

2009. *Libya Archaeological Guides: Tripolitania*. Silphium Press, London.

2013. *Libya Archaeological Guides: Cyrenaica*. Silphium Press, London.

Kiéthéga, J.-B. 1983. *L'or de la Volta Noire: archéologie et histoire de l'exploitation traditionnelle (Région de Poura, Haute-Volta)*, Karthala, Paris.

Killick, D. 1996. On claims for 'advanced' ironworking technology in precolonial Africa. In *The culture and technology of African iron production*, ed. P.R. Schmidt, 247–66. University Press of Florida, Gainesville.

2004. What do we know about African iron working? *Journal of African Archaeology* 2(1), 97–112.

Kim, N.C., and Kusimba, C.M. 2008. Pathways to social complexity and state formation in the southern Zambezian region. *African Archaeological Review* 25(3/4), 131–52.

Kirkman, J.S. 1954. *The Arab city of Gedi: excavations at the Great Mosque. Architecture and finds*. Oxford University Press, London.

1963. *Gedi: the Palace*. Mouton & Co., The Hague.

1964. *Men and monuments on the East African coast*. Lutterworth Press, London.

1966. *Ungwana on the Tana*. Mouton & Co., The Hague.

1975. Some conclusions from archaeological excavations on the coast of Kenya, 1948–1966. In *East Africa and the Orient: cultural syntheses in pre-colonial times*, ed. N. Chittick and R.I. Rotberg, 226–47. Africana Publishing Company, New York and London.

Klee, M., and Zach, B. 1999. The exploitation of wild and domesticated food plants at settlement mounds in north-east Nigeria (1800 cal BC to today). In *The exploitation of plant resources in Ancient Africa*, ed. M. van der Veen, 81–88. New York, Kluwer Academic/Plenum.

Kluckhohn, C. 1960. The moral order in the expanding society. In *City invincible: a symposium on urbanization and cultural development in the ancient Near East*, ed. C.H. Kraeling and R.M. Adams, 391–404. Chicago University Press, Chicago.

Kobishchanov, Y.M. 1979. *Axum*, ed. J.W. Michels. Translated by L.T. Kapitanoff. Pennsylvania State University Press, University Park and London.

Kobish[ch]anov, Y.M. 1981. Aksum: political system, economics and culture, first to fourth century. In *General history of Africa*, vol. 2: *Ancient civilizations of Africa*, ed. G. Mokhtar, 381–400. Heinemann, University of California, UNESCO; London, Berkeley, Paris.

Kraeling, C.H. 1962. *Ptolemais: city of the Libyan Pentapolis*. Chicago University Press, Chicago.

Krencker, D. 1913. *Deutsche Aksum-Expedition*, Band 2. Georg Reimer, Berlin.

Krencker, D., Kruger, E., Lehmann, H., and Wachtler, H. 1929. *Die trierer Kaiserthermen*, Benno Filser, Augsburg.

Kubiak, W.B. 1987. *Al-Fustat: its foundation and early urban development*. The American University in Cairo Press, Cairo.

Kuper, A. 1980. Symbolic dimensions of the Southern Bantu homestead. *Africa* 50(1), 8–23.

1982. *Wives for cattle: bridewealth and marriage in southern Africa*. Routledge and Kegan Paul, London.

Kusimba, C.M. 1999. *The rise and fall of Swahili states*. AltaMira Press, Walnut Creek, CA.

Kusimba, C.M., Kusimba, S.B., and Wright, D.K. 2005. The development and collapse of precolonial ethnic mosaics in Tsavo, Kenya. *Journal of African Archaeology* 3(2), 243–65.

Kusimba, C.M., Kusimba, S.B., and Dussubieux, L. 2013. Beyond the coastalscapes: preindustrial social and political networks in East Africa. *African Archaeological Review* 30(4), 399–426.

Lacovara, P. 1991. The stone vase deposit at Kerma. In *Egypt and Africa: Nubia from prehistory to Islam*, ed. W.V. Davies, 118–28. British Museum Press, London.

Lambert-Zazulak, P. 2000. The International Ancient Egyptian Mummy Tissue Bank at the Manchester Museum. *Antiquity* 74 (283), 44–8.

Lancel, S. 1995. *Carthage: a history*. Translated by A. Nevill. Blackwell, Oxford.

Lankton, J.W., Ige, O.A., and Rehren, T. 2006. Early primary glass production in southern Nigeria. *Journal of African Archaeology* 4(1), 111–38.

Lanning, E.C. 1953. Ancient earthworks in western Uganda. *Uganda Journal* 17(1), 51–62.

1955. The Munsa earthworks. *Uganda Journal* 19(2), 177–82.

1960. The earthworks at Kibengo, Mubende District. *Uganda Journal* 24(2), 183–96.

1970. Ntusi: an ancient capital site in western Uganda. *Azania* 5, 39–54.

LaViolette, A. 1996. Report on excavations at the Swahili site of Pujini, Pemba Island, Tanzania. *Nyame Akuma* 46, 72–83.

LaViolette, A., and Fleisher, J. 2005. The archaeology of sub-Saharan urbanism: cities and their countrysides. In *African archaeology: a critical introduction*, ed. A.B. Stahl, 327–52. Blackwell, Oxford.

2009. The urban history of a rural place: Swahili archaeology on Pemba Island, Tanzania, 700–1500 AD. *International Journal of African Historical Studies* 42(3), 433–55.

Law, R. 1978. Slaves, trade, and taxes: the material base of political power in pre-colonial West Africa. *Research in Economic Anthropology* 1, 37–52.

1980a. *The horse in West African history*. Oxford University Press, Oxford.

1980b. Wheeled transport in pre-colonial West Africa. *Africa* 50(3), 249–62.

Leclant, J. 1973. Glass from the Meroitic necropolis of Sedeinga (Sudanese Nubia). *Journal of Glass Studies* 15, 52–68.

Lehner, M. 1997. *The complete pyramids*. Thames and Hudson, London.

Lejju, B.J., Robertshaw, P., and Taylor, D. 2006. Africa's earliest bananas? *Journal of Archaeological Science* 33(1), 102–113.

Lenoble, P., and Sharif, N.M. 1992. Barbarians at the gates? The royal mounds of El Hobagi and the end of Meroë. *Antiquity* 66, 626–35.

Leslie, M., and Maggs, T. (eds.) 2000. *African naissance: the Limpopo Valley 1000 years ago*. The South African Archaeological Society, Goodwin Series vol. 8.

Levtzion, N. 1973. *Ancient Ghana and Mali*. Methuen, London.

Livingstone, F.B. 1967. The origin of the sickle-cell gene. In *Reconstructing African culture history*, ed. C. Gabel and N.R. Bennett, 139–66. Boston University Press, Boston.

Lloyd, A.B. 2000. The Ptolemaic Period (332–30 BC). In *The Oxford history of ancient Egypt*, ed. I. Shaw, 395–421. Oxford University Press, Oxford.

Lonsdale, J. 1981. States and social processes in Africa: a historiographical survey. *African Studies Review* 24(2 and 3), 139–225.

Lovejoy, P.E. 1986. *Salt of the desert sun: a history of salt production and trade in the central Sudan.* Cambridge University Press, Cambridge.

Lucas, A., and Harris, J.R. 1962. *Ancient Egyptian materials and industries*, 4th ed. Edward Arnold, London.

Lugard, F.D. 1893. In British Parliamentary Papers. Africa. No. 2 (1893). C.–6848, 1–102.

1903. *Northern Nigeria: report for 1902.* Colonial Reports: Annual, No. 409, His Majesty's Stationery Office, London.

Lull, V., and Micó, R. 2011. *Archaeology of the origin of the state: the theories.* (Translated by P. Smith.) Oxford University Press, Oxford.

Mabogunje, A.L. 1968. *Urbanization in Nigeria.* University of London Press, London.

Macamo, S.L., and Duarte, R.T. 1996. Oral tradition and the Songo Ruins. In *Aspects of African archaeology: papers from the 10th Congress of the PanAfrican Association for Prehistory and Related Studies*, ed. G. Pwiti and R. Soper, 561–3. University of Zimbabwe, Harare.

MacDonald, K.C. 1995. Analysis of the mammalian, avian, and reptilian remains. In *Excavations at Jenné-jeno, Hambarketolo, and Kaniana (Inland Niger Delta, Mali), the 1981 season*, ed. S.K. McIntosh, 291–318. University of California Press, Berkeley and Los Angeles.

1998. Before the Empire of Ghana: pastoralism and the origins of cultural complexity in the Sahel. In *Transformations in Africa: essays on Africa's later past*, ed. G. Connah, 71–103. Leicester University Press, London and Washington.

2011. A view from the South: Sub-Saharan evidence for contacts between North Africa, Mauritania and the Niger, 1000 BC–AD 700. In *Money, trade and trade routes in Pre-Islamic North Africa*, ed. A. Dowler and E.R. Galvin, 72–82. Research Publication 176, British Museum, London.

MacDonald, K.C., and MacDonald, R.H. 1999. The origins and development of domesticated animals in arid West Africa. In *The origins and development of African livestock*, ed. R.M. Blench and K.C. MacDonald, University College London and Routledge, London.

MacEachern, S., and David, N. 2013. Monumental architecture in mountain landscapes: the *diy-geδ-bay* sites of northern Cameroon. *Azania: Archaeological Research in Africa* 48(2), 241–62.

McEvedy, C., and Jones, R. 1978. *Atlas of world population history.* Penguin Books, Harmondsworth, UK.

McIntosh, R.J. 1998. *The peoples of the Middle Niger: the Island of Gold*, Blackwell, Oxford.

1999. Western representations of urbanism and invisible African towns. In *Beyond chiefdoms: pathways to complexity in Africa*, ed. S.K. McIntosh, 56–65. Cambridge University Press, Cambridge.

2005. *Ancient Middle Niger: urbanism and the self-organizing landscape.* Cambridge University Press, Cambridge.

McIntosh, S.K. 1994. Changing perceptions of West Africa's past: archaeological research since 1988. *Journal of Archaeological Research* 2(2), 165–98.

1999. Pathways to complexity: an African perspective. In *Beyond chiefdoms: pathways to complexity in Africa*, ed. S.K. McIntosh, 1–30. Cambridge University Press, Cambridge.

McIntosh, S.K. (ed.) 1995. *Excavations at Jenné-jeno, Hambarketolo, and Kaniana (Inland Niger Delta, Mali), the 1981 season.* University of California Press, Berkeley and Los Angeles.

McIntosh, S.K., and Bocoum, H. 2000. New perspectives on Sincu Bara, a first millennium site in the Senegal Valley. *African Archaeological Review* 17(1), 1–43.

McIntosh, S.K., and McIntosh, R.J. 1979. Initial perspectives on prehistoric subsistence in the Inland Niger Delta (Mali). *World Archaeology* 11(2), 227–43.

1980. *Prehistoric investigations in the region of Jenné, Mali*, 2 vols. Cambridge Monographs in African Archaeology 2, BAR International Series 89(i) and (ii), Oxford.

1984. The early city in West Africa: towards an understanding. *African Archaeological Review* 2, 73–98.

1986. Recent archaeological research and dates from West Africa. *Journal of African History* 27, 413–42.

1993a. Cities without citadels: understanding urban origins along the middle Niger. In *The archaeology of Africa: food, metals and towns*, ed. T. Shaw, P. Sinclair, B. Andah, and A. Okpoko, 622–41. Routledge, London and New York.

1993b. Field survey in the tumulus zone of Senegal. *African Archaeological Review* 11, 73–107.

McIntosh, S.K., McIntosh, R.J., and Bocoum, H. 1992. The Middle Senegal Valley Project: preliminary results from the 1990–91 field season. *Nyame Akuma* 38, 47–61.

Mack, J. 2007. The land viewed from the sea. *Azania* 42, 1–14.

McLeod, M.D. 1981. *The Asante.* British Museum, London.

Maggs, T. 1976. Iron Age patterns and Sotho history on the southern Highveld: South Africa. *World Archaeology* 7(3), 318–32.

1993. Sliding doors at Mokgatle's, a nineteenth century Tswana town in the central Transvaal. *South African Archaeological Bulletin* 48, 32–6.

2008. The Mpumalanga Escarpment settlements: some answers, many questions. In *Five hundred years rediscovered: southern African precedents and prospects*, ed. N. Swanepoel, A. Esterhuysen, and P. Bonner, 169–81. Wits University Press, Johannesburg.

Magnavita, C., Breunig, P., Ameje, J., and Posselt, M. 2006. Zilum: a mid-first millennium BC fortified settlement near Lake Chad. *Journal of African Archaeology* 4(1), 153–69.

Magnavita, S. 2003. The beads of Kissi, Burkina Faso. *Journal of African Archaeology* 1(1), 127–38.

2008. The oldest textiles from Sub-Saharan West Africa: woolen facts from Kissi, Burkina Faso. *Journal of African Archaeology* 6(2), 243–57.

Maisels, C. 2010. *The archaeology of politics and power: where, when and why the first states formed.* Oxbow Books, Oxford.

Majno, G. 1975. *The healing hand: man and wound in the Ancient World.* Harvard University Press, Cambridge, MA.

Maliphant, G.K., Rees, A.R., and Roese, P.M. 1976. Defence systems of the Benin empire – Uwan. *West African Journal of Archaeology* 6, 121–30.

Manson-Bahr, P.E.C., and Apted, F.I.C. 1982. *Manson's tropical diseases*, 18th ed. Baillière Tindall, London.

Manton, E.L. 1988. *Roman North Africa.* Seaby, London.

Manyanga, M. 2007. *Resilient landscapes: socio-environmental dynamics in the Shashi-Limpopo Basin, southern Zimbabwe c. AD 800 to the present.* Uppsala University, Sweden.

Manyanga, M., Pikirayi, I., and Chirikure, S. 2010. Conceptualising the urban mind in pre-European southern Africa: rethinking Mapungubwe and Great Zimbabwe. In *The urban mind: cultural and environmental dynamics*, ed. P.J.J. Sinclair, G. Nordquist, F. Herschend, and C. Isendahl, 573–90. African and Comparative Archaeology, Department of Archaeology and Ancient History, Uppsala University, Uppsala, Sweden.

Marcus, H.G. 2002. *A history of Ethiopia.* Updated edition, University of California Press, Berkeley.

Matenga, E. 1993. *Archaeological figurines from Zimbabwe.* Studies in African Archaeology 5, Uppsala University, Sweden, and Queen Victoria Museum, Zimbabwe.

1998. *The soapstone birds of Great Zimbabwe: symbols of a nation*, African Publishing Group, Harare.

Matthews, D., and Mordini, A. 1959. The monastery of Debra Damo, Ethiopia. *Archaeologia* 97, 1–58.

Mattingly, D.J. 1994. *Tripolitania.* University of Michigan Press, Ann Arbor, MI.

2011. The Garamantes of Fazzan: an early Libyan state with trans-Saharan connections. In *Money, trade and trade routes in Pre-Islamic North Africa*, ed. A. Dowler and E.R. Galvin, 49–60. Research Publication 176, British Museum, London.

(ed.) 2013. *The archaeology of Fazzān: Volume 4, survey and excavations at Old Jarma.* Society for Libyan Studies Monograph 9, Department of Antiquities, Tripoli; Society for Libyan Studies, London.

Mattingly, D.J., and Sterry, M. 2013. The first towns in the central Sahara. *Antiquity* 87 (336), 503–18.

Maund, E.A. 1890. Zambezia, the new British Possession in Central South Africa. *Proceedings of the Royal Geographical Society and Monthly Record of Geography.* New Monthly Series 12(11), 649–55.

Mauny, R. 1961. *Tableau géographique de l'Ouest Africain au Moyen-Age d'après les sources écrites, la tradition et l'archéologie.* Mémoires de l'IFAN 61, Dakar.

1970. *Les siècles obscurs de l'Afrique noire: histoire et archéologie.* Fayard.

1978. Trans-Saharan contacts and the Iron Age in West Africa. In *The Cambridge history of Africa*, vol. 2, ed. J.D. Fage, 272–341. Cambridge University Press, Cambridge.

Mayor, A. 1996. Hamdallahi, capital of the Fulani empire of Macina, Mali: a multi-disciplinary approach. In *Aspects of African archaeology: papers from the 10th Congress of the PanAfrican Association for Prehistory and Related Studies*, ed. G. Pwiti and R. Soper, 671–80. University of Zimbabwe, Harare.

Meillassoux, C. 1991. *The anthropology of slavery: the womb of iron and gold.* Athlone Press, London.

Meister, C., and Eggert, M.K.H. 2008. On the Early Iron Age in southern Cameroon: the sites of Akonétye. *Journal of African Archaeology* 6(2), 183–202.

Meskell, L. 2002. *Private life in New Kingdom Egypt.* Princeton University Press, Princeton, NJ.

Meyboom, P.G.P. 1995. *The Nile Mosaic of Palestrina: early evidence of Egyptian religion in Italy.* Brill, Leiden.

Michels, J.W. 2005. *Changing settlement patterns in the Aksum–Yeha region of Ethiopia: 700 BC– AD 850.* BAR International Series 1446, Archaeopress, Oxford.

Miller, D., Desai, N., and Lee-Thorp, J. 2000. Indigenous gold mining in southern Africa: a review. In *African naissance: the Limpopo Valley 1000 years ago*, ed. M. Leslie and T. Maggs, 91–9. The South African Archaeological Society, Goodwin Series vol. 8.

Miller, J.I. 1969. *The spice trade of the Roman Empire, 29 BC to AD 641*, Oxford University Press, London.

Mitchell, P. 2002. *The archaeology of southern Africa.* Cambridge University Press, Cambridge.

　2004. Towards a comparative archaeology of Africa's islands. *Journal of African Archaeology* 2(2), 229–50.

　2005. *African connections: an archaeological perspective on Africa and the wider world.* AltaMira Press, Walnut Creek, CA.

Mitchell, P., and Lane, P. (ed.) 2013. *The Oxford handbook of African archaeology.* Oxford University Press, Oxford.

Monod, T. 1969. Le 'Macden Ijâfen': une épave caravanière ancienne dans la Majâbat Al-Koubrâ. In *Actes du Premier Colloque international d'Archéologie africaine, 1966.* Fort-Lamy, 286–320.

Monroe, J.C. 2012. Building the state in Dahomey: power and landscape in the Bight of Benin. In *Power and landscape in Atlantic West Africa: archaeological perspectives*, ed. J.C. Monroe and A. Ogundiran, 191–221. Cambridge University Press, Cambridge.

　2013. The archaeology of the precolonial state in Africa. In *The Oxford handbook of African archaeology,* ed. P. Mitchell and P. Lane, 703–22. Oxford University Press, Oxford.

　2014. *The precolonial state in West Africa: building power in Dahomey.* Cambridge University Press, New York.

Monroe, J.C., and Ogundiran, A. 2012. *Power and landscape in Atlantic West Africa: archaeological perspectives.* Cambridge University Press, Cambridge.

Moody, H.L.B. [1970]. *The walls and gates of Kano City*, Department of Antiquities, Nigeria.

Morais, J., and Sinclair, P. 1980. Manyikeni, a Zimbabwe in Southern Mozambique. In *Proceedings of the 8th Panafrican Congress of Prehistory and Quaternary*

Studies, Nairobi, 5 to 10 September 1977, ed. R.E. Leakey and B.A. Ogot, 351–4. The International Louis Leakey Memorial Institute for African Prehistory, Nairobi.

Morkot, R.G. 2003. On the priestly origin of the Napatan kings: the adaptation, demise and resurrection of ideas in writing Nubian history. In *Ancient Egypt in Africa*, ed. D. O'Connor and A. Reid, 151–68. Left Coast Press, Walnut Creek, CA.

Mumford, L. 1961. *The city in history: its origins, its transformations, and its prospects*. Secker and Warburg, London.

Munro-Hay, S. 1982. The foreign trade of the Aksumite port of Adulis. *Azania* 17, 107–25.

1989. *Excavations at Aksum: an account of research at the ancient Ethiopian capital directed in 1972–74 by the late Dr Neville Chittick*. Memoir 10, British Institute in Eastern Africa, London.

1991. *Aksum: an African civilisation of late antiquity*. Edinburgh University Press, Edinburgh.

Munson, P.J. 1976. Archaeological data on the origins of cultivation in the south-western Sahara and their implications for West Africa. In *Origins of African plant domestication*, ed. J.R. Harlan, J.M.J. de Wet, and A.B.L. Stemler, 187–209. Mouton, The Hague.

Mutoro, H.W. 1994–5. Tana ware and the kaya settlements of the coastal hinterland of Kenya. *Azania* 29–30, 257–60.

1998. Precolonial trading systems of the East African interior. In *Transformations in Africa: essays on Africa's later past*, ed. G. Connah, 186–203. Leicester University Press, London and Washington.

Negussie, C. 1994. *Aksum and Matara: a stratigraphic comparison of two Aksumite towns*. Department of Archaeology, Uppsala University, Sweden.

Nenquin, J. 1961. *Salt: a study in economic prehistory*. Dissertationes Archaeologicae Gandenses, vol. 6. De Tempel, Bruges, Belgium.

1963. *Excavations at Sanga, 1957: the protohistoric necropolis*. Musée Royal de l'Afrique Centrale, Tervuren, Belgium.

Neumann, K. 1999. Early plant food production in the West African Sahel: new evidence. In *The exploitation of plant resources in Ancient Africa*, ed. M. van der Veen, 73–80. Kluwer Academic/Plenum, New York.

Neumann, K., and Hildebrand, E. 2009. Early bananas in Africa: the state of the art. *Ethnobotany Research and Applications* 7, 353–62.

Neumann, K., Ballouche, A., and Klee, M. 1996. The emergence of plant food production in the West African Sahel: new evidence from northeast Nigeria and northern Burkina Faso. In *Aspects of African archaeology: papers from the 10th Congress of the PanAfrican Association for Prehistory and Related Studies*, ed. G. Pwiti and R. Soper, 441–8. University of Zimbabwe, Harare.

Nevadomsky, J., Lawson, N., and Hazlett, K. 2014. An ethnographic and space syntax analysis of Benin Kingdom nobility architecture. *African Archaeological Review* 31(1), 59–85.

Nikis, N., de Maret, P., Lanfranchi, R., Nsania, J., Goma, J.-P., Clist, B., and Bostoen, K. 2013. Projet KongoKing. Prospections en République du Congo (Brazzaville):

le cuivre et l'origine des anciens royaumes Kongo et Teke. *Nyame Akuma* 80, 32–42.

Nixon, S. 2009. Excavating Essouk-Tadmakka (Mali): new archaeological investigations of early Islamic trans-Saharan trade. *Azania: Archaeological Research in Africa* 44(2), 217–55.

Nixon, S., Rehren, T., and Guerra, M.F. 2011. New light on the early Islamic West African gold trade: coin moulds from Tadmekka [sic], Mali. *Antiquity* 85(330), 1353–68.

O'Connor, D. 1993. *Ancient Nubia: Egypt's rival in Africa*. University of Pennsylvania, Philadelphia.

2011. *Abydos: Egypt's first pharaohs and the cult of Osiris*. Thames and Hudson, London.

O'Connor, D., and Reid, A. 2003a. Introduction – Locating Ancient Egypt in Africa: modern theories, past realities. In *Ancient Egypt in Africa*, ed. D. O'Connor and A. Reid, 1–21. Left Coast Press, Walnut Creek, CA.

O'Connor, D., and Reid, A. (ed.) 2003b. *Ancient Egypt in Africa*. Left Coast Press, Walnut Creek, CA.

Ogundiran, A. 2007. Living in the shadow of the Atlantic World: history and material life in a Yoruba-Edo hinterland, ca. 1600–1750. In *Archaeology of Atlantic Africa and the African diaspora*, ed. A. Ogundiran and T. Falola, 77–99. Indiana University Press, Bloomington, IN.

2014. The making of an internal frontier settlement: archaeology and historical process in Osun Grove (Nigeria), seventeenth to eighteenth centuries. *African Archaeological Review* 31(1), 1–24.

Ogundiran, A., and Falola, T. (eds.) 2007. *Archaeology of Atlantic Africa and the African diaspora*. Indiana University Press, Bloomington, IN.

Okafor, E.E. 1993. New evidence on early iron-smelting from southeastern Nigeria. In *The archaeology of Africa: food, metals and towns*, ed. T. Shaw, P. Sinclair, B. Andah, and A. Okpoko, 432–48. Routledge, London and New York.

Oliver, R. 1953. A question about the Bachwezi. *Uganda Journal* 17(2), 135–7.

1959a. Ancient capital sites of Ankole. *Uganda Journal* 23(1), 51–63.

1959b. The royal tombs of Buganda. *Uganda Journal* 23(2), 124–33.

1993. *The African experience* (1st ed. 1991). Pimlico, London.

Orwell, G. 1966. *Homage to Catalonia: and looking back on the Spanish War*. Penguin Books, Harmondsworth, UK.

Oxford English Dictionary, 1933. Vol. 10. Clarendon Press, Oxford (1970 reprint).

Ozanne, P. 1969. A new archaeological survey of Ife. *Odu* (NS) 1, 28–45.

Pankhurst, R. 1961. *An introduction to the economic history of Ethiopia from early times to 1800*. Lalibela House, distributed by Sidgwick & Jackson, London.

1979. Ethiopian medieval and post-medieval capitals: their development and principal features. *Azania* 14, 1–19.

2004. Arabian trade with Ethiopia and the Horn of Africa: from ancient times to the sixteenth century. In *Trade and travel in the Red Sea Region*, ed. P. Lunde and A. Porter, 19–24. BAR International Series 1269, Archaeopress, Oxford.

Paribeni, R. 1907. Ricerche nel luogo dell'antica Adulis (Colonia Eritrea). *Monumenti Antichi, Reale Accademia dei Lincei* 18, 437–572 and plates I–XI.

Parkington, J., and Cronin, M. 1979. The size and layout of Mgungundlovu 1829–1838. In *Iron Age studies in southern Africa*, ed. N.J. van der Merwe and T.N. Huffman, 133–48. *South African Archaeological Society Goodwin Series 3*.

Patterson, K.D. 1993. Disease ecologies of Sub-Saharan Africa. In *The Cambridge world history of human disease*, ed. K.F. Kiple, 447–52. Cambridge University Press, Cambridge.

Pauketat, T.R. 2007. *Chiefdoms and other archaeological delusions*. AltaMira Press, Lanham, MD.

Pauly, M. 2013. Acoua-Agnala M'kiri (Mayotte-976) archéologie d'une localité médiévale (11e au 15e siècles EC), entre Afrique et Madagascar. *Nyame Akuma* 80, 73–90.

Pawlowicz, M. 2012. Modelling the Swahili past: the archaeology of Mikindani in southern coastal Tanzania. *Azania: Archaeological Research in Africa* 47(4), 488–508.

Peacock, D. 2000. The Roman Period (30 BC–AD 311). In *The Oxford history of ancient Egypt*, ed. I. Shaw, 422–45. Oxford University Press, Oxford.

Peacock, D., and Blue, L. (eds.) 2007. *The ancient Red Sea port of Adulis, Eritrea. Results of the Eritro-British Expedition, 2004–5*. Oxbow Books, Oxford.

Peel, J.D.Y. 2000. Yoruba as a city-state culture. In *A comparative study of thirty city-state cultures*, ed. M.H. Hansen, 507–17. The Royal Danish Academy of Sciences and Letters, Copenhagen.

Perkins, J., Fleisher, J., and Wynne-Jones, S. 2014. A deposit of Kilwa-type coins from Songo Mnara, Tanzania. *Azania: Archaeological Research in Africa* 49(1), 102–16.

Petit, L.P., von Czerniewicz, M., and Pelzer, C. (eds.) 2011. *Oursi hu-beero: a medieval house complex in Burkina Faso, West Africa*. Sidestone Press, Leiden.

Phillipson, D.W. 1994. The significance and symbolism of the Aksumite stelae. *Cambridge Archaeological Journal* 4(2), 189–210.

1997. *The monuments of Aksum*, (based on the work of the Deutsche Aksum-Expedition of 1906). Addis Ababa University Press and British Institute in Eastern Africa, Addis Ababa and London.

1998. *Ancient Ethiopia. Aksum: its antecedents and successors*. British Museum Press, London.

2000. *Archaeology at Aksum, Ethiopia, 1993–7*, 2 vols. Memoir 17, British Institute in Eastern Africa, and Report 65, Research Committee of the Society of Antiquaries of London, London.

2003. Aksum: an archaeological introduction and guide. *Azania* 38, 1–68.

2004. The Aksumite roots of Medieval Ethiopia. *Azania* 39, 77–89.

2005. *African archaeology*, 3rd ed. Cambridge University Press, Cambridge.

2009a. Aksumite civilization, its connections and descendants. *Der Antike Sudan: Mitteilungen der Sudanarchäologischen Gesellschaft zu Berlin* 20, 1–17.

2009b. *Ancient Churches of Ethiopia: Fourth–Fourteenth Centuries*. Yale University Press, New Haven and London.

2009c. The First Millennium BC in the Highlands of Northern Ethiopia and South-Central Eritrea: a reassessment of cultural and political development. *African Archaeological Review* 26(4), 257–74.

2012. *Foundations of an African civilisation: Aksum and the northern Horn 1000 BC – AD 1300*. James Currey (Boydell & Brewer, Woodbridge, Suffolk, UK).

Phillipson, L. 2009a. Lithic artefacts as a source of cultural, social and economic information: the evidence from Aksum, Ethiopia. *African Archaeological Review* 26(1), 45–58.

2009b. *Using stone tools: the evidence from Aksum, Ethiopia*. BAR International Series 1926, Archaeopress, Oxford.

2012. Grindstones and related artefacts from Pre-Aksumite Seglamen, northern Ethiopia, and their wider implications. *Azania: Archaeological Research in Africa* 47(4), 509–30.

2013a. Lithic tools used in the manufacture of pre-Aksumite ceramics. *Azania: Archaeological Research in Africa* 48(3), 380–402.

2013b. Parchment production in the first millennium BC at Seglamen, northern Ethiopia. *African Archaeological Review* 30(3), 285–303.

Phillipson, L., and Sulas, F. 2005. Cultural continuity in Aksumite lithic tool production: the evidence from Mai Agam. *Azania* 40, 1–18.

Phimister, I.R. 1976. Pre-colonial gold mining in southern Zambezia: a reassessment. *African Social Research* 21, 1–30.

Pigafetta, F. 1591. *A report of the Kingdom of Congo*. Translated by M. Hutchinson 1881. Murray, London.

Pikirayi, I. 1992. Loopholed stone structures in a regional and local context: towards a definition of an archaeological tradition in northern Zimbabwe. In *Urban origins in Eastern Africa: proceedings of the 1991 workshop in Zanzibar*, ed. P.J.J. Sinclair and A. Juma, 120–39. Central Board of National Antiquities, Stockholm.

1993. *The archaeological identity of the Mutapa state: towards an historical archaeology of northern Zimbabwe*. Studies in African Archaeology 6, Societas Archaeologica Upsaliensis, Uppsala.

2001a. The physical environment and the landscape(s) of the Zimbabwe Culture states. In *People, contact and the environment in the African past*, ed. F. Chami, G. Pwiti and C. Radimilahy 129–50. University of Dar es Salaam, Dar es Salaam.

2001b. *The Zimbabwe Culture: origins and decline in southern Zambezian states*. AltaMira, Walnut Creek, CA.

2013a. Great Zimbabwe in historical archaeology: reconceptualizing decline, abandonment, and reoccupation of an ancient polity, AD 1450–1900. *Historical Archaeology* 47(1), 26–37.

2013b. Stone architecture and the development of power in the Zimbabwe tradition AD 1270–1830. *Azania: Archaeological Research in Africa* 48(2), 282–300.

Pikirayi, I., and Chirikure, S. 2011. Debating Great Zimbabwe. *Azania: Archaeological Research in Africa* 46(2), 221–31.

Pistorius, J.C.C. 1992. *Molokwane: an Iron Age Bakwena village: early Tswana settlement in the western Transvaal*. Perskor, Johannesburg.

Pitt Rivers, Lieutenant-General. 1900. *Antique works of art from Benin*, Printed privately, London.

Plant, R. 1985. *Architecture of the Tigre, Ethiopia*. Ravens Educational and Development Services, Worcester.

Pole, L. 2010. Recent developments in iron-working research in West Africa. In *West African archaeology: new developments, new perspectives*, ed. P. Allsworth-Jones, 53–65. BAR International Series 2164, Archaeopress, Oxford.

Pollard, E.J.D. 2008. *The archaeology of Tanzanian coastal landscapes in the 6th to 15th centuries AD*. BAR International Series 1873, Archaeopress, Oxford.

Posnansky, M. 1968. The excavation of an Ankole capital site at Bweyorere. *Uganda Journal* 32(2), 165–82.

1969. Bigo bya Mugenyi. *Uganda Journal* 33(2), 125–50.

1980. Trade and the development of the state and town in Iron Age West Africa. In *Proceedings of the 8th Panafrican Congress of Prehistory and Quaternary Studies, Nairobi, 5 to 10 September 1977*. ed. R.E. Leakey and B.A. Ogot, 373–5. The International Louis Leakey Memorial Institute for African Prehistory, Nairobi.

1987. Prelude to Akan civilization. In *The Golden Stool: studies of the Asante center and periphery*, ed. E. Schildkrout, 14–22. Anthropological Papers of the American Museum of Natural History, New York, vol. 65, part 1.

2010. *Reflecting on Begho and Hani: 1970–1998*. Merrick Posnansky, University of California, Los Angeles.

Posnansky, M., and McIntosh, R. 1976. New radiocarbon dates for Northern and Western Africa. *Journal of African History* 17(2), 161–95.

Post Park, D. 2010. Prehistoric Timbuktu and its hinterland. *Antiquity* 84 (326), 1076–88.

Powell, J.E. (trans.) 1949. *Herodotus*, 2 vols. Clarendon Press, Oxford.

Pradines, S. 2004. *Fortifications et urbanisation en Afrique orientale*. BAR International Series 1216, Archaeopress, Oxford.

2009. L'île de Sanjé ya Kati (Kilwa, Tanzanie): un mythe Shirâzi bien réel. *Azania: Archaeological Research in Africa* 44(1), 49–73.

2010. *Gedi: une cité portuaire swahilie: Islam médiéval en Afrique orientale*. Institute Français D'Archéologie Orientale, Le Caire.

2013. The rock crystal of Dembeni, Mayotte Mission Report 2013. *Nyame Akuma* 80, 59–72.

2015. Islamic Cairo: urbanization and town walls. In *Handbook on Islamic archaeology*, ed. B. Walker, Oxford University Press, Oxford.

Price, B.J. 1978. Secondary state formation: an explanatory model. In *Origins of the state: the anthropology of political evolution*, ed. R. Cohen and E.L. Service, 161–86. Institute for the Study of Human Issues, Philadelphia.

Prins, A.H.J. 1982. The mtepe of Lamu, Mombasa and the Zanzibar sea. In *From Zinj to Zanzibar: studies in history, trade and society on the eastern coast of Africa*, (*Paideuma* 28), ed. J. de V. Allen and T.H. Wilson, 85–100.

Pwiti, G. 1996. *Continuity and change: an archaeological study of farming communities in northern Zimbabwe AD 500–1700*. Studies in African Archaeology 13, Department of Archaeology, Uppsala University, Uppsala.

2005. Southern Africa and the East African coast. In *African archaeology: a critical introduction*, ed. A.B. Stahl, 378–91, Blackwell, Oxford.

Radimilahy, C. 1998. *Mahilaka: an archaeological investigation of an early town in northwestern Madagascar*. Studies in African Archaeology 15, Department of Archaeology and Ancient History, Uppsala University.

Ramos, M. 1980. Une enceinte (Monomotapa?) peu connue du plateau du Songo, Mozambique. In *Proceedings of the 8th Panafrican Congress of Prehistory and Quaternary Studies, Nairobi, 5 to 10 September 1977*, ed. R.E. Leakey and B.A. Ogot, 373–5. The International Louis Leakey Memorial Institute for African Prehistory, Nairobi.

Randall-MacIver, D. 1971. *Mediaeval Rhodesia*, reprint, Cass, London, (1st ed. 1906).

Randles, W.G.L. 1968. *L'ancien royaume du Congo*. Mouton, Paris.

Randsborg, K. 2010. Destructive times, constructive measures: Danish funding and collaboration to develop archaeology in Bénin. In *West African archaeology: new developments, new perspectives*, ed. P. Allsworth-Jones, 79–82. BAR International Series 2164, Archaeopress, Oxford.

Rathje, W.L. 1971. The origin and development of lowland Maya classic civilization. *American Antiquity* 36, 275–85.

Ravenstein, E.G. 1898. (Translator and editor.) *A journal of the first voyage of Vasco da Gama, 1497–1499*. Hakluyt Society, London.

Raymond, A. 2000. *Cairo*. Translated by W. Wood. Harvard University Press, Cambridge, MA.

Reader, J. 1997. *Africa: a biography of the continent*. Hamish Hamilton, London.

Redman, C.L. 1978. *The rise of civilization: from early farmers to urban society in the ancient Near East*. Freeman, San Francisco, CA.

   1983. Comparative urbanism in the Islamic Far West. *World Archaeology* 14(3), 355–77.

   1986. *Qsar es-Seghir: an archaeological view of medieval life*. Academic Press, Orlando, FL.

Reefe, T.Q. 1981. *The rainbow and the kings: a history of the Luba Empire to 1891*, University of California Press, Berkeley.

   1983. The societies of the eastern savanna. In *History of Central Africa*, ed. D. Birmingham and P.M. Martin, vol. 1, 160–204. Longman, London and New York.

Reid, A. 1996. Ntusi and the development of social complexity in southern Uganda. In *Aspects of African archaeology: papers from the 10th Congress of the PanAfrican Association for Prehistory and Related Studies*, ed. G. Pwiti and R. Soper, 621–7. University of Zimbabwe, Harare.

   2001. Bananas and the archaeology of Buganda. *Antiquity* 75 (290), 811–12.

   2003. Recent research on the archaeology of Buganda. In *Researching Africa's Past: new contributions from British archaeologists*, ed. P. Mitchell, A. Haour, and J. Hobart, 110–17. Oxford University School of Archaeology, Oxford.

Reid, A., and Robertshaw, P. 1987. A new look at Ankole capital sites. *Azania* 22, 83–8.

Reid, A., and Segobye, A. 2000. Politics, society and trade on the eastern margins of the Kalahari. In *African naissance: the Limpopo Valley 1000 years ago*, ed. M. Leslie and T. Maggs, 58–68. The South African Archaeological Society, Goodwin Series vol. 8.

Reid, A., and Young, R. 2003. Iron-smelting and bananas in Buganda. In *Researching Africa's Past: new contributions from British archaeologists*, ed. P. Mitchell, A. Haour, and J. Hobart, 118–23. Oxford University School of Archaeology, Oxford.

Reisner, G.A. 1923. *Excavations at Kerma*, Parts 1–3, Parts 4–5, Harvard African Studies vols. 5 and 6. Peabody Museum of Harvard University, Cambridge, MA.

Renfrew, C. 1972. *The emergence of civilization: the Cyclades and the Aegean in the third millennium BC*. Methuen, London.

1983. The emergence of civilization. In *The encyclopedia of ancient civilizations*, ed. A. Cotterell, 12–20. Macmillan, London.

Renfrew, C., and Bahn, P.G. 2008. *Archaeology: theories, methods and practice*, 5th ed. Thames and Hudson, London.

Richards, P.W. 1952. *The tropical rain forest: an ecological study*. Cambridge University Press, Cambridge.

Ricks, T.M. 1970. Persian Gulf seafaring and East Africa: ninth–twelfth centuries. *African Historical Studies* 3(2), 339–57.

Robert, D. 1970. Les fouilles de Tegdaoust. *Journal of African History* 11, 471–93.

Robert, S., and Robert, D. 1972. Douze années de recherches archéologiques en République Islamique de Mauritanie. *Annales de la Faculté des Lettres et Sciences Humaines, Université de Dakar* 2, 195–233.

Robertshaw, P. 1994. Archaeological survey, ceramic analysis, and state formation in western Uganda. *African Archaeological Review* 12, 105–31.

1997. Munsa earthworks: a preliminary report on recent excavations. *Azania* 32, 1–20.

Robins, P.A., and Whitty, A. 1966. Excavations at Harleigh Farm, near Rusape, Rhodesia. *South African Archaeological Bulletin* 21, 61–80.

Robinson, K.R. 1959. *Khami ruins: report on excavations undertaken for the Commission for the Preservation of Natural and Historical Monuments and Relics, Southern Rhodesia, 1947–1955*. Cambridge University Press, Cambridge.

Robinson, K.R., Summers, R., and Whitty, A. 1961. *Zimbabwe excavations 1958*. Occasional Papers, the National Museums of Southern Rhodesia, 3(23A), 157–332.

Roese, P.M. 1981. Erdwälle und Gräben im ehemaligen Königreich von Benin. *Anthropos* 76, 166–209.

Roth, H.L. 1903. *Great Benin: its customs, art and horrors*. King, Halifax.

Rousseau, J.J. 1966. *The Social Contract and Discourses*. Translated by G.D.H. Cole. Dent, London.

Rowley-Conwy, P. 1988. The camel in the Nile Valley: new radiocarbon accelerator (AMS) dates from Qasr Ibrim. *Journal of Egyptian Archaeology* 74, 245–8 and plate 35.

1991. Sorghum from Qasr Ibrim, Egyptian Nubia, c. 800 BC–AD 1811: a preliminary study. In *New light on early farming: recent developments in palaeoethnobotany*, ed. J.M. Renfrew, 191–212. Edinburgh University Press, Edinburgh.

Rudd, S. 1984. Excavations at Lekkerwater Ruins, Tsindi Hill, Theydon, Zimbabwe. *South African Archaeological Bulletin* 39, 83–105.

Ryder, A.F.C. 1969. *Benin and the Europeans, 1485–1897*. Longmans, London.

Sadr, K., and Rodier, X. 2012. Google Earth, GIS and stone-walled structures in southern Gauteng, South Africa. *Journal of Archaeological Science* 39, 1034–42.

Saitowitz, S.J., Reid, D.L., and van der Merwe, N.J. 1996. Glass bead trade from Islamic Egypt to South Africa c. AD 900–1250. *South African Journal of Science* 92, 101–4.

Saliège, J.F., Person, A., Barry, I., and Fontes, P. 1980. Premières datations de tumulus pré-islamiques au Mali: site mégalithique de Tondidarou. *C.R. Acad. Sc. Paris Série D* 291, 981–4.

Salzmann, U., and Hoelzmann, P. 2005. The Dahomey Gap: an abrupt climatically induced rain forest fragmentation in West Africa during the late Holocene. *The Holocene* 15(2), 190–99.

Sanmarti, J., Kallala, N., Belarte, M.C., Ramon, J., Telmini, B.M., Jornet, R., and Miniaoui, S. 2012. Filling the gaps in the protohistory of the Eastern Maghreb: the *Althiburos* Archaeological Project (El Kef, Tunisia). *Journal of African Archaeology* 10(1), 21–44.

Sassoon, H. 1980. Excavations at the site of early Mombasa. *Azania* 15, 1–42.

Säve-Söderbergh, T. 1960. The paintings in the tomb of Djehuty-hetep at Debeira. *Kush* 8, 25–44.

Sayce, A.H. 1911. Part II – the historical results. Second interim report on the excavations at Meroë in Ethiopia *[sic]*. *Annals of Archaeology and Anthropology* 4, Liverpool Institute of Archaeology, Liverpool University Press, Liverpool.

Schmidt, P.R. 2009. Variability in Eritrea and the archaeology of the Northern Horn during the first millennium BC: subsistence, ritual, and gold production. *African Archaeological Review* 26(4), 305–325.

Schmidt, P.R., and Avery, D.H. 1996. Complex iron smelting and prehistoric culture in Tanzania. In *The culture and technology of African iron production*, ed. P.R. Schmidt, 172–85. University Press of Florida, Gainesville.

Schmidt, P.R., and Curtis, M.C. 2001. Urban precursors in the Horn: early first-millennium BC communities in Eritrea. *Antiquity* 75 (290), 849–59.

Schmidt, P.R., Curtis, M.C., and Teka, Z. 2008. *The archaeology of Ancient Eritrea*. The Red Sea Press, Trenton, NJ, and Asmara, Eritrea.

Schoenbrun, D.L. 1993. Cattle herds and banana gardens: the historical geography of the western Great Lakes region, ca AD 800–1500. *African Archaeological Review* 11, 39–72.

Schuhmacher, T.X., Cardoso, J.L., and Banerjee, A. 2009. Sourcing African ivory in Chalcolithic Portugal. *Antiquity* 83 (322), 983–97.

Schwartz, J.H., Houghton, F.D., Bondioli, L., and Macchiarelli, R. 2012. Bones, teeth, and estimating age of perinates: Carthaginian infant sacrifice revisited. *Antiquity* 86 (333), 738–45.

Scobie, A. 1986. Slums, sanitation and mortality in the Roman World. *Klio* 68(2), 399–433.

Sears, G. 2007. *Late Roman African urbanism: continuity and transformation in the city*. BAR International Series 1693, Archaeopress, Oxford.

2011. *The cities of Roman Africa*. The History Press, Stroud, UK.

Sernicola, L., and Phillipson, L. 2011. Aksum's regional trade: new evidence from archaeological survey. *Azania: Archaeological Research in Africa* 46(2), 190–204.

Serrano, B.M. 2011. Coins, cities and territories: the imaginary Far West and South Iberian and North African Punic coins. In *Money, trade and trade routes in Pre-Islamic North Africa*, ed. A. Dowler and E.R. Galvin, 21–32. Research Publication 176, British Museum, London.

Service, E.R. 1975. *Origins of the state and civilization: the process of cultural evolution*. Norton, New York.

Shanahan, T.M., Overpeck, J.T., Anchukaitis, K.J., Beck, J.W., Cole, J.E., Dettman, D.L., Peck, J.A., Scholz, C.A., and King, J.W. 2009. Atlantic forcing of persistent drought in West Africa. *Science* 324, 377–80.

Shaw, I. 2012. *Ancient Egyptian technology and innovation: transformations in Pharaonic material culture*. Bloomsbury Academic, London.

(ed.) 2000. *The Oxford history of ancient Egypt*. Oxford University Press, Oxford.

Shaw, T. 1960. Early smoking pipes: in Africa, Europe, and America. *Journal of the Royal Anthropological Institute* 90(2), 272–305 and plates 1–9.

1970. *Igbo-Ukwu*, 2 vols. Faber and Faber, London.

1977. *Unearthing Igbo-Ukwu*. Oxford University Press, Ibadan.

1984. Archaeological evidence and effects of food-producing in Nigeria. In *From hunters to farmers: the causes and consequences of food production in Africa*, ed. J.D. Clark and S.A. Brandt, 152–7. University of California Press, Berkeley.

Shaw, T., and Daniels, S.G.H. 1984. Excavations at Iwo Eleru, Ondo State, Nigeria. *West African Journal of Archaeology* 14, 1–269.

Shaw, T., Sinclair, P., Andah, B., and Okpoko, A. (eds.) 1993. *The archaeology of Africa: food, metals and towns*. Routledge, London and New York.

Shepherd, G. 1982. The making of the Swahili: a view from the southern end of the East African coast. In *From Zinj to Zanzibar: studies in history, trade and society on the eastern coast of Africa*, (*Paideuma* 28), ed. J. de V. Allen and T.H. Wilson, 129–47.

Shinnie, P.L. 1960. Excavations at Bigo, 1957. *Uganda Journal* 24(1), 16–28.

1967. *Meroë: a civilization of the Sudan*. Thames and Hudson, London.

1989. The culture of Meroë and its influence in the central Sudan. *Sahara* 2, 21–30.

1996. *Ancient Nubia*. Kegan Paul, London and New York.

2005. Early Asante and European contacts. *Journal des Africanistes* 75(2), 2–14.

Shinnie, P.L., and Kense, F.J. 1982. Meroitic iron working. *Meroitica* 6, 17–28, 43–9.

1989. *Archaeology of Gonja, Ghana: excavations at Daboya*. University of Calgary Press, Calgary.

Shinnie, P.L., and Shinnie, M. 1978. *Debeira West: a mediaeval Nubian town*. Aris & Phillips, Warminster, UK.

Shipton, P.M. 1984. Strips and patches: a demographic dimension in some African land-holding and political systems. *Man* (NS) 19, 613–34.

Siddle, D.J. 1968. War-towns in Sierra Leone: a study in social change. *Africa* 38(1), 47–56.

Sidebotham, S.E., and Wendrich, W. (eds.) 2007. *Berenike 1999/2000: report on the excavations at Berenike, including excavations in Wadi Kalalat and Siket, and the survey of the Mons Smaragdus region*. Cotsen Institute of Archaeology, University of California, Los Angeles.

Sinclair, P.J.J. 1982. Chibuene – an early trading site in southern Mozambique. In *From Zinj to Zanzibar: studies in history, trade and society on the eastern coast of Africa* (*Paideuma* 28), ed. J. de V. Allen and T.H. Wilson, 149–64.

1984. Some aspects of the economic level of the Zimbabwe state. In *Papers presented in honour of Miss G. Caton-Thompson (Zimbabwea 1)*. National Museums and Monuments of Zimbabwe, 48–53.

1987. *Space, time and social formation: a territorial approach to the archaeology and anthropology of Zimbabwe and Mozambique c. 0–1700 AD*. Aun 9, Societas Archaeologica Upsaliensis, Uppsala.

1991. Archaeology in Eastern Africa: an overview of current chronological issues. *Journal of African History* 32, 179–219.

1995. The origins of urbanism in East and southern Africa: a diachronic perspective. In *Islamic art and culture in Sub-Saharan Africa*, ed. K. Ådahl and B. Sahlström, 99–109. Acta Universitatis Upsaliensis, Figura Nova Series 27, Uppsala.

Sinclair, P.J.J., and Håkansson, T. 2000. The Swahili city-state culture. In *A comparative study of thirty city-state cultures*, ed. M.H. Hansen, 463–82. The Royal Danish Academy of Sciences and Letters, Copenhagen.

Sinclair, P.J.J., and Lundmark, H. 1984. A spatial analysis of archaeological sites from Zimbabwe. In *Frontiers: southern African archaeology today*, ed. M. Hall, G. Avery, D.M. Avery, M.L. Wilson, and A.J.B. Humphreys, 277–88. Cambridge Monographs in African Archaeology 10, BAR International Series 207, Oxford.

Sinclair, P.J.J., Pikirayi, I., Pwiti, G., and Soper, R. 1993. Urban trajectories on the Zimbabwean plateau. In *The archaeology of Africa: food, metals and towns*, ed. T. Shaw, P. Sinclair, B. Andah, and A. Okpoko, 705–31. Routledge, London and New York.

Sinclair, P., Ekblom, A., and Wood, M. 2012. Trade and society on the south-east African coast in the later first millennium AD: the case of Chibuene. *Antiquity* 86(333), 723–37.

Sjoberg, G. 1960. *The preindustrial city*. Free Press of Glencoe, Illinois.

Smith, A.B. 1992. *Pastoralism in Africa: origins and development ecology*. Hurst, London.

Smith, M.C., and Wright, H.T. 1988. The ceramics from Ras Hafun in Somalia: notes on a classical maritime site. *Azania* 23, 115–41.

Smith, M.E. (ed.) 2012. *The comparative archaeology of complex societies*. Cambridge University Press, Cambridge.

Smith, P., Avishai, G., Greene, J.A., and Stager, L.E. 2011. Aging cremated infants: the problem of sacrifice at the Tophet at Carthage. *Antiquity* 85 (329), 859–74.

Smith, P., Stager, L.E., Greene, J.A., and Avishai, G. 2013. Age estimations attest to infant sacrifice at the Carthage Tophet. *Antiquity* 87 (338), 1191–99.

Smith, S.T. 2003. *Wretched Kush: ethnic identities and boundaries in Egypt's Nubian Empire*. Routledge, London.

Soper, R. 1990. Great Zimbabwe tradition sites in local context: the Centenary Survey. In *Urban origins in Eastern Africa: proceedings of the 1990 workshop, Harare and Great Zimbabwe*, ed. P.J.J. Sinclair and G. Pwiti, 67–76. Central Board of National Antiquities, Stockholm.

1992. Observations on the sociopolitical status of Great Zimbabwe tradition sites in northern Mashonaland. In *Urban origins in Eastern Africa: proceedings of the 1991 workshop in Zanzibar*, ed. P.J.J. Sinclair and A. Juma, 140–5. Central Board of National Antiquities, Stockholm.

1993. The palace at Oyo Ile, western Nigeria. In *Imprints of West Africa's past: forum on West African Archaeology at the Conference in Honour of Thurstan Shaw, Founding Editor of WAJA*, ed. B.W. Andah, C.A. Folorunso, and

I.A. Okpoko, 295–311. Special Book Issue, *West African Journal of Archaeology* 22, Wisdom Publishers, Ibadan.

1996. The Nyanga terrace complex of eastern Zimbabwe: new investigations. *Azania* 31, 1–35.

2002. *Nyanga: ancient fields, settlements and agricultural history in Zimbabwe.* Memoir 16, British Institute in Eastern Africa, London.

Soper, R., and Darling, P. 1980. The walls of Oyo Ile. *West African Journal of Archaeology* 10, 61–81.

Soper, R., and Pwiti, G. 1992. Excavations at Zvongombe, Centenary District, Northern Zimbabwe. In *Urban origins in Eastern Africa: proceedings of the 1991 workshop in Zanzibar,* ed. P.J.J. Sinclair and A. Juma, 146–60. Central Board of National Antiquities, Stockholm.

Sowunmi, M.A. 1993. The Quaternary in West Africa: vegetational evidence. In *Proceedings of the 9th Congress of the Pan-African Association of Pre-history and Related Studies: Jos, 11–17 December 1983,* ed. B.W. Andah, P. de Maret, and R. Soper, 12–16. Rex Charles, Ibadan.

Spear, T.T. 1978. *The Kaya Complex: a history of the Mijikenda peoples of the Kenya coast to 1900.* Kenya Literature Bureau, Nairobi.

Speke, J.H. 1863. *Journal of the discovery of the source of the Nile.* Blackwood, London.

Spencer, A.J. 1982. *Death in Ancient Egypt.* Penguin, Harmondsworth, UK.

Stahl, A.B. 1999. Perceiving variability in time and space: the evolutionary mapping of African societies. In *Beyond chiefdoms: pathways to complexity in Africa,* ed. S.K. McIntosh, 39–55. Cambridge University Press, Cambridge.

2001. *Making history in Banda: anthropological visions of Africa's past.* Cambridge University Press, Cambridge.

2005a. Glass houses under the rocks: a reply to Watson. *Journal of African Archaeology* 3(1), 57–64.

Stahl, A.B. (ed.) 2005b. *African archaeology: a critical introduction.* Blackwell, Oxford.

Stanley, H.M. 1878. *Through the Dark Continent,* 2 vols. and maps. Sampson Low, Marston, Searle and Rivington, London.

Staudinger, P. 1889. *Im Herzen der Haussaländer.* Landsberger, Berlin. (Translated by J. Moody 1990 as *In the heart of the Hausa states,* 2 vols. Ohio University Center for International Studies, Athens, Ohio).

Stead, M. 1986. *Egyptian life.* British Museum Publications, London.

Steinhart, E.I. 1981. Herders and farmers: the tributary mode of production in Western Uganda. In *Modes of production in Africa: the precolonial era,* ed. D. Crummey and C.C. Stewart, 114–55. Sage Publications, Beverly Hills, CA.

Sterner, J. 2012. Mandara Mountain basketry in continental context: significance for archaeologists. *Azania: Archaeological Research in Africa* 47(3), 288–313.

Sulas, F., Madella, M., and French, C. 2009. State formation and water resources management in the Horn of Africa: the Aksumite Kingdom of the northern Ethiopian highlands. *World Archaeology* 41(1), 2–15.

Summers, R. 1967. Archaeological distributions and a tentative history of tsetse infestation in Rhodesia and the Northern Transvaal. *Arnoldia (Rhodesia)* 3(13), 1–18.

1969. *Ancient mining in Rhodesia and adjacent areas.* Museum Memoir 3, Trustees of the National Museums of Rhodesia, Salisbury, Rhodesia.

Sutton, J.E.G. 1982. Archaeology in West Africa: a review of recent work and a further list of radiocarbon dates. *Journal of African History* 23(3), 291–313.

1985. Ntusi and the 'dams'. *Azania* 20, 172–5.

1991. The international factor at Igbo-Ukwu. *African Archaeological Review* 9, 145–60.

1993. The antecedents of the interlacustrine kingdoms. *Journal of African History* 34, 33–64.

1997. The African lords of the intercontinental gold trade before the Black Death: al-Hasan bin Sulaiman of Kilwa and Mansa Musa of Mali. *Antiquaries Journal* 77, 221–42.

1998. Kilwa: a history of the ancient Swahili town, with a guide to the monuments of Kilwa Kisiwani and adjacent islands. *Azania* 33, 113–69.

Sutton, J.E.G., and Roberts, A.D. 1968. Uvinza and its salt industry. *Azania* 3, 45–86.

Swan, L. 1994. *Early gold mining on the Zimbabwean Plateau: changing patterns of gold production in the first and second millennia AD.* Studies in African Archaeology 9, Societas Archaeologica Upsaliensis, Uppsala.

Taddesse, T. 1972. *Church and state in Ethiopia 1270–1527.* Clarendon Press, Oxford.

Tainter, J.A. 1988. *The collapse of complex societies.* Cambridge University Press, Cambridge.

Talbot, M.R., and Delibrias, G. 1977. Holocene variations in the level of Lake Bosumtwi, Ghana. *Nature* 268, 722–4.

Theal, G.M. (ed.) 1964. *Records of south-eastern Africa,* 9 vols. Printed for the Government of the Cape Colony, 1898–1903, facsimile reprint, Struik, Cape Town.

Thomassey, P., 1956. Campagne de fouilles de 1950 à Koumbi Saleh (Ghana?). *Bulletin de l'IFAN,* Dakar, 18(B), 117–40.

Thomassey, P., and Mauny, R. 1951. Campagne de fouilles à Koumbi Saleh. *Bulletin de l'IFAN,* Dakar, 13(1), 438–62.

Thompson, A.H., Chaix, L., and Richards, M.P. 2008. Stable isotopes and diet at Ancient Kerma, Upper Nubia (Sudan). *Journal of Archaeological Science* 35(2), 376–87.

Thompson, H.N. 1910–1911. The forests of Southern Nigeria. *Journal of the African Society* 10(38), 121–45.

Thorp, C.R. 1995. *Kings, commoners and cattle at Zimbabwe Tradition sites.* National Museums and Monuments of Zimbabwe, Harare.

Thruston, A.B. 1900. *African incidents: personal experiences in Egypt and Unyoro.* John Murray, London.

Thurman, C.C.M. 1979. The textiles. In *Ancient textiles from Nubia: Meroitic, X-Group, and Christian fabrics from Ballana and Qustul,* ed. C.C.M. Thurman and B. Williams, 36–46. The Art Institute of Chicago, Chicago.

Togola, T. 2008. *Archaeological investigations of Iron Age sites in the Mema Region, Mali (West Africa).* Cambridge Monographs in African Archaeology 73, BAR International Series 1736, Archaeopress, Oxford.

Tooley, A.M.J. 1995. *Egyptian models and scenes*. Princes Risborough, UK, Shire Publications.

Török, L. 1992. Ambulatory kingship and settlement history: a study on the contribution of archaeology to Meroitic history. In *Etudes Nubiennes: Conférence de Genève, Actes du VIIe Congrès international d'études nubiennes 3–8 septembre 1990*, ed. C. Bonnet, vol. 1, 111–26, Genève.

　1997. *Meroe city: an ancient African capital: John Garstang's excavations in the Sudan*, Parts 1 and 2. Egypt Exploration Society, London.

Townshend, P. 1979. Mankala in Eastern and Southern Africa: a distributional analysis. *Azania* 14, 109–38.

Trigger, B.G. 1965. *History and settlement in Lower Nubia*. Yale University Publications in Anthropology No. 69, New Haven, CT.

　1969. The myth of Meroë and the African Iron Age. *African Historical Studies* 2(1), 23–50.

　1973. Meroitic language studies: strategies and goals. In *Sudan im Altertum*, ed. F. Hintze. Internationale Tagung für meroitische Forschungen in Berlin 1971. *Meroitica* 1, Akademie–Verlag, Berlin, 243–72.

　2003. *Understanding early civilizations: a comparative study*. Cambridge University Press, Cambridge.

Trimingham, J.S. 1975. The Arab geographers and the East African coast. In *East Africa and the Orient: cultural syntheses in pre-colonial times*, ed. H.N. Chittick and R.I. Rotberg, 115–46. Africana Publishing Company, New York.

Tsheboeng, A. 2001. Late Iron Age human responses and contribution to environmental change in the Shashe-Limpopo river basin: north eastern Botswana. In *People, contact and the environment in the African past*, ed. F. Chami, G. Pwiti, and C. Radimilahy 124–28. University of Dar es Salaam, Dar es Salaam.

Turner, G. 1984. Vertebrate remains from Lekkerwater. *South African Archaeological Bulletin* 39, 106–8.

UCL. 2013. *Issues in the archaeology of Nubia. Course Handbook 2013*. Undergraduate course coordinated by D.Q. Fuller, Institute of Archaeology, University College London. www.ucl.ac.uk/archaeology/studying/undergraduate/courses/coursehandbooks/ARCL3050_ArchNubia.pdf (Accessed 6 January 2015.)

Uganda. 1967. *Atlas of Uganda*, 2nd ed. Department of Lands and Surveys, Uganda.

Uganda National Parks, n.d. *Queen Elizabeth National Park (North Sector)*. Guide leaflet, Kampala. (Acquired 1990.)

Ullendorff, E. 1960. *The Ethiopians: an introduction to country and people*. Oxford University Press, London.

Usman, A.A. 2004. On the frontier of empire: understanding the enclosed walls in Northern Yoruba, Nigeria. *Journal of Anthropological Archaeology* 23, 119–32.

van Beek, G.W. 1967. Monuments of Axum in the light of South Arabian archeology. *Journal of the American Oriental Society* 87(2), 113–22.

van der Veen, M. 1991. The plant remains. In *Soba: archaeological research at a medieval capital on the Blue Nile*, ed. D.A. Welsby and C.M. Daniels, 264–73. Memoir 12, British Institute in Eastern Africa, London.

　1999. *The exploitation of plant resources in Ancient Africa*. Kluwer Academic/Plenum, New York.

2011. *Consumption, trade and innovation: exploring the botanical remains from the Roman and Islamic ports at Quseir al-Qadim, Egypt.* Journal of African Archaeology Monograph Series 6, Africa Magna Verlag, Frankfurt am Main.

Van Noten, F.L. 1972. *Les tombes du Roi Cyirima Rujugira et de la Reine-Mère Nyirayuhi Kanjogera: description archéologique.* Musée Royal de l'Afrique Centrale, Tervuren, Belgium.

1982. The Iron Age in the north and east. In *The archaeology of Central Africa*, ed. F.L. Van Noten, 69–76. Akademische Drück — und Verlagsanstalt, Graz, Austria.

Vansina, J. 1969. The bells of kings. *Journal of African History* 10(2), 187–97.

1973. *Oral tradition: a study in historical methodology* (first published in French in 1961). Penguin, Harmondsworth.

1990. *Paths in the rainforests: toward a history of political tradition in Equatorial Africa.* James Currey, London.

2004. *How societies are born: governance in West Central Africa before 1600.* University of Virginia Press, Charlottesville and London.

Vantini, G. 1970. *The excavations at Faras, a contribution to the history of Christian Nubia*, Nigrizia, Bologna.

van Waarden, C. 1998. The Later Iron Age. In *Ditswa Mmung: the archaeology of Botswana*, ed. P. Lane, A. Reid, and A. Segobye, 115–60. The University of Botswana, Gaborone.

2012. *Butua and the end of an era: the effect of the collapse of the Kalanga state on ordinary citizens; an analysis of behaviour under stress.* BAR International Series 2420, Archaeopress, Oxford.

Vercoutter, J. 1959. The gold of Kush: two gold-washing stations at Faras East. *Kush* 7, 120–53.

1962. Un palais des 'Candaces', contemporain d'Auguste (Fouilles à Wad-ban-Naga 1958–1960). *Syria: Revue d'art oriental et d'archéologie* 39, 263–99.

Vérin, P. 1986. *The history of civilisation in north Madagascar.* Translated by D. Smith. Balkema, Rotterdam.

Vernet, T. 2003. Le commerce des esclaves sur la côte Swahili, 1500–1750. *Azania* 38, 69–97.

Verschuren, D., Laird, K.R., and Cumming, B.F. 2000. Rainfall and drought in equatorial east Africa during the past 1,100 years. *Nature* 403, 410–14.

Vivian, B.C. 1996. Recent excavations at Adansemanso. *Nyame Akuma* 46, 37–42.

Vogel, J.O. (ed.) 1997. *Encyclopedia of precolonial Africa: archaeology, history, languages, cultures, and environments.* AltaMira Press, Walnut Creek, CA.

von Endt, D.W. 1978. Was civet used as a perfume in Aksum? *Azania* 13, 186–8.

von Hellermann, P. 2010. Was Benin a forest kingdom? Attempting to reconstruct landscapes in Southern Nigeria. In *West African archaeology: new developments, new perspectives*, ed. P. Allsworth-Jones, 93–101. BAR International Series 2164, Archaeopress, Oxford.

von Heuglin, T. 1874. *Reise nach Abessinien, den Gala-Laendern, Ost-Sudan und Chartum in den Jahren 1861 und 1862.* Griesbach, Gera, Germany.

Waller, H. 1874. *The last journals of David Livingstone, in Central Africa, from 1865 to his death …*, 2 vols. Murray, London.

References

Walton, J. 1956. *African village*. Van Schaik, Pretoria.

Ward, C. 2006. Boat-building and its social context in early Egypt: interpretations from the First Dynasty boat-grave cemetery at Abydos. *Antiquity* 80 (307), 118–29.

Watson, D.J. 2005a. Straws within a glass house: a reply to Stahl. *Journal of African Archaeology* 3(1), 65–8.

2005b. Under the rocks: reconsidering the origin of the Kintampo Tradition and the development of food production in the savanna–forest/forest of West Africa. *Journal of African Archaeology* 3(1), 3–55.

2010. Within savanna and forest: a review of the Late Stone Age Kintampo Tradition, Ghana. *Azania: Archaeological Research in Africa* 45(2), 141–74.

Watson, E.J., and Watson, V. 1990. 'Of commoners and kings': faunal remains from Ondini. *South African Archaeological Bulletin* 45, 33–46.

Wayland, E.J. 1934. Notes on the Biggo bya Mugenyi: some ancient earthworks in northern Buddu. *Uganda Journal* 2(1), 21–32.

Weeks, K.R. 1967. *The Classic Christian townsite at Arminna West*. Publications of the Pennsylvania-Yale Expedition to Egypt, No. 3. New Haven and Philadelphia.

Welsby, D.A. 1996. *The Kingdom of Kush: the Napatan and Meroitic Empires*. British Museum Press, London.

1998. *Soba II: renewed excavations within the metropolis of the Kingdom of Alwa in Central Sudan*. Memoir 15, British Institute in Eastern Africa, and British Museum Press, London.

2002. *The Medieval Kingdoms of Nubia: Pagans, Christians and Muslims along the middle Nile*. British Museum Press, London.

Welsby, D.A., and Daniels, C.M. 1991. *Soba: archaeological research at a medieval capital on the Blue Nile*. Memoir 12, British Institute in Eastern Africa, London.

Wengrow, D. 2006. *The archaeology of Early Egypt: social transformations in North-East Africa, 10,000 to 2650 BC*. Cambridge University Press, Cambridge.

Wenig, S. 2001. Musawwarat es-Sufra: interpreting the Great Enclosure. *Sudan and Nubia* 5, 71–88.

Wheatley, P. 1975. Analecta Sino-Africana Recensa. In *East Africa and the Orient: cultural syntheses in pre-colonial times*, ed. H.N. Chittick and R.I. Rotberg, 76–114. Africana Publishing Company, New York.

Whitelaw, G. 1997. Southern African Iron Age. In *Encyclopedia of precolonial Africa: archaeology, history, languages, cultures, and environments*, ed. J.O. Vogel, 444–55. AltaMira Press, Walnut Creek, CA.

Wildung, D. 1997. Meroitic ceramics. In *Sudan: ancient kingdoms of the Nile*, ed. D. Wildung, 341–68. Flammarion, Paris and New York.

Wilkinson, T.A.H. 1996. *State formation in Egypt: chronology and society*. BAR International Series 651, Tempus Reparatum, Oxford.

2011. *The rise and fall of Ancient Egypt: the history of a civilisation from 3000 BC to Cleopatra*. Paperback edition, Bloomsbury Publishing, London.

Willett, F. 1966. On the funeral effigies of Owo and Benin and the interpretation of the life-size bronze heads from Ife, Nigeria. *Man* (NS) 1(1), 34–45 and plates 1–4.

1967. *Ife in the history of West African sculpture*. Thames and Hudson, London.

Willett, F., and Fleming, S.J. 1976. A catalogue of important Nigerian copper-alloy castings dated by their thermoluminescence. *Archaeometry* 18(2), 135–46.

Willett, F., and Sayre, E.V. 2006. Lead isotopes in West African copper alloys. *Journal of African Archaeology* 4(1), 55–90.

Wilson, A. 2012. Saharan trade in the Roman period: short, medium and long-distance trade networks. *Azania: Archaeological Research in Africa* 47(4), 409–49.

Wilson, J.A. 1960. Egypt through the New Kingdom: civilization without cities. In *City invincible: a symposium on urbanization and cultural development in the ancient Near East*, ed. C.H. Kraeling and R.M. Adams, 124–64. Chicago University Press, Chicago.

Wilson, R.T. 1984. *The camel*. Longman, London and New York.

Wilson, T.H. 1978. *The monumental architecture and archaeology north of the Tana River*. National Museums of Kenya, Xerox.

   1980. *The monumental architecture and archaeology of the central and southern Kenya coast*. National Museums of Kenya, Xerox.

   1982. Spatial analysis and settlement patterns on the East African coast. In *From Zinj to Zanzibar: studies in history, trade and society on the eastern coast of Africa, (Paideuma 28)*, ed. J. de V. Allen and T.H. Wilson, 201–19.

Wilson, T.H., and Lali Omar, A. 1997. Archaeological investigations at Pate. *Azania* 32, 31–76.

Winterbotham, H.S.L., Smith, E.G., and Longland, F. 1944. *The Belgian Congo, Geographical Handbook Series*. Naval Intelligence Division, Oxford.

Wittfogel, K.A. 1957. *Oriental despotism*. Yale University Press, New Haven.

Wolf, P. 1997. Recent fieldwork at Musawwarat es Sufra. *Sudan and Nubia* 1, 20–29.

Wolf, P., Nowotnick, U., and Wöß, F. 2014. Meroitic Hamadab – a century after its discovery. *Sudan and Nubia* 18, 104–20.

Wood, M. 2000. Making connections: relationships between international trade and glass beads from the Shashe-Limpopo area. In *African naissance: the Limpopo Valley 1000 years ago*, ed. M. Leslie and T. Maggs, 78–90. The South African Archaeological Society, Goodwin Series vol. 8.

   2011. A glass bead sequence for southern Africa from the 8th to the 16th century AD. *Journal of African Archaeology* 9(1), 67–84.

Woodhouse, J. 1998. Iron in Africa: metal from nowhere. In *Transformations in Africa: essays on Africa's later past*, ed. G. Connah, 160–85. Leicester University Press, London and Washington.

Woolley, C.L. 1911. *Karanòg: the town*. Eckley B. Coxe Junior Expedition to Nubia, vol. 5, University Museum, University of Pennsylvania, Philadelphia.

Woolley, C.L., and Randall-MacIver, D. 1910. *Karanòg: the Romano-Nubian cemetery*. Eckley B. Coxe Junior Expedition to Nubia, vols. 3 and 4. University Museum, University of Pennsylvania, Philadelphia.

Wright, D.K. 2005. New perspectives on early regional interaction networks of East African trade: a view from Tsavo National Park, Kenya. *African Archaeological Review* 22(3), 111–40.

Wright, H.T. 1984. Early seafarers of the Comoro Islands: the Dembeni Phase of the IXth–Xth centuries AD. *Azania* 19, 13–59.

1992. Early Islam, oceanic trade and town development on Nzwani: the Comorian Archipelago in the XIth–XVth centuries AD. *Azania* 27, 81–128.

1993. Trade and politics on the eastern littoral of Africa, AD 800–1300. In *The archaeology of Africa: food, metals and towns*, ed. T. Shaw, P. Sinclair, B. Andah, and A. Okpoko, 658–72. Routledge, London and New York.

Wright, H.T., and Johnson, G.A. 1975. Population, exchange, and early state formation in southwestern Iran. *American Anthropologist* 77, 267–89.

Wright, H.T., and Rakotoarisoa, J.-A. 1990. The archaeology of complex societies in Madagascar: case-studies in cultural diversification. In *Urban origins in Eastern Africa: proceedings of the 1989 Madagascar workshop*, ed. P.J.J. Sinclair and J.-A. Rakotoarisoa, 21–31. Central Board of National Antiquities, Stockholm.

Wright, H.T., Vérin, P., Ramilisonina, Burney, D., Burney, L.P., and Matsumoto, K. 1996. The evolution of settlement systems in the Bay of Boeny and the Mahavavy River Valley, north-western Madagascar. *Azania* 31, 37–73.

Wrigley, C.C. 1958. Some thoughts on the Bacwezi. *Uganda Journal* 22(1), 11–17.

1989. Bananas in Buganda. *Azania* 24, 64–70.

Wynne-Jones, S. 2012. Exploring the use of geophysical survey on the Swahili coast: Vumba Kuu, Kenya. *Azania: Archaeological Research in Africa* 47(2), 137–52.

Wynne-Jones, S., and Croucher, S. 2007. The central caravan route of Tanzania: a preliminary archaeological reconnaissance. *Nyame Akuma* 67, 91–5.

Xella, P., Quinn, J., Melchiorri, V., and van Dommelen, P. 2013. Phoenician bones of contention. *Antiquity* 87 (338), 1199–207.

Yegül, F. 2010. *Bathing in the Roman World*. Cambridge University Press, Cambridge.

Ylvisaker, M. 1982. The ivory trade in the Lamu area, 1600–870. In *From Zinj to Zanzibar: studies in history, trade and society on the eastern coast of Africa, (Paideuma 28)*, ed. J. de V. Allen and T.H. Wilson, 221–31.

Yoffee, N. 2005. *Myths of the archaic state: evolution of the earliest cities, states and civilizations*. Cambridge University Press, Cambridge.

Yoffee, N., and Cowgill, G.L. (eds.) 1988. *The collapse of ancient states and civilizations*. University of Arizona Press, Tucson.

York, R.N. 1973. Excavations at New Buipe. *West African Journal of Archaeology* 3, 1–189.

Zabkar, L.V. 1975. *Apedemak, lion god of Meroë: a study in Egyptian-Meroitic syncretism*. Aris & Phillips, Warminster, UK.

Zazzaro, C., Cocca, E., and Manzo, A. 2014. Towards a chronology of the Eritrean Red Sea port of Adulis (1st–early 7th century AD). *Journal of African Archaeology* 12(1), 43–73.

Index

gold mining, 285–6
Gondar, 144
gourds, 133, 188
The Grain Coast, 185. *See also* West African
    forest region
Grains of Paradise, 188
grapes, 133
Grat-Be'al-Guebri, 120
Great Crescent of population, 266, 292
Great Zimbabwe
    archaeological evidence for, 260–1, 267–86
    as archaeological riddle, 260–2
    architectural evidence in, 272–3
    Bantu Cattle Pattern in, 284, 290–1
    building and construction practices in, 269–70,
        284, 287–8
    Centenary Survey of, 281
    daga in, 264, 269–70, 272, 288
    external trade throughout, 293–7
    gold mining in, 285–6
    historical evidence in, 266–7
    ideology in, 293
    Maund Ruin, 274
    metallurgy in, 288
    population pressures in, 291–2
    pottery production in, 289
    social systems in, 289–91
    technology in, 287–9
    urbanization in, 278, 290–1
    Zimbabwe Plateau, 262–6
Greece, ancient, 44–6
groundnuts, 303
Gudit Stelae Field, 124

Haas, Jonathan, 6
Hall, Richard, 260–1
Hamadab site, 86–7
Hambarketolo, 157–60
Hamdallahi, 164
Haoulti-Melazo, 119–20
Hausaland (old state), 154–5
Herodotus, 75
heterarchy, 352–3
Hierakonpolis, 17, 23
Hiernaux, Jean, 307–8
hieroglyphic texts, 75
Hill Ruin, 284–6
historical evidence
    in East African coastal region, 231–2
    in Ethiopian and Eritrean highlands, 116–17

in Great Zimbabwe, 266–7
for North Africa, 44–8
in Nubia region, 75–6
in Pharaonic Egypt, 21–2
in West African savanna, 154–5
History of Pate, 231–2
History of the Yorubas (Johnson), 190
Holl, Augustin, 9
Horn of Africa, 229
horses, 66, 114–15, 173
house power, 234
Huffman, Thomas, 274–8
Hull, Richard, 9
human development, archaeological evidence of,
    3–4
Hunwick, John, 154–5
Husuni Ndogo, 238

ibn Battuta, 154, 221, 231–2, 294
ibn Fartua, 154
Ibn Hawqal, 154, 162–4
ibn Khaldun, 154
ibn Said, 154
ideology
    East African coast and, 253–4
    in Ethiopian and Eritrean highlands, 143–4
    in Far Western Africa, 325
    in Great Zimbabwe, 293
    in Interlacustrine Region, 325
    in North Africa, 63–5
    in Nubia region, 104–5
    in Pharaonic Egypt, 36–7
    in South Africa, 344–5
    in Upemba Depression, 325
    urbanization and, 105
    in West African forest region, 215
    in West African savanna, 179
al-Idrisi, 154, 231–2
Ife, 198, 209, 211, 215, 218–19
Ifriqiyah, 48
Igbo people, 206–8
Igbo-Ukwu, 206–9, 217
Ijebu-Ode, 195
Iliffe, John, 9
impluvia courtyards, 202
Indicopleustes, Cosmas, 126, 146–7
infant cemetery. *See tophet*
Ingombe Ilede, 296
Inland Niger delta
    archaeological evidence in, 157–60